Education Reform in Japan

THE NISSAN INSTITUTE/ ROUTLEDGE JAPANESE STUDIES SERIES

Education Reform in Japan

A Case of Immobilist Politics

Leonard J. Schoppa

London and New York

First published 1991
by Routledge
11 New Fetter Lane, London EC4P 4EE
Simultaneously published in the USA and Canada
by Routledge
a division of Routledge, Chapman and Hall, Inc.
29 West 35th Street, New York, NY 10001

Typeset by Pat and Anne Murphy,
Highcliffe-on-Sea, Dorset.
Printed in Great Britain by
Billing & Sons Ltd, Worcester

370.952
S373e

British Library Cataloguing in Publication Data

Schoppa, Leonard James, *1962–*
    Education reform in Japan: a case of immobilist politics
    (The Nissan Institute/Routledge Japanese studies series)
    1. Japan. Education policies. Formulation
    I. Title
    379.52
    ISBN 0-415-02062-X

Library of Congress Cataloging in Publication Data

Schoppa, Leonard James, 1962–
    Education reform in Japan: a case of immobilist politics/
    Leonard James Schoppa.
        p.   cm. – (Nissan Institute/Routledge Japanese studies
    series)
    Originally submitted as the author's thesis (Oxford, 1988).
    Includes bibliographical references and index.
    ISBN 0–415–02062–X
    1. Education – Japan – History – 1945–   2. Politics and
    education – Japan – History.   3. Education and state –
    Japan – History.
    I. Title.   II. Series.
    LA1311.82.S33   1990   90–43470
    370′.952–dc20   CIP

To my father

Contents

Figures and tables

Acknowledgements

In the years I spent working on this book (originally a thesis submitted in 1988), I have become indebted to many individuals who have helped me at every stage of the research and writing-up process. Above all, I must thank my academic supervisor, Professor Arthur Stockwin, who introduced me to the workings of the Japanese political system and provided immeasurable assistance and encouragement throughout my time in Oxford. Professor Ronald Dore of London Imperial College and Dr Vincent Wright of Oxford also provided insights through their service as examiners for the thesis. Dr Roger Goodman, the Nissan Institute's resident expert on Japanese education, was also always there to help me put my ideas together – as were the rest of the Nissan staff. David Finegold, through our discussions comparing education reform in Britain with that in Japan, provided numerous insights. I owe a special debt to Cecil Rhodes and the Rhodes Trust for funding my studies at Oxford and providing further financial assistance to make possible two research trips to Japan. The entire staff of Rhodes House and especially the Warden, Dr Robin Fletcher, were always friendly and helpful. I must also thank Pembroke College and the Sasakawa Fund for providing further assistance toward those research trips.

In Japan special thanks goes to Munakata Miyo, the staff of the compulsory education division of the Kumamoto-ken school board and the many teachers I worked with during my year teaching in the lower secondary schools of that city. It was through them that I first became acquainted with the Japanese education system. In Tokyo my research would not have been possible without the assistance of Yasudu Izumi of *Bunka kaigi*, Takeda Michiyo and Nawashiro Aoi of the Diet Library, Yamanaka Shinichi of the Ministry of Education, Soejima Takeyoshi of *Nikkyōso* and Masuzoe Yōichi of Tokyo University. I must thank all of those who gave generously of their time for interviews, but especially Nakajima Akio, Kuroha Ryōichi and Watase Noriyuki, who were particularly helpful at the time when I was just beginning my research and maintained an interest in its progress. David Morris deserves special mention for all of his help in introducing me to the art of connection-building in Tokyo.

Finally, a special note of thanks to Roger Goodman again and Bonnie Saint John for their assistance in proofreading the original thesis under the time pressure of an approaching submission date.

Glossary of abbreviations

AHCE   Ad Hoc Council on Education (*Rinji kyōku shingikai* or *Rinkyōshin*) – supra-cabinet advisory council under Prime Minister Nakasone's office, established by law in 1984 and functioning until 1987

ANUP   Association of National University Presidents (*Kokuritsu daigaku kyōkai* or *Kokudaikyō*)

AS   *Asahi shimbun*, daily newspaper

AVM   Administrative vice-minister (*jimujikan*) – the senior career post in most Japanese ministries, including the MOE

CCE   Central Council on Education (*Chūō kyōiku shingikai* or *Chūkyōshin*) – permanent advisory council set up to advise the minister of education in 1952

DSP   Democratic Socialist Party (*Minshu shakaitō* or *Minshatō*)

DY   *Daily Yomiuri*

ERC   Education Reform Committee – Occupation period committee composed primarily of Japanese educators

ESRC   Education System Research Council (*Bunkyō seido chōsakai*) – one of the two primary education committees of the LDP's Policy Affairs Research Council

FLE   Fundamental Law of Education (*Kyōiku kihon-hō*) – law passed by the Diet in 1947 setting out the philosophy of post-war Japanese education

JCER   Japan Council for Economic Research (*Nihon keizai chōsa kyōgikai*) – policy research organ of the business community

JCP   Japan Communist Party (*Nihon kyōsantō*)

JSP   Japan Socialist Party (*Nihon shakaitō*)

KS   *Kyōiku shimbun*, weekly newspaper

LDP   Liberal Democratic Party (*Jiyū minshutō* or *Jimintō*)

MAFF Ministry of Agriculture, Forestry and Fisheries (*Nōgyō nōrin suisanshō* or *Nōrinshō*)

MFA   Ministry of Foreign Affairs (*Gaimushō*)

MITI   Ministry of International Trade and Industry (*Tsūshō sangyōshō* or *Tsūsanshō*)

MHW Ministry of Health and Welfare (*Kōseishō*)

MOE   Ministry of Education, Science and Culture (*Mombushō*)

MOF   Ministry of Finance (*Ōkurashō*)

MS   *Mainichi shimbun*, daily newspaper

NKS   *Nihon kyōiku shimbun*, weekly newspaper

PARC Policy Affairs Research Council (*Seimu chōsakai* or *Seichōkai*) – policy review organ of the LDP

PESA Prefectural Education Superintendents' Association (*Todōfuken kyōikuchō kyōgikai*)

PMO   Prime Minister's Office (*Sōrichō*)

RD   *Rinkyōshin dayori*

SS   *Sankei shimbun*, daily newspaper

TEU   Tokyo Education University (*Tokyo kyōiku daigaku*)

USEM United States Education Mission – group of US educators who visited Japan in 1946 and made recommendations for the reform of Japanese education. There were in fact two such missions. The reference in the text refers to the first.

YS   *Yomiuri shimbun*, daily newspaper

Glossary of Japanese terms

bukai	the divisions of the LDP's Policy Affairs Research Council, organized to correspond to the ministries of the cabinet
chūgakkō	lower secondary schools (the seventh, eighth and ninth years of formal schooling, serving ages 12 to 14)
funsō	the university 'troubles' of the late 1960s
genba	the actual site at which education is delivered (i.e. the schools and universities)
genjō iji	status quo maintenance
Hinomaru	the 'Sun Flag' used in many settings as Japan's national flag but opposed by the Left as a symbol of pre-war militarism
hōjinka	incorporation – refers to an education reform proposal calling for all national universities to be converted into autonomous corporations receiving block grants from the government
Jinkakuhō	the short Japanese name for the Law to Guarantee the Quality of Compulsory Education Teaching Personnel in order to Maintain and Improve the Quality of School Education
jiyūka	liberalization – refers to the set of policies promoted by a group of reformists on the AHCE. In this book it is used to refer specifically to those policies aimed at introducing free-market competitive forces into the education system as a means of forcing improvements
jūnanka	'flexibilization' – is used in this book to refer to education reform policies aiming to reduce the regulation of educational content

Keizai dōyūkai	Japanese Committee for Economic Development – one of the leading *zaikai* organizations
'Kimigayo'	a hymn to the emperor used in many settings as Japan's national anthem but opposed by the Left as a symbol of pre-war militarism
Kōmeitō	Opposition party which in English calls itself the Clean Government Party
kōtōgakkō	upper secondary schools (the tenth, eleventh and twelfth years of formal schooling, serving ages 15 to 17)
Kyōtsū-ichiji	the unified first-stage university entrance examination used by all national universities as the first step in the process whereby students are selected
Nikkeiren	*Nihon keieisha renmei* (Japanese Federation of Employers' Associations) – one of the leading *zaikai* organizations
Nikkyōso	*Nihon kyōshokuin kumiai* (Japan Teachers Union)
Rinchō	*Rinji gyōsei chōsakai* (Provisional Commission for Administrative Reform) – a supra-cabinet council, 1981–3, which called for a whole range of budget cut-backs and put the government on a strict diet of zero-budget ceilings
shiho	a long-standing reform proposal calling for new teachers to be classified as 'probationary' for a year before being fully employed, during which time they would receive training
shimon	a formal request for advice issued to advisory councils
shoninsha kenshū	a reform proposal similar to the *shiho* idea but emphasizing the one-year training programme rather than the probationary aspect
shūbetsuka	division into classes – one of the diversification proposals for higher education in the CCE

round of reform calling for post-secondary institutions to be divided into a number of more specific categories

shunin   teachers serving in positions of responsibility, such as the chief of instruction, the heads of grade, the heads of department and counsellors. Reforms introduced in the mid-1970s made these formerly unofficial positions into official mid-level management positions qualifying for a special salary bonus

zaikai   the Japanese business community, specifically those businessmen active in the peak economic organizations

zoku   unofficial cliques composed of LDP Dietmen sharing an interest in a particular area of public policy, typically composed of those Dietmen having served in PARC posts and cabinet positions related to that field. In this book the term is often used to refer to the education clique, the *bunkyōzoku*

1

Introduction and theoretical background

Today on the eve of the twenty-first century we are facing an age of transition – transition to an internationalized society, transition to an information-centred civilization, and transition from a fifty-year life span to an eighty-year life span. The further advance of science and technology in the twenty-first century will require a re-examination of our way of living and a careful effort to maintain our humanity. Education must respond to these requirements of the new age.

The Ad Hoc Council on Education, 1985[1]

Japan is known as an adaptable nation – famous for its success in achieving two great transformations in its modern history. First, following the Meiji Restoration in 1868, a cadre of reformists were able to transform feudal Japan into a fast-growing modern nation state by directing all of the nation's energies toward the goal of catching up with 'the west'. Then, after the Second World War, Japan was able to adjust equally efficiently to a new world order dominated by the United States – incorporating new democratic institutions and continuing its campaign to achieve economic parity with the western powers. In each of these great transformations, education reform played a central role. In the Meiji period, the reformist leaders' decision to institute universal primary education and a meritocratic system gave Japan an educated and trainable workforce and a talented elite at a time when the nation needed to make maximum use of its human resources in its effort to catch up. Later, following the war, the reforms carried out under the Allied Occupation succeeded in creating a more egalitarian and democratic education system, making it even more efficiently

1

meritocratic at a time when the nation needed skilled workers to power its post-war recovery.

By the beginning of the 1970s, however, Japan found itself at another critical juncture in its history. It had succeeded in its 'catch up' campaign, but having pursued the goal of economic growth relentlessly for some one hundred years, it was faced with the task of adjusting to a new role as one of the leading economic powers in a fast-changing and competitive world. Among the many demands for change which accompanied this new status were a need to adjust the nation's industrial structure to emphasize industries on the cutting edge of scientific and technological change; demands that the government stop emphasizing growth at the cost of damage to the environment; demands that Japan open up its markets to international competition; and demands that the nation assume more of the burden of its own defence. In addition, the government was forced to look once more at its education system. Successful though it was in terms of past performance, it had been designed for the catch up phase of Japan's development − structured to produce a large number of workers of a standard quality and to emphasize the selective function of examinations. With the Japanese economy increasingly dependent on international business and fast-changing science and technology industries, therefore, the government faced demands from many quarters calling on it to reform its education system to bring it into line with the growing need for more diversely talented and creative workers and a 'life-long learning system'.

In many areas the government adapted once again with efficiency: through an effective industrial policy, it was able to take the lead in several high-technology areas;[2] reversing its growth-at-all-costs position, it instituted firm anti-pollution laws in the early 1970s;[3] and by the mid-1980s it had opened many of its markets to international competition.[4] In the area of defence and in the case of certain market-opening disputes, the government was hampered to a greater degree by 'immobilist' forces. Nevertheless, it was able to achieve some change.[5]

In one area, however, the Japanese government's inability to achieve reform was particularly conspicuous. Twice in the twenty-year period between 1967 and 1987, it embarked on major education reform initiatives. The first reform campaign, culminating in the publication of a comprehensive programme for reform in 1971, sought to introduce a greater degree of diversity into the education system. The second, centred on the activities of a cabinet-level advisory body set up in 1984, similarly tried to achieve a freer and more flexible education system capable of producing the type of workers required for the next stage in Japan's economic advance. As indicated in the passage cited at the beginning this chapter, the aim of both initiatives was to create an education system in line with the transition to a 'new age'. Though both of these initiatives were accompanied by great fanfare and backed by the authority of the full government, however, neither produced significant changes in the education system. It is this failure of the government to achieve its objectives in the area of education reform which serves as the focus of this case study in Japanese policy-making.

THE FIRST INITIATIVE

The first of the two recent attempts to transform Japan's education system began when the Minister of Education, Kennoki Toshihiro, made a little-noticed 'request for advice' from the Central Council on Education (CCE, *Chūkyōshin*) in 1967. Kennoki and the Ministry of Education, Science and Culture (MOE, *Mombushō*) wanted the council to examine the whole school system – pre-school through to higher education – and produce 'basic guidelines for the development of an integrated educational system suited for contemporary society'. Despite its grand mandate, however, the 1967 CCE would probably have had little publicity or impact were it not for the university disturbances which suddenly put education reform at the top of the political agenda in the late 1960s. After making an emergency recommendation on how to resolve the university crisis in 1969, the council went on to produce a comprehensive, high-profile set of 'basic guidelines' for reform in June 1971.

Among its numerous recommendations the council proposed that Japan experiment with alternatives to its strictly standardized '6–3–3 system' (six years of elementary education, three years of lower secondary school and three years of upper secondary school). Pilot projects were to be set up to test the specific ideas of a lower school-starting age and a unified secondary education. In addition, the council proposed to increase the diversity of the school system by making the upper

3

secondary education curriculum more flexible and by allowing streaming and grade-skipping. Aiming to strengthen the management of schools and improve the quality of teachers, the council also proposed to increase the ranks of school administrators, raise teachers' salaries, create a new salary scale recognizing graduate-trained teachers and require new teachers to undergo a full probationary year before being fully employed. The report's section on university reform concentrated primarily on a call for administrative reforms aimed at increasing central management authority and responsibility.

While other recommendations calling for increased aid to kindergartens, education for the handicapped and private education were gradually implemented, the more controversial reforms listed above met a stormy response. Although some were implemented over vehement protests from the teachers' union and other progressive organizations, the central recommendation calling for pilot projects and the most controversial reforms concerning teachers (a reformed salary scale and the probationary year) were abandoned. As the 1970s drew to a close, the most telling sign of the first initiative's failure was the state of the school system. For all of the CCE's calls for flexibility and diversity, Japanese students continued to have no alternative to the standard 6−3−3 system. In fact, with more students than ever seeking to enter university, individual teachers and upper secondary schools were given little opportunity to take advantage of more flexible curriculum guidelines: virtually all classes had to be directed towards helping students pass the standard national university entrance examination. Universities, with a small number of exceptions, remained wedded to decentralized forms of administration long criticized as barriers to their ability to adapt to social and economic change.

THE SECOND INITIATIVE

In initiating a second reform campaign in 1984, the Prime Minister, Nakasone Yasuhiro, essentially confirmed that the 1971 reform attempt had fallen a long way short of its goals. The reason the previous initiative had not succeeded, he argued, was that it had been dominated by the MOE. As a single bureaucracy, it could not build the support necessary for more than 'minor improvements' in the system, whereas the Japanese education system required major structural and philosophical changes.[6] Consequently, Nakasone sought and won Diet approval of his plan to establish a supra-cabinet advisory body directly under his office – the Ad Hoc Council on Education (AHCE, *Rinkyōshin*). Its task, as outlined by the Prime Minister at its inaugural meeting, was to address the immediate problems of growing school violence and misbehaviour as well as the more basic problems of 'a social climate that places too much value on the academic background of individuals, a uniform and inflexible structure of formal education and a need for internationalizing Japan's educational institutions'. The challenge, Nakasone concluded, was to 'create an educational system which copes with the change in times', one which would help 'build up a society full of vitality and creativity relevant to the twenty-first century'.[7]

Established at a time of heightened public concern about violence and misbehaviour in the schools, the AHCE started its work in August 1984 with a large majority of the public convinced of the need for some change. Yet, despite such support and the broad mandate it enjoyed from the Diet and the Prime Minister, the council gradually discarded most proposals for real change. The most significant debate concerned suggestions that elements of diversity and competition be introduced into the school system through the liberalization of government regulations. While the council in the end gave the principle some support, it expressly rejected proposals to deregulate textbooks and allow free parental choice in the selection of compulsory (elementary and lower secondary) schools. Even in its comments on the need to minimize the amount of detail in the curriculum and similar regulations, the council left its recommendations vague enough to allow substantial room for MOE non-implementation. While the council considered Nakasone's suggestion that the national university entrance examination be abolished, in the end it decided merely to abolish the old test and create a new one. The AHCE could not even agree on a plan to shift the starting date for the school year from April to the September start which is most common in the west.

As for the proposals which survived the AHCE debate, the record on implementation up to the end of 1987 was decidedly mixed. Some recommendations – such as those calling for the internationalization of the education system and its adjustment to the 'information age' – enjoyed broad support and looked

5

likely to win gradual approval. The council's more controversial proposal to require a 'training year' for all new teachers was in the pilot project stage and appeared likely to be expanded nation-wide as funds allowed. Likewise, such conservative-supported proposals as those calling for increased moral education and greater use of the 'national flag' and 'national anthem' were quickly being written into MOE guidelines.

Other proposals, however, were languishing for a lack of MOE enthusiasm. The proposal to allow prefectures to establish six-year secondary schools – contained in the council's 1985 report – remained 'under study'. The vague call for a minimization of regulations was not being taken very seriously by the MOE. Despite broad support, the AHCE's proposals aimed at reducing the emphasis on academic credentials were simply too vague to produce concrete action: the government itself continued to hire its top bureaucrats almost exclusively from the University of Tokyo. After three years of high-profile deliberations by a powerful advisory body, the state of the education system had changed very little: children still had no choice besides the 6−3−3 system; almost all of the 99 per cent of parents who sent their elementary school children to public schools still had a choice of only one school; and entrance examinations continued to dominate secondary schooling. If it was true – as Nakasone asserted – that Japan was in need of a less standardized and less credential-orientated system to meet the challenge of the twenty-first century, the AHCE reform had not produced it.

EDUCATION REFORM AS POLICY-MAKING

Were this study concerned merely with the content of Japan's recent reform packages, it would not have to go much further than the above analysis. The results of the initiatives were not very impressive. This book, however, is not a study of educational policies. Rather, as a work which treats education reform as a case study in Japanese policy-making, it is interested not so much in the quality of the results as in the way those results were produced. While the limited nature of the final reform packages might dampen the interest of an educationalist, the fact that so many reformist ideas failed to be implemented actually makes Japanese education reform more interesting as a study in politics.

The primary aim of this book is to explain this failure. It asks: why did the Japanese government fail to achieve its reform objectives in the sphere of education? The study will focus on the nature of education issues, the actors involved in education policy and the education policy-making process and ask what it is about the sphere of education which explains the government's 'immobilism' in that area. The use of such words as 'failure' and 'immobilism' perhaps produces the impression that this study is based on the idea that education reform is necessarily desirable in Japan. In fact, it seeks to avoid that normative issue. Observers inside and outside Japan have pointed to many strengths of the Japanese education system, and it may be that some of the changes sought by the government were not desirable. Immobilism may or may not be 'good' depending on one's viewpoint. Maintaining a formal neutrality on this normative issue, the study aims to explain empirically the inability of the government leadership to achieve its reform objectives.

While the book is concerned above all with explaining the reasons for immobilism in the case of education reform, it is ultimately interested in the degree to which the Japanese policy-making process in general is or is not adaptable: to what extent are Japanese leaders able to achieve the policy changes they see as necessary? The introductory discussion outlined some of the numerous policy challenges facing Japan in its new position at the forefront of the world economy. In addition, like all nations, Japan faces a continuous stream of policy challenges arising out of a need to adapt to a fast-changing world. While not all of these challenges demand radical policy 'change', all of them demand a policy-making process which allows the nation's leadership, based on a broad view of social and economic needs, to change those policies which need changing. In its response to the policy challenges in the areas of industrial and environmental policy, the Japanese policy-making process has definitely met that test. At other times, however, the system has been characterized by what has been termed 'immobilism' – 'an inability to do more than accommodate competing pressures and effect a "lowest common denominator" compromise between them'.[8] This study seeks to explain this variation in the Japanese system's responsiveness.

Japan is, of course, not unique in being more responsive in its approach to some policy challenges than to others. All governments will naturally be able to arrive at solutions to some issues which are 'dynamic' while in other cases being totally stymied by immobilism. The government's responsiveness depends on many factors specific to a given issue. The aim of this book, therefore, is to examine the government's inability to achieve education reform in an effort to identify at least some of the issue-specific factors which account for the range in the Japanese system's responsiveness to specific policy challenges. By explaining what factors determine the level of policy-making effectiveness in specific cases, the study aims to locate that point at which the Japanese system becomes 'immobile'. In other words, the study seeks to locate what can be termed 'the limits of change in Japanese policy-making'.

This final phrasing of the central question in terms of 'the limits of change' points towards the secondary concerns which lie behind it. Ultimately, the study is interested in the issue of whether or not a system like Japan's – wedded to a single predominant party and committed to a form of 'consensual' decision-making – can cope with demands for change. Both of these features of the Japanese political system are well known. The Liberal Democratic Party (LDP, *Jimintō*) has remained in power continuously since its founding in 1955, ruling alone for all but a brief period (1983–6) when it took in the tiny New Liberal Club as a coalition partner. It has maintained its rule, furthermore, by broadening its political base and seeking consensus decisions whenever possible. While this oversimplified description of Japanese politics is developed in much greater detail below, it clearly raises interesting questions about the ability of such a system to deal with new circumstances and demands. To what degree can a system firmly set in patterns of one-party dominance and consensus rule maintain the vitality needed to meet new policy challenges?

A THEORETICAL FRAMEWORK

Before focusing on the actual case study of education reform, it is necessary first to examine the basic structure of the Japanese policy-making system. Other case studies and broader studies of the system have provided important insights into the way in which policy-making works in Japan – insights which will aid in the analysis of the government's education reform efforts which follows. The goal of this section, therefore, is to provide a framework for an issue-specific study through an examination of the theories about the way policy is made in Japan. The effort to develop this framework is concentrated in two stages: (1) an attempt to discover *who* makes policy in Japan and (2) an attempt to determine *how* policy is made.

Power and conflict in the Japanese policy-making system

Theories about the division of power in Japan have undergone substantial change in recent years. Up until at least the early 1970s, the orthodox line of argument had it that Japan was run by a uniquely unified power elite – a 'triad' of bureaucracy, business and the LDP. As one often-quoted passage described it, these were the 'three legs of the tripod on which the Japanese political system rests'.[9] Focusing on the left–right polarized divide which was so visible particularly in the first two decades following the war, advocates of this model emphasized the manner in which the three 'establishment' actors effectively succeeded in excluding organized labour and the opposition parties in order to settle most issues among themselves.[10]

In recent years, however, a growing number of scholars have focused on divisions within and among the three elite actors in arguing that the Japanese system is actually much more plural-istic than suggested by the power elite model's image of a system neatly balanced on the three legs of a tripod.[11] Some have also disputed the model's primary contention that the progressive opposition is irrelevant to the policy process.[12] While these various studies have attempted to present alternative visions of how policy is made in Japan, however, their contributions are perhaps better seen as *modifications* of the older power elite model. For while all of them portray a system which is much more complex than the 'tripod' conception, few dispute that the Japanese policy-making system remains fundamentally elitist: due to the extended tenure of the LDP and its close co-operation with the bureaucracy and certain interest groups, some actors have more direct influence on the policy process than others. There is 'pluralism', but it is an unbalanced kind of pluralism. The following survey of the literature on power and conflict in Japanese policy-making helps define what has been called 'patterned pluralism'.[13]

The central role of the bureaucracy

While advocates of the elite model of Japanese politics have emphasized the overall power of bureaucracy,[14] pluralists have pointed to the importance of its various parts as representatives of diverse interests.[15] Both agree, however, that the ministries play a central role in the Japanese policy process. As a parliamentary democracy (with a structure similar to that of the United Kingdom), the system is naturally centred on the bureaucracy to a greater extent than, for example, the United States. As in the United Kingdom, the ministries are charged with the task of drafting legislation. They also have access to more information than do politicians.[16] They are able to use powers of administrative guidance,[17] and the various ministries oversee many advisory bodies which are often used to legitimize policy positions held by the parent departments.[18]

Finally, it is also significant that bureaucrats in Japan seem to maintain a superior attitude towards politicians, seeing themselves as guardians of 'neutral' policy-making based on their expert examination of objective facts.[19] Such a self-image naturally leads them to seek a more assertive role in the policy process. Several scholars have concluded, based on these features of the Japanese system, that the Japanese Diet is in the end a mere ratifier of decisions reached within the bureaucracy.[20] While such comments overstate the case for the bureaucracy's dominance, there can be no doubt that the ministries do have substantial powers with which to influence policy outcomes.

The growing role of the LDP

While many studies of Japanese policy-making have emphasized the importance of the nation's bureaucrats, most recent studies have found that the LDP has – over time – increased its influence in the policy process.[21] The major cause of this shift in power has been the simple fact of the party's continuing rule. While it may have been true that the LDP once left many details of policy-making to the government ministries and agencies,[22] it has used its dominance of electoral politics since 1955 to take increasing control over the decision-making process. Most importantly, the party organ charged with overseeing the policy-making process – the Policy Affairs Research Council (PARC, *Seichōkai*) – has emerged as an effective partner (some would say dominator) of the government ministries. With divisions (*bukai*) set up to correspond to each government ministry, and research committees (*chōsakai*) established to deal with most major policy issues, PARC serves as an effective organization for promoting the party's interests in the policy-making process.[23]

In addition, while the LDP remains dependent on the ministries for some of its information, many of its members have acquired at least as much policy expertise as can be claimed by even the most senior bureaucrats. With Dietmen specializing in a particular area from early in their often very long careers, many LDP Diet members rival or surpass their bureaucratic colleagues in the years they can claim to have spent working on any particular policy area. Typically, young Diet members become active in one or two PARC divisions corresponding with a specialized policy field. Those who are successful and remain in office then move up through the party ranks while consistently serving in positions related to their area of specialization: political vice-minister of the relevant ministry, chairman of the relevant PARC division, chairman of the relevant Diet committee and finally the occupant of the relevant cabinet post. Such Dietmen, known as members of unofficial policy-specialized cliques called *zoku*, exercise significant power and leadership in their areas.[24]

The continuing rule of the LDP and the development of *zoku* have given the LDP an increasing ability to influence the policy formulation activities of the ministries. Particularly the top ministry officials (bureau chief and above) tend to respect the political priorities of the LDP members influential in their area, consulting with them throughout the legislative and budget processes and getting their consent prior to all major decisions.[25] The LDP and the *zoku* have succeeded in increasing their influence in this way at least partly through their power over ministry personnel decisions.[26] The party has also gained leverage over the bureaucracy in the recent period of tight budgets as ministries have learned that they cannot succeed in getting new programmes or even in maintaining their share of the budget without the support of their *zoku*.[27] Finally, the party has taken advantage of the increasing 'complexity' of problems – the fact that they are beyond the realm of any single ministry – to assert its influence. Problems such as administrative reform, involving the need to co-ordinate the policies of numerous ministries and agencies, and issues such as agricultural policy, which have increasingly acquired an international dimension beyond the purview of the ministry nominally in charge, have called for the type of broad view and flexible leadership which only the party has been capable of providing.[28]

The importance of subgovernments

While much of the literature on Japanese policy-making has been preoccupied with the question of whether the bureaucracy or the LDP is the dominant partner in the process, there is a danger in overemphasizing this issue. As a substantial number of case studies and broader analyses have pointed out, the most significant conflicts explaining policy outcomes are often not the conflicts between the LDP and the bureaucracy but sectoral conflicts based on cleavages which cut across party and bureaucratic lines to create distinct issue-orientated divisions.[29]

One of the most important of the studies emphasizing the importance of these 'subgovernments' was John C. Campbell's 1977 study of the budget process. Borrowing the terminology from studies of the American political system, he describes Japanese subgovernments as units centred on the various government ministries, each of which is linked to a corresponding division of the LDP's Policy Affairs Research Council and the interest groups concerned with that ministry's activities.[30] Thus the health and welfare subgovernment, for example, is composed of the Ministry of Health and Welfare (MHW, Kōseishō), the PARC Health and Welfare Division and such interest groups as the Japan Medical Association, while the agriculture subgovernment is composed of the agricultural bureaux of the Ministry of Agriculture, Forestry and Fisheries (MAFF, Nōrinshō), the PARC Agriculture Division and such groups as the agricultural co-operatives. Competition between doctors and farmers for their share of the budget is not reflected in fights between political parties or in disputes between the LDP and the bureaucracy but rather takes the shape of a battle between these two separate subgovernments. While Campbell admits that varying degrees of internal conflict can be found *within* individual subgovernments, he finds that the budget process at least is dominated by competition *between* the units.[31]

At the centre of this subgovernmental conflict – as Campbell describes it – is the Ministry of Finance (MOF, Ōkurashō). Receiving numerous demands from the peripheral ministries and their supporters, the MOF is charged with providing a 'balanced' final budget which goes as far as possible in meeting requests while staying within the limits imposed by the government's fiscal capabilities.[32] The LDP leadership too is at least superficially involved in guiding this process through its decisions on spending priorities. While Campbell's judgement on the superficiality of the LDP budget role might be disputed – particularly in view of changes which have taken place since restrictive budget ceilings were applied in the 1980s – his placement of the two actors at the centre of subgovernmental conflict completes a picture of the Japanese budget process which serves as a useful paradigm of the broader policy-making process.[33]

While Campbell did not immediately seek to extend his findings about the budget process to the Japanese policy-making process as a whole, he does so in a more recent work. He writes:

> Subgovernments thus constitute a set of interest-based cleavages that divide the entire decision-making system. These cleavages are crucially reinforced by the deep formal-organization cleavages between the ministries. Interactions *within* subgovernments must be taken into account in analyzing the conflict patterns of nearly all policy issues, and moreover the relationships *between* subgovernments are the key to understanding most issues that are broader than the jurisdiction of a single ministry.[34]

Campbell thus describes the Japanese policy process in a way which is clearly more complex than the simple idea of a 'power elite', a 'dominant bureaucracy' or a 'dominant party'. For him the most significant dynamic of the process is not the elite–progressive conflict or the bureaucracy–party rivalry. Rather, he locates the crucial dynamic *within* a single subgovernment in the case of narrowly focused issues while emphasizing the importance of conflict *between* subgovernments in the case of broader issues. Thus, for example, while the narrow question of where to build a road might involve primarily a bargaining process between the transportation *zoku* and the Ministry of Transportation, a broader issue such as the government-wide competition for budget resources would be likely to bring the two actors together to battle with the rest of the government for a larger transport allocation.

'Patterned pluralism'

In important respects, the policy-making system described by Campbell is 'pluralist'. A whole range of interest groups, through their respective ties with different sections of the bureaucracy and different sections of the LDP, take part in the policy-making process. To that extent, the system is not very different from the policy processes in many other modern democracies. The way pluralism operates under the Japanese system, however, has been fundamentally affected by the extended one-party dominance of the LDP. Without the ebb and flow of party alternation, interest groups have lost any incentive to maintain their party neutrality. With the exception of those groups such as organized labour and citizen's groups which have maintained their distance for ideological reasons, virtually all interests have developed close ties with their respective sections of the party and bureaucracy. As several studies have found, the LDP and the ministries have come to be 'penetrated' by interest groups who over the years have developed close working relationships based on mutual support: the interests help the ministries lobby to increase their budgets, and the ministries help the interest groups by representing their points of view.[35] Another effect of the LDP's extended rule has been a blurring of the LDP and bureaucratic roles in the policy-making process. While studies of policy-making in other nations have discovered similar trends towards 'hybridization', this process seems to have progressed to a particularly significant degree in Japan due to the lack of party alternation.[36]

The close ties between the LDP, the bureaucracy and certain interest groups are in contrast to the lack of such ties on the part of the opposition parties and progressive interest groups. These actors are effectively frozen out of the policy-making process.[37] Progressive interests do, however, enjoy close ties with the opposition parties, and together they are able to influence the process to a degree from outside formal channels. As several studies have revealed, the opposition has at times been able to exercise a significant blocking power when certain of its fundamental interests have been at stake and when the public has been sympathetic with its position. This was true particularly during the period in the mid to late 1970s, when the Diet was almost evenly split between the LDP and the opposition parties.[38] Nevertheless, such influence must be seen as clearly distinct from that exercised by the LDP and the large numbers of interests tied to various sections of the bureaucracy and party.

While there is real pluralism in the Japanese system, therefore, it is pluralism which has developed a particular 'pattern' over the many years of LDP rule. Coining the term 'patterned pluralism', Muramatsu Michio and Ellis Krauss describe the basic structure of Japanese policy-making as follows:

> Policymaking conflicts under patterned pluralism are *pluralist* in that many diverse actors whose alliances may shift participate, but *patterned* in that the shifting coalitions occur within the framework of one-party dominance and of a bureaucracy that procedurally structures the types of possible alliances and policymaking patterns.[39]

Other recent studies have summed up the Japanese system in similar terms. All of them describe a division of power which is pluralist – but in a way which is slanted towards a particular side of the political spectrum.[40]

Conflict resolution and policy-making in Japan

The above description of pluralism in one-party dominant Japan provides a general outline of the Japanese policy-making system but leaves certain key questions unanswered. It identifies the primary actors and the most important cleavages, yielding a framework for answering the question, 'who governs?' It does not, however, provide much of a hint as to *how* policy is produced in such a system. Specifically, while pointing out the extensive links between different sections of the government and a large variety of interest groups, the outline of the policy-making system as developed thus far provides few clues as to how conflicts are resolved to produce policy within such a system.

This question is given added impetus when one considers that one of the primary mechanisms for conflict resolution available in many liberal democracies is not an option in Japan: because of the LDP's continuing dominance, conflicts cannot be resolved through party alternation. Thus, for example, whereas another nation might resolve a dispute over whether to favour declining industries or new industries through an election in

15

which the party allied to new industries replaced the party allied to declining industries, such a resolution could not be expected in one-party dominant Japan. This limitation has become particularly notable as more and more interests have flocked to the LDP banner over its prolonged period of rule. Several recent studies have documented this trend.[41] The LDP is the party of both rising industries and declining industries, of both small business and large business, of both farmers and consumers. At budget time, virtually every organization with a claim to a share of government funds has a connection with some part of the LDP and/or some part of the bureaucracy. Without the option of party alternation, all conflicts must be resolved (or at least avoided) within the stable system of LDP rule.

There is of course a danger in overemphasizing the importance of party alternation in resolving conflicts in liberal democracies. Many nations only seldom see a change in government, and even those that do often rotate power inevitably face situations in which the ruling party or coalition wants to please both sides of a dispute. Nevertheless, the prolonged rule of the LDP has created an extreme situation which definitely raises questions about its ability to avoid succumbing to immobilism. Given the primary concern of this book with the degree to which the Japanese system is able to overcome such pressures in order to deal constructively with policy challenges, the issue of how conflict is actually resolved in Japan is a central concern.

Most of the literature of relevance to this question has been in the form of case studies. Numerous studies have recorded how conflicts were resolved to produce policy in specific instances.[42] Two scholars in particular, however, have sought to move beyond specific cases to make generalizations about conflict resolution in Japanese policy-making: T.J. Pempel and, as previously cited, John C. Campbell. Neither provides a theory that is perfectly explanatory, though elements in both theories provide important insights.

The Pempel contribution

Although his study (published in 1978) is somewhat dated, Pempel's attempt to describe how certain types of issues tend to produce certain types of conflict resolution techniques provides a useful starting-point for this attempt to develop a framework for an issue-specific study. According to his analysis, based on a study of policy in the area of high education, conflict resolution

16

techniques tend to depend on the 'divisibility', 'scope' and 'affect' of the issue. As Pempel explains it, 'divisibility' refers to the degree to which a certain decision can be compromised: does it call for a clear-cut Yes or No answer or are there choices in between? 'Scope' refers to the nature of the group affected by a policy proposal: will the decision have a wide scope (affecting many people a little bit) or will it have a narrow scope (affecting a few people a lot)? Finally, Pempel uses the term 'affect' as a measure of an issue's emotional content.[43]

His thesis is that Japanese policy-making generally tends to follow one of three patterns depending on the nature of the issue as defined by the above concepts. If an issue is characterized by low divisibility, narrow scope and high affect, it will tend to deteriorate into a polarized 'camp conflict' style of decision-making with one side (inevitably the progressive Opposition) forced to use extreme means like street protests and boycotts of the Diet so that the other (always the government) is forced to decide the issue with a show of force. At the other extreme, if an issue is highly divisible, wide in scope and low in its affect, it will probably be settled quietly through a process of 'incremental change'. Issues which are somewhere between these extremes – for example those involving narrow scope but low affect – are likely to be settled through 'pressure group pluralism' involving hard but good-faith bargaining between affected groups.[44]

While Pempel's analysis offers important insights into the relationship between conflict and policy-making patterns in Japan, it suffers from one major oversight. In limiting his discussion on 'high affect' conflicts to those matching the conservatives against the progressives, he fails to allow for the possibility of serious conflict *within* the conservative camp. The assumption is clearly stated in Pempel's more comprehensive study *Policy and Politics in Japan*:

> So long as policymaking involves members of the conservative coalition, the process will be largely consensual and bureaucratic; when the conservative circle can no longer encapsulate the preponderant forces relevant to a policy decision, there is a strong likelihood that jarring conflict will result.[45]

According to Pempel, the two main forces outside the 'conservative circle' include foreign actors and the progressive Opposition. While serious conflict certainly tends to arise when such outside groups get involved, Pempel goes too far in his assertion that policy-making will be 'consensual and bureaucratic' as long as such actors are not involved. The past decade is full of examples of conflictual issues which have sparked serious disagreement *within* rather than just outside the conservative coalition. The government proposal to cut rice prices, administrative reform, the sales tax and education reform are just a few of the cases which have involved significant intramural conflict.[46] Pempel himself, perceiving a rise in centrifugal tendencies in the conservative camp, has recently begun to concentrate his study on such internal conflict.[47] Given that he has yet to integrate these 'new' conflicts into his model, however, the 'Pempel model' must be seen as incomplete. It provides important insights into how the system functions in relation to the dominant left–right conflict but leaves one wondering whether conflictual issues (low divisibility, narrow scope and high affect) involving purely intra-camp conflict are resolved in the same way as those involving inter-camp disagreements.

Campbell's contribution

Campbell's study, focusing on conflict *within* the conservative camp, serves as a natural complement to the incomplete Pempel model. While he does not offer a clear set of policy-making patterns along the lines of Pempel's analysis, his discovery that internal conflicts often lead to 'conflict avoidance' rather than the 'forced resolution' marking disagreements with external interests suggests a need to add to Pempel's threefold categorization of policy-making patterns.

Campbell's emphasis on subgovernmental conflict (within the conservative camp) was noted above. His most interesting argument, however, is his assertion that the Japanese system fails to resolve many of these internal conflicts due to the way in which policy-makers attempt to abide by rules of consensus policy-making which often do not fit the circumstances.[48] Despite the reality of significant intramural conflict, Campbell argues, Japanese policy-makers tend to abide by an implicit theory which 'holds that a pure consensus model, when it can work, will produce the best output: decisions that not only satisfy all relevant participants but are speedily reached and appropriate to the problem'.[49] That Japanese small groups tend to prefer the consensus form of decision-making to adversarial majority-rule has been widely asserted in sociological literature.[50] Campbell argues that Japanese policy-makers too tend to prefer such a consensus style – despite the fact that small group dynamics are not readily transferable to national policy-making. The policy-making process is complicated by this difficulty in transference.

In some cases, Campbell found, policy-makers are able to overcome disagreements through the means of 'contrived consensus' involving the use of inter-agency project teams, top-level advisory bodies and mediation from above.[51] In many cases, however, the conflicts are simply too deep and too intense. No common interest can be found and a consensus compromise cannot be reached. In such cases, rather than deciding an issue by majority vote, Japanese policy-makers tend simply to run away from the problem. While such conflict avoidance can be found in many societies, Campbell argues, it is unusually common in Japan. Disagreements, he writes, tend to be 'ignored, papered over, postponed in hopes they will go away, or arbitrarily settled by imposing some mechanical and therefore acceptable decision-making rule'.[52] This policy-making pattern is clearly different from the 'forced resolution' of Pempel's left–right conflicts.

A final modification

While Campbell's analysis serves to fill in one of the holes in Pempel's analysis, one weakness remains. Neither of the two studies provides for a pattern of conflict resolution which recognizes the fact that the progressive opposition sometimes succeeds in blocking government initiatives. Campbell does not see the opposition camp as playing any role whatsoever. As he writes, 'In Japan, except perhaps for a brief period in the 1970s, the partisan cleavage is not directly relevant to the formulation of public policy.'[53] While such a conclusion may be understandable given Campbell's background in budget policy where the opposition is indeed all but irrelevant, it does not change the fact that the opposition has played an important part in numerous recent policy-making conflicts – including education reform. While Pempel recognizes the opposition's role in making the government 'force' a resolution in certain cases, he too does not adequately account for its limited blocking power.

It is possible to account for this opposition role, however, without throwing out the Pempel–Campbell emphasis on policy-making which revolves around the need for conservative consensus. As will be shown in this study's examination of the role played by the opposition in the case of education reform, the opposition's ability to block certain initiatives may best be seen as an *indirect* power arising from its ability to 'break the conservative consensus' by raising vocal protests and convincing a segment of the conservative camp to back down.

The Pempel–Campbell model

The arguments of Pempel and Campbell, if modified to allow for a limited opposition role, thus provide the basis for a fairly complete model of conflict resolution patterns in Japanese policy-making: (1) low-conflict disputes – some combination of high divisibility, wide scope and low affect – tend to result in incremental change or pressure group pluralism involving 'contrived consensus' type decision-making; (2) high-conflict disputes involving *outside forces* – again defined on Pempel's scale – result in camp conflict and either (a) forced resolution by the government or (b) opposition success in convincing at least some conservatives to back down – thereby creating a situation not unlike the next category; (3) high-conflict disputes involving primarily *conservative camp actors* result in conflict avoidance and little change. At the centre of this categorization is the idea of conservative consensus: the policy-making process requires a consensus *within* the conservative camp while not requiring the approval of non-conservative forces.[54] It recognizes, however, that progressive forces are sometimes able to play an indirect role by 'breaking the conservative consensus'.

Education reform within the Pempel–Campbell framework

This modified synthesis of the Pempel and Campbell models forms the starting-point for this study of recent education policy-making in Japan. In seeking to understand why the government failed in its education reform attempts, this book will therefore concentrate on the following questions: (1) What are the basic conflicts which animate the education reform debate? (2) How intense are these conflicts? (3) Are these conflicts internal or external? (4) How do all of these factors affect the patterns of conflict resolution and policy development? By exploring the way conflicts in the education sphere have affected conflict resolution patterns and policy outcomes, the study seeks to explain why Japan has had difficulty reforming its education system – thereby providing a partial answer to the broader question regarding the ability of the government to achieve change in contemporary Japan.

The organization of the book is structured to correspond closely to the questions suggested by the Pempel–Campbell framework. First, in Chapter 2 the study begins the process of identifying the conflicts which animate the contemporary education reform debate by focusing on the historical background and immediate issues which prompted the two recent initiatives. Chapters 3, 4 and 5 focus closely on conflicts within the conservative camp, revealing significant divisions within the LDP (Chapter 3), within the bureaucracy (Chapter 4) and within the interest groups close to the government (Chapter 5). These cleavages are found to reflect conflicts over 'turf' as well as serious disagreements over issues. Chapter 6 takes a close look at the role of the progressive opposition in the recent initiatives, examining in particular the role of the Japan Teachers Union (*Nikkyōso*). Chapters 7 and 8 then examine how all of these actors and all of these conflicts have fitted together in the recent reform initiatives. Confirming many of the observations of the previous chapters, each concludes with a comprehensive analysis of the record of reform in the respective reform campaigns, graphically illustrating how the failure of key reform proposals can be explained by two major reform-blocking factors: the absence of a conservative consensus and Opposition aggravation of conservative disagreements. Finally, Chapter 9 returns to the broader question of Japan's ability to adapt, examining closely the factors behind the government's failure to achieve its education reform objectives and seeking to determine the degree to which these factors might be relevant to other policy challenges.

2

Background to the recent debate

On the surface, the debate over education in Japan since 1967 has been about immediate concerns: the university protests of the late 1960s, the school violence of the 1980s and the growing need for a 'flexible' education system to meet the needs of the twenty-first century. As with most political debates, however, recent arguments over education reform cannot be explained merely in terms of the latest problems. To many of those involved, the new issues are almost irrelevant. Conditioned by years of hard-fought ideological combat, these actors show few signs of noticing the shift in subject-matter – preferring to fight from the safety of trenches dug and fortified long ago. The modern debate, therefore, is very much a reflection of the long-running battle which has divided the education world since the war – a battle which in turn is rooted in the broader history of education politics in Japan.

The history of education politics, like that of Japan in general, is dominated by the two great transformations which have marked its modern history. First, the Meiji Restoration brought to power a group of reform-minded leaders who sought to use education as part of their broader effort to build a strong, centralized nation-state. Then, following the Second World War, the Occupation gave Japan a strong dose of 'democratization', applied in the field of education as well as to society in general. The combination of these successive transformations has left a system with often divergent tendencies. Today the centralized nation-building conception of the role of education must compete with the more decentralized, democracy-building conception. What has remained constant is the premiss of both conceptions, that education should play a key society-building role. The struggle is over what form of society it should foster – a question which explains the continuing national preoccupation with education issues.

An understanding of 'education reform 1967–1987' thus requires a basic appreciation of the history of education in Japan – the policies and systems which preceded the current ones and the conflicts of the past which continue to shape the views of individuals and institutions today. This chapter provides a brief summary of that history, emphasizing in particular those aspects of the past which most affect the character of the recent debate. The final section traces the history right up to the recent reform initiatives, outlining the immediate issues which prompted the government's twenty-year struggle to bring about another great reform in the education system.

THE BIRTH OF JAPAN'S 'MODERN' EDUCATION SYSTEM

Although the Meiji Restoration of 1868 marked a turning-point in Japan's emergence from its long period of international isolation, it was almost twenty years before the nation could settle on an education system seen as able to meet the foreign challenge. During this period the nation was divided into numerous factions, each advocating what it considered to be the best course. Some argued that Japan should import the American model of liberal education along with its textbooks and scientific know-how. Others resisted such a radical approach, pointing to the emptiness of a 'victory' over the west which entailed the sacrifice of traditional values. A final group sought to have it both ways, aiming to maintain basic Japanese values while also mobilizing the talents of the nation through a centralized, meritocratic, 'modern' educational system. The outcome of this earlier education reform debate – resolved in favour of the final group – was to have a major effect on the attitudes and political positions of all actors involved in the modern education debate.

The Tokugawa legacy

Even before the birth of 'modern' education, Japan already had a large number of schools and a comparatively literate population. Ronald Dore estimates that by 1870, some 40 to 50 per cent

23

of boys and 15 per cent of girls were receiving at least some formal schooling.[1] Commoners – especially the children of the wealthier villagers and townspeople – could get a basic education in their local *terakoya*, privately-run schools which provided their students with practical training in reading, writing and arithmetic along with some moral guidance.[2] A well-developed network of schools administered by the various feudal authorities (the local *han* and the central *bakufu*) served the 7 per cent of the population who were of the samurai class. Although these schools too offered some practical training in the skills necessary for effective civil administration, they were set up primarily to provide the ruling class with moral values rooted in the study of the Chinese Confucian classics.[3]

Both in its class-orientated organization and in its emphasis on Confucian ethics for the elite, the Tokugawa system of education was dedicated above all to maintaining the social order. The Sung school of Confucianism – emphasized in the *han* and *bakufu* schools for most of the Tokugawa period – taught samurai-class students the values of virtuous living and harmonious relations.[4] Individuals received education according to their place in society, enabling each to fulfil the role assigned to him by his class. Partly because of the success of these order-enhancing aspects of Tokugawa education, the Shogunate was able to survive for over 250 years. While the era came to a close with the Meiji Restoration, it left behind a tradition which emphasized this ability of education – particularly *moral* education – to preserve order.

The end of class-based education

The strict class-based structure of the Tokugawa system, however, did not survive the Meiji reforms. Even under the feudal system, some horizontal movement based on ability and education had become possible by the late Tokugawa period.[5] The Meiji reformers – themselves lower-ranking samurai – realized early in their campaign that a new educational system designed to meet the challenge of the west would have to be designed to mobilize the talents of the whole nation, regardless of class. As Fukuzawa Yukichi wrote, 'All the people of the country, whether noble or base, whether high or low, must feel that they have a personal responsibility for the country.'[6] The Meiji leaders therefore drew up an elaborate plan for a vastly expanded educational system, aiming to provide a compulsory elementary education of four years for all boys and girls, a great expansion in the number of middle schools and a network of national universities. While it took many years to achieve the government's targets, by the early 1900s Japan had a system of almost universal primary education – increased to a compulsory six years in 1907.[7] This growth in elementary education served as a base from which increasing numbers of talented individuals (of all classes) went on to secondary and higher education. By 1937 some 10 per cent of boys were proceeding to the academic middle schools, seeking to be numbered among the few able to enter one of the prestigious national universities.[8]

Japan's decision to embark on this course of educational expansion reflected the conviction of the Meiji reformers that education was what the nation needed to provide it with the trained workers and talented leadership needed to 'catch up' with the west. Mori Arinori, an early minister of education, expressed the goal quite succinctly:

> Our country must move from its third-class position to second class, and from second class to first; and ultimately to the leading position among all countries of the world. The best way to do this is [by laying] the foundations of elementary education.[9]

This belief in the ability of education to foster industrialization and economic growth – confirmed by the nation's subsequent economic advance and left in place by the Occupation reformers – has continued to serve as a basic principle of Japanese education until today.

'Catch up' education

Several features of Japan's 'catch up' system deserve further analysis. First, as it developed in the decades following its establishment, the system was rigidly meritocratic. Entrance examinations controlled access to each higher level of education, and growing numbers of students competed to pass those tests and improve their educational (and hence economic) attainment. At the pinnacle of the whole hierarchy was Tokyo Imperial

25

University whose graduates staffed the elite levels of the national government. Below it and the several other universities were the higher schools designed primarily as preparatory schools for these institutions. And below these schools, separating the elite few from the masses of elementary students, were the middle schools. As noted above, only one in ten elementary school boys went on to middle school. In 1937 only one in thirteen of these passed the examination leading to the higher schools and hence to university.[10] The net effect was that only one in 1,000 elementary students made it to the top – to Tokyo Imperial University. Even in the 1930s, following the expansion of the Imperial University system, only one in 100 primary school entrants survived to enter one of these universities.[11]

Motivating the whole process was the fact that job prospects were closely tied to educational performance. Without university, students could not expect to enter the higher levels of business or government. The talented students of the whole nation were thus driven to compete through the educational system. The system worked as a ranking mechanism, identifying the relatively talented among the masses and providing the motivation for even moderately able students to study as hard as they could. In short, it served as an efficient mechanism for maximizing the nation's use of its precious manpower resources.

While the system was thus well suited for this period of Japan's development, it has come to have a disruptive effect in the day of 'mass' education. In the 1930s the examination competition involved primarily the 10 per cent of the male students who made it to middle school. Most of the others recognized the limited chances for succeeding through educational competition and therefore devoted their studies to more practical matters. Today, however, middle school is compulsory and some 94 per cent of students proceed to high school. Virtually all harbour some hope of becoming one of the 30 per cent who go to university. Not just the top business and government jobs but middle-level positions as well increasingly require a college education. As a result, virtually the whole education system has come to concentrate on examinations and the race for a university degree. Japan has become a 'qualification society'.[12] As further discussion below will show, this aspect of the pre-war legacy came to be a major source of problems in the 1970s and 1980s.

A second feature of the pre-war 'catch up' system was the

diversity and 'rationality' of its post-elementary education. The system sorted out students early in the process (at the start and finish of middle school) and then concentrated on giving each an education closely related to his future career. An academic education of the type needed for university was only provided for the small number who made it to the higher schools – almost all of whom went on to university. Teachers were trained at normal schools designed exclusively for that purpose. Soldiers went to military school. Colleges and higher technical schools provided further professional training for those middle-school graduates who failed to pass the higher-school examination. For those who failed to enter the five-year middle schools which served as the gateway to all of the above courses, there were a variety of opportunities for education terminating at the middle-school level: girl's high schools for girls, and vocational, technical and further elementary schools for boys (Figure 2.1).[13] While such a system might be characterized as anti-egalitarian for the way in which it separated students at such a young age, it nevertheless served as an extremely efficient mechanism for providing education appropriate to the future career of each individual, an important consideration given the limited resources available for education in pre-war Japan.

This aspect of the pre-war system, however, did not survive the post-war 'democratic' reform. Compulsory education was extended to include a three-year lower secondary school, and the whole multi-track system was unified into a single co-educational '6–3–3–4 system'. While the system thus became more egalitarian, the pre-war model of diversified education has continued to live in the minds of post-war conservatives. These men – most of whom were socialized in elite middle and higher schools – looked at the post-war system and saw their old selective institutions falling into mediocrity.[14] Particularly as more and more students began attending upper secondary schools and universities, conservatives began to bemoan the lack of elite institutions to serve the brightest of those age groups. 'Diversification' – the reintroduction of multiple tracks at the secondary and university levels – has therefore become a consistent goal of the conservatives in their post-war education reform campaigns.

Figure 2.1 The Japanese school system in 1937

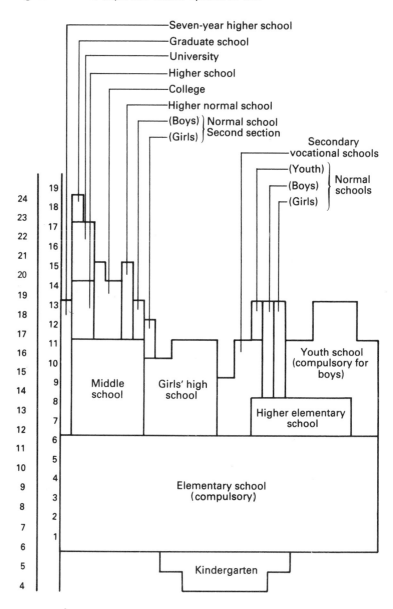

Source: Herbert Passin, *Society and education in Japan* (Columbia University Press, New York, 1965), p. 308.

The nationalism of pre-war education

The final major current running through pre-war education has had a much more complex effect on the post-war debate. The system's nationalism, especially in the militarist form it took in the years leading up to the Second World War, has been the root cause of the ideological polarization which has dominated discussions of education policies since the war. On the one hand, the system's excesses – the government's complete control over the training of teachers, textbooks and the philosophy of education and its manipulation of all of these powers to turn the education system into a militarist tool – served to provide those involved on the progressive side of the post-war education debate with a deep sense of distrust and antagonism toward central government attempts to control the education system. At the same time, the pre-war model provided a 'tradition' of central control over education which was not readily conceded by the ruling conservatives, despite their willingness to reject the excesses of the pre-war authorities.

The Meiji system did not start out with extreme central control and nationalism; it tended towards liberalism in the first decade after 1868.[15] By the 1880s, however, the nation as a whole had started to react against the rapid pace of 'westernization'. The Education Minister, Kōno Togama, appointed in 1880, set the process of centralization in motion,[16] and Mori Arinori, the first education minister appointed under the new cabinet system of government established in 1885, incorporated the idea of education-for-the-nation in the education system he set up and developed during his four-year tenure.[17] Although he was assassinated in 1889, the following two years saw the trends he had set in motion produce what was to become the key statement on the nationalist philosophy of education in Japan, the Imperial Rescript on Education.[18] To a degree, this document was classically Confucian. In particular, its passages about the need for 'filial piety', balanced relationships and modest living strongly echoed the Confucian precepts of elite Tokugawa education. As such, the Rescript was firmly grounded in traditional morality. In its calls to civic service ('offer yourselves courageously to the state') and in its emphasis on the special virtue of the Japanese nation, however, it added a new, distinctly Japanese nationalist element. Recited by generations of school children amid the pomp of school ceremonies and taught by teachers dedicated to the goal of training a corps of loyal citizens, this document formed the basis for the nationalist morality of the pre-war education system.

For Meiji reformers like Mori, such an emphasis was the perfect complement to the rational, meritocratic structure of its 'catch up' system. The new morality directed each individual, regardless of class, to make the best of his talents in service to the state. When combined with an effective meritocratic selection process, it provided for Japan to make optimum use of her human resources. Given later abuses of this nationalist morality, it is easy to ignore the positive appeal of the educational philosophy embodied in the Imperial Rescript. In fact, it maintains enough positive appeal to keep it alive (like the pre-war higher schools) in the minds of post-war conservatives. While recognizing the impossibility of maintaining the imperial aspect of the Rescript, Japan's traditional conservatives have never given up on its basic moral precepts. They credit it above all with having given Japanese a unique 'ethic' (not unlike the 'Protestant ethic') which turned pre-war generations of Japanese into loyal, self-sacrificing servants of Japan's rise among the company of nations.[19] Confronted with signs that post-war youth are no longer as self-sacrificing or obedient, these conservatives decry the Occupation reform which killed the Rescript. The solution to such problems, they claim, lies in new education reforms aimed at restoring the traditional morality and work ethic swept away with the Rescript.

Militarist abuses of the pre-war system

For *Nikkyōso* and other elements of the post-war progressive camp, however, the Imperial Rescript and virtually all aspects of the pre-war system were tainted beyond redemption by the abuses of the wartime militarists. By the 1930s the normal schools for training teachers had become *de facto* military institutions. Army officers trained teachers not only in discipline but in weapons firing, marching and military leadership as well. After 1927 teachers were required to serve at least five months in the military prior to actual work in the schools in order to understand the 'military spirit'.[20] Officers were also assigned to all public schools, bringing military attitudes right into the classroom.[21]

Virtually no aspect of the educational process was free of central government control. Local education offices and the Ministry of Education itself were run by officials of the pre-war Home Ministry (*Naimushō*), the agency charged with maintaining control of the nation's population. Textbooks, containing increasingly nationalistic and distorted accounts of Japanese history and geography, were written and published by the Ministry of Education.[22] The whole ideology of the system – describing teachers as 'servants of the emperor' and exhorting students to offer themselves courageously to the state – worked to eliminate the possibility of dissent. Not all teachers accepted such changes without a fight, but those who resisted through such organizations as the pre-war teachers' unions were soon suppressed.[23] In the end, schools became effectively preparatory institutions for the military.

The effect of this militarist abuse of the pre-war system was to leave teachers and other elements of the post-war progressive camp with a strong aversion to government intervention in education and the schools. Having been used by the pre-war government in its disastrous military campaign, teachers were ready to fight any post-war government attempts to reimpose central controls. Many teachers, experiencing feelings of guilt over their role in sending numerous students off to war, reacted by taking active parts in the post-war teachers' union – set up to defend the 'democratic' reforms of the Occupation period. They were joined by veterans of the pre-war unions. Under the slogan 'never send our children to the battlefields again', these teachers stood ready to resist any government attempt to increase its control over the curriculum, textbooks, teacher training or school administration. Any such measures would be 'a retreat to pre-war militarism'.[24]

Even before the Occupation forces arrived in Japan, therefore, the pre-war system had provided the stimulus for both of the two opposing post-war 'camps'. On the one hand, its success in mobilizing the talents of the nation through its espousal of a 'Japanese ethic' and its meritocratic/rational structure left post-war conservatives with a strong desire to maintain these features of the system. They were willing to reject the militarism of the late pre-war period, but they did not want to lose the 'traditional Japanese morality' of the Imperial Rescript. Neither did they want to see the efficiency of the pre-war system sacrificed in the name of 'western' egalitarianism. On the other hand, the pre-war experience gave the post-war progressives the high moral ground in their struggle to resist all attempts to reinstate elements of the old system. The whole package was tainted by militarism and defeat. Confronting later government attempts to increase central control, re-emphasize Japanese morality or diversify higher education, the progressives could appeal to popular revulsion towards the wartime abuses of the education system. Education, they could insist, is a particularly dangerous tool in the hands of the government. The pre-war experience had given the education issue a special 'sensitivity'. The experience of a foreign occupation and foreign-dominated reform was only to exacerbate this tension.

THE OCCUPATION

The Japanese surrender aboard the USS *Missouri* on 2 September 1945 ushered in the most turbulent period in the history of education in Japan. Where previously the central government had asserted its control over education in areas ranging from the minutest detail of textbooks to the regimentation of its teachers, the new government would have to deal with criticism and disturbances in response to almost every action. While reflecting underlying contradictions already existing in the pre-war educational system, this transformation was largely shaped in the emotional pressure-cooker of the immediate post-war period. Defeat had discredited old patterns of education politics, but the patterns brought in to replace them by the Occupation were also somewhat tainted by their sheer novelty and 'foreignness'. As a result, a country accustomed to bold education-based nation-building was left arguing about 'what education?' and 'what nation?'. Much of the antagonism still hampering educational policy-making in the 1980s can be traced to the events of this crucial period.

The Occupation reforms

The changes introduced under the American-led military occupation were swift and substantial. First, the occupying authorities set about dismantling the militarist and ultra-nationalist aspects of the old system. Teachers and education officials were purged; textbooks and courses in Japanese history, geography and morals were banned; and, after extended debate, the Imperial Rescript as well was proscribed.[25] If all of these measures were basically aimed at dismantling the old system, the early Occupation period also saw an active effort to build a new system in its place. The goal of the reform programme was the 'democratization' of Japanese education and society. It had two central themes. First, the reforms sought to prevent a recurrence of the pre-war abuses by limiting central government control. Responsibility for curriculum and textbooks was to be devolved to the level of individual schools and teachers. Local autonomy was to be encouraged through the establishment of elected school boards based on the US model. The authority of the MOE was to be limited to that of issuing outlines, suggestions and teaching guides. Finally, as a safeguard, moral education was to be eliminated as a separate subject, partially subsumed in 'social studies' classes and more generally taught through school activities.

Second, the reform programme aimed to end the undemocratic elitism of the multi-tracked pre-war system through a number of measures designed to create an extremely egalitarian structure. The old compulsory six-year elementary schools were to remain. The secondary education which had formerly taken place in selective five-year middle schools was to be divided such that all children would attend compulsory three-year lower secondary schools (*chūgakkō*), while further secondary education was to be provided in three-year American-style comprehensive upper secondary schools (*kōtōgakkō*). All higher education, including that which had formerly taken place in normal schools and lower-status technical colleges, was henceforth to be provided in undifferentiated four-year universities. The old elite higher schools were essentially to be squeezed out – transformed into lower-status local universities or absorbed into other universities as 'general studies departments' (*kyōyō gakubu*).[26] All institutions were to be co-educational. In short, the reforms aimed to create a unified, single-track 6−3−3−4 system based on a simplified US model.[27]

In the three years following the end of the war, virtually all of these reforms were adopted – an amazing pace given the radical changes involved. The only reform which was not implemented as envisaged was the plan for comprehensive upper secondary schools. Due to the shortage of funds, most were set up as selective institutions. In addition, many prefectural authorities quickly began differentiating between vocational and academic institutions. All other reforms – including the radical proposals calling for the establishment of elected local authorities, compulsory three-year lower secondary schools and consolidated universities – were adopted as planned (Figure 2.2). The crowning achievement of the early occupation period, however, was the 1947 passage of the Fundamental Law of Education (FLE, *Kyōiku kihon-hō*).[28] Together with provisions in the new constitution, this law laid the foundation for the new system of education, in effect replacing the pre-war Imperial Rescript. The law provided for equal opportunity and co-education, and in a key provision set forth that 'Education shall not be subject to improper control, but it shall be directly responsible to the whole people.' The FLE thus served to confirm the two central themes of the Occupation reform: democratic control and egalitarianism.

The effect of the post-war reforms on education politics

Although the Occupation was able to implement most of its reform proposals, it did not do so without arousing substantial opposition. Progressive forces, of course, were fully supportive. Seeing the Occupation's plans for local autonomy and greater equality as major improvements on the pre-war system, they quickly attached themselves to the whole of the post-war reform programme. 'Democratic control' and 'egalitarianism' became their battle-cries, and the FLE became their creed. Conservatives, however, felt the Occupation had gone too far in some of its reforms. They were willing to reject the militarism of the wartime system and agreed with the need to extend compulsory education, but they stood ready to defend other essential features of the pre-war system. As anticipated earlier in this chapter, they were not ready to give up the Japanese ethic or the diversified rationality of the system which had done so much to propel the nation's pre-war economic advance.

The conservatives in the MOE went along with the Occupation as long as it had control, but their co-operation was not freely given, and many vowed to reverse the 'excesses' of the reforms they were implementing. The 'excesses' which most concerned them were the following:

Figure 2.2   The Japanese school system in 1983

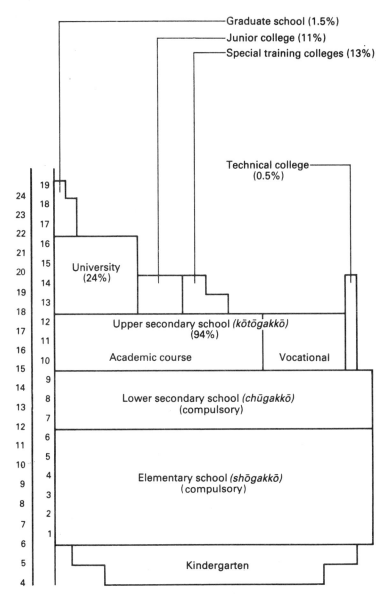

Source: Statistics cited for post-secondary education are from the MOE Higher Education Bureau, *Higher education in Japan*, October 1984, p. 18. The upper secondary school figure is from Mombushō daijin kanbō chōsa tōkeika, *Shōwa 61-nendo gakkō kihon chōsa chokuhō (shotō-chūtō kyōiku)*, August 1986, p. 9.

1   The abolition of the Imperial Rescript; they had hoped to preserve the 'traditional Japanese morality' at the centre of the document.
2   The abolition of moral education as a separate course.
3   The emasculation of the MOE, particularly the removal of its power over local authorities, the curriculum, textbooks and teachers.
4   The division of the previously unified secondary schools (five-year middle schools) into two three-year segments; many conservatives had hoped to preserve some sort of elite course similar to the old middle school/higher school track.
5   The total lack of differentiation at the *kōtōgakkō* and higher education levels; they wanted some sort of vocational track, and many could not accept the way the Occupation had put together dozens of inferior institutions and called them 'universities'.[29]

While the conservatives have argued for the reversal of these so-called excesses based primarily on their conviction that the Occupation *policies* were wrong, the tone and content of their rhetoric makes it clear that they have sought and continue to seek a 'resettlement' also because of the *way* in which the post-war reforms were implemented. To many conservatives, the fact that the reforms were basically forced on Japan by foreign military authorities calls into question the legitimacy of the entire post-war system. By focusing on the foreign nature of the implementation, they insinuate that some of the ideas at the heart of the post-war system – 'local autonomy' and 'individualism' – may be alien as well. Such ideas were rejected once, in the Meiji years, after liberal reformers were discredited for being too 'western'. The 'foreignness' of the Occupation settlement served in the same way to bolster the case of conservatives who sought to defeat those ideas again.

Thus, although the real issue has been a question of whether 'democracy' or 'individualism' have a place in Japan, the post-war debate has become concerned to an absurd degree with the history of the Occupation. At the centre of the controversy is the question of the relative roles of Japanese and Americans in the process whereby key provisions of the reform programme were drawn up and implemented. Specifically, the various sides have focused on the roles of two key groups: the United States

Education Mission (USEM) and the Education Reform Committee (ERC). The former was a group of American education experts who came to Japan for three weeks in March 1946 and left behind a set of recommendations which formed the basis of the Occupation reform programme. The latter was the Japanese successor to the USEM, established after its departure to draw up more detailed plans and make formal recommendations on exactly which parts of the USEM programme should be implemented.

This book will not attempt to document the actual historical series of events. More important for this study are the differing ways in which the various sides *perceive* this history. Many of the conservative actors were present while the Occupation was pursuing its reforms, and so their perceptions are those of having individually been forced to do something they did not want to do by foreign military authorities. Typical are the comments of Kennoki Toshihiro, then a top MOE administrator:

> The Mission began drafting its report on returning from Kyoto and it presented its expansive set of education reform recommendations on the 25th (of March 1946). It is true that the group was composed of first-class US educators, but the idea that a group of people who came to Japan with not even a child's knowledge about the Japanese education system could – in just 24 days in the country – get a grasp on how the system really works and propose a set of reforms is simply unbelievable. I guess it's all right for me to say this now, but my theory is that the whole Education Mission was just a trick (*karakuri*) of the Occupation.[30]

Kennoki's assertion that the USEM was a 'trick' is just part of his conspiracy theory. Basing his arguments on his personal recollections, he argues that the ERC was also manipulated by the Occupation authorities. While admitting that it was composed of respected Japanese educators, he claims that it was dominated by its steering committee, a body which included Occupation representatives. The steering committee, he claims, forced the ERC to endorse the Occupation's radical plans for secondary and higher education despite the fact that a majority of its members disagreed.[31] Other conservatives have focused on this same body's role in the drawing up of the FLE to claim that it too was largely the Occupation's work.[32]

Kennoki, who later went on to serve as an LDP member of the Upper House and minister of education (1966–7), came away from his experience under the Occupation vowing to undo what he had been forced to do.[33] But he was not the only one. Morito Tatsuo, later to become the chairman of the Central Council on Education, was the minister of education charged with implementing much of the Occupation reform programme. 'Taking responsibility' for the post-war reforms, he devoted the later years of his life to righting the 'mistakes' the foreigners had made.[34] Naitō Yosaburō, later to become MOE administrative vice-minister (AVM, *jimujikan*) and an influential LDP member of the Upper House, was one of Kennoki's colleagues in the MOE section charged with implementing the 6–3–3–4 system. Both as an MOE bureaucrat and LDP politician, he made the reversal of Occupation 'excesses' a top priority.

The progressive camp's perception of this historical record is quite different. *Nikkyōso* and other opposition groups sympathize with the Occupation's work, and so have not worried so much about the degree to which foreigners were involved. Nevertheless, the conservative attack has forced them to defend the 'Japaneseness' of the post-war reform, and left-leaning scholars have produced detailed work documenting the Japanese involvement in drawing up the reform programme.[35] In the end, it is difficult to determine exactly to what degree the post-war reforms reflected foreign pressure and involvement. As noted above, however, the importance of this history has less to do with facts than with perceptions. Due to the Occupation's involvement in the whole process, conservatives continue to believe that many aspects of the post-war reform – including the 6–3–3 division of years – were forced on Japan by foreign military authorities. These men were predisposed to defend many aspects of the old system even without the involvement of foreigners. Their experience under the Occupation only hardened their resolve to restore the 'Japaneseness' of the education system.

The 'reverse course'

Even before the Occupation authorities left Japan in 1952, a change in their attitudes signalled a retreat from the ideals of the immediate post-war years. Their major new concern – in the developing Cold War climate – was the threat of left-wing influence among university staff and in the teachers' union movement. By 1947, 95 per cent of elementary school teachers had joined the newly unified *Nikkyōso*.[36] Faced with what he saw as a dangerous trend towards union radicalism, the Occupation commander General Douglas MacArthur decided in 1948 to reduce drastically the rights of all public-sector unions. *Nikkyōso* would no longer be respected as an agent of collective bargaining; teachers would not be allowed to strike; and the political rights of teachers to run for office and to campaign would be restricted.[37] Two years later MacArthur initiated the 'Red Purge', an anti-communist campaign which led to the firing of some 1,200 teachers.[38] Viewing universities too as a source of left-wing radicalism, the Occupation authorities did not object when the MOE sought to strengthen central control of left-leaning faculty councils. After vocal opposition, this proposal was dropped.[39]

This series of actions, part of what was known as the 'reverse course', had two effects. First, by showing Japanese conservatives that even their democratic tutors could bend their principles in the face of 'the communist threat', it encouraged them to use the same logic in arguing for an even broader retrenchment in the years that followed. At the same time, by taking away instruments of moderate opposition and compromise (collective bargaining) and poisoning the atmosphere with its Red Purge, these policies only succeeded in radicalizing the progressive Opposition. In effect, the final moves of the authorities served to push the two opposing sides of the education debate even further apart.

'RE-REFORM' SINCE THE OCCUPATION

The polarization which continues to characterize the education debate today owes much to the events of the Occupation period. The battle lines are still drawn essentially as they were then. Nevertheless, the fact that the cleavage remains so deep cannot be explained merely by pointing to the origins of their disagreement. It reflects as well the numerous struggles of the intervening years. What follows, therefore, is a brief history of the repeated skirmishes which have dominated the education policy process in the post-war period. Like the original post-war settlement, these struggles can be grouped under two basic themes: democratic control and egalitarianism.

The struggles over democratic control

For various reasons the government was much more active in seeking to reverse the Occupation's 'excesses' in the area of 'democratic control'. First, the MOE realized that regaining central control of education policy was a prerequisite to any other action it might want to take. Japan had little experience with the American idea of local autonomy, and the MOE did not see central control (under a democratically elected government) to be contrary to the FLE provision that education be controlled 'by the whole people'. Equally important, however, was the fact that both the MOE and the LDP saw centralization as a way of countering *Nikkyōso* influence. The MOE needed to defeat the union in order to effect its education policies; the LDP wanted to weaken the union because of its prominent role in building up the vote of the opposition, the Japan Socialist Party (JSP, *Nihon shakaitō*).

Nikkyōso and other progressives, on the other hand, saw the government's centralization efforts as an attempt to regain the power it needed to control once again the minds of the nation's children. They saw themselves as a force dedicated to preventing such a retreat. For them democracy meant a devolution of educational control to local authorities and teachers so that no government could again stand able to do what the militarists had done to Japan. The fact that the early efforts of the MOE and LDP were aimed at destroying *Nikkyōso* only served to stiffen the union's resolve.

The government's strategy, as it developed, was as follows. Not having the legislative votes to move immediately to reassert central control, the government sought first to reduce *Nikkyōso* influence over education by requiring the 'political neutrality' of teachers and by limiting their political rights. Measures introduced under the Occupation had already restricted the political rights of teachers at the local level. Now the government wanted to extend such limits to the national level as well. In addition, it aimed to require all teachers to be 'politically neutral' in their teaching. In 1954 the government succeeded in pushing such legislation through the Lower House, but the measures were made effectively unenforceable by amendments introduced by the Upper House.[40]

Despite this setback, the government embarked on another offensive in 1956, this time strengthened by the formation of the LDP as a unified conservative party. Its aim was to take direct control of education policy by greatly weakening the Occupation-imposed system of local autonomy. The legislation introduced abolished the system whereby local school boards were elected, instead providing for board members to be appointed by prefectural governors and mayors. At the same time, MOE powers were to be enhanced by making the local boards subject to ministry 'demands'. Despite vocal and united progressive opposition, both measures were passed.[41]

The next step in the government's campaign was to use its new authority to reassert national control over the school curriculum and textbooks. The Occupation had left the MOE with only the authority to issue curriculum 'guidelines'. In 1958 the ministry made its curriculum mandatory.[42] Concurrent changes required that textbooks conform with the curriculum – a provision enforced by a group of ministry 'reviewers'. Through these ordinances, the MOE succeeded in re-establishing national control over textbooks without a legislative change. Additional changes in the textbook approval process introduced in 1963 further reduced teacher autonomy: henceforth, texts were to be selected by local authorities rather than individual teachers, a move which had the effect of reducing the variety of textbooks available.[43]

Having established strict national standards, the only remaining step in the government's effort to regain control of education was to force teachers to comply. Local authorities had been brought under conservative influence, but individual schools and a great many teachers were still quite independent. In the first of two initiatives aimed at rectifying this situation, the MOE set out to make all teachers subject to efficiency ratings. As originally suggested by the ministry, the Teachers' Efficiency Rating Plan would have linked salary increases to a teacher's efficiency rating, thereby giving the government great potential leverage over teachers in its campaign to encourage co-operation. *Nikkyōso* naturally opposed the plan as a threat to its very existence; few teachers would participate in union activities if they felt their salary was on the line. In the battle which followed (1957–9), the union fought this initiative in every prefecture and most schools – with numerous strikes, police intervention and court cases. Although it failed to stop the MOE from making national-level decisions to implement the plan, it succeeded in making deals at the prefectural and individual school level which rendered the rating largely irrelevant.[44]

The second government attempt to gain teacher compliance with its national education policies was more subtle. Its 1961 proposal called merely for the administration of standard achievement tests to all students in given age groups. The government presented these tests as necessary to fulfil its task of assuring that students across Japan were receiving adequate education. The union, however, saw them as a back-door attempt to force teacher compliance with the 1958 MOE curriculum. If all students were evaluated by tests closely linked to the curriculum, the authorities could determine which teachers were not following the prescribed course of study and force them to fall in line. While again *Nikkyōso* failed to block the national-level decision to order such testing, through local opposition and non-co-operation (most importantly its success in getting schools to make the tests anonymous) it rendered the tests useless as measures of individual student or teacher evaluation.[45]

While these struggles were the most heated of the period, other government actions were also related to its overall campaign to alter the post-war settlement on democratic control. In 1958 the government once again established a separate morals class, although it left details to individual schools and teachers.[46] Twice during the period, the MOE led campaigns to increase central and administrative control of national universities. Although both ended without much success, the attempts left university teachers with a strong distrust of ministry proposals.[47] Finally, the MOE's refusal to deal with *Nikkyōso* even on questions related to teachers' salaries might also be considered part of its retrenchment campaign. In all of the 1960s the Minister of Education met with the leader of *Nikkyōso* only once – despite the 1965 ruling of the International Labour Organization that such contact should take place.[48] Although the *Nikkyōso*–MOE battle quietened down somewhat in the mid-1960s as the government increasingly sought to concentrate on economic issues, the preceding years of sometimes violent struggle between the two sides was still fresh in the minds of individuals on both sides as the government embarked on its major reform initiative in 1967.

The struggles over egalitarianism

As noted above, the government was much more active in seeking to reverse the post-war settlement on democratic control than it was in pulling back from the extreme egalitarianism of the Occupation system. Partly, this emphasis reflected the fact that the LDP was preoccupied with its struggle to reduce *Nikkyōso* influence. Also important, however, was the general public support for the 6−3−3−4 structure. Even before the war, the public had demanded greater access to higher levels of education. The new unitary structure − with private institutions expanding to meet public demand − gave more and more young people the chance to reach higher levels of educational attainment. The 6−3−3−4 system was not so much a reverse of the pre-war system as an extension. More education and greater equality of opportunity meant that the meritocratic mechanism would provide even greater numbers of better qualified workers.

Nevertheless, certain elements in the conservative camp − notably the business sector and older-generation MOE bureaucrats − were vocal in their assertion that the Occupation had gone too far. They supported the idea of educational expansion in principle but felt that the unitary structure of the 6−3−3−4 system was overly standardized. In its attempt to keep everyone on the road to university as long as possible, the system ended up training too many mediocre generalists and not enough trained workers and specialists. They advocated a return to the rational pre-war system whereby those students not bound for university would be given a more practical education. They succeeded early on in maintaining vocational upper secondary schools. Junior colleges (two-year institutions of higher education) were authorized as well before the Occupation forces left Japan.

The big push, however, did not come until 1958. In that year the government embarked on a three-year plan to increase by 8,000 the number of trained scientists and technicians. In the same year the Central Council on Education (set up as a permanent MOE advisory body in 1952) issued a report calling for the establishment of several diversified tracks to train greater numbers of specialized workers: five-year technical colleges combining the three years of upper secondary education with two years of higher education and six-year vocational institutions combining the lower and upper secondary years. It also urged the expansion in the number of vocational upper secondary schools.[49]

Progressives (led by *Nikkyōso*) opposed most of these proposals both because they saw them as reflecting 'undemocratic' business influence and because the proposals to emphasize diverse tracks threatened the egalitarianism of the post-war 6−3−3−4 system. After several failed attempts, the government finally succeeded in getting Diet approval for five-year colleges of technology (*kōtō semmon gakkō*) in 1961.[50] No action was taken on the CCE recommendation concerning six-year vocational secondary schools.

In the 1960s, as Prime Minister Ikeda embarked on his income-doubling plan, the conservatives' diversification campaign continued. The report outlining Ikeda's famous plan included, in addition to a broad call for increased 'investment' in education, a specific target of an 86,000 increase in the number of technical upper secondary school students. In 1966 the CCE went further in proposing such an emphasis on vocational secondary education as part of an official policy of diversification. Upper secondary education, it said, should be 'diversified in response to careful consideration of societal demands'. Arguing that education should 'conform to the various aptitudes, abilities, life courses and environments of individuals', it pointed to the need to consider the establishment of a mechanism for providing special training for students with special talents. It was the first time since the war that an MOE organ had called for 'elite education' in such clear terms.[51] *Nikkyōso* opposed both the proposal for elite education and the broader call for diversification as 'discriminatory'. Although the MOE authorized the creation of special *kōtōgakkō* for those talented in mathematics and science, these schools never became popular.[52] The government succeeded in having prefectures establish great numbers of new technical and industrial *kōtōgakkō*, but at the end of the 1960s the total share of vocational upper secondary education remained steady at 39 per cent.[53]

As the situation stood in 1970, therefore, the conservatives had not had much success in their effort to diversify the post-war education system. Due to *Nikkyōso*'s ideological opposition and the broad public support for the egalitarian structure of the 6−3−3−4 system, they had totally failed in their campaign to re-create an elite academic track. While the colleges of technology and vocational *kōtōgakkō* went some way towards their goal of re-emphasizing practical education for those not bound for university, these were already suffering from a lack of public interest. More and more parents wanted their children to go to university and therefore resisted attempts to take students off that track any earlier than was absolutely necessary.

By the late 1960s, as such parental attitudes led to rapidly rising staying-on rates, the issue of 'egalitarianism vs diversification' actually became more of an issue. In 1955, with only 51 per cent of *chūgakkō* students staying on for *kōtōgakkō*, it was still possible to consider upper secondary education (particularly the college preparatory institutions) an elite course. Ten years later the *kōtōgakkō* share had increased to 71 per cent, and by 1975 fully 92 per cent of *chūgakkō* students were staying on for *kōtōgakkō*.[54] Likewise, universities which had catered to the brightest 8 per cent of students in 1955 were serving 27 per cent by 1975.[55] Such quantitative growth meant that neither *kōtōgakkō* nor universities could remain elite institutions. Either they would have to lower their standards to accommodate the broader range of ability, or they could persist in teaching the 'masses' the same material which they had taught to the elite.

The Japanese system went some way towards addressing this problem of a broad ability range by using examinations to rank students. Those with the best scores coming out of *chūgakkō* would go to the 'best' *kōtōgakkō*, while those with the top scores on the university entrance examinations would go to the University of Tokyo and the other most prestigious universities.[56] Nevertheless, conservatives saw the trends towards higher staying-on rates as constituting even greater cause for pursuing their long-cherished policy of diversification. They realized that while examinations sorted students by ability, they did so on a single scale of measurement. Because the University of Tokyo was at the apex of the system, all *kōtōgakkō* were judged on how well they performed in getting their students into that institution. In turn, local *chūgakkō* and individual teachers were judged on how well they performed in getting their students into the 'best' local *kōtōgakkō*. When only a portion of students aimed for the top, the examination system did not reach down and dominate school education at the lower levels. But with increasing numbers of aspiring *kōtōgakkō* and university students all judged on such a single-dimensional, hierarchical scale, the system was becoming very exam-dominated and standardized. While the exams provided an important motivating force for individual students, teachers and schools, the uniformity they fostered was increasingly seen in Japan as inappropriate for the future needs of the nation.

IMMEDIATE ISSUES IN THE RECENT REFORM DEBATE

Issues in the CCE reform debate

The above discussion forms a good starting-point for this final section, for in 1967 such concerns about the need for diversification were uppermost in the minds of those who initiated the CCE reform project. The way they worded the council's mandate – asking it to suggest changes which would make the education system more 'suited for contemporary society' – reflected their conviction that rising staying-on rates required some significant modifications in the structure of the system. The CCE had only a year earlier submitted a report wherein it had pointed to the need for diversification in upper secondary education. The MOE expected the new council to emphasize a similar approach in proposing structural changes for the system as a whole.[57]

Although those who initiated the CCE project were broadly in agreement about the 'problem' they were addressing, the situation in 1967 was not what could be described as an educational crisis. From the conservative perspective, the problem was merely one which had been getting worse since the Occupation imposed a unified 6–3–3–4 system in 1947. The year 1967 was chosen primarily because it marked the twentieth anniversary of the post-war structure. Twenty years was considered to have been enough time to let the system 'settle'. Now it needed evaluating.[58] The initiation of the CCE project, therefore, was not purely a function of the immediate concern over rising staying-on rates. Also involved were the whole range of complaints about the post-war settlement which conservatives had been nursing since the war: university administrative reform, the need to increase the co-operation of teachers, and so on. It was not a coincidence that those most active in the CCE initiation were those who had been personally forced to implement Occupation demands. Morito, education minister under the Occupation, was now chairman of the CCE. Kennoki, then a top MOE bureaucrat, was the new education minister. Amagi Isao, then a junior MOE bureaucrat, was a senior ministry official and soon to be administrative vice-minister (AVM).

Within a year, however, the whole CCE project had been transformed by more immediate developments. The nation's universities had erupted in a series of student demonstrations, strikes and other actions which came to be known as the 'university troubles' (*daigaku funsō*).[59] Although the student disturbances reflected a range of political and social problems, at least part of the responsibility lay with the universities themselves. Many institutions – especially private ones – had expanded too rapidly in the face of the rapidly growing demand for higher education. Facilities were inadequate and the price of tuition was rising too fast. The government was also at fault for having relied to such an extent on unsubsidized private institutions to take in the growing numbers of students.[60]

For many conservatives, however, the 'problem' was more a matter of the failure of university administrators to control their students. The conservative 'hawks' (*takaha*) had long been calling for university presidents to be given greater central power to control left-wing teachers and students. When the *funsō* spread to national universities like Tokyo University, these conservatives could contain their ire no longer. LDP members concerned with law and order issued urgent demands that the government deal strictly with the leaders of the demonstrations. In addition, Naitō Yosaburō – another veteran of the Occupation and a new LDP Dietman – issued a plan for university reform which would have greatly strengthened the power of central university administrators.[61] In response to such demands, the MOE referred the matter to a subcommittee of the CCE. Based on the recommendations of this group, the government acted quickly in the summer of 1969 to pass legislation authorizing MOE intervention in universities experiencing prolonged disturbances.[62] More fundamental changes were to await the conclusion of the CCE's comprehensive review of the post-war system.

It was in this atmosphere of crisis and action that the CCE entered the peak of its deliberations. Although its mandate had been bold from the beginning, the *funsō* gave the council a sense of urgency. Political actors outside the original core of MOE initiators were suddenly interested in education reform, and the public seemed to agree that 'something' needed to be done. Meeting often throughout 1969, it produced a mid-term report on university policy in May 1970 and another on elementary and secondary policy in November of that same year. The following

June, it issued the report which effectively set the agenda for education policy-making in the 1970s.

Issues in the Nakasone reform debate

The issues of the most recent round of the education debate cannot be understood without seeing the Nakasone initiative first as part of a *set* of reforms pursued by the Prime Minister. Under the banner 'the total clearance of the post-war political accounts' (*sengo seiji no sōkessan*), Nakasone advocated reform in a range of policy areas: administrative reform, tax reform, abolition of limits on defence spending and education reform. Not only in the area of education but in these other areas as well the Prime Minister sought to review the post-war legacy. He was concerned that too many areas of Japanese politics had become 'taboo' due to the nation's experience of militarism and defeat, and he sought to face these issues head on through reform programmes which would 'clear' the post-war settlement. In education, this philosophy led Nakasone to make issues of many Occupation 'excesses' the conservatives had been complaining about since the 1950s. Like those before him, he sought to re-emphasize traditional Japanese morality, reassert government authority over teachers and alter the 6−3−3−4 structure of the system.

The 1980s reform debate, however, was not entirely divorced from immediate issues. In fact, the prime minister made a particular attempt to link his reform proposals to the future needs of the nation. Teacher training and increased moral education were essential, he argued, because of the increasing disorder (violence, bullying) in the schools. Japanese children needed more training in Japanese tradition because they needed to know their own culture before they could understand and appreciate other cultures in an increasingly internationalized world. The 6−3−3−4 system needed changing because its standardized and overly egalitarian nature prevented the training of the creative geniuses necessary in the next stage of Japan's economic advance.

The immediate problem most responsible for making education reform a leading political issue in the 1980s was that of school violence and delinquency (*kōnai bōryoku to hikō*). These phenomena had started to make headlines in 1980. In that year the city of Tokyo reported a 44 per cent increase in cases of school violence. The next year, the National Police Agency reported a 50 per cent increase in the number of cases nationwide – with a doubling of attacks on teachers.[63] Figures continued to grow for the next two years, reaching a peak in 1983.[64] Thus by 1984, when Nakasone embarked on his reform initiative, incidents of school violence were receiving nation-wide publicity in a way which created the feeling of a real educational crisis. Two incidents within the period of a week in February 1983 particularly served to focus national attention on problems in the schools. In the first, a group of *chūgakkō* and *kōtōgakkō* youths in Yokohama were arrested after they attacked a number of sleeping vagrants, killing three.[65] Just three days later, the media headlined reports that a Tokyo *chūgakkō* teacher had stabbed a student in the chest, resorting to the use of a knife in order to protect himself from his violent students.[66] Both stories received wide media attention and served to dramatize what the statistics showed was a rapidly growing problem in the schools. Shortly after the above incidents, Nakasone spoke for the first time about the need for a 'radical solution' to deal with problems in the schools.[67]

Traditional conservatives, reading about increasing school violence and later about widespread vindictive bullying (*ijime*), immediately blamed the problems on the lack of moral education under the post-war system.[68] Students were not being taught the value of human life. They were hearing too much about freedom and not enough about the responsibilities that go with rights in Japanese society. What Japan needed was to go back to the basics of Japanese morality prescribed in the Imperial Rescript.

While these conservatives considered the problems of school violence and *ijime* to be almost exclusively a function of the moral decline of youth, others saw these phenomena as symptoms of deeper problems in the Japanese education system as a whole. Many articles were published linking the rise in violence to the pressure of examinations. It was noted, for example, that the bulk of incidents were concentrated in the *chūgakkō* – the level marking the transition between mixed ability compulsory education (grades 1 to 9) and the rigid hierarchy of *kōtōgakkō* and universities.[69] Other problems were also linked to the examination system. It was noted that more and more children were being forced to attend cram schools (*juku*) in order to keep up with their peers.[70] Exams were seen to be fostering a kind of 'cramming education' (*tsumekomi kyōiku*) which, while providing a solid basis of knowledge, was failing to encourage creativity or critical thinking.[71] Education after the examinations was also seen to be suffering as universities found it difficult to motivate students who were more interested in enjoying their post-examination freedom than in furthering their education.[72]

Many of these problems were not new to the Japanese education system.[73] Emphasis had always been placed on cramming. The nation's examination system had put pressure on students for generations. The universities had never been very successful in motivating students. Progressives had been pointing to these problems for some time. Until the 1970s, however, most others had been willing to view them as necessary evils in a system which had proven so successful in providing the nation with the skilled manpower needed to propel its economic advance. What had changed in 1984 was the economic context. Increasingly, even certain conservatives had started to recognize that the 'qualification-based social structure' (*gakureki shakai*) so useful in the 'catch up' phase of Japan's economic advance might prove to be a barrier in its next phase. They argued that the economy of the 1980s (and even more, the economy of the future) required creative scientists, fluent foreign-language speakers, specialists in extremely complex technology and workers who could express their views rather than just follow orders. The examination-based system – and the broader social system which gave little credit to talents demonstrated outside that system – was seen to be less suited to meeting these new economic needs.

Among those sounding such alarms was Amaya Naohiro, a former senior official of the Ministry of International Trade and Industry (MITI, *Tsūsanshō*) who served on Nakasone's education council:

Japan's schools, successful in supplying large numbers of homogeneously trained workers, contributed greatly to the nation's economic growth in the second half of the twentieth century. But will what was successful in the twentieth century prove to be successful in the twenty-first? Business must consider such things carefully and plan its strategy. In the pre-war military, a soldier's rank in the army and navy schools determined his place in the military for the length of his career. Japan's defeat in war was linked to this system which had those who were successful in school manage the battles. I'm afraid that businesses which today remain dependent on an education system which serves primarily as a ranking mechanism are in danger of repeating that mistake. I believe that both businesses and schools must work to correct this point.[74]

Japan would be risking its future, Amaya was saying, if it continued to value success in the qualification-orientated education system as the primary determinant of a person's place in society. The fact that Nakasone placed such men as Amaya on his Ad Hoc Council indicates that the Prime Minister as well was sympathetic towards such concerns. As noted in the previous chapter, Nakasone himself described his initiative as one designed to bring Japan into the twenty-first century. The most recent education debate was thus very much concerned with immediate and future education problems.

CONCLUSIONS

The history of education in Japan – described in the first three sections of this chapter – serves as the starting-point for this case study of recent education reform in Japan. The traditions inherited from pre-war systems and the conflicts born of militarism and foreign occupation all contribute to the ideology and priorities of the actors involved in the modern debate. Most of the conservative actors (notably the MOE and the education-alists of the LDP) approach the argument from a perspective heavily influenced by their experience of the post-war Occupation and respect for the way education was conducted before then. Equally, the progressive actors have been shaped by their memory of pre-war subjugation and their experience of the con-servatives' forty-year campaign to restore pre-war policies.

Through these actors, history has also played a major role in shaping the issues of the most recent reform debates. The 1970s round of reform, in retrospect, seems to have been concerned almost exclusively with issues left over from the post-war settle-ment. It began in 1967 not because of any urgent crisis but because that was the year in which the post-war system turned 20.

Both the diversification proposals which served as the initial focus of the debate and the university reform proposals which were added following the outbreak of the late-1960s *funsō* were primarily old ideas reflecting the conservatives' desire to bring back elements of the pre-war system.

The issues in the 1980s have been somewhat more complex. Again, the old issues – the need to restore moral education to its old central position and the demand for reform of the strictly egalitarian 6–3–3--4 system – reflected Prime Minister Nakasone's desire to achieve a 'total clearance of the post-war political accounts'. At the same time, however, the recent debate has also been shaped by changes in Japan and the world which have raised new issues less tied to the historical experience of the actors. Growing concern about the need for Japan to adapt to its new position of economic strength has led to growing criticism of the standardization and 'qualificationism' of Japanese education.

This combination of history and issues provides the basic constraints for the policy-making process under study. The various actors in the process, approaching the debate from positions heavily influenced by history, are forced to work within the limits imposed by the issues. In the 1970s the left–right character of the issues naturally led to a pattern of conflict which varied little from the left–right struggle of the entire post-war period. As will be seen in following chapters, disagreement did exist within the conservative camp, but these were less outright conflicts than what might be described as shades of the same colour. Under Nakasone, the greater complexity of the issues led to a more complex conflict pattern. A strong element of left–right polarization remained, but the new standardization/qualification issue left both camps disorientated with some conservatives advocating less central control and some progressives seeking to maintain government authority. Through their influence on conflict patterns, history and issues serve as important factors in determining the outcome of the policy-making process as a whole.

3

Internal actors: the Liberal Democratic Party

In introducing the politics of education, the study thus far has concentrated on the major force which has shaped the debate: the disagreement between the government and progressive interests over the issues of democratic control and equality in education. As the previous chapter revealed, post-war education policy-making has been largely a history of the battle between the Ministry of Education and the teachers' union. In terms of the analysis in Chapter 1, the dominance of this polarized, 'left–right' divide points to the basic validity of the 'power-elite model'. As it predicted, the process has consisted primarily of a struggle between the ruling 'conservative camp' and the opposition 'progressive camp'. The analysis, however, went on to argue that the power-elite model was an oversimplification of the policy-making process. The conservative camp, it found, is composed of various actors who often compete for power, money and 'turf' as well as policy: bureaucrats battle politicians and subgovernments fight other subgovernments. In most cases, it concluded, it is conflict *within* the conservative circle which determines policy outcomes. This chapter and the three which follow represent the first step in the effort to see how this process works in the case of the debate over education reform.

The chapters in this section demonstrate clearly that education policy-making – as the pluralists predicted – is not merely a function of conflict along a one-dimensional, ideological cleavage. Chapters 3 and 4 focus on the 'internal actors' (the party in power and the bureaucracy) and find numerous differences: between members of the LDP education *zoku* and other party members; between the MOE and other parts of the bureaucracy; between the *zoku* and the MOE; within the *zoku*;

and within the MOE. Chapters 5 and 6 examine the effect of various external actors (those outside the government) and find that these groups – those which are close to the conservatives as well as those which oppose them – tend to aggravate the government's conflicts. Once each of the actors has been introduced, with both its 'attitudes' and 'place in the process' explained, the stage will be set for the evaluation of the total policy-making process in the final two chapters.

As the predominant political party of Japan, the LDP has naturally come to play a leading role in education policy. From the method of selecting boards of education to the content of textbooks, the education system bears the marks of forty years of conservative party rule. This analysis of 'actors', therefore, begins with an examination of the LDP. While the analysis finds the party to have a certain set of basic goals related to education reform, it finds that the LDP is far from being a monolithic force in the policy-making process.

ATTITUDES

The LDP's nationalism

In pursuing education reform, the most basic attitude of the LDP is its nationalism. Above all, it is seeking an educational system which is 'more Japanese', more orientated towards moral training and less under the influence of the left-wing teachers' union. This concern with nationalism explains, for example, the party's periodic campaigns to rewrite textbooks so that they describe the nation's role in the Second World War in a less negative light; its attempts to push the traditional Japanese concept of social 'responsibility' through a moral education curriculum; and its teacher-training proposals aimed at fostering a more 'dedicated' teaching corps. While the LDP certainly is not concerned exclusively with these nationalistic aims, its vocal pursuit of such policies has nevertheless dominated its image in this sphere. It is therefore natural that this analysis of the party's education 'attitudes' begins with an examination of what are sometimes referred to as its 'reactionary' aims.

Undoing the 'excesses' of the Occupation

Although the word 'reactionary' has negative connotations which make it dangerous to use in an academic context, it nevertheless describes a certain tendency which has been present in LDP education policy to one degree or another throughout the post-war period. This is the consistent argument of many conservatives that the radical education reforms introduced by Occupation authorities following the Second World War went too far in embracing 'western' values and structures. As described in Chapter 2, the story of education policy-making since that time can be seen as a series of efforts by these conservatives to undo the 'excesses' of the Occupation reforms and re-establish certain aspects of the pre-war system.

The comment of Education Minister Kiyose Ichirō in initiating one early effort to undo Occupation reforms is typical of the LDP attitude at the time:

> The fundamental reforms of the education system carried out after the end of the war were epochal in the history of Japanese education and played a considerable role in educational development, but on the other hand, since these reforms were carried out under the special conditions of occupation, there are quite a few points at which they do not accord with reality.[1]

The quote is interesting in that it emphasizes less the problems with actual policies than the fact that the policies were *tainted* due to the way in which they were introduced. This concern with cleansing the post-war system of foreign influence has continued to dominate the party's education ideology in recent years.

In its cleansing efforts, the party has concentrated first and foremost on the centrepiece of the post-war settlement in the area of education: the Fundamental Law of Education. On numerous occasions LDP politicians have criticized the FLE both for being 'forced on Japan' by the Occupation authorities and for its failure to champion traditional Japanese values. Araki Masuo, for example, began a personal campaign to revise the FLE shortly after becoming education minister in 1960, criticizing the law for its failure to allow the 'full cultivation of the excellence of the Japanese race'.[2] More recently, Minister of Education Sunada Shigetami received front-page news coverage when he spoke of the 'mistake' of having totally abandoned the Imperial Rescript.[3]

The effort to reverse Occupation reforms has influenced other aspects of the party's education platform as well. As noted in

Chapter 2, many conservatives felt particular resentment at the way in which Japan had been forced to adopt the '6−3−3 system' and radical reforms in the area of higher education − both based on the US model. The cleansing effort has therefore focused on these aspects of the post-war system as well. During the CCE debate in the late 1960s, for example, the reform plan advocated by Naitō Yosaburō, an LDP Upper House member, would have brought back many controversial aspects of the pre-war system. It would have turned the seven old imperial universities into elite 'graduate universities' (restoring them to unrivalled superiority as in the pre-war system); created six-year elite secondary schools in each prefecture with attendance similar to the number of places available in the graduate universities (a resurrection of the old elite higher schools); abolished the general studies departments of universities (returning them to their pre-war emphasis on specialist studies); and created special government schools to train a 'mainstay' corps of teachers (resurrecting the old normal schools).[4] While few LDP plans have been so blatantly backward-looking, many have reflected similar nostalgia for pre-war institutions.

Prime Minister Nakasone's effort to 'clear' the post-war accounts in the education sphere (outlined in Chapter 2) is perhaps the best example of the LDP's continuing concern with the foreign origins of its post-war education system. His approach was somewhat different from Naitō's, however, in that he sought to cleanse the system, partly by returning to pre-war patterns but also by the mere act of *changing* a system which had come to be viewed as untouchable (a 'taboo') in post-war politics. Merely by adopting new policies in an area influenced by the Occupation, he aimed to re-establish its 'Japaneseness'. To an extent, therefore, Nakasone's interest in radical education reform (e.g. his desire to change the 6−3−3 division of years) can be seen as a reflection of his desire simply to erase a symbol of Japan's defeat.

Nakasone's treatment of education as just one item in a set of taboos was noted in the previous chapter. For him and for others on the *seishin* (ideological right) wing of the party, the FLE, the '6−3−3 system' and the 'Peace Constitution' are all symbols of Japan's emasculation after the war. In seeking to undo the Occupation's 'excesses' in the area of education, therefore, these politicians have been aiming to broach the even more sensitive issue of constitutional revision. A successful reform of the post-war education system would symbolically break the taboo against altering sensitive post-war institutions, thereby paving the way for a revision of the Constitution's 'peace clause'.

Nakasone expressly linked the issue of education reform with constitutional revision when he remarked that reform in that sphere would 'also be a way of dealing with the constitutional problem'.[5] It is no coincidence that many of those Dietmen active in the LDP's education *zoku* tend to be from the party's *seishin* wing.[6] Many are active in party organs committed to other nationalist causes, most notably that of a bolder Japanese defence policy. Virtually all Dietmen in the education *zoku* are long-time members of the Dietmen's League for the Realization of an Independent Constitution – a group closely associated with the late Prime Minister Kishi Nobusuke (Table 3.1). Key members of the *zoku* were also active in Dietmen Nakagawa Ichirō's right-wing mini-faction, the *Seirankai*.[7]

Restoring national values to a central place in the system

To a large extent, undoing the Occupation's 'excesses' represents the negative manifestation of the party's nationalism: it is concerned with undoing rather than doing. In its positive manifestation, LDP nationalism is concerned primarily with the goal of restoring national values to a central place in the post-war system. While the party has been thwarted in its campaign to revise the FLE, this failure has not stopped it from seeking to make the system more nationalistic. As noted in Chapter 2, the party succeeded in re-establishing moral education classes in 1956. More recently, its policy goals in this area have included the following: (1) using schools and these morals classes to assure that future generations of youth accept traditional Japanese values; (2) stiffening textbook controls to ensure that students are taught to love their country; and (3) increasing the use of Japan's *Hinomaru* flag and '*Kimigayo*' song as its national flag and anthem in school ceremonies.

The party's commitment to the teaching of traditional Japanese values was evident in Nakasone's first Diet address:

Post-war education has achieved success by establishing the idea of respect for individual autonomy as its focus. In the process, however, it has neglected the basic ingredient necessary for fostering human growth. I want to refocus our system

57

Table 3.1 The education *zoku* (after the 1986 election)

Name of Dietman	Times elected	Faction	Former* Seirankai	Diet League† on Constitution
Sakata Michita	17	None	No	Yes
Inaba Osamu	14	Nakasone	No	Yes
Hasegawa Takashi	12	Abe	No	Yes
Kaifu Toshiki	10	Kōmoto	No	Yes
Okuno Seisuke	9	None	No	Yes
Fujinami Takao	8	Nakasone	No	No
Nishioka Takeo	8	None	No	No
Tanikawa Kazuo	8	Kōmoto	No	Yes
Kondō Tetsuo	7	Kōmoto	Yes	Yes
Mori Yoshirō	7	Abe	Yes	Yes
Sunada Shigetami	7	Nakasone	No	Yes
Matsunaga Hikaru	7	Nakasone	Yes	Yes
Mitsuzuka Hiroshi	6	Abe	Yes	Yes
Aoki Masahisa	6	Nakasone	Yes	Yes
Ishibashi Kazuya	5	Abe		Yes
Ōtsuka Yūji	5	Abe		Yes
Nakamura Yasushi	5	Nakasone		Yes
Funada Hajime	4	Tanaka		Yes
Kudō Iwao	4	Kōmoto		Yes
Nakagawa Yukio	2 (upper)	Tanaka		Yes
Yanagawa Kakuji	1 (upper)	Nakasone		N.A.

* 1977 Data. The *Seirankai* disbanded soon afterward, so younger Dietmen did not have a chance to participate.

†1983 Data. The full name of the group is the Dietmen's League for the Realization of an Independent Constitution (*Jishu kempō kisei giin dōmei*).

Sources: There is no such thing as an official 'membership' of a *zoku*. Nevertheless, most actors involved in education recognize the existence of such a group and have an idea of who is 'in' and who is not. This list was compiled by Inoguchi Takashi and Iwai Tomoaki, in their book *'Zoku giin' no kenkyū* (Nihon keizai shimbunsha, Tokyo, 1987). It was largely confirmed in my interviews with education actors (including Dietmen) and in other sources.[8]

to emphasize the training of 'sympathetic hearts' (*omoiyari no kokoro*) and the training of internationalists who love their country and are willing to work hard for its development.[9]

In this speech and in many others, the Prime Minister voiced his argument that the post-war system was essentially averse to the teaching of things 'Japanese'. Students were taught to be individuals in the western sense but they were not taught the importance of the community in Japanese culture. Education systems in many nations play a role in providing their citizens with a basic understanding and appreciation of their national culture and social values. Nakasone's argument was that the post-war Japanese system failed in this task. One of the consistent themes of his education reform campaign, therefore, was an effort to reintroduce Japanese content into the education system. Young people needed to be trained, he argued, in the 'living culture of the nation' (*minzoku no seikatsu bunka*). They needed to be taught to recognize the 'obligations' and 'responsibilities' that go with the 'rights' of their culture.[10] The party's platform for the 1986 election campaign emphasized similar themes. The nation needed an education system, it argued, 'which will train our people to respect individuals, carry on the traditional culture of our country and contribute to international society while maintaining their consciousness of being Japanese'.[11]

The LDP's stands on the more controversial issues of textbooks and *Hinomaru/Kimigayo* follow naturally from its demand for more moral education. Arguing that 'national pride' and 'love of country' are essential elements in the Japanese emphasis on community values, party nationalists insist that textbooks and school functions should encourage these feelings as well. The LDP politicians active in the area of education have in recent years become more closely associated with the issue of textbook control than with virtually any other education issue – particularly after they launched a vocal offensive aimed at stiffening the MOE review process in the early 1980s (see p. 61). In the most recent round of reform, the nationalists put greater emphasis on their demand that schools be forced to display the 'national flag' and play the 'national anthem' at school functions.[12]

Weakening Nikkyōso

Another consistent aim of LDP education policy has been its anti-union element. To an extent, this objective has simply been a 'means' towards the above goals. Since *Nikkyōso* has been the main force blocking LDP efforts to re-establish pre-war patterns and reintroduce traditional Japanese values, it has naturally become a corollary of these policies that the union must first be weakened. Over the years, however, the suppression of the union has also become a goal in itself. It follows from the conviction on the part of many in the older generation in the party that 'teaching is a holy profession' unsuited for those who would call themselves 'education workers' and seek personal economic gain through unions.[13] While even the 'hawks' in the party have stopped publicly making an issue of this distinction,[14] the image of an ideal teacher continues to animate party thinking. As described by journalist Yamazaki Masato, the party's ideal teacher would 'never do anything like strike, never say a word about politics and never get involved in union activities. Instead, he would subscribe to the idea that teaching is a holy profession and simply concentrate on educating children.'[15] Given this attitude, the weakening of the union (or at least its transformation into one more in line with this view) thus becomes a goal independent of other goals. As party literature phrases it, the party's aim is 'to improve the quality of teachers' (*kyōin shishitsu kōjō*).[16]

The combination of these direct and indirect aims has made fighting the union a consistent and visible part of LDP education politics. The series of anti-union measures promoted by the LDP in the 1950s and 1960s was recorded in Chapter 2. In general, these policies sought to give the central government the power to force teachers to leave the union and teach what the government wanted them to teach. They were partly successful but also had the effect of radicalizing the union and increasing teacher distrust of the government. The 1970s saw a continuation of this pattern, but with a slightly 'softer' approach. LDP Dietman Funada Hajime explained the logic behind the new tactic. Relating the party's policy to an Aesop's Fable, he likened the old and new LDP strategies for dealing with the union to the competition between the North Wind and the Sun to get a wandering traveller to take off his coat. In the fable, the North Wind tried to blow the coat off the man, but the traveller only pulled it around himself more tightly. The Sun simply turned up the heat, whereupon the man voluntarily took off his coat. Thus, while the old 'smash the union' strategy had encouraged *Nikkyōso* to fight harder, the new strategy sought to create incentives for teachers to co-operate.[17]

The centrepiece of the 1970s strategy was a plan to raise overall teachers' salaries and create incentives for co-operation by establishing salary gradations dependent on administrative approval. Although only partially implemented, the changes which were put into effect (most notably a 30 per cent salary rise) did succeed in reducing the radicalism of the union by establishing teaching – in the minds of the public and many teachers – as a 'special profession' and by eliminating many of the old economic arguments behind union activism. In the 1980s the LDP's anti-union activities continued with an effort to establish a one-year probationary training year for new teachers. While the party did not publicly advocate the training year as an anti-union pro-gramme, *Nikkyōso* leaders charged that it was an attempt to encourage new teachers to stay out of the union. These two initiatives will be explored in detail in Chapters 7 and 8.

Disagreements over tactics

The above LDP goals – undoing the Occupation's 'excesses', restoring traditional Japanese values to a central place in the education system and fighting the union – all reflect the party's basic nationalist ideology and to that extent are supported at least to some degree by most party members. Disagreements which do exist concern tactics more than the goals themselves. Nevertheless, such disagreements over 'means' play a significant part in the policy-making process and therefore require closer analysis. Many Japanese observers tend to express these differ-ences in simplified terms: the LDP 'hawks' (*takaha*) are said to favour tough policies of anti-unionism and nationalism; 'doves' (*hatoha*) tend to prefer more subtle 'soft' anti-unionism and would rather avoid harsh nationalist rhetoric – particularly of the kind which offends Japan's sensitive neighbours. While such terms inevitably gloss over the complex reality, they nevertheless provide insights into this first basic 'conflict' within the con-servative camp.

The textbook controversy of the early 1980s was a typical 'hawk' versus 'dove' conflict. In the 1980 general election the LDP had just won a 'stable' (*antei*) majority for the first time since the early 1970s, and the 'hawks' were consequently feeling more assertive. In the months which followed, therefore, they began to voice criticism of the MOE's textbook review process. It was not tough enough, they argued. It was letting textbooks through which were not teaching 'love of country' (*aikokushin*). Leading the offensive was LDP 'hawk' and education *zoku* Dietman Mitsuzuka Hiroshi. When the party decided to estab-lish a Textbook Problem Subcommittee as a subunit of the PARC education committees, Mitsuzuka was named chairman.

The party, however, was not uniformly enthusiastic about

Mitsuzuka's 'hawkish' offensive. *Zoku* leaders Fujinami Takao, Nishioka Takeo, Sakata Michita and Sunada Shigetami all criticized Mitsuzuka's approach. Long active in the area of education policy (Mitsuzuka was a relative newcomer), they realized that his public demand for more nationalist textbooks risked prompting a strong counter-reaction. They preferred the long-standing approach of quiet, steadfast support for the MOE review process. They did agree, however, with the Textbook Subcommittee's proposals for reforms in the MOE review procedure.

Inevitably, the 'counter-reaction' happened. The MOE's review of *kōtōgakkō* social studies texts – leading up to the issuing of new texts in the summer of 1982 – included a request that authors 'improve' on their use of the term 'invasion' to describe Japan's wartime action against China. The media, reporting (inaccurately) that textbooks had actually been changed to describe the action as an 'advance into' China, quickly turned the issue into an international controversy with the Chinese and Korean governments demanding an MOE climbdown. Faced with pressure to adjust the textbook review process to international pressure, LDP 'hawks' were even more adamant. The *zoku* hawks (Mitsuzuka, Ishibashi Kazuya, Aoki Masahisa) defended the MOE review process, and other politicians not as closely associated with education (Matsuno Raizō, Fujio Masayuki) demanded that the party leadership stand up to foreign 'interference' in Japan's domestic affairs. On the other hand, the LDP's internationalist 'doves' (such as Kosaka Tokusaburō) and even education *zoku* leaders like Fujinami recommended moderation. In the end, the leadership apologized to the Koreans and Chinese. Although the government subsequently implemented some of the procedural changes recommended by the Textbook Subcommittee, the textbook screening process in effect became *less* strict as a result of the international controversy.[18]

Similar patterns have characterized the LDP's other significant hawk versus dove conflicts over education policy. In the late 1960s, the party's educationists were split over how to deal with a court challenge by *Nikkyōso* demanding compensation for overtime work. The 'hawks' (Naitō, Nadao Hirokichi, Inaba Osamu) insisted that teachers ought to perform such work in a spirit of selfless dedication to their profession – and therefore argued that the party should rewrite the contested labour law to exempt teachers from its provisions. A newly recruited group of young *zoku* activists, however, sought to avoid a confrontation by compromising with the union. The group included Nishioka and Fujinami, as well as the later New Liberal Club leader Kōno Yōhei. Nishioka (still in his thirties at the time) negotiated with union leader Makieda Motofumi and came back with a proposal: in exchange for a flat 4 per cent salary bonus, all teachers would be expected to work overtime – but headmasters would be restricted in how much overtime they could demand. The bonus, eventually accepted by the party, became the first step in Nishioka's 'soft' strategy for dealing with the union.[19]

In both of the above episodes, there was significant hawk versus dove conflict. While the antagonists in both cases essentially agreed on the goals (nationalist textbooks and reducing union influence), they advocated different tactics. The result in both cases was a moderation of the LDP approach. The textbook review process was rewritten, but the MOE was made to recognize the limits in how much nationalism it could encourage. The government forced the union to accept a proposal requiring teachers to work overtime, but in exchange it had to offer compensation and a negotiated limit on how much overtime teachers could be forced to work. While issues have not always been fought out in this way, there can be no doubt that the hawk versus dove cleavage has limited LDP nationalism. The party has consistently sought to rewrite the Fundamental Law of Education and create a 'merit' salary scale for teachers which would truly pressure the union – but its doves (reacting to foreign and *Nikkyōso* pressure) will not let the party press too hard.

Lest one overestimate the power of the doves, however, a final case deserves attention. In the mid-1970s the MOE faced a decision on whether to implement a controversial new salary bonus for department head-level teachers (*shunin*). The LDP had advocated the measure as a means of extending the power of the administration within schools while *Nikkyōso* vocally opposed it as an attempt to divide teachers. Minister of Education Nagai Michio and some *zoku* doves like Fujinami encouraged moderation. In this case, however, Nishioka joined the hawks in angrily demanding that the MOE go ahead with its plans. He convinced Fujinami to go along with his tough approach, and the *shunin* bonus was implemented as planned (see Chapter 7). The case illustrates that when the LDP can agree on a firm stand, it usually gets its way.

Education for the economy

According to Kobayashi Tetsuya, the author of a history of education in Japan, the Japanese government's post-war education policy has had two basic aims: nationalism and utilitarianism.[20] As seen above, the LDP has been consistent and fairly unified in its pursuit of the first of these goals – differing only on the issue of tactics. At least it has agreed on what it means to pursue a 'nationalist' education policy. It has consistently sought a strong central administration, a weak teachers' union, a Japanization of the system and the incorporation of Japanese values into the curriculum.

The LDP has also been unified in its pursuit of 'utilitarianism'. It has always sought to pursue the education policies which would best help the nation continue its economic advancement. As noted in Chapter 2, the government pursued this aim consistently in the 1950s and 1960s, encouraging the expansion of university and secondary education and the 'diversification' of these sectors in favour of greater emphasis on science and technology. Throughout this period, while the demands almost always originated from the business community and while the policies were usually developed and implemented by the Ministry of Education, the LDP acted as the middle man in ensuring that business demands were put into effect. Chapter 2 also noted, however, that establishment opinion had started to change and break down by the 1970s and 1980s. Whereas before it had been unified in its advocacy of expansion and specialization, by the 1970s some voices had started to call for more radical reform. Men like Amaya Naohiro argued that the twenty-first century would require an education system with a whole new emphasis: less rigid in its emphasis on academic background, less stress on memorization and more concentration on work-related ability, creativity and self-confident expression. Japan's 'catch-up' phase was over, these men argued, and it therefore needed to re-examine its educational system which had been built around this goal.

Such shifts in opinion left the LDP somewhat unsure *which* policies were the most utilitarian in the post-industrial age. While it could agree as to which policies were most nationalist, it found – as economic needs changed – that it was more difficult to determine which ones were most utilitarian. Thus, although the LDP remained unified in its commitment to education for the economy, it found itself increasingly divided as to what this meant. Various LDP politicians in the 1970s and 1980s used economic arguments as a basis for advocating such reforms as (1) an increased emphasis on ability-based streaming of students; and (2) a radical liberalization of the system. Neither, however, earned broad party support. Instead, large parts of the LDP remained convinced that the status quo system was best for the economy, and therefore advocated no change. This failure of the LDP to agree on a course for dealing with the changing demands of the economy contributed greatly to the breakdown of the government's recent education reform initiatives.

The debate over earlier selection of students by ability

Within the LDP the reformist course most often advocated on utilitarian grounds was the proposal that schools and the education system as a whole put an increased emphasis on ability. As noted in Chapter 2, the Occupation reforms introduced following the Second World War greatly increased the egalitarianism of the system by extending compulsory education (where students were educated as equals) from six to nine years. Ever since, there have been at least some LDP members who have wanted to restore earlier selection. While some of these conservatives were motivated largely by a desire to erase Occupation influence on the system, they always made their case on utilitarian grounds: earlier sorting would allow for the training of a more talented elite.

In 1969 the LDP's Education System Research Council (ESRC, *Bunkyō seido chōsakai*) – one of the two permanent PARC education committees – issued a report outlining its plan for education reform. The government, it said, should consider establishing six-year or five-year secondary schools in order to promote 'gifted education' (*eisai kyōiku*). Its proposals for higher education similarly emphasized a diversification of institutions so that some could specialize in research and the training of an elite while others could concentrate on more specific job- and skill-related training.[21] After the CCE's similar recommendations (1971) encountered widespread opposition, however, it became apparent that interest in such radical changes was limited to a core of education activists. As Dietman Nishioka explained, 'The rest of the party simply didn't have an opinion, and I did not yet have the influence to advance a reform agenda on my own.'[22]

65

Since that time, even the core of education activists has been unable to agree on significant steps towards greater emphasis on ability. In 1980 the PARC ESRC set up a special School System Problem Subcommittee to draw up a plan for bringing the nation's education system into line with the needs of the twenty-first century. When the subcommittee reported to the main body in 1981, however, *zoku* moderates declared that it was too far ahead of its time.[23] The plan – referred to as the 'Kondō Plan' due to the active role played by the chairman Kondō Tetsuo – called for changes allowing 'grade skipping' (*tobikyū*) by bright students and 'holding back' (*ryūnen*) for students who were not keeping up. In addition, it proposed that the School Education Law be amended to allow alternatives to the 6–3–3 division of years.[24] In an extremely unusual move, the full ESRC refused to accept the report. It planned to put the subcommittee back to work with a new chairman, but the new subcommittee never produced a report.[25]

The education *zoku*'s failure to reach agreement on a reform plan (other than on nationalist principles) is a reflection of its inability to separate itself from the status quo system – a system which it played such a large role in developing. In the late 1960s when it agreed on a concrete plan for radical reform, it was still possible for LDP Dietmen to make the case for change by attacking the 'Occupation-imposed system'. By the 1980s, however, many *zoku* members were finding that in order to make the case for change they had to attack a system which they had overseen for forty years. Some *zoku* members remained enthusiastically reformist. Nishioka, for example, remained a vocal advocate of such proposals as six-year secondary schools and examination reform. Kaifu Toshiki once proposed that Japan consider the introduction of a 'voucher system' – a revolutionary reform which would have eliminated the school district system and allowed parents to choose their elementary and secondary schools.[26] Both men were unable, however, to build a *zoku* consensus around their proposals. Kaifu's plan was quickly smothered by moderates after the MOE explained the serious nature of the proposed reform.[27] Nishioka encountered a lack of enthusiasm from his colleagues who felt that the established system was all right as it was. As one *zoku* member commented, 'Nishioka has always been a little ahead of the times.'[28]

Illustrative of the *zoku*'s generally conservative attitude towards change were the comments of various educationist Dietmen in a 1986 article prepared by the LDP periodical *Gekkan jiyū minshu*. In this profile of politicians active on the party's education committees, *zoku* members such as Nakamura Yasushi were quoted speaking almost defensively about the established system:

> These days, people talk a lot about how bad *ijime* is and about examination hell – and there are various such problems. But Japanese education has many good points too. It's not as if everything is bad. That's why my goal is to expand on these good points.

He went on to emphasize the importance of moving cautiously in the process of education reform and concluded by describing the positive reviews which Japan's education system was getting from foreign visitors.[29] In the entire article (profiling the reform opinions of several leading *zoku* members), only one Dietman mentioned the idea of 'gifted education' – and only in an effort to describe what his plan was not. Sunada Shigetami suggested that 'in the future, we would like to train people who will be able to develop creative science and technology'. In explaining what he meant, however, he was careful to insist that he was not talking about anti-egalitarian, gifted education. His proposal was merely that 'the government should spend more money on starting [the training of scientists] at the lower and upper secondary school levels'. Neither he nor any of the other quoted Dietmen mention the ideas of earlier selection or six-year secondary schools.[30]

The debate over liberalization

Not all members of the LDP, however, have been as closely tied to the status quo education system as the education *zoku*. In the most recent round of reform, it was a non-educationist – Prime Minister Nakasone – who emerged as the most vocal advocate of far-reaching utilitarian (as well as nationalist) reform. Borrowing much of his rhetoric from men like Amaya, he criticized the established system for its inability to meet the needs of the future and advocated the *jiyūka* (liberalization) and *jūnanka* (flexibilization) of the system. His main concern was the degree to which the established system was rigidly standardized. Such a system had worked well in producing highly skilled manpower for Japan's economic advancement, he admitted, but Japan needed more than just that for the twenty-first century. It needed creativity, high-level talent and internationalism as well. Basing his arguments on future economic needs, Nakasone was making a classic utilitarian case for change.

The Prime Minister had not always been an advocate of such reforms. In the early 1970s round of reform, his comments on education had been limited to demands that the government take a tough stand against the leaders of university disturbances.[31] He was also known as a strong advocate of nationalism in the schools – having been one of the leaders of an early attempt to reverse much of the Occupation settlement.[32] In the lead-up to the establishment of his Ad Hoc Council on Education, however, he began to advocate changes which went beyond the usual nationalist proposals.

Nakasone's interest in broader educational change can be traced to his association with the cause of administrative reform in the early 1980s. As Director of the Administrative Management Agency under Prime Minister Suzuki Zenkō, Nakasone had worked closely with the high-profile Provisional Commission for Administrative Reform (*Rinchō*) set up in 1981 as a means of dealing with Japan's chronic budget deficits. Through his work with *Rinchō* – a major force in the politics of the period as it put the Japanese government on a strict diet of zero-budget ceilings – Nakasone had become committed to a philosophy of fiscal conservatism and its companion ideology of privatization and free-market competition. As prime minister, he went on to oversee the privatization of Japan National Railways, Nippon Telephone & Telegraph and the Japan Monopoly Corporation.

While *Rinchō* did not propose the privatization of education, such a policy would have been consistent with its philosophy. Some of its members, in fact, were known to espouse ideas about the activization of free-market forces in education. Kumon Shumpei, a close associate of the Prime Minister who had served as a leading force behind the *Rinchō* ideology, was known for having argued that 'given the advent of the information age . . . the most important thing is that the Ministry of Education and other ministries and agencies shed their old insistence that "education is basically a job for the bureaucracy" '. Arguing that a wealthy Japan did not need to depend so much on public education, he advocated reforms in the basic laws governing the education system (including the FLE) to allow the expansion of diverse forms of private education even at the level of compulsory education.[33]

Just as Nakasone was embarking on his education reform campaign in March 1984, a report from the Kyoto Group for the Study of Global Issues issued a report which elaborated on Kumon's ideas. The Group – which included Kumon as well as others from among Nakasone's former *Rinchō* associates – proposed that the principles of free competition be fully applied to the sphere of education:

> The sort of education that can match the needs of the twenty-first century must be ruled by the principle of fair competition in all areas. A diversified and technologically sophisticated society requires many different types of talented citizens. For that, the school must be a place where students are motivated to learn. An environment must be created which encourages free competition not only among students but also among teachers to become better educators.
>
> Ideally, education should be free and independent of constraints and interference from public authorities. In particular, we would like to see as much decontrol as possible – if not the outright abolition of restrictions – in the education system.[34]

In order to introduce competitive forces into the education system, the group proposed specifically that both school establishment rules and the school district system be relaxed. Such steps, it argued, would give parents a greatly expanded choice in the selection of schools and teachers and would therefore force bad schools to improve – or go out of business.[35]

A pair of memos prepared by Nakasone advisors in the early months of 1984 pointed in essentially the same direction, both proposing that the philosophy of *jiyūka* be made one of the pillars of the new education reform. As one of the memos argued:

> The time has come for us to demand a thorough re-examination of the education bureaucracy's current emphasis on administration through licensing and financial assistance. It is imperative that we move towards a new emphasis on reduced regulation (*kisei kanwa*) in order to achieve the activization of education in Japan.[36]

Although the memos – intended for distribution within the Nakasone camp only – were not signed, newspapers reported that a key figure in their preparation had been Kōyama Kenichi, a Nakasone advisor who was to go on to serve on the Ad Hoc Council.[37]

While Prime Minister Nakasone himself was never very specific in his comments about *jiyūka*, he did express his support for the concept on several occasions. Appearing on the NHK programme 'Ask the Prime Minister', he came out expressly in favour of the positions being taken by his advisors, arguing that 'it is important that we introduce an element of competition into the whole school system through policies of *jiyūka* and *jūnanka*'. He added that while public education would continue to be important, 'we cannot keep thinking that everything has to be done by the government. Things which can be handed over to the private sector should be handed over.'[38] Similar statements regarding the need to expand the role of private education can be found dating back to the beginning of Nakasone's involvement with *Rinchō*.[39] When the time came to appoint members of the Ad Hoc Council, he showed his sympathy for the *jiyūka* line by choosing known advocates of such policies, including Kōyama, Kumon and Amaya.

The policies advocated by the Prime Minister can be summarized as follows. First, he argued that MOE regulations should be made more flexible (*jūnanka*) in order to reduce the uniformity of the education system. Free to emphasize different subjects, materials and teaching techniques, schools would be able to teach students more according to their different interests and levels of ability, and in the process would help meet future demands for high-level and diverse talent. Second, he advocated the liberalization of the rules governing school choice (*jiyūka*) in order to activate the schools through free-market competition. Forced to compete for students and money, schools would have to improve in order to survive. In the actual comments of Nakasone and his advisors, these two concepts seem to have been joined as one – usually the two ideas were referred to together as 'liberalization' (*jiyūka*). In fact, however, they are clearly distinct. One could have free competition (*jiyūka* as narrowly defined above) without an increase in flexibility. Schools would merely compete on a standard scale. Likewise, one could have *jūnanka* without free-market competition.

School choice would continue to be regulated, but educational content and methods would be freer and less uniform.

Within the LDP, there seems to have been some support for at least part of what the Prime Minister wanted to do. Many Dietmen outside the education *zoku* viewed the Ministry of Education as too conservative and behind the times. These politicians pointed to the growing trend towards liberalization and reduced regulation throughout the government and argued that the MOE should not be exempt. Typical of this group was Aichi Kazuo, a recent chairman of the Diet Education Committee but definitely not a part of the party's education *zoku*.[40] He argued:

> The education *zoku*, both its left and right factions, is committed to central control over education. They think the more power the MOE has, the better, because they exercise their power through the ministry. Personally, I think it would be better to reduce the authority of the MOE. Nakasone was thinking this too. And so he raised the issue of *jiyūka*, and the AHCE itself was established with this purpose in mind: reduce MOE authority and do things freely.[41]

Aichi went on to emphasize the need to allow regions and localities to have more control over what was taught in their areas. The MOE, he said, should require only the basics. What he was talking about was *jūnanka* – reduced government control of educational *content*. It is difficult to determine the degree to which Aichi's views were shared by other Diet members. Saitō Taijun, the MOE official in charge of the AHCE's secretariat, estimated that up to a quarter of the LDP were sympathetic towards the Prime Minister's intentions.[42]

In expanding the scope of his reforms to embrace free-market competition as well as the *jūnanka*, however, Nakasone seems to have gone beyond what even those sympathetic with his programme were willing to accept. Aichi noted, for example, that 'there was a problem with the way *jiyūka* was sold – it was pushed too hard. Nakasone saw the need to make a splash in order to really change the way the MOE does things, but he just went too far.'[43] If Aichi thought the Prime Minister had gone a little too far, the MOE and the LDP's own education *zoku* were much stronger in their criticism. Kaifu Toshiki, the Minister of

Education during the AHCE's crucial second year, and an influential leader of the party later to serve as prime minister, was a leading opponent of Nakasone's plans for *jiyūka*:

> Look at what's happened in Britain. There they have too few standards and – as a result – low quality. Britain now wants to improve the quality of its schools by establishing standards. Japan has standards and high quality now – so why change? As far as regulations go, there is no plan to do away with them. There's no way Japan will see an end to the school district system.[44]

Kaifu was opposing not just the abolition of the school district system (*jiyūka*) but also the idea of any reduction in regulations (*jūnanka*). Pressed further, Kaifu revealed the depth of his opposition: 'There absolutely will not be any *jiyūka*. The party decides!'[45]

That the *zoku* came out opposed to *jiyūka* was not at all surprising. The inability of the *zoku* to agree even on specific steps to increase the education system's emphasis on ability (a much less radical reform) was noted above. *Zoku* members were simply too attached to the status quo. 'The system was working all right, so why change it?' they asked. The Prime Minister's ideas for liberalizing the whole system, therefore, sparked immediate and firm opposition. Such steps would drastically reduce the MOE's (and therefore the *zoku*'s) control over the system. The battle between the *zoku* with its opposition to any regulatory relief and the Prime Minister with his plan to liberalize the education system radically was the critical line of cleavage in the most recent round of reform. Both sought the utilitarian goal of creating an education system best able to serve the economy, but their ideas of what this goal required were radically divergent.

Money, power and 'turf'

While the chapter thus far has focused on the LDP's *policy* goals, the party as a whole (and individuals and factions within it) have also sometimes based their position on non-policy considerations – such as power. In order to affect policy, politicians and parties have to have power, and so the LDP's education policy has sometimes reflected the goals of 'money, power and "turf" ' as much or more than long-term policy aims. Leaders of the LDP have pursued education reform in order to win elections and extend their term in office; opposition factions within the party have opposed leadership education initiatives in order to end the leader's tenure as head of the party; and education policy has often been affected by the quarrels of the party's various *zoku* among themselves and with the 'centre' over money and 'turf'.

Winning elections

Although easy to overlook given the party's often dogmatic approach to education issues, the ever-present interest of the LDP in this as in other policy areas is to get re-elected. While its general orientation may be explained by its ideology, its actions – the timing of initiatives, the content and, most importantly, the degree to which they are pushed – may often be explained primarily by the immediate need of the party to maintain power. Thus in the 1974 Upper House elections, for example, Prime Minister Tanaka made education policy a major issue, not as much for its direct value as for its potential as a means of drawing the attention of the electorate away from the problem of inflation.[46] Similarly, Prime Minister Nakasone's decision to emphasize education reform in 1983 was at least partially related to his desire to do well in the 1983 Upper House (June) and Lower House (December) elections. In both campaigns he made major speeches on the need for education reform – outlining a concrete 'seven-point proposal' for reform at the height of the December campaign.

Similar concerns about getting elected have also caused the party to *down*grade education issues. In 1971, in the period immediately following the issuance of the CCE report, leading LDP figures such as Prime Minister Satō pledged full support for the council's plan. It was not long, however, before the combination of diminished public concern about the university crisis and vocal opposition from a broad section of the labour and academic communities convinced many party members to tone down their efforts. Even as they continued to voice respect for the reform plan, the party quietly stopped working for some of the more far-reaching proposals.[47]

Party leadership and factional conflict

An LDP leader has to worry about winning elections, but he also has to worry about winning leadership contests within his party. Every two years a prime minister must win re-election to the presidency of his party – a process which requires that he maintain the support of at least enough party 'factions' (*habatsu*) to constitute a majority. In the most recent round of education reform, Nakasone was also clearly motivated by his need to win re-election within his party. The Prime Minister's use of education in the 1983 general election was noted above. When he followed through on his campaign promises by proposing the AHCE in the spring of 1984, however, this too was politically motivated. Approaching the end of his first term as party president, he wanted to be able to point to the wide public support for his education initiative as a means of gaining re-election within his own party – a goal which he achieved in October 1984.

Two years later, when he faced a general election and a party presidency decision once more, he again used the education issue to his advantage. He pushed the Ad Hoc Council to produce major reform proposals in its second report (April 1986) and campaigned on the basis of the AHCE recommendations in the June 1986 'double' election. He used his success in that election (the LDP won by a landslide) to win an extension of his term as party president in October of that same year. Again, as in the case of the 1971 reform initiative, however, the months after all of these elections saw the LDP put increasing distance between itself and the AHCE. Having used the issue to earn a landslide victory at the polls and to have his term as party president extended twice, Nakasone showed much less interest in putting priority on council proposals in the final year of his tenure as prime minister.

When a party leader uses an issue in an attempt to extend his tenure, his action usually yields an equal and opposite counteraction: the leader's factional opponents will also take positions on that issue which reflect their interest in *ending* his tenure. When Nakasone tried to use the education issue to his advantage, therefore, his factional opponents (the Kōmoto and Fukuda/Abe factions) naturally tried to stop him. His opponents did not mind when Nakasone used education as an issue to win the 1983 Lower and Upper House elections. When he tried to make the issue his own by setting up a cabinet-level advisory council, however, they immediately tried to block him. In a rare *majority* party parliamentary inquiry, a leading member of the Fukuda/Abe faction – Fujio Masayuki – attacked the Prime Minister's proposal, saying, 'Right here in our party we have a fine Education Division and Education System Research Council, and the Diet has a fine standing committee. My point is that we can carry out this exercise through these existing arrangements!'[48]

Fujio and the 'opposition' factions were particularly upset with Nakasone's proposal for a cabinet-level council because, in taking charge of education reform, Nakasone was 'taking away' an issue which was of particular interest to the many Fukuda and Kōmoto faction members in the education *zoku*. Not only was Nakasone using an issue to extend his tenure, he was using *their* issue. Table 3.1 above lists the *zoku* members and their factional affiliations. While the largest block of *zoku* members were from the Nakasone faction – and were therefore not so resentful of the Prime Minister's move – nine out of eighteen committed members were from either the Fukuda/Abe or Kōmoto factions, including the Minister of Education (Mori), the recent past chairman of the LDP Education Division (Ishibashi), *zoku* veteran Hasegawa, as well as textbook activist Mitsuzuka – all from the Fukuda/Abe faction; and an influential Kōmoto faction member, Kaifu Toshiki, the chairman of the LDP's Education System Research Council. Fujio, the Fukuda faction leader who spoke up in the Diet, was also close to the *zoku* although not generally seen as a 'member'. In the party's internal debate over education reform, Nakasone found the *zoku* members of the opposition factions to be the most difficult to convince.[49]

Quarrels over money and 'turf'

While factional considerations helped shape the above conflict, the disagreement clearly reflected deeper divisions over the question of who within the party was due to make education policy. *Zoku* members naturally felt that they – who had dedicated their Diet careers to the education issue – had the right to speak for the party on education reform. They knew the history of what the party had tried to do in the past, and they knew the education system and its 'problems' better than any other group of party members. Nakasone, however, argued that

75

the breadth and depth of the problems being experienced by the education system required wider involvement in the education reform process. The previous initiative in 1971 had failed, he insisted, exactly because it was built on a narrow base. He put forward his Ad Hoc Council – with its cabinet-level status directly under his office – as the proper place for developing the education reform proposals necessary to bring the system up-to-date with the needs of the twenty-first century. The conflict, therefore, was essentially a fight over 'turf'. In the terms used by John Campbell, it was a battle between the education 'sub-government' (the *zoku* and the MOE) and the 'centre' (Nakasone). The *zoku* saw education reform as a narrow issue – which under the Japanese system was supposed to be handled *within* the relevant subgovernment. Nakasone saw the issue as a broad one which called for the involvement of the centre.

In the battle between the two views, Nakasone won the first round. He compromised with the *zoku* leaders – agreeing to share in the running of the council in exchange for their backing. As will be seen in Chapter 8, however, this initial compromise failed to resolve the basic tensions between the subgovernment and the centre. When it came time to appoint the members of the AHCE, Nakasone and the *zoku* actually had to divide the membership between them. Their disagreements were replicated within the council. The compromise failed because the conflict between these two forces over 'turf' involved other factors as well – it was also a battle over issues and money. The conflicting positions taken by the Prime Minister and the *zoku* on the issues of *jiyūka* and *jūnanka* were described above. In addition, as in most conflicts between centre and subgovernment, the two sides disagreed over what share of the budget should be devoted to education.

Nakasone, through his association with the *Rinchō* administrative reform, was known as a budget-cutter. Specifically, he was associated with *Rinchō*'s proposals for deep cuts in the education budget: such policies as those calling for a cut in aid to private universities; a delay in the implementation of the MOE's plans for reducing the size of school classes from forty-five to forty; and a re-examination of the policy of providing free textbooks for students.[50] Nakasone's advocacy of a greater private role in education, noted above, was also seen by many of the educationists as an excuse for reducing government funds for education.

On the other hand, increasing or at least preserving the size of the education budget was one of the basic purposes of the LDP education *zoku*. Throughout the 1970s *zoku* members had worked to expand the size of the education budget, gradually building the government's aid programme for private universities, its programme for funding school construction and its plan for reducing the size of school classes. They did not easily give up on these programmes when they were attacked by *Rinchō*. On the contrary, many felt that the education crisis provided reason for further increases in funding. Problems in the classroom, they argued, proved the need for smaller classes and increased funding for teacher training. The goal of the *zoku* as a whole was to have education designated a priority budget category on a par with defence and Overseas Development Assistance.[51]

The conflict over 'turf' between the Prime Minister and the *zoku* thus corresponded with a basic disagreement over issues (*jiyūka/jūnanka*) and money. The cleavages overlapped and were mutually reinforcing. While the initial compromise resolved the disagreement over 'turf' by providing for the two sides to share oversight of the Ad Hoc Council, it did not do anything to resolve their disagreement over these other factors. As the detailed discussion of the council's deliberations in Chapter 8 will reveal, Nakasone's initiative failed to achieve its objectives largely because it never succeeded in resolving these fundamental tensions between the centre and the subgovernment.

PLACE IN THE PROCESS

As the predominant party since its founding in 1955, the LDP has consistently played an important part in the education policy-making process. Its role, however, has changed dramatically over this period. From being concerned almost exclusively with the destruction of *Nikkyōso* in the early years, the party increased its involvement in the process to the point that by the mid-1970s it was exercising influence over virtually all aspects of education policy-making. Whereas previously the party had been content to let the ministry develop its own budget, curriculum and other policies as long as it remained steadfast in its opposition to the union, by the 1970s the party had taken a lead in developing its own policies and drawing up its own budget priorities. On the one hand, the LDP education *zoku* emerged as a strong player in the policy-making process – dominating but also working with the MOE. On the other, the party's 'centre' (particularly under Prime Minister Nakasone) was deeply involved as well. The education debate of the recent period (1967–87) cannot be understood without an appreciation of the changing and complex role of the LDP in this period.

The formal structure

The formal structure of the LDP – specifically the shape of its policy-making apparatus – has changed little since the party's founding in 1955. Then, as now, the job of developing, reviewing and approving policy has been the function of Policy Affairs Research Council and its various divisions (*bukai*), research councils (*chōsakai*) and special committees (*tokubetsu iinkai*).[52] Of the various PARC bodies, those with the largest formal part in the process are the *bukai*. These divisions, set up on an issue-specific basis corresponding with the various ministries on the one hand and the Diet standing committees on the other, each work to co-ordinate the party's policy in their own area. Thus the Education Division (*Bunkyō bukai*), for example, deals with all legislation coming from the Ministry of Education and going to the Diet Education Committee. These divisions serve as the forum in which the ministries present their legislative proposals for party review (*shinsa*) as the first step in the LDP deliberative process in which the party decides which legislation to send to the Diet.[53] The *bukai* spend a great deal of their time dealing with a particular kind of legislation – the annual budget.

The other PARC bodies, the *chōsakai* and *tokubetsu iinkai*, have less defined roles. In general *chōsakai* are responsible for conducting long-term research into basic, important policies in established areas. *Tokubetsu iinkai* deal with specific measures or particular problems, especially those which do not fall neatly into the jurisdiction of an established council.[54] In the area of education, the Education System Research Council, a body which has existed since the party was established in 1955, is responsible for examining education issues from a long range perspective. Among the other councils dealing with education in 1987 were the Infant and Childhood Problem Research Council; the Special Education Reform Research Council; and the Special Committee for Developing Countermeasures to Deal with Young People.[55] In general, the education *bukai* includes the younger, junior Dietmen while the *chōsakai* is dominated by veteran education activists, particularly the former ministers of education. The younger Dietmen are thus employed doing the day-to-day work on legislation and budgets while the veterans are free to take a longer-term look at education issues.[56]

The changing party role in education

The LDP's first decade

While the LDP's structure as described above existed from the day of the LDP's founding, the bodies of the Policy Affairs Research Council did not play a very significant role in the party's first decade. The party, still new to power and intent on solidifying its political base, delegated most of its policy-making power to the bureaucracy and devoted its energy to the more political task of dealing with the opposition parties in the Diet. As a result of this division of responsibilities, the party's policy-related positions (such as those in PARC) were considered to be less prestigious than its party-political posts.[57] In the area of education the most influential party figures were not those who worked on the PARC education committees but rather the senior 'political' Dietmen who specialized in fighting the Socialists and the unions (and therefore *Nikkyōso*).

The party's 'education' policy, therefore, was in those early years largely subsumed in its broader political campaign against the progressive camp. Many of the Dietmen most active in pushing the party's anti-*Nikkyōso* education policies were not even part of the PARC education policy-making apparatus. Ōdachi Shigeo and Araki Masuo, both graduates of the pre-war bureaucracy, were known more for their tough positions in favour of law and order than for their views on education. If they were part of any *zoku*, they were part of the law and order group (*chian zoku*). Nadao Hirokichi maintained a long-term interest in the party's education policy (he was an early chairman of the ESRC) but was known almost exclusively for his stand against the teachers' union. He too, like Ōdachi, was a former top bureaucrat in the pre-war Home Ministry. Another group of Dietmen – such as Moriyama Kinji – became involved in the party's education policy through their leadership of the LDP's anti-union labour policy. Again, these men were not 'educationists' as much as they were law and order labour specialists.[58]

As a result of the LDP's decision to emphasize politics over policy in the area of education, there were few LDP 'educationists' in that early period. Among the few were Sakata Michita and Kennoki Toshihiro. Sakata, elected to the Lower House in the first post-war election at the age of only 29, was slowly gaining experience in the education sphere through his work on PARC education bodies. He was chairman of the ESRC for two extended periods between 1961 and 1968. Kennoki, the Occupation-era MOE official mentioned in Chapter 2, had entered the Upper House in 1953 and had since been seeking to get the party to take a greater interest in reforming the education system. He recalled, however, that there were few Dietmen interested in education in those days. The issue was seen as a jinx, he explained, with many young Dietmen discouraged from getting involved by the belief that 'those who get involved with education lose elections'. At the peak of the LDP's offensive against *Nikkyōso*, Kennoki had to make 'home visits' just to fill the LDP's share of seats on the Diet Education Committee. 'I told them that all they had to do was come to meetings and sit quietly,' he recalled.[59]

The ideological nature of the LDP's early involvement in education meant that it played an influential but narrow part in the policy-making process. The party's primary avenue of influence was its group of law and order ministers. (Ōdachi, Araki, and Nadao all served as ministers of education.) These men intervened in MOE personnel affairs and used various other tactics to convince the ministry to become as avidly anti-*Nikkyōso* as the party itself. They then went on to encourage the ministry's various anti-union policy proposals, concentrating their efforts on pushing those laws through the Diet. The party remained relatively uninvolved, however, in the MOE's non-union-related education policies. Lacking a core of dedicated educationists, the LDP did not have the expertise to get involved in most areas of education policy. Until the late 1960s, the party played what journalist Yamazaki describes as a 'handmaiden' role. Apart from its primary concern of assuring that the ministry maintained its anti-union posture, it was satisfied to do the minimum of work regarding its budgetary and legislative needs.[60] Kennoki agreed: 'Before the *zoku*,' he admitted, 'most education policy was made by the MOE.'[61]

The birth of the zoku

In the late 1960s, at the height of the student movement, the LDP's educationists finally took charge of the party's education policy. The old law and order group (led by Araki as head of the party's Student Problem Discussion Group and Moriyama of its Education Normalization Committee) were using the occasion of the university demonstrations to seek a tough new law to provide the government with greatly increased power over the universities. The problems would be resolved, they argued, if university officials would simply take a harder line in dealing with the student leaders of the demonstrations.

Educationists like Sakata insisted, however, that the problems in the universities were not merely an issue of law and order; the disturbances reflected real deficiencies in the institutions of higher education. Using his position as chairman of the ESRC, Sakata took the initiative in September 1968 by convening a special investigation. Over a period of two months the council met regularly to hear testimony from university officials, professors, students and others about the problem. It was the first time the LDP had conducted serious research into an education issue and foreshadowed the coming, more activist pattern of LDP involvement in education policy-making. Following a vigorous internal debate, the ESRC published a set of proposals calling for changes in the structure of university administration, the diversification of higher education, aid to private universities and limited consultations between students and university officials.[62] The proposals, while still too radical for much of the progressive camp, nevertheless marked a significant change from previous party statements on education because they sought to address the educational problems at the root of the university disturbances rather than relying on discipline and control as advocated by the law and order 'hawks'.

Soon after the publication of these recommendations, Prime Minister Satō named Sakata as his new minister of education – signalling the ascendancy of the educationists and the success of their campaign to have the university disturbances treated as an education problem. Sakata worked quickly to stem the demand for government intervention in the universities by pushing through the 'Special Measures Law Relating to the Management of Universities', a law which accomplished its mission merely by *threatening* such intervention.[63] He then set out to follow the advice of his own ESRC by addressing the root causes of the disturbances. The first step was to be the establishment of the government programme for providing private universities with greatly expanded financial assistance (see Chapter 7).

Sakata was not alone in this campaign. He was joined by a whole new group of young Dietmen who had been attracted to the education sphere as the university protests pushed the education issue to the top of the political agenda. Nishioka, one of the new group, explained that he joined 'because the Diet Education Committee was becoming important'. He did not accept the old argument that 'education loses elections' but felt instead that it would serve as an effective platform on which to build his Diet career.[64] Several other up-and-coming young Dietmen agreed. Among the others attracted to the party's various education organs in this period were Kōno Yōhei, Fujinami Takao, Hashimoto Ryūtarō, Matsunaga Hikaru, Mori Yoshirō and Tanikawa Kazuo – all destined to become cabinet ministers. All were of the 'Shōwa generation' (born variously between 1928 and 1937) and therefore had undergone some or all of their schooling in the post-war years. Nishioka, Kōno, Mori and Hashimoto were barely in elementary school when the war ended. They were the first Dietmen produced by the 6–3–3 system.

The decision of all of these young Dietmen to join the party's education organs at this time was not entirely coincidental. The LDP's leadership – particularly senior educationists such as Sakata and Hasegawa Takashi – realized that the party needed young Dietmen who had grown up with the post-war education system in order to deal with the system's problems. The party leadership was seeking to put a greater emphasis on the policy side of politics in all spheres, and education seemed particularly in need of young talent. The young Dietmen were therefore talked into joining Sakata's education workshops.[65] The university disturbances gave the young men a great deal of experience very quickly. Within a few years, the new group were given positions of responsibility in the education sphere. The education *zoku* was born.

The maturing of the zoku

The *zoku* thus emerged as a new participant in the education policy-making process in the late 1960s and early 1970s – just as the CCE was drawing up its education reform proposals. At that time, however, the *zoku* was still in its infancy. Although Sakata was minister of education for virtually the entire period of the council's deliberations, and although Nishioka was MOE political vice-minister in the CCE's final year, their input seems to have been limited. They helped give the report its general shape and tone, but the details were worked out entirely between the council and the MOE. Nishioka himself admits that he had only limited influence at the time.[66] Suzuki Shigenobu, a CCE specialist member at the time, was more blunt:

> Nishioka was part of a 'reformist faction' then, but he had absolutely no input. There was really no input from any politicians. Morito (the chairman) just would not allow it. He had a real samurai-type character, and he just would not listen even if the LDP voiced its opinion. For example, Morito was never even called before the Diet (or the LDP) to testify on the progress of the CCE's deliberations. I really respected this.[67]

Up through 1971 at least, therefore, the MOE remained the dominant force in shaping education reform policies.

The CCE report, however, was only the first step in the reform process. In the implementation stage (which lasted well into the late 1970s), the *zoku* played a much more significant role. By this time, the young Dietmen had gained much more experience in the area of education. Nishioka – who had served as a director (*riji*) of the Diet Education Committee starting in 1967; vice-chairman of the PARC Education Division starting in 1968; and MOE political vice-minister from 1970 to 1971 – was named chairman of the PARC Education Division in 1971 and went on to serve for four and a half years. Tanikawa, Fujinami and Mori served in a similar number of posts (Table 3.2). Such career paths gave these Dietmen a base of knowledge and experience from which they could exert much more influence on the education policy-making process. Okuda Shinjō, an MOE official who saw the *zoku* come of age, remarked on the transformation:

> In the 1950s and 1960s, MOE officials played the leadership role. But during this time, LDP Dietmen were getting elected at a younger and younger age. Many were second-generation politicians. . . . In the late 1960s, these Dietmen got together and set up study sessions to learn about education policy.

When these were first established, I was called on to lecture at these meetings – as an MOE elder to these younger Dietmen. Today, those same Dietmen are able to come up with their own ideas and formulate their own policies. They tell the MOE what to do.[68]

The long years of working on LDP education organs gave the *zoku* members the ability to play an active role.

Table 3.2 The careers of education *zoku giin* (numbers indicate order of positions assumed)

Name of Dietman	D-DEC	V-ED	PVM	C-DEC	C-ED	M-MOE	C-ESRC
Sakata Michita	1			2		4	3
Inaba Osamu	1		2	5	3	4	
Hasegawa Takashi	3		1		2		
Kaifu Toshiki						1	2
Okuno Seisuke						1	2
Fujinami Takao		1	2		3		
Nishioka Takeo	1	2	3		4	5	
Tanikawa Kazuo	1	2	3	5	4		
Kondō Tetsuo	2	2	1				
Mori Yoshirō	2	1			3	4	
Sunada Shigetami						1	2
Matsunaga Hikaru	2	1				3	
Mitsuzuka Hiroshi	1	2	3				
Aoki Masahisa				1	2		
Ishibashi Kazuya	1	2	3		4		
Ōtsuka Yūji	2	3	1		4		
Nakamura Yasushi	2	1	3		4		
Funada Hajime	1	2	3				
Kudō Iwao		1	2		3		
Nakagawa Yukio		1					
Yanagawa Kakuji		1					

Key: D-DEC = Director–Diet Education Committee
V-ED = Vice-chairman–PARC Education Division
PVM = Political vice-minister–MOE
C-DEC = Chairman–Diet Education Committee
C-ED = Chairman–PARC Education Division
M-MOE = Minister of education
C-ESRC = Chairman–PARC Education System Research Council.

Sources: Jiyū minshutō, *Jiyū minshutō-shi: shiryō-hen* (Jiyū minshutō shuppankyoku, Tokyo, 1986), pp. 1448–552, for dates of C-ED and C-ESRC; Mombushō, *Mombushō* (Mombushō, Tokyo, 1985), pp. 45–7, for dates of PVM and M-MOE; dates on D-DEC and V-ED estimated based on information in issues of *Kokkai benran*. Updated as far as the last Takeshita cabinet of 1989.

The Dietmen who made up the *zoku* in the 1970s were not only able to play a role, however, they were also eager. In many ways, they were a special kind of politician. Some (such as Kaifu) were former ministers of education who only got involved in the education sphere *after* they served in the cabinet. Most, however, were Dietmen who decided early in their careers to devote themselves to education. They chose education and then worked their way up in the party by taking steadily higher-ranking education posts.[69] Given the lack of political pay-offs and the actual risk of defeat associated with the education issue, the fact that these men chose to devote their careers to education marks them out as particularly policy-orientated politicians.

Most Dietmen choose to get involved in areas such as construction, commerce and agriculture in order to secure votes and/or political funds. Those who gain influence in the areas of construction and commerce can be sure of getting ample political donations from the concerned industries. Dietmen representing rural areas can secure their electoral base by getting involved in the agriculture *zoku*. As a result, these three *bukai* are the most popular of the PARC divisions. Education, on the other hand, promises neither political funds nor votes. As a result it tends to attract 'strong' politicians – many of them second-generation Dietmen – who do not need to worry very much about their political base. Instead of representing any outside interest, they can simply push the party's policy directly on the bureaucracy.[70] Some Dietmen – particularly but not exclusively those of the older generation – joined because they believed in the importance of controlling *Nikkyōso* and limiting its ability to 'distort' the education offered to future generations. Others joined because they believed in the critical importance of both moral and academic education. In both cases, however, these Dietmen tended to have set views which they sought to push within the policy-making process.[71]

The influence of the mature *zoku*

With its ability and eagerness to shape education policy, the education *zoku* emerged in the 1970s as the dominant actor in the education sphere. Whereas previously the old law and order activists had been content with perpetuating an anti-*Nikkyōso* attitude in the MOE, this new group of educationists sought to

85

supervise and direct all aspects of the ministry's work. The apparatus of this influence, as noted at the beginning of this section, had not changed since 1955. The difference was that the new group sought to *use* this apparatus.

The PARC Education Division, which had previously limited its role to that of reviewing proposals initiated by the ministry, began to take the initiative itself. Under Nishioka, the *bukai* set up 'project teams' (*purojekuto chīmu*) to develop party positions on key problems. Among those set up in the period after Nishioka took over in 1971 were teams for 'teacher policy', 'higher education', 'private education', 'educational content', 'school lunch' and 'culture'. These small groups, each composed of a few *bukai* members, investigated problems and developed their own policy proposals. The Education Division under Nishioka was the first *bukai* to employ project teams, although this innovation was subsequently adopted by most other PARC divisions.[72] The education *zoku* in particular made intensive use of its project teams and subcommittees (*shoiinkai*) in the 1970s and early 1980s, producing a steady stream of reports which gave the *zoku* the policy-making initiative for virtually the whole period.

The *zoku*'s new activist role, however, did not end with planning and issuing proposals. While it generally let the MOE develop the details of its favoured policies, it played a much more aggressive part in encouraging it. The *zoku*'s primary tool in its early campaigns was the budget. The PARC's role in co-ordinating budget requests was described briefly above. Whereas the *bukai* had previously been only minimally involved in supervising the MOE budget, however, the new activists became involved in the entire budget process.

In the early 1970s, the budget process of the Japanese government was still largely dominated by the bureaucracy. The spending ministries battled with the Ministry of Finance, and the LDP leadership became involved only in the final stages. It was basically a three-step process: Step One (August) – the spending ministries (including the MOE) issued their budget 'demands'; Step Two (December) – the MOF, following consultations with the spending ministries, issued its version of the budget, usually granting only a few of the ministries' demands for new spending; Step Three (late December–January) – the LDP issued its final budget proposal which used the MOF draft as a base but added a few new programmes which it considered to be special priorities.[73] Under this system, the minimally involved

PARC *bukai* would be doing its job if it merely took part in the final December–January stage. There it would simply take up a few of its ministry's demands and serve as the ministry's advocate in the PARC debate leading to a decision on which new programmes the LDP would decide to fund.

Until around 1971, the education *bukai* had been a typical, minimally involved *bukai*. In the next few years, however, it became more and more involved in earlier stages of the budget process. It would meet with MOE officials in July and August, before the ministry issued its demands, to pass on its own ideas as to which new programmes should be funded. Between September and December it would work behind the scenes, using influence with Finance officials to have them include its priorities in the MOF draft budget. And in the final stage, it would work actively to have the LDP give its support to MOE demands (particularly those which it had supported all along). In the early 1970s the *zoku* used this more active role in the budget process to push in particular its policies of aid to private universities and higher teachers' salaries – earning the sobriquet '*Kantō gun*' (the Japanese army which swept into Manchuria in the 1930s) for its aggressive tactics.

In the period after the Oil Shock of 1973–4 the budget process (and the *zoku*'s role) changed somewhat. Because of the shortage of funds caused by the slow-down of the nation's economic growth, the government was forced to issue national bonds, and their redemption left the government with fewer funds available for new programmes. The government leadership was thus forced to bring the budget process under greater central control through the use of strict budget ceilings. Where previously the spending ministries had been able to demand as many new programmes as they wished, these ceilings forced them to choose their priorities earlier in the process. In effect, there was a new three-step process: Step One (July) – the MOF, in consultation with the LDP leadership, set a budget ceiling; Step Two (August) – the spending ministries issued demands, limited already by the ceiling; and Step Three (December) – the MOF issued its budget draft. Under the new budget system, the December–January step became a mere formality: the final government budget proposal differed very little from the MOF draft. The ceiling thus forced budget decisions to be made much earlier in the process. With the spending ministries writing their budget demands based on an already-decided budget framework, the budget was largely determined by the end of August.[74]

The new circumstances effectively reinforced education *zoku* influence in the budget process. With only limited funds available, the ministry had to depend on *zoku* support more than ever in its campaigns to fund new programmes. After *Rinchō* began its assault on education spending, it had to rely on the *zoku* just to maintain its existing level of spending. The ministry thus had to work even more closely with the *zoku* through the entire budget process – a pattern of co-operation which by the 1980s was fully institutionalized. In July and August, in the lead-up to the issuing of its budget demands, the ministry meets on a regular basis with the PARC Education Division to establish spending priorities. The *bukai* also hosts forums which bring together various education interest groups in order to demonstrate support for its spending demands. When the MOE issues its demands in August, therefore, the requests closely reflect *zoku* priorities. The *zoku* and MOE then co-operate to assure that their spending priorities are faithfully reflected in the MOF draft budget and the LDP final budget plan.[75]

The rise in *zoku* influence can be measured by the increasing degree to which it effects even the personnel affairs of the MOE. Under the Japanese system, decisions on promotions are officially the prerogative of cabinet ministers. Well-established precedent dictates, however, that these decisions are made by the administrative vice-minister (AVM, the top civil servant) following a complex set of rules. When the AVM retires, he names his successor. In the MOE, however, the AVM's decisions often reflect the preferences of the education *zoku*. Because of the importance of the MOE–*zoku* relationship, the MOE cannot afford to offend its LDP sponsor. While this influence is rarely exercised overtly, it provides the *zoku* with another means of subtly affecting MOE decisions.[76] One case in which the *zoku* did overtly intervene demonstrated its power. In the mid-1970s, the *zoku* forced the MOE to go along with its plan to implement the controversial *shunin* plan by forcing the premature resignation of an uncooperative official (see Chapter 7).

Since its arrival on the scene in the early 1970s, therefore, the LDP education *zoku* has established itself as the dominant player in the education subgovernment. Specifically, it has gained a great deal of influence over its ministry, the MOE. Yung Ho Park, in his extensive writings on the MOE–*zoku* relationship, focuses on the *zoku*'s strength and labels it the 'senior partner'.[77] He notes in particular the *zoku*'s important part in establishing the government's policies of aid to private education, higher teachers' salaries and the *shunin* system – all examples cited above. While the *zoku* may have a great deal of influence on MOE decision-making, however, the MOE–*zoku* relationship is not the only relationship relevant to education policy-making. The education subgovernment must also compete with other subgovernments for funds and convince the 'centre' to support its decisions.

The role of the LDP centre

Ironically, even as the LDP education *zoku* was gaining influence over the MOE in the 1970s, the LDP centre was taking greater control over the government as a whole. An important catalyst in both cases was the government's policy of fiscal restraint. The way in which this policy gave the *zoku* leverage over the MOE has been noted. While the arrival of tight budgets thus strengthened the *zoku* relative to the ministry, however, it may have lessened the group's influence in the overall policy-making process. The fact that less funds were available (to the point that the MOE could expect to win approval for virtually no new programmes) meant that the *zoku* had less room to shape policy through the process of initiating new programmes. Nishioka emphasized this negative effect of the budget ceilings. According to his analysis, the ceilings did increase the LDP's role in the budget process, but it was the LDP centre which gained the most, not the *zoku*. In setting low ceilings, the LDP centre gained power at the expense of both the MOF and the spending subgovernments (the MOE and the education *zoku*). Where previously much policy had been determined through their interaction, fiscal restraint greatly limited their latitude.[78]

The greater role played by the LDP centre was clearly evident in the *Rinchō* administrative reform campaign. The Commission, a cabinet-level advisory body under the Prime Minister's Office (PMO, *Sōrichō*), issued recommendations for budget cuts and administrative changes which affected virtually every area of government. As noted earlier, it called specifically for extensive education budget cutbacks – all of which had major implications for education policy. Since that time, the LDP leadership has maintained its more active role in all areas of policy-making through its control of the purse-strings. In the most recent round of education reform, the party centre greatly limited the possibilities for reform by steadfastly refusing to agree to larger increases in the education budget. In the summer of 1986, when the education *zoku* campaigned to have the LDP leadership exempt education from the strict budget ceilings, it came away empty-handed (see Chapter 8).

Prime Minister Nakasone in particular sought to increase the centre's role in all areas of policy-making – including education. He took the initiative in establishing personal and cabinet-level advisory councils. He expanded the staff of the PMO and gave it new responsibilities for co-ordinating government policy. As Nakasone himself described it, his aim was to be a 'presidential prime minister'.[79] In education, of course, the prime mechanism for Nakasone's involvement was the Ad Hoc Council on Education. The council was set up at his insistence, it was placed under his office and it was filled with his appointees. With it, the Prime Minister staked his claim to a leadership role in education policy-making.

CONCLUSIONS

The LDP clearly plays a complex role in the Japanese education policy-making process. The party has consistently sought to reduce *Nikkyōso* power in the education system. On numerous other issues, however, it has been divided. Part of the party advocates higher levels of education spending while another part advocates cutbacks. Part of it urges an increased emphasis on ability/selection and a decrease in standardizing MOE regulations, while another points to the success of the status quo and insists on the need for standards. Part of it urges the introduction of free-market forces into education while another part refuses to allow the privatization of (particularly compulsory) education. Even in the case of its attitude towards *Nikkyōso*, some party politicians urge a hard line in dealing with the union while others have urged moderation.

Furthermore, these differences have increasingly been reflected in the different roles played by different parts of the party policy-making apparatus. Until the early 1970s the party's education policy was dominated by a group of law-and-order 'hawks' who were concerned almost exclusively with limiting

Nikkyōso influence in the education system. The party left most other areas of education policy to the MOE. By the 1980s, however, *two* parts of the party were seeking to take greater control of education policy-making. The education *zoku*, having established its expertise in the sphere, sought to build on the success of the established system by adding new programmes. The party leadership, aiming to save funds and reduce MOE regulatory control over the system, sought budget cuts and, under Nakasone, the radical 'liberalization' of the system.

As will be seen in subsequent chapters, the failure of the Japanese government to make progress in its education reform efforts (particularly in the case of the most recent initiative) can largely be explained by these divisions within the predominant party. While both the *zoku* and the LDP centre gained authority and influence in the policy-making process over the course of the 1970s and early 1980s, neither could implement its desired policies without the other.

4

Internal actors: the bureaucracy

Although this thesis has dealt thus far with only one of the actors of the conservative camp, it has already revealed significant rifts in the conservative consensus on education reform. The conflicts within the LDP alone were shown to be substantial enough to threaten the government reform initiatives. The party, though committed to a basic set of education reform goals, was often divided on the question of how these goals should be pursued: party reformists advocating greater nationalism in the schools had to deal with 'doves' in their own party, while reformists like Nakasone advocating the diversification, 'flexibilization' and liberalization of the education system encountered strong opposition from LDP educationists closely tied to the status quo. With the conservative camp already thus divided, the addition to the scene of the other major conservative actor – the bureaucracy – reveals an even more complex set of conflicts.

The most important bureaucratic actor in the education sphere is, of course, the Ministry of Education. As the ministry charged with administering education policy, it is by necessity a central participant in the policy-making process. It gathers the data and information which form the basis for rational policy-making, and it pulls the administrative levers which put policies into practice. To a large extent, it is the 'centre' of education policy-making with all other actors seeking to move it one way or another. Nevertheless, while many MOE officials seek to portray their ministry as the defender of neutral, rational policy-making and administration, the MOE is in fact just as much an 'actor' as the LDP. An examination of its part in the recent reform debate – its 'attitudes' and 'place in the process' – reveals the ministry's contribution to the failure of the conservative consensus on education reform. The MOE itself was not always united, and, more significantly, it stood in defence of the status quo in a way which brought it into sustained conflict with the reformists of the LDP.

The MOE is not the only part of 'the bureaucracy' concerned about education policy. Among other ministries with a stake in the education reform debate, the Ministry of Finance seeks to assure that the MOE does not spend too much money on its reform projects; the Ministry of Health and Welfare refuses to allow the MOE to encroach on its control of the nation's nursery schools; the Ministry of International Trade and Industry seeks to assure that the MOE's education policies will provide Japan with the talent needed to maintain the nation's international economic competitiveness; and, finally, the Ministry of Foreign Affairs seeks to make sure that the MOE's textbook control activities do not damage Japan's diplomatic relations with her neighbours. All of these cleavages – following the pattern of subgovernmental conflict outlined by John C. Campbell – serve to fragment the conservative consensus and make education reform more difficult. While these other ministries too are thus part of the conservative camp, this chapter concentrates on the role of the most important bureaucratic actor, the Ministry of Education. The other ministries – their attitudes and roles in the process – are discussed primarily in terms of their interaction with the MOE.

ATTITUDES

Bureaucratic conservatism

The predominant 'attitude' of the MOE, across the whole range of policy issues, has been its desire to maintain existing practices and policies. This 'bureaucratic conservatism' reflects, first, the simple fact that the MOE has developed an attachment to the status quo over its many years of supervising the existing education system. The preceding chapter described how the LDP education *zoku* developed such an attachment in the years since it began overseeing the system in 1955. The Ministry of Education, having also presided over the post-war system since its establishment, has also developed a stake in preserving what it created and nurtured.

Kida Hiroshi, a former MOE administrative vice-minister (AVM, 1976–8), reflected on the growth of this attachment over the course of the post-war period. The first post-war MOE bureaucrats, he explained, were accustomed to the pre-war and wartime way of educational administration and therefore tried to change certain aspects of the post-war settlement. His generation – those bureaucrats who reached the MOE's top positions in the late 1960s to early 1970s – had a greater commitment to 'the post-war way of doing things', but nevertheless were willing to consider change. 'We had experienced the post-war process of rebuilding and had seen the need to change with the times,' he explained. The bureaucrats who followed his generation, however, were not so flexible. Kida characterized their attitude as one of 'status quo maintenance' (*genjō iji*):

> That next generation, having finally put the system in place by the mid-1960s, thought it best just to maintain the system as it was. They were the people who had come through the ranks advocating the new post-war order as the best. Aside from Morito [the chairman of the CCE which produced the 1971 recommendations], Kennoki [the Minister of Education in 1966–7] and people like Amagi [the MOE AVM, 1969–71], the great majority of people inside and outside the MOE thought it fine to maintain the post-war order.[1]

In the period of the recent education reform initiatives, therefore, the vast majority of MOE bureaucrats were committed to perpetuating the established system.

The commitment of MOE bureaucrats to the status quo, however, cannot be explained merely in terms of their personal pride in maintaining what they built. It is also a reflection of their positions in the administration of the existing system. Dealing on a daily basis with educational administrators closer to 'the actual site' (*genba*) at which education is being delivered, they naturally come to represent the views of these local officials – officials who, because of their fears of disruptive opposition from *Nikkyōso* teachers in their area and their worries about more immediate needs in their schools, tend to be opposed to change. Kuroha Ryōichi, a longtime education reporter and recently a member of several MOE councils, explained the pattern as follows:

The key officials are those in the middle levels of the MOE – the division chiefs who deal with their sector on a day-to-day basis. These men, whatever their personal opinions, represent the conservative attitudes of the education *genba*. The Elementary School Division Chief, for example, hears the opinions of the Elementary School Headmasters Association and effectively is forced to represent their opinions.[2]

The conservatism of MOE bureaucrats thus does not necessarily reflect their personal opinions. Their positions simply lead them to represent the conservative views of those closer to the education *genba*.

While the bureaucratic conservatism of the MOE thus reflects the conservatism of Japanese educators in general, the tendency is reinforced by the Japanese bureaucratic system – a system which gives officials close to the conservative *genba* a particularly important role in the decision-making process. That system, in the MOE as in other Japanese ministries, is based on the idea of bottom-up consensus-building, a process known as *nemawashi*. *Nemawashi* refers to the practice – common in Japan but particularly important in the nation's bureaucracy – whereby Japanese officials are forced to 'dig around the roots' of a decision in order to have their favoured policy put into effect. They must build broad support among their fellow officials, ideally establishing a consensus position, before openly advocating a certain course. The process is formalized in a system known as the *ringi sei*. Decisions – recorded on a formal document (the *ringisho*) – are drawn up by lower- to middle-ranking administrators who are closer to the problem and know more about details. These official statements of policy are then circulated up through the ministry hierarchy where officials can contribute insights based on their broader knowledge and responsibilities.[3]

Such structures serve to compound the effect of MOE conservatism because of the emphasis they place on the role of lower- and middle-ranking officials – the division chiefs and the assistant division chiefs (Figure 4.1). These officials, as Kuroha argued above, are the bureaucrats closest to the conservatizing influence of the education *genba*, and it is they who are charged with the actual drafting of policy proposals. Nakajima Akio, an MOE bureaucrat at the councillor level, described the effect of the MOE *ringi sei* on education reform proposals:

When the AHCE puts out a recommendation for a reform, these are sent to the relevant MOE division, and these divisions start the process of gathering opinions about the idea. This is strange, really, when you realize that you are asking those who have been responsible for bringing along the present system to judge a reform proposal. Of course they are going to object. The *ringi sei* is fine if you are asking the lower administrators to suggest a policy in line with the established direction of policy-making. In such cases the system works well. It makes sure there are no mistakes. In the case of reform proposals, however, there really is a need for a new structure of policy-making.[4]

Nakajima added, however, that the MOE has been unable to devise a more successful 'new structure' for dealing with reform proposals. The *ringi sei* way of thinking simply does not allow the ministry to overcome the conservatism of officials attached to the status quo. While the MOE has attempted to provide a greater leadership role for higher officials by establishing top-level conferences of bureau chiefs (*kyokuchō kaigi*) to deal with certain education reform proposals, this system has failed to overcome the problems associated with the *ringi sei*. Given that the *kyokuchō kaigi* can act only when it has a consensus, the bureau chief representing the division chief who represents the established policy retains the power to veto reform proposals. 'That is the dilemma,' Nakajima concluded.[5]

Still, while the structure of the Japanese bureaucracy further explains the conservatism of the Ministry of Education, it does not explain the particular conservatism of that ministry. As processes common throughout Japanese officialdom, *nemawashi* and the *ringi sei* serve to make all ministries more conservative.[6] The MOE, however, is for some reason *especially* conservative. Yung Ho Park notes that 'Most serious Japanese observers, and LDP Dietmen who have had extensive dealings with the MOE, rate the agency as one of the most conservative and reactive offices in the Japanese officialdom.'[7] Expanding on this statement, Park quotes various Japanese officials who describe MOE bureaucrats as less able to cope with 'long-term policy problems like education reform' and less interested in getting involved in much more than their routine work.[8] The final factor contributing to the MOE's conservatism, therefore, is a factor more unique to the Japanese Ministry of Education.

Figure 4.1 Organizational chart of the Ministry of Education

Minister of education (*mombu daijin*)
(political appointee, member of the cabinet)
|
Political vice-minister (PVM, *seimujikan*)
(political appointee)
|
Administrative vice-minister (AVM, *jimujikan*)
(senior career post for MOE officials)
|

Bureau chiefs (*kyokuchō*)	One for each of the following:
|	Minister's Secretariat
Councillors (*shingikan*)	Elementary and Secondary
	Education Bureau
	Educational Assistance and
	Administrative Bureau
	Higher Education Bureau
	Science and International Affairs
	Bureau
	Social Education Bureau
	Physical Education Bureau
Division chiefs (*kachō*)	In the Elementary and Secondary
	Education Bureau, for example,
Assistant division chiefs	there are one *kachō* and one or
(*kachō hosa*)	two *kachō hosa* for each of the
	following:
	Upper Secondary School Division
	Lower Secondary School Division
	Elementary School Division
	Kindergarten Division
	Vocational Education Division
	Special Education Division
	Textbook Authorization Division
	Textbook Administrative Division

Source: Ministry of Education, Science and Culture, *Education in Japan: A Brief Outline*, 1986, p. 17.

The MOE, more than other ministries, seems to have grown more conservative in response to its experience of numerous ideological conflicts over education policy in the post-war period.

Park himself sees the conservatism of the MOE as a natural result of the post-war experience of MOE bureaucrats. Having survived repeated confrontations over policy in the ideologically polarized environment of post-war education policy-making, these officials came to shy away from doing anything that might provoke unnecessary controversy. 'Thus,' Park concludes, 'the career officials have acquired the habit of acting only when sufficient pressure has built up within the party for agency action, as far as major and controversial matters are concerned.'⁹ This tendency of MOE officials to avoid action until 'sufficient pressure has built up', a practice which grew out of their experience of repeated ideological skirmishes, goes a long way towards explaining the particular conservatism of that ministry. When, in past battles, MOE officials went too far in advocating textbook control or early selection, they were vilified in the Japanese press. When on a few occasions they sought to reduce tensions by dealing with *Nikkyōso*, they were attacked by LDP 'hawks' in the education *zoku*. Most officials learnt, therefore, that the safest course was to avoid action of any kind unless there was 'sufficient pressure'.

MOE conservatism on the issues

While the bureaucratic conservatism of the MOE has been discussed thus far in fairly general terms, this general orientation of the ministry is also visible in the positions it took on the specific education reform issues of the recent debate. As a government ministry, the MOE does not actually take formal 'positions' on political questions. Nevertheless, it reveals how it stands through its actions (or inactions), through the reports of its advisory councils and through the comments of its officials. Its conservative attitude towards the whole range of reform proposals, as outlined below, illustrates the degree to which the MOE stands as a barrier to change.

Nationalist reform proposals

The reforms favoured by LDP nationalists, as outlined in the previous chapter, included the following: (1) the reform of structures imposed by the foreign Occupation; (2) an increase in the teaching of traditional Japanese moral values; (3) the revision of textbooks and the use of national flag and anthem to emphasize love of country; and (4) changes in school management and an increase in teacher training 'to improve the quality of teachers'. With the exception of the first, MOE officials generally seem to have agreed with these LDP aims – at least in principle.

The ministry in particular supported the reformers' calls for more moral education. In numerous reports and public statements, MOE officials focused on the need for moral education as an explanation for the problems of Japanese education.[10] Similarly, the ministry also stood in favour of stricter control of textbooks. Ishiyama Morio, in his thorough study of the MOE role in the 1981–2 textbook incident, concludes that ministry bureaucrats approached the subject from the perspective of long having wanted to consolidate ministry control over texts. This control has been based on an *ad hoc* set of regulations ever since the LDP failed to push through formal legislation authorizing textbook control in 1956. At a minimum, therefore, the MOE wanted to see these regulations written into a formal 'textbook law' in order to safeguard ministry authority.[11]

Finally, on the specific issue of 'improving teacher quality', ministry officials also seem to have started from a position sympathetic towards the LDP reformists. The proposal to establish a salary bonus for middle-management *shunin* teachers, for example, was actually conceived by a ministry official who advocated the change as a means of recognizing and rewarding particularly dedicated teachers.[12] The ministry has similarly supported the expansion and improvement of teacher training. In a 1978 special report on 'Improving Teacher Quality and Ability', one of its advisory councils recommended a whole list of such programmes, including expanded graduate university retraining for teachers and more substantial training for new teachers.[13]

Nevertheless, while MOE officials favoured all of the above nationalist reforms *in principle*, the ministry was often timid when it actually faced the prospect of having to put such changes into effect. First, as was noted above, the MOE has not advocated the most radical LDP nationalist reform goal: the reform of the Fundamental Law of Education. As one reporter observed:

Ministry officials feel that the FLE does not have much to do with what they do; it's merely a statement of philosophy. On the other hand, they fear it would cause major difficulties if they tried to reform it. Thus they try to avoid tampering with it.[14]

While not so timid on morals and textbooks, the MOE was nevertheless more 'dovish' than the LDP 'hawks'. In emphasizing the need for moral education, MOE officials tended to concentrate on the need for basic good behaviour – the need for students to remain quiet in their classes, learn to obey their teachers and learn good manners (*shitsuke*). They tended not to talk about the idea of teaching children to 'love their country' – a kind of moral education which they see as too controversial.[15] In dealing with textbook control, the MOE was similarly more conservative in its actions. Despite its long-standing desire to consolidate its control over textbooks, it did not act until the LDP took a vocal lead. Ishiyama notes that Morosawa Masamichi – the MOE AVM long known as 'Mr Textbook' – never took any steps to initiate a review of the textbook control process until the LDP embarked on its campaign to strengthen textbook control in 1981.[16] He waited, in typical MOE conservative fashion, 'until sufficient pressure had built up'.

The most striking example of MOE conservatism in the face of pressure to implement nationalist reforms, however, was its handling of the *shunin* policy when it actually came time for it to change its regulations. Legislation passed in 1974 providing funds for a teachers' salary increase gave the MOE the opportunity to establish a new bonus for *shunin* teacher-managers. By 1975, however, it was apparent that such a bonus – promoted by the LDP *zoku* as an anti-*Nikkyōso* measure – would provoke the vocal opposition of the teachers' union. In this atmosphere, the MOE leadership attempted to work *with* the union in order to implement the bonus without causing excessive disruptions in the schools. Throughout the controversy which ensued, the MOE evidenced a desire to compromise if necessary in order to avoid controversy while the LDP hawks pressed for rapid and uncompromising implementation.

In summary, the MOE position on nationalist issues can be likened in some ways to that of LDP doves. While agreeing with the general goal of increasing the nationalist content of education, both the ministry and the doves were not always in agreement with the LDP *zoku* and other party hawks on the means through which such goals should be pursued. Having experienced repeated ideological battles over the post-war period, the ministry preferred to be cautious.

Diversification issues

A second set of reform proposals, also outlined in the previous chapter, were those reforms advocated by conservatives concerned about the single-track uniformity of the post-war education system. Mourning the loss of pre-war-style elite secondary and higher education, they called for the 'diversification' (*tayōka*) of the 6–3–3 system. The LDP was quite divided in its attitude towards these proposals. Reformists advocated major changes such as the establishment of six-year secondary schools, the introduction of earlier 'streaming' of students by ability and other proposals to provide 'gifted education' for the nation's most talented students. Other LDP members, however, were either disinterested or unwilling to support such controversial departures from the status quo. The MOE's position can again be described as 'ambiguous'. While officials seem to have sympathized with the LDP reformists in principle, they were often too timid to act in accordance with this sympathy.

Throughout the post-war period, the ministry consistently expressed support for the idea of diversification, advocating what it termed 'education appropriate for the ability and aptitudes of students' (*seito no nōryoku tekisei ni ōjita kyōiku*) – a phrase repeated often in MOE advisory council reports.[17] In the 1960s this meant that the ministry advocated such policies as an increased emphasis on vocational education and other steps to maintain the elite nature of the academic upper secondary schools at a time when growing numbers of students were staying in school up to the age of 18.[18] While the MOE softened its position somewhat by 1971, it still argued that education should be better matched to the ability of individual students. In the CCE report of that year, it advocated greater diversity in the curriculum and increased use of streaming as well as steps towards the legalization of grade-skipping.[19]

While the MOE thus sympathized with the LDP reformists' advocacy of ability-based diversification, it generally failed to follow through on its rhetoric. Most significantly, it consistently resisted efforts to achieve a greater diversity through changes in the structure of the 6–3–3 education system. In 1971, after the MOE's own CCE proposed that the government establish six- and/or five-year secondary schools as part of a series of 'pilot projects', the majority of MOE officials resisted. In the end, the lack of support on the part of the ministry helped kill this centrepiece of the 1971 reform campaign. Likewise, in the more recent reform campaign, ministry officials again sought to avoid implementing the AHCE recommendation on six-year secondary schools – even after they had succeeded in convincing the council to limit its recommendation to *non-academic* schools in areas such as art, music and physical education. Both of these cases will be explored in detail in Chapters 7 and 8.

Even in the case of less radical reform proposals for providing ability-based or gifted education, however, the MOE has tended to hesitate at the stage of implementation. Despite the 1971 recommendation that grade-skipping be legalized, the MOE never acted. The ministry has also been slow to encourage streaming by ability – particularly at the lower secondary school level. This record reveals that MOE bureaucrats, despite their rhetoric calling for 'education matched to the abilities of individual students', are actually quite committed to the egalitarianism of the status quo – especially for the compulsory years. As one bureaucrat commented, 'Anyone who wants to move away from the egalitarianism of the present system – the strong point of post-war education – cannot be truly concerned with education!'[20]

Suzuki Isao, a ministry 'old boy', tried to account for the gap between the MOE's rhetoric and its action in the recent round of reform. The ministry, he said, had long felt that there was a need for gifted education. At the same time, however, it was reluctant to push the idea in the absence of broader agreement – among policy-makers and the public – on the need for such change.

> The ministry cannot do it alone. There's got to be – well, if not a consensus – at least a general agreement on direction. This idea is not even very well developed in the *zoku*.[21]

Lacking a consensus in the LDP and sensing that public opinion too was not ready, the MOE as a whole therefore resisted attempts by reform-minded bureaucrats and politicians to initiate changes in this area. It did not want to act, again, until 'sufficient pressure had built up'. On this issue, therefore, the MOE was once again more conservative than the LDP reformers.

'Flexibilization' and liberalization issues

The final set of education reform proposals, closely related to the previous set, were those calling for the 'flexibilization' (*jūnanka*) and liberalization (*jiyūka*) of Japanese education. Advocates of both courses, like those who advocated diversification by ability, argued for a move away from the standardized, uniform status quo. Those urging *jūnanka* and *jiyūka*, however, sought to create room for diversity rather than seeking to force students into ability-differentiated courses. The *jūnanka* advocates argued for policies aimed at increasing the flexibility and range of educational content – a more flexible set of curriculum guidelines, greater opportunities for subject-specialization at the secondary level, and a greater variety of textbooks. Those pursuing *jiyūka*, on the other hand, aimed to provide parents and students with a greater variety of educational choices by reducing government regulation of school choice and school establishment. The previous chapter revealed that despite Nakasone's support for *jūnanka* and *jiyūka* and the sympathy among others in the LDP for at least some move away from the standardized nature of the established system, the LDP education *zoku* largely stood in the way of these changes. To a great extent, the MOE's position on these issues mirrored that of the *zoku*.

There was within the MOE at least some support for a moderate amount of *jūnanka*. Saitō Taijun, himself a relatively reform-minded MOE bureaucrat, notes that the 1970s saw a gradual increase in MOE support for 'flexibilization'. He emphasizes in particular the ministry's role in implementing more flexible curriculum guidelines for *kōtōgakō* which were designed to allow a greater selection of subjects at that level.[22] Moving away from the previous emphasis on 'education matched to ability', the ministry increasingly started using the phrase, 'education matched to the individuality of each student' (*kosei ni ōjita kyōiku*) – a shift which pointed towards the ministry's increasing tendency to portray its philosophy in terms of student choice rather than in terms of pushing students into ability-differentiated tracks.[23]

Nevertheless, the MOE's support for *jūnanka* was reluctant and, in the end, insufficient to yield real change. Kuroha Ryōichi summarized the overall MOE attitude:

MOE bureaucrats have their own opinions about emphasizing individuality (*kosei-jūshi*). Some support it, others do not. As an organization, however, it has a pretty consistent line. Some of the young MOE people, being more open, have taken

103

the idea of *jūnanka* to heart. But those at the division chief level and above – those over 40 – are fairly set in their rigid way of doing things.[24]

This 'rigid' mind-set has meant that while the MOE has authorized greater choice in curriculum, it has not done enough to overcome the established tendency towards standardization. As will be seen in Chapter 7, the ministry's continued active support for a uniform university entrance examination system throughout the period under study has created a situation in which, despite the greater choice given to *kōtōgakkō* students under the new curriculum guidelines, almost all have continued to pursue a uniform academic course. Despite its reformist rhetoric, therefore, the MOE has remained wedded to the standardized general course emphasis of the status quo.

The ministry was less subtle in its opposition to the reformists' liberalization proposals. While it expressed support for *jūnanka* at least in principle, it did not even go that far in its evaluation of the more controversial proposals for *jiyūka*. It was strongly and openly opposed to any liberalization whatsoever – as its 1985 testimony before the AHCE revealed:

1 Regarding the proposal that rules be liberalized so that anyone would be able to establish a school freely, we fear that such a reform would raise various problems in our effort to maintain the quality of education. Specifically, such a change could lead to the establishment of schools set up purely for profit-making purposes or the establishment of schools without a sound financial basis. In general, we fear that it would make it impossible for us to guarantee the continuity and public nature of education in this nation. In the future, we feel, proposals for regulatory relief in this area should be studied while keeping in mind that we cannot afford to lose the continuity, stability and public nature of education.

2 There is also a proposal – aimed at providing parents with a free choice of schools at the compulsory education level – calling for the abandonment of the current system of designating schools for fixed school districts. We can foresee that, if we were to do this, students would naturally converge on particular schools. Given that such a result would make it impossible for us to predict the number of students

(due to attend any given school), planning for school provision and construction would become troublesome – requiring extensive financial resources for such things as increased (excess) school construction. Even assuming that these problems can be solved, however, we foresee major problems: competition to get into preferred schools will get worse beginning at the compulsory school level, and the feeling of dissatisfaction will remain among those parents and children who do not get into their school of choice – leading to an actual amplification of their feelings that they are not free to choose their schools.[25]

While the passage is lengthy, it illustrates the degree to which the MOE was opposed to *jiyūka*. Both the proposal for allowing free establishment of schools and the one for allowing parents to choose their school at the compulsory-school level were attacked in very direct terms – especially considering the tendency of bureaucracies (particularly Japanese bureaucracies) to use more discreet language.

The MOE's testimony before the AHCE also revealed the ministry's more general attitude towards regulations. It stood firmly in favour of maintaining them. It argued that regulations were necessary to 'maintain the quality of education' and emphasized the role of regulations in preserving the 'stability, continuity and public nature of education'. At various times throughout the post-war period, the ministry has used the same arguments to defend its continued control over the details of curriculum and over textbooks. The attitude explains why the Ministry of Education, on both the liberalization and 'flexibilization' issues, stood in defence of the status quo and in opposition to reformists in its own conservative camp. It was not going to yield its regulatory control of the education system without a fight.

Divisions within the MOE

The analysis thus far has treated the MOE as a unified entity. While it has recognized some diversity of attitudes within the ministry, it has emphasized the dominant strand of bureaucratic conservatism. This attempt to identify the most important 'attitude' within the ministry, however, should not lead one to assume that the MOE is some kind of homogeneous unit. As with the LDP, business and the teachers' union, there are sometimes differences of opinion within the ministry. Particularly in the CCE-round of reform in the late 1960s and early 1970s, the difference of opinion between the conservative MOE mainstream and a more reform-minded group of top officials marked a crucial cleavage in the conservative consensus.

While MOE officials quickly dismiss suggestions that their ministry is characterized by factionalism, they themselves use the term 'faction' (*ha*) to describe various groupings which have arisen in the ministry. Thus the group of reform-minded bureaucrats most involved in shepherding the comprehensive set of reform proposals through the CCE in 1967–71 was known variously as the 'internationalist faction' (*kokusai-ha*) and the 'theorist faction' (*risōka-ha*). These officials – such men as Amagi Isao and Nishida Kikuo – were known as 'internationalists' because they tended to have served in 'international posts' within the ministry, positions which brought them into contact with foreign education officials and such international bodies as the Organization of Economic Co-operation and Development (OECD) and the United Nations Economic and Social Council (UNESCO). They were therefore familiar with foreign education systems and international trends in education reform and sought to bring this knowledge to bear in their efforts to reform the Japanese education system. They were known as 'theorists' because they tended to approach reform issues from a theoretical perspective, arguing for a change to six-year secondary schools, for example, based on child development theories.[26]

The actual number of officials in this group was very small. Kida Hiroshi – himself sometimes listed as a member of the group – jokingly commented that Amagi Isao was effectively a 'faction of one'.[27] Amagi (AVM, 1969–71) was definitely a central figure among the internationalists. He had extensive experience dealing with international organizations and during his tenure as AVM worked to encourage the CCE's reformism. The most active member of the group, however, was a relatively junior official named Nishida Kikuo. A bureaucrat with the unusual work history of having come to the ministry after originally starting his career as a university physics instructor, Nishida put his scientific skills to work in his capacity as the councillor in charge of the CCE.[28] As will be detailed below and in Chapter 7, he used this position to push the council in a generally reformist direction, based largely on new educational theories to which he subscribed. The CCE's later proposals for pilot projects, the *shunin* system and a more individual-student-orientated education system reflected to a large extent his personal involvement in managing the CCE. Kida and Saitō Sei (AVM, 1967–9) have also been described as 'internationalists'.[29]

The majority of MOE bureaucrats, however, were less inclined to support the reformist ideas of the internationalists. They were occupied with the day-to-day running of the established system and tended to disregard many of Nishida's proposals as mere ideas written down on paper. When faced with the task of implementing the CCE's controversial recommendations in 1971, many of these officials resisted – opposing in particular the council's emphasis on changing the structure of the 6–3–3 system and arguing that the council's proposal calling for educational pilot projects would 'treat children as if they were guinea pigs'. While this group – encompassing virtually all of the MOE's officials – could hardly be referred to as a faction, it was nevertheless known sometimes as the 'status quo maintenance faction' (*genjō iji-ha*).[30] As might be expected based on the analysis of MOE conservatism above, it was led by those officials dealing most directly with the education *genba* – the officials responsible for elementary, secondary and higher education.[31] The interaction between this 'mainstream' and the so-called internationalists will be a major topic of interest in the discussion of the CCE initiative in Chapter 7.

In the years following this battle over the CCE recommendations, the MOE was much less divided. This greater cohesiveness followed the departure of men like Amagi (retired in 1971) and Nishida (exiled to UNESCO in 1971). The new top officials were much less inclined to take the initiative on education reform. They were busy enough with the day-to-day running of the education system and had concluded – based on their experience of the 1971 upheaval over the CCE recommendations – that the ministry should not seek to change anything until 'sufficient pressure had built up'. They were much less inclined to be individualists or leaders in pursuit of education reform. Before doing anything, they would make sure they had an MOE consensus.[32]

PLACE IN THE PROCESS

Much has been written in recent years about the role of bureaucrats in the Japanese policy-making process. As the discussion in Chapter 1 noted, the previous emphasis on the dominant role played by bureaucrats has recently given way to descriptions of a bureaucracy increasingly dominated by long-serving LDP politicians. The analysis of the LDP in education policy-making in the previous chapter provided evidence for this recent line of argument, showing how the rise of the education *zoku* in the 1970s served to make the LDP the 'senior partner' in its relationship with the Ministry of Education. The place of the MOE in this changing environment, however, has not yet been explored. The discussion below reveals the importance of examining the MOE role from two perspectives: first, from its perspective as a 'politically neutral' bureaucracy dealing with an activist LDP education *zoku*, and second, from its perspective as a member of the education subgovernment (allied with the *zoku*) dealing with the 'centre'. In both capacities the MOE emerges as an important player in the conservative camp where its bureaucratic conservatism serves to disrupt the consensus on education reform and makes change in that sphere more difficult.

The MOE as a 'neutral' bureaucracy dealing with the *zoku*

Despite the growing power of the LDP education specialists relative to their MOE counterparts, ministry officials have not become mere tools of the predominant party – as some observers have suggested.[33] Rather, they retain a view of their role which emphasizes the 'political neutrality' of the bureaucracy and use the levers of power at their disposal to limit partisan 'interference' in education policy-making. That MOE officials see themselves as more than 'tools' in the education policy-making process is clear from their comments in interviews. Almost without exception they express concern about the growing dominance of the LDP in the running of their department and argue that the MOE has a crucial role to play in protecting the education system from majority-party domination. Typical of their opinions is that expressed by Saitō Taijun (the official in charge of the AHCE Secretariat) in his study on 'The Policy-making Process – Seen from the Perspective of Educational Administration'. He writes:

What is important is the degree to which politics, respecting the way in which the bureaucracy has built up its basic plan based on its fair and objective judgement of social necessity . . . , recognizes the relative neutrality of the bureaucracy. Especially with regard to guaranteeing the political neutrality of education, more than in other spheres, the neutrality of education administration should be prudently considered.[34]

Essentially, Saitō is arguing that the bureaucracy is better at making policy. It makes a 'fair and objective judgement based on social necessity' and builds rational policies on this basis. Although he recognizes the rightful role of politicians in a parliamentary democracy at other points in his analysis, he insists that the bureaucracy has a legitimate role to play in checking political interference – especially in education.[35]

Particularly interesting is Saitō's argument that the bureaucracy plays a critically important part in checking party interference in a *one-party dominant* political system like Japan's. According to his analysis, a ruling party in a parliamentary democracy plays two functions: first, it pursues its 'private interest' as a political party, and second, it pursues the 'public interest' as the government of the whole people. According to democratic theory, the party which spends too much time pursuing its private interest will be thrown out and replaced by another party – assuring that in the long term the public interest will be pursued. Saitō is concerned that in the absence of party-alternation, Japan lacks a crucial mechanism for assuring that policy-making is based on the interest of 'all the people'. In such circumstances, he insists, the role of the politically-neutral bureaucracy becomes particularly important. From its 'objective, neutral' position, it must make sure that policy accurately reflects the points of view of *all* groups in society. The bureaucracy's role, Saitō concludes, is to make sure that policy reflects a social *consensus*.[36]

That MOE officials perceive their mission in this way, of course, does not necessarily mean that they can actually fulfil that mission. In fact, their concern reflects their general feeling that LDP influence has been growing at the expense of MOE authority over the past thirty-plus years of one-party rule. None the less, Saitō's arguments point to the bureaucrats' determination and hint at the means through which they can (and do) influence the policy-making process. By emphasizing their role as objective, neutral participants in the process, MOE officials actually do check LDP power.

The MOE role at the policy-drafting stage

The previous chapter described the budget and legislative processes from the LDP perspective, emphasizing the growth in the predominant party's role. The fact that the LDP's part has grown, however, should not be allowed to overshadow the fact that the MOE (like other bureaucracies) retains significant influence. The MOE does not have the ability to push through legislation or increase budgets in areas where it does not have LDP support. In those situations in which the LDP advocates legislation or budgets which the MOE opposes, however, the ministry is not powerless. It has an important blocking power.

In the legislative process, the LDP relies on the ministry for the actual drafting of legislation. While the LDP *zoku* heavily influences what the MOE does in this capacity, the ministry retains the ability to transform or block policies which it especially opposes – particularly in cases in which the LDP is not unified or emphatic in its support for some change. One MOE official quoted by Ishiyama describes the ministry's role as follows:

> Compared to Dietmen of the past, the education Dietmen of today know a great deal about administration and make an effort to study about it. Still, when it comes to the actual drafting of policy, that is the part we bureaucrats play. The various Dietmen merely tell us what they think – all together in a muddle. With their various factions and ideologies, their opinions do not come together. So there are cases when we 'neutrals' have to step in as moderators.[37]

Given the range of opinions about education reform in the LDP – as seen in the previous chapter – this power to come in and mediate at the policy-drafting stage can often be crucial. If there are just a few *zoku* members sympathetic towards the ministry's position (usually the cautious, conservative one), the MOE can mediate a settlement which follows the cautious course.

The MOE has used this technique most notably in its confrontations with reformist *zoku* members over their demands for a change in the 6–3–3 structure of the education system. In the aftermath of the 1971 report and in the course of the Nakasone reform initiative, there were many voices in the LDP urging changes in structure of the education system. Some wanted six-year secondary schools, others a complete change to a 5–4–4 system, and still others supported the CCE recommendation of pilot projects. The MOE, on the other hand, was of the opinion that system reform should be considered only as a last resort. In 1971 the MOE capitalized on the lack of an LDP consensus to avoid drafting any legislation which would have implemented pilot projects or any other change in the structure of the education system. The MOE used similar techniques to avoid drafting legislation on six-year secondary schools in the recent round. These and other examples of the MOE's 'blocking' ability at the legislative-drafting stage will be examined in Chapters 7 and 8.

Legislation, however, is only one kind of policy-drafting. Many education reform policies are of a type which can actually be implemented through changes in MOE regulations – an area in which the ministry naturally has even more influence. A whole set of education policies – including the national curriculum – are actually nothing more than ministry demands (*yōkyū*) enforced on the basis of legislation which authorizes the MOE to demand that local school boards follow certain instructions. The process of changing these demands, therefore, is purely an MOE-internal one. Other policies which are largely based on MOE-issued regulations include the controversial text-book control system and the system whereby the establishment of universities is regulated. In all of these areas, the ministry maintains the power to block or alter substantially LDP-demanded policy changes at the policy-drafting stage. In fact, with its control over the regulatory process, the MOE actually has some power to effect change on its own by *initiating* changes in regulations.

The best example of the MOE's ability to block change through its control over regulations was its success in avoiding substantive action on the AHCE recommendation that it relax its regulatory control (*kisei kanwa*) across a range of spheres. The AHCE, seeking greater flexibility in the system, recommended in its 1986 report that the MOE relax its control over the details of educational content 'to enable individual educational institutions to implement creative and innovative ideas and practices'. Specifically, it pointed to the need for the MOE to broaden its university establishment regulations and the national curriculum for elementary and secondary schools.[38] While the

MOE was in 1987 gradually moving along in the process of rewriting these regulations, there were few signs that it planned to introduce significantly greater flexibility in these areas (see Chapter 8).

In all of the above cases in which the MOE used its role at the policy-drafting stage to prevent changes to which it was opposed, it founded its actions on claims that it was acting on the basis of its neutral evaluation of what would constitute rational policy. In the case of its refusal to act on the CCE's pilot projects proposal, for example, MOE officials based their action on the claim that the objectives of the council's recommendation could be obtained without resorting to the drastic step of pilot projects or structural reform. They saw it as their responsibility to prevent the LDP from causing unnecessary disruptions purely because it sought a high-publicity symbol for its education reform campaign.[39] Likewise, MOE officials defended their inaction on the AHCE's recommendation calling for the authorization of six-year secondary schools by arguing that such a change would cause more problems than it would solve.[40]

These examples illustrate that while the LDP has enlarged its role in the policy-drafting process, it has not excluded the MOE. The ministry maintains control over certain levers of power (the power to draft legislation and regulations) and, based on its claim to represent a 'netural' position, can and does block LDP-supported changes to which it objects. It is able to use this influence particularly in cases in which the LDP is not united on the need for any specific change. In those cases, it can use its 'neutral' position to push the policy which it favours.

The MOE's use of advisory councils

In the process whereby the ministry seeks to bring its 'neutral and objective' perspective to bear on policy issues, it relies heavily on a set of advisory councils (*shingikai*). While they are often used to pursue objectives which the MOE and LDP *zoku* share, these councils also serve as one of the most important levers of power at the disposal of ministry officials intent on protecting education policy from excessive political interference. The councils are important to the MOE (as they are to other ministries) because they give the ministry's policy-making activities a degree of legitimacy. Composed of 'outside experts', the councils serve to highlight both the *neutrality* and *rationality* of the MOE's point of view. The fact that experts (presumably of different views) all agree to recommend a certain course lets the MOE claim that it has found a policy which is supported by a consensus. Having found a consensus, it can describe the policy as 'politically neutral' and 'in the public interest' – hence giving the MOE's position a certain democratic legitimacy. At the same time, the fact that the members of the council are experts serves to demonstrate the rational basis for ministry policy-making. The MOE can claim that the policies recommended by its councils (unlike the politically motivated ideas of the LDP project teams) are based on knowledge, experience and facts. This combination lets the MOE use councils to set an agenda of 'neutral' and 'objective' policy proposals which become the centre of the political debate. By manipulating the councils, the MOE has a chance to greatly influence the education policy-making process.[41]

As of 1983, the Ministry of Education was being advised by some seventeen councils ranging from the overarching CCE – set up as the supreme advisory organ of the MOE in 1952 – to more specialized councils on textbook content, teacher training policy and even one on the Japanese language.[42] Between 1984 and 1987 it was also receiving advice from the Ad Hoc Council on Education – actually a cabinet-level council organized under the Prime Minister's Office. Typically, the CCE serves as a forum for debating *broad* education policy issues – with the AHCE playing this role only in the latest reform initiative. Then, in either case, *specific* policy proposals are debated by more specialized councils. In the case of the recent plan for instituting a 'training year' for newly-hired teachers, for example, the idea was first suggested by the AHCE in its April 1985 report. It was then handed over to the MOE's permanent Teacher Training Council for further discussion on exactly how such training ought to be administered. Only after the second council issued its report did MOE officials begin drafting formal policy documents. By the time bureaucrats and politicians get involved in the drafting of legislation and budget requests, therefore, proposals like the training-year example have often already been extensively studied and developed by two independent advisory councils.

Officially, as noted above, these councils provide expert outside advice and serve to establish a consensus position in favour of a particular policy. While they do play these roles to some extent, the MOE councils are more important as legitimators of preconceived courses of action.[43] The 'expert members' of councils are often picked based on their sympathy towards the MOE position. The councils are frequently given a 'request for advice' which is heavily weighted towards the course of action favoured by the ministry. And the councils' deliberations are often manipulated through the use of MOE-provided information, staff assistance and hints as to which sort of policy the ministry might find acceptable.[44] To a large extent, therefore, the arguments that the councils provide expert advice and produce a consensus are just a cloak behind which the MOE legitimizes its point of view.

That the MOE manipulates its advisory councils is not a big secret.[45] Particularly interesting is a study of the CCE Textbook Subcommittee (1981–3) in which Ishiyama Morio describes the expert way in which ministry officials controlled the council.[46] Morosawa Masamichi (MOE AVM, 1980–2) is quoted actually admitting that the council's recommendations came out exactly as he had envisaged before the council began its deliberations.[47] Describing Morosawa's domination of the council as machine-like, Ishiyama highlights the following techniques employed by the ministry: it chose the council's membership so that fifteen of the twenty members were veterans of other MOE advisory councils with a proven willingness to listen to MOE guidance; it chose as chair a man known for his public statements in favour of the MOE position; the management of the CCE secretariat was placed under the Elementary and Secondary Education Bureau (the one closest to the *genba*) rather than the more far-sighted Planning Office; top MOE officials (including Morosawa) attended virtually every meeting; while the council's 'request for advice' was not too specific, the council used an LDP *zoku* report on textbook control (actually drafted by MOE officials) as a starting-point for its deliberations; when council members voiced opinions not totally in line with the MOE position, ministry officials were quickly sent around to 'explain the problems with the member's point of view'; and the ministry secretariat, through its role in preparing the summaries of deliberations and the final report, brought the council's recommendations even more closely into line with the MOE position.

The ministry is not always so successful in controlling its councils. In the lead-up to the publication of the CCE's report in 1971, the ministry itself was split: the council's secretariat and the top administrative position in the MOE were both under the control of relative reformists (Nishida and Amagi) while the bureaux responsible for the day-to-day running of the education system were in the hands of men less inclined to support significant reforms. Naturally under such circumstances the council could not please all factions. As it turned out, Nishida and Amagi did do a great deal to manipulate the council. They chose men sympathetic towards their reformism and carefully led the council to their conclusions through the use of facts and data supplied by the secretariat. It is widely acknowledged that Nishida personally drafted the final report. Nevertheless, although the final report was still too radical for most MOE officials, Nishida was forced to temper some of the council's proposals in response to opposition from others in the ministry.

In the case of the AHCE as well, the council was not as easily manipulated as the Textbook Subcommittee described above. Technically, the council was not even under the jurisdiction of the ministry. In the course of negotiations between the Prime Minister and the LDP *zoku*, however, the ministry secured the right to help choose the council's membership and provide the council's secretariat. By making the most of these powers, the ministry was in the end able to gain a great deal of influence over the council's recommendations: many of the members chosen were sympathetic towards the ministry's position; the MOE employed its secretariat as usual to provide the council with extensive information supporting its point of view; and perhaps most importantly, the MOE (together with the *zoku*) made sure that the council realized that it could not expect them to implement the radical reforms being promoted by some of the members. While the AHCE maintained a fairly independent line for the first year of its existence, it had been brought under control by the time it issued its first report and never came out in favour of the radical reforms originally feared by MOE officials.

The record of these councils, to be examined closely in Chapters 7 and 8, reveals an important if complex mechanism through which the MOE is able to influence the policy-making process. By influencing council recommendations at a stage before politicians and bureaucrats formally enter the debate, the ministry is able to have its point of view (usually the bureaucratic conservative one) reflected in the 'neutral' and 'objective' policy proposals which form the starting-point for the policy-drafting process. Examples of cases in which the ministry has used this lever of power to promote its conservative viewpoint are numerous. In 1971 the conservative ministry 'mainstream' succeeded in having Nishida phrase the controversial recommendation for a probationary year for new teachers in 'should be studied' terms. In the recent round, the MOE succeeded to an even greater extent in assuring that the AHCE would not support the most radical reforms supported by Nakasone and *zoku* reformists: the council recommendation on reforming the university entrance examination process called only for modest changes rather than abolition as favoured by the Prime Minister; the proposal for six-year secondary schools called for schools specializing in talents like art and sports rather than academic elite schools; the recommendation on changing the starting date of the school year from April to September was heavily qualified; and finally, the council's recommendations in the areas of *jiyūka* and *jūnanka* were all either vague or non-existent.

The ability of the MOE to block or at least limit reform proposals through advisory councils once again illustrates the MOE's use of its 'neutrality' and 'objectivity' to claim a role in the policy-making process. Particularly in education – with its official designation as a sphere which is supposed to be 'politically neutral' – the ministry is able to capitalize on its 'neutral' status. Interestingly, the ministry's ability to appeal to the need for neutrality in education policy-making is closely related to the strategy of opposition groups like the teachers' union. These groups seek to defeat reform proposals which threaten their interests by demanding that politicians keep their hands off the education system – a line of argument which neatly opens the way for bureaucrats to become involved. These bureaucrats, more conservative than the LDP reformists, in turn help the opposition meet its objectives by applying the brakes to reform proposals which threaten to disrupt the smooth administration of the education system. This linkage is explored in much greater detail in Chapter 6.

The MOE as a member of the subgovernment dealing with the centre

The analysis of the ministry's place in the process has concentrated thus far on the MOE's role as a neutral bureaucracy dealing with an activist LDP. Despite the growth in the party's (particularly the *zoku*'s) dominance, the discussion revealed that the MOE does have various avenues of influence through which it can bring its bureaucratic conservatism to bear on the process. This emphasis on bureaucracy–party conflict, however, should not be allowed to obscure the important way in which the MOE and the LDP *zoku* are often on the same side in debates over education reform. In the majority of cases, the ministry and the *zoku* work in a mutually-supportive way to pursue their common interests as members of the education subgovernment in dealings with other subgovernments and the centre.

To a large extent, the ministry's role as a member of the education subgovernment parallels that of the *zoku* – described in the previous chapter. The MOE works with the *zoku* to fight for its share of the budget and similarly co-ordinates its activities with its LDP allies on substantive issues involving conflict with other subgovernments. In the discussion of the budget process in Chapter 3, the *zoku*'s growing role was highlighted. One must recognize, however, that the MOE does not object to this assistance; it welcomes it. In many cases, in fact, the new programmes championed by *zoku* politicians are projects conceived and developed by the ministry. The programme to reduce the size of classes from forty-five to forty, for example, was an MOE priority long before the *zoku* began to make it a priority in the budget negotiations. In the Nakasone round of reform, the *zoku* and the MOE worked hand in hand in an effort to secure AHCE endorsement of higher spending for education programmes.

The co-operation between the MOE and the *zoku* was visible, for example, in the case of their campaign to fight a *Rinchō* recommendation calling for an end to the provision of free textbooks to students in the compulsory years.[48] In the case of non-budgetary subgovernmental conflicts as well, the MOE works *with* the *zoku*. LDP education *zoku* Dietmen are among the leading supporters of the MOE's effort to expand its control over pre-school education – something the Ministry of Health and Welfare (with its nursery schools) opposes. Likewise, in the conflict with the Ministry of Foreign Affairs which followed the international outcry against the MOE's textbook control activities, the MOE relied on *zoku* members to prevent the MFA from intervening in its area of responsibility. In both cases, the

117

cleavages were between subgovernments rather than between the MOE and the LDP.

The area of MOE–*zoku* co-operation most relevant to this study, however, concerns their co-operation in the recent education reform initiatives. In some cases the two actors work together in *favour* of reforms. Especially when reforms call for an expansion of the MOE budget, the direction of their co-operation is generally positive. Examples include the programmes for expanding aid to private education; making compulsory the education of all handicapped children; reducing the size of classes; creating new teacher-training programmes; and funding new moral education 'camps' for school children. In all of these cases, the *zoku* was often a major force advocating the programmes, but the MOE worked to provide data supporting the changes and drafted the actual policies.

In the case of many reform proposals, however, the co-operation between the *zoku* and the MOE is *opposed to change*. This has been the pattern, most obviously, in the case of Nakasone's radical reform proposals in the most recent round of the education debate. These reforms – the *jiyūka* and *jūnanka* proposals – called for a reduction in MOE regulatory authority and (in some cases) a reduction in its budget. Naturally, therefore, they became the subject of subgovernmental conflict between the education subgovernment and the centre. As in the other cases of subgovernmental conflict described above, the MOE and the *zoku* worked together to prevent the adoption of the controversial reforms. The ministry's success in having the AHCE propose only those reforms it could support reflected the efforts of the LDP *zoku* as much as it did the MOE's own activities.

CONCLUSIONS

Yung Ho Park, in his various writings on the MOE and its relationship with the LDP, calls the party's education *zoku* the 'senior partner' and labels the MOE the 'junior partner'. To prove his point, he focuses on the trend towards greater party involvement in the ministry's decision-making process and concludes that 'the LDP, in power well over quarter of a century, has been the key locus of power'. The MOE, he says, is merely 'reactive'.[49]

There is a great deal of validity to Park's argument. The *zoku* is probably the 'senior partner' in the party–bureaucratic relationship. The analysis of this chapter has revealed, however, that the MOE cannot be dismissed as *merely* reactive. It *is* reactive, but this reactiveness (or bureaucratic conservatism, as it has been referred to in this chapter) plays an important role in determining the outcomes of education debates. As a member of the conservative camp and a key actor in the policy-making process, the ministry brings its bureaucratic conservatism to bear on education reform proposals promoted by other members of the camp. Through its advisory councils and in the policy-drafting process, it puts its 'neutral' and 'objective' weight behind positions which are usually opposed to significant change. In numerous cases, it has demonstrated an ability to *block* proposals for real educational reform.

Yamagishi Shunsuke, a veteran education reporter for *Asahi Shimbun*, describes the Ministry of Education as a 'protective mother' in the sense of a wild animal. It is not very strong in expanding its territory, but it is a determined fighter when it comes to defending its baby.[50] The analysis in this chapter has supported this description. The ministry does not have the power on its own to promote education reform – and it is not really very interested in doing so. Rather, it prefers to defend the existing system and, in that capacity, is an effective combatant.

Park seems to overstate his dismissal of the MOE in another sense as well. By emphasizing the conflict between the bureaucracy and the party, he fails to consider the many cases in which the MOE teams up with part of the party (the *zoku*) to promote its subgovernmental interests. In these cases, it makes little sense to describe one or the other of the two actors as 'senior'. They are both pursuing the same objectives – an expanded budget, opposition to Nakasone's intervention in education reform – and therefore act in a mutually supportive fashion. While the *zoku* may in these cases be taking the more public role, in many cases it is merely acting on behalf of the MOE. In both of the above ways, the MOE emerges as an important actor contributing its share to the breakdown in the conservative consensus on education reform.

5

External actors:
incorporated interests

In addition to the LDP and the MOE – the two actors most involved in the formal process of formulating education policy – numerous other organizations have an interest in the results of this policy-making process and seek to influence the outcome. Most prominent among these 'external actors' are the business community, the association of local education superintendents, the other national associations of educational administrators, the teachers' union and the various associations of university faculty and officials. All of these groups are technically 'external' in that they are not officially a part of the national government. Some, however, are more external than others.

Over the years since the LDP began its one-party dominant rule of Japan, the interest groups involved in various spheres of policy-making have tended to establish themselves as either 'for' or 'against' the ruling conservative camp. Those lining up on the side of the conservatives have developed close ties to the LDP and the bureaucracy and have come to have substantial input into the planning of policy even before it reaches the point of public debate. To a large extent, they have been 'incorporated' into the conservative camp. On the other hand, the set of groups closer to the progressive camp has been systematically excluded from policy deliberations and left to seek ways of influencing government decisions outside formal channels. Perpetually opposed to government initiatives, these groups have come to be described as 'opposition interests'.[1] In fact, of course, interests do not fall so neatly into these two categories. Within each category, there are some groups which are less firmly 'incorporated' or 'opposed' than others. For the purposes of this discussion, however, the simple dual format serves to highlight the differing ways in which these two sets of interest groups affect the process.

To a large extent, the 'incorporated interests' which serve as the subject of this chapter's analysis can be seen as 'members' of the conservative camp. The business community, for example, was long considered one of the three partners of the conservative coalition – a full member of the 'ruling triumvirate' along with the LDP and the bureaucracy.[2] While the proponents of this view probably overstated the power of Japan's business leadership, the *zaikai* (as the business community is known) must nevertheless be seen as an important part of the broader constellation of actors known as the 'conservative camp'. On education issues, its views are taken very seriously by the LDP leadership and the MOE bureaucracy, and leading businessmen are regularly invited to sit on the government's education advisory councils. The other education groups in this category – the various associations of educational administrators – also work closely with the government to a degree which makes them almost a part of the formal governmental structure. These organizations, many of whom maintain their national offices in a government building situated conveniently next-door to the Ministry of Education, are in touch with their counterparts in the ministry on a daily basis. As with the *zaikai*, a share of the seats on advisory councils is systematically reserved for their leaders.

As should be clear from the discussion thus far of the LDP and the MOE, however, the fact that these various interest groups are part of the 'conservative camp' should not be interpreted to mean that they are part of some monolithic force. On the contrary, they too contribute to the general absence of a conservative consensus on education reform in a way which has made change in that sphere more difficult.

BUSINESS INTERESTS

As noted above, students of Japanese politics (particularly those advocating the 'power-elite model' of Japanese politics) have traditionally described the influence of the business community in Japan as uniquely dominant – ranking it on a par with that of the LDP and the bureaucracy. Andō Yoshio, for example, wrote that business 'literally presides over Japanese society'.[3] In the years since the 'power elite' thesis was put forward, however, these observations about *zaikai* influence have come to be criticized as an oversimplification. Gerald Curtis, examining the arguments about the supposedly unique mechanisms for *zaikai* dominance in Japan, found that the idea of business omnipotence was a 'myth'. Others have examined the power of business in specific spheres and found it lacking. Ogata Sadako studied the role of business in the normalization of relations with China and found the economic community more divided and reactive than united and influential.[5] John C. Campbell found a similarly less significant role for business in the budget-making process.[6] What these critiques and case studies showed was that the *zaikai* was not an all-powerful interest group dominating the whole range of policy issues.

This analysis of business influence on the education reform process largely corroborates the findings of these studies. Business interests, viewing education as a critical factor in Japan's economic success, maintain a high profile in the education debate. Their demands for reforms are taken seriously by the LDP and the MOE. In the end, however, the business community is just one actor in the conservative camp. *Zaikai* reformism must eventually compete with the more timid attitudes of other equally important actors such as the associations of educational administrators. In addition, the business community is handicapped by the fact that it is not itself united on education reform issues. While part of the business community has provided vocal support for the reformism of the MOE internationalists (within the MOE) and Nakasone (within the LDP), another segment has been sceptical or even opposed to ideas like 'flexibilization' and liberalization. Divided and isolated, the *zaikai* has been unable to forge a conservative consensus in favour of its ideas.

Before proceeding, the term '*zaikai*' itself needs clarification. The term literally means something like 'the financial world'. In practice, however, it refers to a more limited segment of the economic community: the leading business organizations generally listed as including the Federation of Economic Organizations (*Keidanren*); the Japanese Federation of Employers' Associations (*Nikkeiren*); the Japanese Committee for Economic Development (*Keizai dōyūkai*); and the Japan Chamber of Commerce and Industry (*Nisshō*). Even more precisely, the term is used to refer to a relative handful of leaders in these organizations who, as Gerald Curtis writes, 'spend an extraordinary amount of time in so-called *zaikai* activities – activities that are not directly related to their own companies, but which seek to represent the interests of the business community as a whole'.[7]

Attitudes

Not surprisingly, the business community's main concerns with the education system arise from its position as an employer seeking a labour force which meets its employment needs. This emphasis is reflected initially in the division of responsibility for education among the *zaikai* groups. *Keidanren*, the organ representing Big Business as a whole, rarely concerns itself with education issues. Viewing education as a labour concern, it tends to leave the drafting of position papers in that sphere to its 'employers' arm', *Nikkeiren*. These position papers – like those issued by *Keizai dōyūkai* – naturally emphasize issues related to the quality of the workforce. They criticize the education system for being closed to changing business demands for workers skilled in growing sectors of the economy and call for reforms designed to force schools and universities to respond to employers' needs for specialized, creative and disciplined workers.

An end to uniformity

If there was a unifying theme to the policy positions taken by the business community over the 1967–87 period, it was their campaign to reduce the uniformity of Japanese education. Business was satisfied with the general level of education provided to workers but was concerned that the system was not meeting its more specific needs for technically skilled labour and creative, high-level talent. In the 1960s the key word in business demands was 'diversification'. The *zaikai* wanted students to be separated into diverse tracks earlier in their school years so that they could be sorted by ability and trained to meet the specific needs of the economy. This theme was emphasized repeatedly, for example, in one 1969 *Nikkeiren* position paper which used the term 'diversification' a total of ten times. Arguing that the advent of mass advancement to higher levels of education had created a 'gap' between the idea of a standard curriculum and the reality of diverse abilities, the report demanded that the education system be transformed to meet the 'diverse demands of society'. Specifically, it called for the 'diversification of secondary education' to produce more 'specialized workers as required by industrial society' as well as the 'diversification of higher education' to allow its various institutions to specialize in such areas as 'high-level scientific research, higher professional training, general learning, teacher training and fine arts'.[8] More recent reports have continued to focus on this idea of diversification. Two such reports by *Keizai dōyūkai*, for example, were entitled 'The Challenge of Diversification' (1979) and 'Demanding Creativity, Diversity and Internationalism' (1984).[9]

By the time of the Nakasone initiative in the 1980s, however, the business community (or at least part of it) was expressing its demand for less uniformity in a subtly different way. Where previously it had urged that students be channelled into a rigid hierarchy of diverse secondary- and higher-education courses, it had begun to speak of the need to let individuals and educational institutions develop their own individuality. It wanted the government merely to reduce its regulatory intervention in the education system to allow students to pursue studies at their own pace and enrol in diverse courses of their own choosing. The new approach was most apparent in *Keizai dōyūkai*'s proposals for the restructuring of higher and secondary education (1984). Rather than proposing that the government devise a new classification system as part of a forced diversification of higher education institutions, it suggested that rules be made more flexible to allow institutions to develop their own unique orientations. To promote diversity at lower levels, it emphasized the need to reform business hiring practices and university admission policies to favour diverse talents rather than just success on the standard examination. And finally, directing its attention to secondary education, the report suggested that this segment of the school system be revitalized by letting institutions (particularly private ones) pursue new institutional structures.[10] In short, business (or at least *Keizai dōyūkai*) was proposing the 'flexibilization' and liberalization of the education system.

A disciplined workforce

Another persistent theme in business reports, however, was a demand for disciplined workers. While the *zaikai* wanted its workers to be trained in the technical and professional skills, it also wanted them to be taught proper attitudes towards work, life and society. It wanted new generations of workers to be as self-sacrificing as the one which helped rebuild Japan after the war. This second major priority was apparent first in the timing of business position papers: the peak years for business activity in the education sphere coincided closely with years in which the schools and universities experienced particularly marked breakdowns in their ability to discipline and control students. In 1969, the peak year of the university disturbances, *Nikkeiren* issued a record six reports on education issues. Then, after a relatively quiet period from 1972 to 1982 when it issued only two brief reports, it was again prompted to issue a major position paper by the increase in secondary school violence in the early 1980s.[11]

The content of these reports also highlighted business demands for greater emphasis on discipline-training. *Nikkeiren*'s position paper on university reform (1969), for example, began by emphasizing the deplorable state of discipline in higher education and demanded that authorities be firm, that they punish violence and bring in the police when necessary and that the government close down universities with particularly prolonged disturbances.[12] The business community was concerned that Japanese youth – if left undisciplined in their universities – would not acquire the conscientious work habits of their elders. This line of argument was actually spelt out in *Nikkeiren*'s report on secondary school violence (1983):

From the perspective of business managers, we are particularly concerned about the effects of school violence and juvenile delinquency. It being one of the objects of school education to teach students about the relationship between society and the individual, the disrespect for rules inherent in school violence and the situation in which brute force rules supreme – the undermining of the basic foundations of education – cannot be tolerated.

While we recognize the delicate changes taking place in the rising generation's attitudes towards work, we nevertheless felt we must try to maintain the Japanese worker's diligence and group-consciousness which have been so crucial in helping to push up the nation's economy. Thus it is vitally important that the schools guide students in such a way that they have a proper outlook on society and work.[13]

Nikkeiren thus outlined exactly what it was seeking when it demanded that the schools teach 'discipline': it wanted them to

125

train young people to become 'diligent' workers willing to dedicate themselves to their job and their company; and it wanted the schools to help hold off the 'delicate changes taking place in the rising generation's attitudes towards work' – changes which it feared would produce a new generation of selfish, leisure-loving individualists. Interestingly, the business community's solution to the crisis of school indiscipline was the same as that advocated by the LDP nationalists: it wanted more 'moral education'. The *zaikai* version of 'moral education', however, put less stress on nationalist values like 'love of country' and more on the secular values of work and dedication to the group.

Indirect aims: open and rational universities

The *zaikai* demands for a diversely trained and disciplined workforce could be described as its 'direct' aims. In the end, business was interested in its employment needs. As a means towards those ends, however, it was concerned about other, sometimes more controversial education issues. Most significantly, it stood in favour of reforms which would serve to make the education system (particularly the relatively autonomous universities) more responsive to changing economic developments – and changing business needs. The primary business complaint was that the administration of national universities in particular had devolved into a sort of feudalism under the banner of 'university autonomy'. Individual departments were more powerful than the central administration, and even within departments some professors were more influential than the department as a whole. Any proposal for change, therefore, required a complex process of consensus-building within each department and then within the university as a whole. The *zaikai*'s concern was that this process made it impossible for universities to change with the times, an immobility made worse by what business called the 'ivory tower' mentality of the academic community. Not only were universities unable to change, they were so insulated from society that they had no interest in changing.[14]

The *zaikai*'s interest in university administration peaked during the student riots of the late 1960s when it came to judge the ineptitude of the fragmented university leadership as being primarily responsible for the problem growing out of control. Typically, *Keizai dōyūkai* began its 1969 report on university reform by finding that, 'We can only conclude that the chief responsibility for the university disturbances lies with the universities themselves.' Echoing the criticisms outlined above, it criticized in particular 'the closed and self-righteous attitude of "omnipotent" faculty conferences and their treasured university autonomy' and 'the weakness of university management given the lack of a responsible decision-making mechanism'.[15]

As a solution to these problems, the *zaikai* offered a complete programme for reform. *Nikkeiren* proposed that all management matters not related to research and teaching be removed from the jurisdiction of the faculty conferences. Instead, these matters would be charged to a new, strengthened central administration, bolstered by the addition of professional managers and the introduction of a vice-presidential organization.[16] *Keizai dōyūkai* proposed an even more radical programme. Arguing that the power of central administrators was weakened by the MOE's monopoly on university finance decisions, it suggested that national universities be reorganized as essentially private corporations under boards of directors. The concentration of power in the hands of this board would allow greater central leadership, while the board could also serve as a source of input from outside the academic world. The same report also proposed the replacement of lifetime employment (tenure) for faculty with a system of short-term contracts such that universities could shift directions more easily.[17]

In these ways, business proposed to make universities 'open' and 'rational': open in that the participation of non-academics (including businessmen) on boards of directors would make institutions more aware of 'social needs'; rational in that the consolidation of central authority in the hands of such a board would make them more able to meet those needs. Faculties and departments could be reorganized to emphasize new fields of science and technology as the economic demand for such changes developed. Strict codes of discipline and order could be enforced without the delay and inconsistency of the established system. In short, the *zaikai* envisaged that its direct demands for trained and disciplined manpower could be met indirectly. In the twenty-year period under review, the business community probably devoted more attention to these university reform efforts than to any other education issue.

Fiscal conservatism and a preference for privatization

A final complicating demand of the business community arose from its broader aim of limiting the role of government. Its preference for less regulation was reflected in several of its positions noted above: it wanted less standardization and more flexibility in the structure of school education, and it suggested that national universities be reorganized as private institutions. Beginning in the late 1970s, business also began to demand that the government reduce spending on education as part of its 'administrative reform'. *Nikkeiren* questioned the whole constitutional basis for aid to private education in a 1984 report.[18] Returning to the theme in 1985, it noted, 'Where higher education is concerned, public monies are being wasted on some students, particularly those in the humanities, who have become more interested in recreation than academic achievement.'[19] *Keizai dōyūkai* in 1982 published a detailed proposal for a net saving of ¥68.4 billion (US$285 million) a year in the sphere of education. Specifically, it proposed that the established system of providing free textbooks to students in the compulsory grades be abolished, that proposals for reducing class size be abandoned and that public university tuition in 'expensive' subjects like medicine and science be raised relative to 'cheap' subjects. Unlike *Nikkeiren*, it proposed increasing scholarships and aid to private education to reflect the importance of private institutions in providing cheap (for the government) higher education.[20] While these concerns with saving funds and increasing the role of the private sector were part of *zaikai*'s broader political agenda, they clearly were significant for the education sphere as well. The business community wanted top-quality workers, but at the best price.

Differences of opinion within the business community

Up to this point, 'the *zaikai*' has been treated as a single body. It has been asserted, for example, that 'the *zaikai* demands trained and disciplined workers'. While this statement may accurately express the opinion of the *zaikai* as a whole, it nevertheless glosses over crucial differences of emphasis within the business community. While some businessmen are most concerned about whether or not the education system provides adequate training, others worry more about discipline. Particularly in the latest reform initiative, this subtle divergence of opinion grew into a basic cleavage dividing the business community and limiting its ability to influence policy.

Perceptive readers may have noticed a difference of opinion between *Keizai dōyūkai* and *Nikkeiren* in the various position papers cited above. One might have noticed that all of the references regarding the *zaikai* demand for disciplined workers referred to *Nikkeiren* reports while, on the other hand, virtually all of the reports discussing the need for a more flexible and creativity-orientated education system were issued by *Keizai dōyūkai*. This pattern is not merely coincidental. It reflects the differing (and to an extent conflicting) emphases of these two organizations.

Keizai dōyūkai, as an organization, is much more concerned about the rigidity of the established system and the need for bold reforms to make the system more flexible. In its various position papers, it suggested that public universities be privatized, that all universities be encouraged to develop their unique strengths and that the university entrance system be changed to emphasize diverse talents rather than just exam numbers.[21] It also called for a reduction in central regulations such that students would be able to pursue courses of secondary education varied in terms of length, subject and type of institution.[22] In all of these recommendations, it stressed the need to reorientate the education system towards training the creative, diversely talented corps of workers required to keep Japan's economy growing as it moved towards the uncertain, competitive twenty-first century. None of the *Dōyūkai*'s reports were particularly concerned with whether or not that future workforce was to be disciplined. In fact, in four reports on education issued in the period after school violence emerged in the early 1980s, the organization did not once mention the problem of school indiscipline.

On the other hand, *Nikkeiren* was more cautious in its proposals calling for reduced uniformity and was much more concerned about discipline. Its reform proposals in 1969 – prompted by the indiscipline of university students – emphasized the need for a stronger, more centralized administration of universities. Even its broader proposals for reform were limited to general calls for 'rigid' diversification. While *Keizai dōyūkai* began to articulate proposals for a more 'flexible' kind of diversification beginning in the late 1970s, *Nikkeiren* remained silent. In its only detailed discussion of education policy since the early 1970s (its 1983 report on school violence) *Nikkeiren* in fact chose to emphasize the opposite approach. Rather than proposing reduced regulation and a greater emphasis on individuality, it stressed the need for the stricter management of schools and a more detailed moral education curriculum.[23] Only after the Ad Hoc Council on Education put the term 'liberalization' on the agenda did *Nikkeiren* come out in favour of the principle – but only at the 'higher levels' of the education system.[24]

This divergence of opinion can be traced at least partly to differences between the two *zaikai* organizations. *Nikkeiren* is constrained in its ability to express its views, first, by the nature of its membership. Like its parent organization *Keidanren*, it is composed of trade associations and corporations.[25] The individuals involved in its various activities act as representatives of their companies and associations, not as private citizens, and are therefore limited in their ability to speak and act freely. *Keizai dōyūkai*, on the other hand, is an organization of approximately a thousand individual businessmen.[26] Thus, as it points out in its own promotional literature, 'its members can express their views clearly and frankly without heed to the interests of any particular company or industry'.[27] This difference in the organizational basis of the two bodies partly explains the greater reformism of the *Dōyūkai*.

Perhaps more significantly, however, the opinions of the two groups also reflect their distinct traditions and goals. *Keizai dōyūkai*, founded shortly after the Second World War by a group of young managers intent on modernizing and democratizing the business world, remains relatively 'forward looking'. While its membership today is older and more mainstream, it is still composed of self-selected, socially concerned individuals. Naturally, its views reflect its activist role. Addressing the question of the degree to which government should be involved in education, the *Dōyūkai* education division chief sounded almost evangelical:

> Basically, *Dōyūkai*'s position is that we need deregulation of everything. Privatization is our ideology. When the country was poor – like in the Meiji era – the government had to pay for education. That was the idea behind compulsory education, and it worked well. The economy flourished. Now, however, the people are wealthy. They can afford their own books, their own school lunches. We need to change the old idea that the government must provide everything.[28]

Nikkeiren, on the other hand, is an umbrella organization for management in its relations with labour and therefore includes relatively disinterested members as well as activists. As one *Nikkeiren* official explained, 'Many of them think the present education system is fine.'[29] Addressing the same question which inspired the above statement from his *Dōyūkai* counterpart, this *Nikkeiren* official replied:

> Most members aren't opposed to the *theory* of liberalization and actually support certain changes like the shortening of compulsory education and reducing the regulation of higher education. But when it comes especially to the question of deregulating compulsory education, they tend to emphasize the good points of the current system. It's taken Japan a long way. They hesitate, therefore, to mess with success.[30]

The 'don't mess with success' attitude of *Nikkeiren* thus contrasts with *Keizai dōyūkai*'s 'we need to change'. The significance of this conflict is explained further in the following section.

Place in the process

Avenues of influence

Unlike the MOE and the LDP, the *zaikai* is not a formal part of the government and therefore does not have official 'levers of power' which it can pull. Nevertheless, as an important interest group in the conservative camp, it does have a number of means through which it is able to influence the policy-making process. At a most basic level, it can simply publish reports such as those cited above. Between 1948 (when it was founded) and 1987, *Nikkeiren* published forty-six position papers on education issues – ranging from single-page statements on subjects like 'The Need to Accelerate the Establishment of Graduate Schools of Technology' (1972) to lengthy documents calling for the reform of the entire education system (1969). Similarly, between 1946 and 1987 *Keizai dōyūkai* published twelve reports, almost all fairly broad-ranging policy statements.[31] Simply by virtue of the close relations between these *zaikai* groups and their fellow conservatives in the government, these reports tend to receive a close reading from those who make education policy.

In addition to publishing its own reports, the *zaikai* also supports a number of 'think-tanks' which add academic weight to some of its ideas. Typically, these organizations receive substantial funds from business and are composed variously of university professors, bureaucrats and businessmen. They are important not only because their reports (like those of the *zaikai* organizations themselves) are read by conservative policy-makers, but also because the think-tanks themselves provide businessmen with a chance to interact with academics and bureaucrats who play a more direct role in formulating policies.

The most important of these think-tanks has been the Japan Council for Economic Research (JCER, *Nihon keizai chōsa kyōgikai*) set up in 1962 by the major *zaikai* organizations as their research unit. In the lead-up to the publication of the 1971 CCE report, the JCER made sure its views were known through the work of its Education Committee, headed by Dokō Toshio, the chairman of Tōshiba Electric Company and a *zaikai* heavyweight. Although the committee did not publish its report until 1972, after the CCE report, it provided a forum (as described above) for frequent contact between businessmen and bureaucrats. Prominent members included Hiratsuka Masunori and Koga Issaku, key CCE members, as well as Amagi Isao and Inumaru Tadashi, top MOE bureaucrats.[32] In the latest round of reform, the JCER played a similar role. Its Education Committee – this time headed by Iwasa Yoshizane, the former president of Fuji Bank – published its report on education reform in 1985. Again, it included key business figures as well as influential academics and MOE bureaucrats.[33]

Another think-tank, though not an official organ of the business community, also served to promote business views on education policy in the recent round of reform. Actually more of a 'study group' than a think-tank, the Kyoto Group for the Study of Global Issues (*Sekai o kangaeru Kyōto zakai*) was founded by Matsushita Kōnosuke, a leading business entrepreneur and one of the wealthiest individuals in Japan, as part of his personal complex of policy research, publishing and lobbying organizations.[34] As noted in Chapter 3, the Kyoto Group emerged as one of the leading advocates of 'liberalizing' the education system in the lead-up to the establishment of the AHCE and influenced Prime Minister Nakasone's thinking about education reform. Members of the Kyoto Group's 'Education Working Group' included businessmen like Ushio

Jirō (vice-chairman of *Keizai dōyūkai*) as well as leading academic and government figures who went on to serve as members of the AHCE: Amaya Naohiro, chairman of the Ad Hoc Council's first subcommittee, Ishii Takemochi, chairman of the AHCE's second subcommittee, as well as two 'specialist' members of the Council.[35] Like the JCER's Education Committee, therefore, the Kyoto Group served as a forum for contact between business and those with influence in the making of education policy.

The most obvious way in which businessmen influence education policy, however, is by sitting on actual advisory councils. In the case of the 1971 Central Council on Education, *Keizai dōyūkai* senior vice-president Fujii Heigo played an influential role as a long-standing member of the council, as did fellow CCE members Koga Issaku, Yorozu Naoji and Shinojima Hideo – all businessmen (see Table 7.1, pp. 176–7). In the latest round, five of the twenty-five Ad Hoc Council members – including three on the council's executive committee – were businessmen with close ties to *zaikai* organizations (see Table 8.1, pp. 220–2). In addition, one of the 'specialist' positions was filled by Ishii Kōichirō, the head of *Keizai dōyūkai*'s Education Committee. As actual members of these councils, these businessmen were able to participate directly in the policy-making process – using their influence to have *zaikai* priorities written into council reports. The business community's participation in the work of government advisory councils, combined with its use of think-tanks and position papers, thus gave the business community a great deal of access to the policy-making process.

Degree of influence

Access alone, however, does not equal influence. A true understanding of the business community's place in the policy-making process requires also an evaluation of the degree to which it succeeded in taking advantage of its privileged position. In the two rounds of reform under study there can be no denying that business views did indeed have some impact. In the 1971 round, the idea of 'diversification' – a key business demand as seen above – served as the basic philosophy of the reform package put together by the MOE 'internationalists'. Business ideas for reforming university administration were also included in the report. In the recent round, *zaikai* ideas were again at the centre of the debate, with Nakasone serving as the chief advocate for the business community's demands that the education system be made more flexible, international and creativity-orientated.

In the end, however, the government's reformists were only partially successful in having the business community's ideas put into practice. Universities – with a few exceptions discussed in Chapter 7 – emerged almost entirely unchanged: they continued to be decentralized organizations dominated by fiercely territorial faculty departments. The school curriculum was still very standardized with virtually no movement toward diversification or 'flexibilization'. Proposals for liberalization were rejected outright. In some areas (moral education, internationalization), the business community was more successful in having its ideas reflected in actual practice, but these successes were only a small part of the *zaikai* agenda for education reform (see Chapters 7 and 8 for detailed accounts of the fate of business-backed proposals). An analysis of why the business community failed to get its way in the education debate despite its level of access goes to the heart of the issues this book is trying to address: to put it simplistically, business failed because it could not forge a conservative consensus in favour of its ideas. It won the support of government reformists, but it could not overcome the 'status quo maintenance' attitude of other important sectors of the conservative camp.

Business was not able to forge a consensus, first, because it was just one conservative interest group among many. Other equally influential interest groups were arguing against cuts in the education budget, an increased role for private education, earlier streaming of students by ability and reduced MOE regulation. Also important, however, was the fact that the business community itself was not united – particularly in the latest round of reform. While the *Keizai dōyūkai* wing of business emerged as a vocal proponent of reduced MOE regulation and a generally more flexible education system, *Nikkeiren* worried primarily about moral education. Nothing better illustrated the significance of this cleavage than the sight of Arita Kazuhisa – a *zaikai* member of the AHCE and the former head of *Nikkeiren*'s Education Committee – arguing *against* business-backed proposals. As other AHCE businessmen like Nakayama Sōhei and Ishii Kōichirō argued for the *Keizai dōyūkai* point of view, Arita – as chairman of the council's crucial third subcommittee – emerged as the leading defender of the status quo.

While the others urged reform, he helped the Ministry of Education block change (see Chapter 8).

The final factor which limited the influence of the business community, however, was its lack of any claim to 'expertise' in the area of education policy. While it was able to convince the government to implement some of its priorities, these successes were all in areas in which business had the support of MOE 'experts'. Moral education, internationalization and curriculum reform were all MOE priorities as well as business priorities. In areas where business wanted to go further than the MOE experts, it had great difficulty. One *Keizai dōyūkai* official openly admitted that MOE opposition was largely responsible for the ineffectiveness of his organization's lobbying efforts in favour of ideas like privatization, a relaxation of rules to allow skipping grades and the option of studying outside the school system. 'In such cases,' he explained, 'we have a problem because the ministry is a specialist in education issues while the *zaikai* is not.'[36] Many of those involved on the receiving end of business pressure expressed similar opinions about the limits of *zaikai* influence. Several AHCE members argued that the effectiveness of businessmen on the council was limited by their lack of knowledge about education issues.[37] Particularly interesting were the comments of Kuroha Ryōichi, a man who observed business lobbying-activities as a reporter for *Nihon keizai shimbun* and more recently as a member of MOE councils serving next to business representatives. He argued that business influence in the sphere of education – though significant in the 1950s – has been on the decline since that time. 'They still have a lot to say,' he admitted, 'but they don't have that much influence.'[38]

LOCAL EDUCATIONAL ADMINISTRATORS

In Japan, as in most modern nations, the provision of educational services to the nation's school children involves multiple layers of administration. The role of the MOE at the national level was reviewed in the previous chapter, and the part played by teachers (at the most localized level) will be treated in Chapter 6. The layers of administrators between these two extremes, however, also play an important role in the policy-making process. Immediately below the central government are the forty-seven prefectural education authorities, each composed of a lay board of education (*kyōiku iinkai*) headed by a lay board chairman and a professional staff led by a professional superintendent (*kyōikuchō*).[39] Below this level are the various city, town and village authorities, also composed of lay boards and professional staff. Finally, at the school level, the role of the immediate administration of schools is charged to each school's principal (*kōchō*) and assistant principal (*kyōtō*).

Like local educational administrators in other nations, these officials play a dual role in the policy-making process. On the one hand, they are part of the official governmental machinery. They carry out and administer national policy and, within limits, innovate and develop their own policies at the local and individual school levels. On the other hand, they have a large stake in decisions made at the national level and therefore seek – as an interest group – to influence the central government. In Japan, with its tradition of centralization in the sphere of education, the part played by administrators is most significant in the latter capacity. Through their various national organizations (listed in Figure 5.1), officials seek to assure that their interests are reflected in MOE regulations and directives as well as national legislation. Particularly as regards the education reform policies which serve as the focus of this study, individual local authorities are severely constrained in their ability to affect policy at the local level.

Partly as a result of this balance of power, local educational administrators in Japan serve very much as 'incorporated interests' in the policy-making process. They work closely with the conservative actors at the national level – particularly the MOE. As was stressed in the introduction to this chapter, however, the fact that educational administrators are part of the conservative camp does not necessarily mean that they are part of a monolithic entity. Rather, through their various means of influencing government decisions, educational administrators often advocate positions exactly opposite to those advocated by the other incorporated interest group considered in this chapter – the business community. As the analysis below reveals, local officials generally serve to reinforce the bureaucratic conservatism of the MOE.

Before entering into an analysis of the attitudes and role of local officials, however, the context in which they operate requires further elaboration. This section therefore focuses first

Figure 5.1 National Associations of Local Educational Administrators*

National Public Kindergarten Principals Association
National Combined Elementary School Principals Association
All-Japan Lower Secondary School Principals Association
National Upper Secondary School Principals Association
National Agricultural Upper Secondary Principals Association
National Industrial Upper Secondary Principals Association
National Technical Upper Secondary Principals Association
National School for Handicapped Principals Association
National Prefectural School Board Chairmen Association
Prefectural Education Superintendents Association
Designated City School Board Chairmen Association
National City–Town–Village School Board Co-operative Association
National City Education Superintendents Association
National Town–Village Education Superintendents Association

* The organizations listed here are those which testified before the Ad Hoc
  Council. There are others as well.

Source: *RD*, special edition 2–3, June 1985, pp. 73–4.

on the way in which the centralized nature of the education
system in Japan limits the ability of local educational administrators to make a difference – particularly as regards education
reform policies. It then examines the attitudes of local officials
within this system and concludes with an analysis of the role
these administrators play both at the national and local levels. In
the examination of the role played by local administrators at the
national level, the analysis focuses in particular on the Prefectural Education Superintendents Association (PESA,
Todōfuken kyōikuchō kyōgikai) – the group which includes all
of the forty-seven officials who are the highest-ranking professional administrators in each prefecture. While other groups,
particularly the largest principals' associations, are quite vocal
and important as well, the views and role of these groups vary
very little from those of PESA. The analysis concludes with a
brief review of the *local-level* role of local officials – looking at
the role of local officials in a few specific prefectures.

The limits of local autonomy

The attitudes and role of local authorities in Japan reflect
several institutional, historical, political and social conditions
which place limits on local autonomy in the sphere of education.

137

Localities are restricted first by the legally centralized nature of the education system in Japan. The curriculum, for example, is written entirely at the national level. Textbooks are reviewed by the Ministry of Education as well. In addition, many policies involving the expenditure of finances, though nominally under the jurisdiction of local authorities, are effectively controlled by the national government through its role as the provider of a large share of locally-spent education funds.[40]

Given these legal constraints, local authorities in Japan are left with only limited ability to innovate at the local level. They cannot, for example, set up their own six-year secondary schools or set up *kōtōgakkō* based on a credit system simply due to the fact that national standards require that all schools follow the 6−3−3 pattern. They are also effectively limited in their ability to improve local school conditions by spending more, for example, on teachers' salaries. While these institutional barriers do not prohibit local authorities from acting as a pressure group at the national level, they also limit this role by leaving them with very little leverage with which they might seek concessions.

Equally important in explaining the lack of local initiative, however, is the fact that localities have no historical tradition of educational autonomy on which to build. Particularly under the rigid, centralized system set up following the Meiji Restoration, locals simply followed national guidelines. There were no lay school boards, and local administrators looked directly to the MOE for directions. Although the Occupation authorities sought to transplant the American idea of local control over education through the introduction of school boards, the idea had not taken root when the conservative government ended the system of directly elected boards in 1956. Henceforth, lay board members were to be appointed − by the prefectural governors at the prefectural level and by mayors at the city, town and village level. Although local school boards were still entitled to nominate their professional superintendent, this power too was curtailed by adding the requirement that their choice be approved by the minister of education.[41]

Not surprisingly, local autonomy has failed to emerge under these constraints. Even when localities have the authority to act independently, this system guarantees that most of those in a position to exercise that power will not be interested in doing so. While lay boards technically set the 'basic direction from above',[42] the fact that most of them are chosen by conservative governors and mayors helps guarantee that few will be very assertive. Local education superintendents, many of whom come from purely administrative backgrounds, rarely exercise innovative leadership.[43] The MOE works hard to keep it this way.[44]

Another important factor limiting the latitude of local authorities is essentially political. As the government officials closest to the education *genba* (the actual site at which education is delivered), local administrators must deal with a whole range of local political forces – most significantly, the teachers' union. More than the MOE (which is insulated from direct contact with teachers), local administrators must come to terms with the union in their area. Seeking to avoid complicating their job of administering the schools, local administrators generally prefer to let the national government take a lead before initiating any controversial change in their area. In some cases – particularly in areas where unions are strong – local authorities actually work to convince the central government to refrain from initiating changes which threaten to disrupt the schools.

A final barrier to local assertiveness lies in the social pressures which greatly handicap any reform effort short of a national one. Given the existence of a national hierarchy of universities and a national examination for getting into those universities, the ability of localities to make a difference purely through local reform is severely limited. Typical of failed local reform efforts are those which have tried to ease pressure on *chūgakkō* students by making local *kōtōgakkō* less selective. The Tokyo Metropolitan School Board, for example, instituted major reforms in 1967 which sought to narrow the gap between its 'best' and 'worst' *kōtōgakkō*.[45] These efforts, however, only succeeded in lowering the prestige of public *kōtōgakkō* at the expense of elite private schools. Competition formerly directed at getting into the top public schools was re-routed into the effort to gain admission to top private institutions. Pressure was not reduced, and the public school system suffered as a result. In the case of the Tokyo reforms, the drain of top students from public to private schools had created such a degree of public dissatisfaction by the mid-1970s that, in 1976, major alterations back towards selectivity were introduced.[46] Even when local authorities have succeeded in breaking out of legal, political and attitudinal barriers to local initiative, they have encountered the immovable barrier of 'society'.

Attitudes

Given these various constraints on local initiative, it is not surprising that the predominant attitude of local administrators – both in their capacity as national-level interest groups and in their role as policy implementers at the local level – is one of passivity and a preference for the status quo. Beholden to the powers above them (especially the MOE) and unable to initiate change on their own, they tend to await MOE leadership passively before taking a position or acting. While waiting, however, they subtly reinforce the bureaucratic conservatism of the ministry by transmitting the conservatism of the *genba* to their superiors.

Passivity

The generally passive attitude of local administrators is reflected clearly in the activities and statements of national organizations of local administrators like PESA. In the lead-up to national policy decisions, that organization's biggest concern is inevitably about whether or not adequate finances will be provided. Even when it goes so far as to express its views on policy alternatives, it most often uses the form: 'if you decide on policy A, please be sure you do this; and if you choose policy B, please do it this way.'[47] After decisions are announced, most local authorities act quickly to get into line with new central directives.

Typical of this passivity has been the local authorities' attitude towards the idea of six-year secondary schools, a proposal which if enacted would become a major focus of local debate, decisions and planning. Despite this reason for its involvement – and the fact that this idea has been on the agenda for some time – PESA has never made its position clear. In a 1979 report, a PESA project team devoted eleven lines to the subject, listing six-year secondary schools as one idea among several for reforming *kōtōgakkō* education. The key word is *list*. PESA did not express a preference for any particular reform, choosing only to describe the various 'new-type *kōtōgakkō*' that might be tried.[48]

By 1985 the idea was definitely on the agenda for the new reform initiative. Nakasone had come out in favour of the 6–6 reform and the Ad Hoc Council was due to decide on the issue in its first report. Nevertheless, in its testimony before the council, PESA avoided committing itself to any specific concept, calling simply for 'the testing of a system of secondary education consistent between the lower and upper divisions'. It did not elaborate.[49]

Finally in May of 1986, the organization published the results of a survey on the idea. The impact of the report in terms of its use in pressuring central government policy, however, was limited this time by the form of the questions. Question 1, for example, asked the superintendents how they were responding to the proposal, not whether or not they supported it. Almost all responded that they were reserving their opinion until the government developed the idea further. While other questions asked the officials to specify the type and number of such schools they might wish to establish, nowhere in the survey were they asked for an opinion on the idea itself.[50]

A preference for the status quo

While organizations like PESA thus exhibit a generally passive attitude towards central government action, they nevertheless have an underlying preference for the status quo which shapes their role in the policy process. While this conservatism reflects several different factors, three seem particularly important: (1) like the MOE and the LDP zoku, local administrators have a personal commitment to a system which they have built and nurtured; (2) as the officials responsible for implementing policy changes, local administrators have a natural aversion to changes which might require them to put in extra work; and (3) particularly as regards changes opposed by the teachers' unions, local officials prefer to avoid the long, drawn-out conflicts which can accompany controversial reforms.

A striking illustration of this attitude was PESA's 1985 testimony before the Ad Hoc Council:

Regarding education reform, in order that it realise the educational objectives set out in the FLE, we demand the following: (1) that the reforms respect the strong points of the current education system; (2) that you respect the opinions of those concerned with education; (3) that you consider the need for continuity and co-ordination in education; (4) that you provide the necessary finances; and (5) that you strengthen and improve the school board system.

Regarding the important issues confronting us, we demand: (1) that you maintain the educational standards and equality-

141

orientated mechanisms of compulsory education – the responsible maintenance of educational conditions; a respect for the school district system; and uniform standards for educational content.[51]

PESA did go on in the remainder of its testimony to call for some specific changes: the diversification of secondary (particularly upper secondary) education, the upgrading of the quality of teachers and reform of the entrance exam. What is most interesting about the testimony, however, is the strong emphasis on the status quo in the first part of the testimony quoted above, clearly directed at those members of the Ad Hoc Council who would prefer to see a less regulated education system. Despite the fact that localities would gain a great deal of freedom and responsibility under a less regulated system, the major organization of local administrators was pleading that the established centralized, standardized system be maintained.

While the various organizations of educational administrators thus tend to exhibit a generally conservative attitude towards reform, their conservatism is most apparent in their respective attitudes towards changes which affect the parochial interests of their own group. In the 1971 round of reform, for example, one of the leading opponents of the plan to establish pilot projects with a 5–4–4 division of years was the organization of elementary-school principals. It objected to the idea of reducing the length of elementary schools from six to five years. Also vocally opposed was the group representing private kindergartens which saw the MOE's attempt to lower the school entering age (which would result in a transfer of 5-year-olds from largely private kindergartens to predominantly public primary schools) as a threat to their very existence. Similar examples can be cited for virtually all reform proposals of the period under study. Reforms inevitably affect the parochial interests of one sector or another, and the educational administrators representing that sector naturally emerge as a leading force opposed to change.

Structure

At the national level

While educational administrators thus advocate a much more conservative attitude towards education reform than that favoured by the other major incorporated interest group (the business community), the ways in which they influence national policy are not that different. Like the *zaikai*, the organizations of administrators voice their views through reports, participation on advisory councils and by otherwise exploiting their close relationship with the conservative government. Typically, the reports of organizations like PESA take the form of membership surveys. One 1985 PESA survey of local authority opinion regarding education reform, for example, revealed: (1) that virtually all superintendents favoured the established system of textbook review, and (2) that most supported expanding the training requirements for teachers.[52] Such pronouncements – especially when backed up by virtual consensus opinion among administrators – naturally have a strong influence on MOE decisions. The ministry cannot ignore the views of this important constituency. In many cases, of course, organizations like PESA tend to parrot the MOE line. Even in such cases, however, their role is significant in that they give the ministry something to point to in support of its positions.

When opinion within administrative circles is divided, the effect of these survey-style reports is less easy to determine. In the case of the above survey on local authority attitudes towards teacher training, for instance, the PESA summary revealed that the forty-seven superintendents were quite divided on the *extent* to which training requirements should be strengthened: eleven superintendents were reported to be in support of the strongest proposal – one which would institute a strict probationary training period for new teachers. Seven others were reported to be in support of less strict versions of the same idea. The fact that the remaining twenty-nine superintendents did not appear to want to attach conditions to the employment of teachers was not mentioned.[53] While one can only speculate on the impact of such a divided finding, it seems reasonable to suppose that this evidence of a lukewarm attitude towards the probationary (*shiho*) system on the part of these important local officials helped convince the MOE to work for a more moderate version of the idea, one which would emphasize training rather than probation. Evidence of a *lack* of consensus among administrators can thus be almost as important as evidence of unanimity, serving to moderate proposals for controversial change.

Local administrators also work to influence national policy

through their role as members of education advisory councils. Typically, the various organizations of education administrators provide an even greater number of council members than *zaikai*. The 1971 CCE, for example, included one PESA representative and three representatives of the principals' associations. The Ad Hoc Council – noted for its lack of education specialists – still included one superintendent and one principal. One MOE council in the 1970s (The Discussion Group on Upper Secondary Education) included among its ten members two prefectural superintendents and six principals.[54] Like the *zaikai*, local administrators use these positions to bring their opinions to bear directly on the policy-making process. In the 1971 round of reform, the elementary-school representative on the CCE (Takahashi Sanae) was a leading voice opposed to the pilot project proposal.[55] In the most recent round, the two administrators on the AHCE both served as members of the MOE 'block' opposed to the reformism of the Nakasone 'block'. Through these various means, therefore, local administrators serve as an important conservatizing force in the national-level debate over education reform.

At the local level

Local administrators are equally conservative in their capacity as implementers and innovators at the local level. As noted above, much of this conservatism must be attributed to the limits placed on local initiative by the centralized nature of the Japanese system. Even in cases where they are allowed a great deal of latitude, however, local authorities have failed to overcome their tendency towards 'status quo maintenance'. This pattern was visible, for example, in the local authorities' response to recent demands that they reduce the emphasis on examinations at the stage where students are sorted between upper secondary schools. The emphasis on exams at this level was one of the factors widely held to be responsible for the upsurge in *chūgakkō* violence in the early 1980s. Despite the fact that local officials possessed the power to change the local selection criteria, however, few authorities initiated significant reforms. PESA, in its 1984 report on such reform efforts, reported that the ability of localities to initiate change was greatly limited by the need to establish a local consensus. 'It might be easier,' the report continued, 'if the national government set the basic direction.'[56] Just two months later the MOE obliged, issuing an official communication (*tsūchi*) urging local authorities to reform their *kōtōgakkō* entrance selection processes to emphasise interviews, admission by nomination and tests formulated with their effect on lower levels of the school system in mind.[57] Local authorities were much more active in formulating such reforms after this MOE intervention.[58]

While the above example demonstrates the general weakness and conservatism of local authorities, the tendency can best be seen through an examination of the record of local initiative in individual prefectures. Generalizations are difficult because localities in Japan range from those which tend to follow every move of the conservative central government to those which elect Socialist mayors and governors and claim to be 'progressive'. In the end, however, the record of local initiative in the area of education reform reveals that while the 'conservative' prefectures indeed undertake few independent reforms, even the 'progressive' prefectures do little which deviates from MOE policy. This pattern can be illustrated by looking briefly at the two extremes:

Kumamoto Prefecture: Tucked away in the centre of Kyūshū, the southernmost of the four main islands of Japan, Kumamoto is perhaps typical of the conservative, relatively rural prefectures which lie outside the Kantō–Kansai areas. Not surprisingly, most local officials I spoke with there echoed the MOE line as they pointed to the decline in traditional morals and the need for dedicated teachers as they sought to explain the problems of Japanese education.[59] The prefecture's local reform effort has reflected these values. Asked to explain how Kumamoto was responding to education problems, officials in the prefectural education office pointed to the following reforms:

1   Increased teacher training. Beginning in 1976, new teachers were required to attend twenty days of training sessions in their first year, starting with a three-day, three-night 'camp'. In addition, training requirements of six days for sixth-year teachers (1979) and three days for third-year teachers (1983) have since been added.
2   Student camps. Starting in 1983 with a portion of first-year *chūgakkō* students, the prefecture has organized and required students of certain grades to participate in overnight 'camps' in facilities located in nature spots. The aim of this programme

has been 'to provide students with a chance to play with friends and relax with teachers – to experience things like cooking, cleaning and the beauty of nature'.

3 *Ijime denwa*. In response to the growing problem of bullying in the schools, the prefecture established a hotline for those who wished to report incidents.

4 Guidance. The prefecture established procedures for dealing with problems in specific schools. When efforts at the school and community level fail, an eight-member team of professors, headmasters, police and others gets together to suggest means of dealing with the crisis.[60]

What is interesting about these policies is the degree to which they reflected MOE directives and advice. The teacher-training policies (except for the first-year camp) were formally required by the ministry. The others, notably the policies requiring student camps, setting up the *ijime denwa* and establishing procedures for dealing with school crises, all reflected ministry advice.[61]

That even these locally-orientated policies all originated from above points out the degree to which prefectures like Kumamoto look to the Ministry of Education for virtually all of their activities. Perhaps the best illustration of the attitude of these local officials, however, was the boast of one Kumamoto official that his prefecture had been the *first* to introduce many of these reforms. His office, he explained, had a mole in Tokyo (someone with close ties to the LDP education *zoku*) who often leaked to them information about forthcoming MOE directives and advice. Knowing what to anticipate, Kumamoto could arrange to be the first to introduce the suggested reforms.[62]

The progressive prefectures: Not all prefectures, of course, are as eager to follow MOE advice as Kumamoto. Some, like Kanagawa and Saitama, for example, actually pride themselves on being progressive and innovative. A look at what they have been doing, however, reveals that even these more liberal localities have not strayed far from the MOE line.

Saitama, for example, has a policy of 'promoting the establishment of distinctive *kōtōgakkō*'. Choosing from among the various 'new-type' *kōtōgakkō* listed by the PESA project team (see p. 140), Saitama has concentrated on experimenting with '*kōtōgakkō* groups' and 'comprehensive vocational schools'. A school complex representing a combination of the two ideas –

Ina Gakuen – was set up in 1984. By putting several separate schools in a concentrated 'group' area, it allows students to enjoy a wider selection of electives than would be possible in any single school (this is the 'group' idea). By bringing together vocational and university preparatory schools, it allows general course students to get some vocational education while letting top vocational students get the general courses they need to reach higher education (this is the 'comprehensive vocational' idea). The prefecture has also made sure that each new school it has established (it has built seventy-nine since 1973) has had some distinctive course – foreign language, computer science, industrial design, and so on.[63]

Kanagawa prefecture has followed a similar policy, emphasizing streaming and group education in addition to the above type of efforts to provide increasing opportunities for distinct education.[64] While both programmes are impressive for the initiative displayed, neither is especially radical. Diversification of the type represented by the building of specialized *kōtōgakkō* and the establishment of specialized courses is exactly what the reformists in the MOE have been seeking for years. Similarly, streaming at the high-school level is something the MOE has been pushing since the early 1970s. Kanagawa and Saitama are original only in that they have started to overcome the inertia of standardization and have succeeded in actually turning some of the ministry's still rather limited reform rhetoric into action. The fact that these cases are treated as the 'foremost' examples of local initiative actually points again towards the fact that local administrators in Japan remain in general a very conservative group.

CONCLUSIONS

At one level the two sets of incorporated interests considered in this chapter are a study in contrasts. The business community – particularly its *Keizai dōyūkai* wing – served as perhaps the most reformist force within the 'conservative camp' in both of the recent rounds of the education debate. Basing their demands on their perception of the future needs of the nation's economy, these businessmen argued for bold moves away from the standardization of the established system. The various associations of educational administrators, on the other hand, were arguably the most conservative set of actors in the same 'conservative camp'. In the recent rounds of reform, they stood at the opposite extreme of the debate over standardization, urging the MOE to maintain its regulatory control and opposing virtually all suggestions for significant change.

While these two groups differ in their attitudes towards reform, however, their respective roles in the policy-making process are very similar. Both enjoy special positions of access to the formal governmental actors of the conservative camp – with the business community, on the one hand, able to boast of close links to the LDP while the educational administrators, on the other, are able to rely on an almost symbiotic relationship with their superiors in the Ministry of Education. Both can be sure that their policy statements and reports will receive a close reading by their fellow conservatives, and both are assured of getting at least some representation on the government's education advisory councils. These two groups – with such dissimilar attitudes – are thus both fully integrated, fully 'incorporated' members of the 'conservative camp'.

The fact that these two groups are *both* full members of the conservative camp serves as just one more illustration of the way in which Japan's conservatives have failed to achieve a consensus on education reform. Their failure to agree – combined with the failure of the MOE and the LDP to agree – largely explains the conservatives' inability to achieve movement towards significant change in the sphere of education. The cleavage between business and the educational administrators, however, should not be seen as totally independent of the cleavages within and between the LDP and MOE as discussed in previous chapters. Rather, the split between these interests can actually be seen as a cause of the divisions within the government. Thus the reformism of Nakasone can be explained partly by his links with the business community (particularly the reformist wing) while the status quo maintenance attitude of the MOE can be seen to reflect the desire of the educational establishment to preserve the order of the established system. This analysis of the 'incorporated interests' of the education sphere therefore provides a clear illustration of the one-party dominant dilemma: too many interests grouped in one camp make it difficult to achieve agreement on the direction of change.

6

External actors: opposition groups

In contrast to the special position of access enjoyed by 'incorporated interest groups' like the business community and local educational administrators, another set of education policy actors have virtually no official avenues for influencing government decisions. Typically, these 'opposition interest groups' are excluded from bureaucratic advisory councils, greatly limited in their official and unofficial contacts with government policymakers and isolated in general by an official attitude which places them outside the circle of power. What is more, these groups have been locked in this position at least since the formation of the united LDP in 1955 and appear likely to remain excluded as long as Japan remains wedded to its current predominant party power structure.

That such 'opposition interest groups' have no official access, however, does not mean they do not play a role in education policy-making. On the contrary, their vocal defence of the 'postwar settlement' on education policy – the 'democratic', egalitarian system set up by the Occupation – has placed significant limitations on the government's ability to introduce education reform. While they have not been able to stop reform efforts through electoral muscle, they have succeeded through the strident tone of their opposition in setting a mood of confrontation which has made smooth and quiet education reform virtually impossible. This technique of the opposition – described in Chapter 1 as one of 'breaking the conservative consensus' – is explored in detail in this chapter.

As in the case of the incorporated groups, opposition interests also work at various degrees of exclusion. Organizations like the Association of National University Presidents – despite a

149

generally wary attitude towards government initiatives – enjoy regular access to MOE councils dealing with university issues and sometimes actually endorse government reform plans. *Nikkyōso*, on the other hand, has been systematically excluded from all government councils and has experienced extended periods in which its officials have been barred from even meeting top MOE bureaucrats. The opposition groups to be treated in this chapter include the above – *Nikkyōso* and university groups like the ANUP – as well as the opposition parties. Focusing in particular on *Nikkyōso* as the classic case of an opposition group in this sphere, this chapter will examine the attitudes of opposition groups and their place in the education policy-making process.

NIKKYŌSO

While *Nikkyōso* is not in fact the only teachers' union in Japan, it is by far the largest. With its membership numbering at least 580,000 and encompassing around half of the total number of public school teachers, it has many times the membership of any competing teachers' union.[1] The next largest union, the All-Japan Teachers League (*Zennikkyōren*), includes just 2.7 per cent of teachers and is basically only a minor group propped up by the MOE in an effort to create an alternative to *Nikkyōso*.[2] Spending much of its energy criticizing its larger rival and taking positions in favour of government priorities like teacher training and moral education, *Zennikkyōren* has little independent effect on education policy.[3] In effect, *Nikkyōso* is the only broad-based union expressing the views of teachers in Japan. Though it is smaller than it used to be,[4] it continues to play a major role in setting the tone of the education policy debate.

The union's attitudes

Defence of post-war 'democratic' education

As argued in Chapter 2, the position of the union in the recent education debate can be seen as a natural reaction to the pre-war and post-war experience of teachers. Teachers were suppressed and used in the wartime nationalist campaign, and *Nikkyōso* was immediately targeted by post-war conservative governments concerned about the union's central role in the progressive opposition. Given this experience, the militant opposition of *Nikkyōso* to government recentralization policies is not at all surprising. Holding tight to Occupation-introduced policies of 'democratic' education, it has resisted with all of its strength each effort to increase central control over curriculum, textbooks, teacher training and general administration. Despite having lost some battles, the union today still stands firm on several issues:

(1) Opposition to revision or even reinterpretation of the legal foundations of post-war education. While the government has slowly reclaimed various central powers over education policy, it has not succeeded in modifying the laws which laid the foundation for 'democratic' education: the Constitution and the Fundamental Law of Education. The union has thus focused on these two documents with crusade-like zeal in an attempt to prevent further centralization of power over educational administration.

In 1971, one of the primary concerns of the union was the MOE's attempt to reinterpret the FLE provision requiring that education 'shall not be subject to improper control, but shall be directly responsible to the whole people' (Article 10). The ministry maintained that this provision meant simply that the government, as the elected representative of the people, was responsible for education. The union, on the other hand, maintained and continues to insist that the provision was written specifically to prevent government excesses in the sensitive area of education. *Nikkyōso* argues that education policies must meet *a higher standard of democracy* – something approaching a consensus of 'the whole people'.[5] The union's strong opposition to reinterpretation was again apparent in the latest round of reform. Despite the fact that the AHCE was committed by law to respect the spirit of the FLE, it continued to concentrate its attacks on the few *suggestions* of reinterpretation which were buried in the council's reports.[6]

(2) Opposition to increased teacher training. Despite repeated efforts of the government to increase training requirements, *Nikkyōso* has opposed every attempt. Efforts to increase course requirements for university training programmes have been opposed because the union feels such standards should be kept minimal in order to allow a broad range of graduates to become

teachers. It fears that increased course requirements would force many departments in regular universities to close and leave teacher training increasingly to government-run teacher-training colleges. It opposes all government-organized training for new and veteran teachers on the grounds that such sessions could be used to turn teachers into government tools. In the latest round of education reform, the union was most concerned by the council's proposal to introduce a one-year training requirement for new teachers and vocally opposed it on the above grounds.[7]

Nikkyōso is also opposed to the government's efforts to increase control of teachers through administrative means. The CCE's 1971 proposal to create three levels of teachers with the top grade reflecting graduate teacher training, for example, was opposed on these grounds. Fearing that promotions would be subject to administrative control through the process whereby teachers would have to be granted leave in order to obtain the necessary further education, the union charged that the scale was just another attempt by the government to force teachers to quit their union and ingratiate themselves with administrators.

(3) Opposition to increased moral education. While the union is not opposed to instilling students with a certain moral sense through the various activities of school life,[8] it is strongly opposed to government efforts to set up special moral education classes (this is already required), regulate a moral curriculum (also done) and encourage the use of government-prepared 'special materials' for moral education courses (a proposal of the AHCE). The degree to which the union sees such actions as being linked to pre-war patterns is seen in the following passage from its response to the second Ad Hoc Council report:

> There is a danger that [the policies recommended by the Ad Hoc Council] neglect the scientific consciousness of education, that they would wrap up the whole school system in moral education, and that they could lead to a re-establishment of the pre-war system under which a moral code was enforced through militarism, the Imperial Constitution and the Imperial Rescript on Education.[9]

As with teacher training, therefore, the union opposes all government attempts to add to the content of moral education in the curriculum and to increase its control of what is already there.[10]

(4) Opposition to increased administrative centralization. While this goal is visible in the union's positions on training and moral education detailed above, it is also a general goal of union politics. Since the government has already succeeded in introducing such centralizing policies as a national curriculum and school board reform, recent union efforts in this sphere have concentrated on opposing government efforts to strengthen MOE regulation of textbooks.

In all of the aims outlined above, the emphasis is on opposition to change. The government wants to increase training, increase moral education and increase centralization – and the union is opposed to all of it. In fact, the union does have a programme for positive action on education policy. Even in its positive documents, however, the stress is on the wonders of the post-war 'democratic' system. It proposes the 'substantialization' (*jūjitsuka*) of what is already there.[11] Specifically, it proposes that teacher training be left to teachers, that the national curriculum be limited to 'guidelines', that school boards be elected once again and that textbook regulation be kept to a minimum.[12] Given the out-of-power position of *Nikkyōso*, however, these proposals have no prospect of being implemented. In effect, they serve only to illuminate further the points on which the union opposes government reforms. Being limited to a role of opposition, the best the union can do is to defend the status quo.

Defence of egalitarian education

A similar pattern of opposition to reform and defence of the status quo has characterized the union's role in pursuing its other major objective: maintaining the system's emphasis on equality. Here again *Nikkyōso* is seeking to hold onto a system introduced during the Occupation. The post-war reforms replaced the pre-war multi-track education system with a single 6−3−3−4 track for all young people. Since that time, conservative reformers have been seeking to 'diversify' the system and recreate a new elite track. Particularly in the past twenty years, as the government has sought to diversify the upper years of the 6−3−3−4 system, *Nikkyōso* has emerged as a major force defending the current level of egalitarianism. Specifically, it has taken the following positions:

(1) Opposition to diversification at the *chūgakkō* level. Here the main issue has been the idea – proposed by both the 1971 CCE and the Ad Hoc Council – that the currently standardized 6–3–3 system be made more flexible with the introduction of a parallel 6–6 track. Charging that the new six-year secondary schools would inevitably become elite university preparatory institutions, the union has insisted that students be educated as equals *at least* through the *chūgakkō* years.[13]

(2) Opposition to the further diversification of upper secondary education. Critical even of the current degree of diversity and hierarchy within the *kōtōgakkō* system, *Nikkyōso* has opposed all efforts to increase that diversity through such means as the establishment of 'new-type high schools' and the creation of specialized courses. It urges that as many students as possible be given an academic secondary education in order to put off the need for selection in the system.[14]

(3) Support of efforts to extend equal education through the *kōtōgakkō* years. Arguing that many of the problems of Japanese education can be traced to the competitive pressures which accompany the current system of selective admission to upper secondary schools, *Nikkyōso* has made the idea of '*kōtōgakkō* for all' one of its top *positive* priorities. Specifically, it has proposed that the period of compulsory schooling be extended to include at least some upper secondary education and that the current hierarchical system of *kōtōgakkō* be replaced by 'regional comprehensive secondary schools' (*chiiki sōgō chūtō gakkō*) which would admit students on an equal basis within a small district without resort to competitive examinations.[15]

Despite the reformist tone of this final policy position, however, *Nikkyōso* remains essentially on the defensive on this front as well. While its ideas for *kōtōgakkō* reform have received significant attention (many local reforms have tried to move in that direction), they nevertheless are most important in their role as a hypothetical counterplan to be used in the more real battle against central government policies which are moving increasingly in the other direction. Standardization today is out of vogue in Japan, and *Nikkyōso* will be lucky if it can simply prevent further diversification. Once again, therefore, the teachers' union is essentially limited to the role of opposition in preserving as much as it can of the egalitarianism which remains in the system.

Other aims

The union has been less negative in its efforts on several other fronts. It has taken a firm positive stand, for example, in its campaign to improve conditions in the schools. Having successfully pressured the government into working towards a reduction in class size from forty-five to forty, it has recently begun to demand that thirty-five or even thirty be set as the goal.[16] It has also been vocal in its positive pursuit of a reduction in the size of 'mammoth' schools, an increase in aid to private education and the maintenance of systems under which compulsory school students receive free textbooks and subsidized school lunches.[17] In these latter aims, it has earned the MOE's sympathy, if not always its funds.[18]

Nikkyōso's conservatism

The idea of *Nikkyōso*'s essential conservatism has already been suggested. As the major defender of the Occupation's reforms, the union has been primarily concerned with maintaining the post-war system of 'democratic' and egalitarian education and preventing a retreat to pre-war policies. Even its programme for positive 'reform' has been basically a call for an *expansion* of post-war public education. What is more interesting is the way in which the union's conservatism serves to reinforce the conservatism of government authorities. Despite the fact that *Nikkyōso* and the MOE remain ideological enemies, they stand together in support of broad aspects of the present system of public education in Japan.

This congruity of interest has been particularly notable with regard to the union's second major objective: its defence of egalitarianism. While the ministry continues to call for some diversification, it remains essentially committed to equal public education, especially through the compulsory years. As noted in Chapter 4, a large share of ministry officials feel that the provision of equal education through the compulsory years has been a major 'plus' of the post-war system and therefore hesitate to meddle with success.

Recent changes in the nature of the education debate – notably the rise of the *jiyūka* argument – have made this congruence of positions even more visible. The opposition of the MOE to such policies has already been noted. What is more surprising is the degree to which *Nikkyōso* supported the ministry's position in the recent debate. Based on the union's first objective (democratic education), one would expect it to have been enthusiastic about the pluralism promised by the *jiyūka* advocates. One would expect, for example, that the union would have supported ideas like 'regulatory relief' and 'decentralization', both leading goals of the liberalizationists. Instead, it came out opposed to the whole idea, warning of the 'dangers' of *jiyūka* in its testimony before the Ad Hoc Council. The application of the philosophy to the upper and lower secondary schools, it argued, would lead to a greater emphasis on ability-based selection at those levels.[19] Another reason for the union's position was suggested by its comments on the council's second report:

> The idea of 'regulatory relief' in education administration actually means a rethinking of public education and funding cut-backs. This is clear from (the council's) emphasis on diverse new private educational institutions visible in its call for 'an increase in the establishment of private elementary and middle schools'. These policies simply promise an acceleration in the privatization of education and a speeding up of the process in which schools are increasingly being treated as just another piece of merchandise.[20]

The union thus put its goal of keeping Japanese education equal and public *above* its goal of reducing government control of education. It still wanted to reduce the control of its ideological enemies in the government, but not at the cost of the privatization and diversification of the education system.

Unstated was another reason for the union's stake in maintaining public control over the education system. The ministry would not be the only institution to lose power if public education gave way to private. The union also has a significant stake in maintaining the current system. It may have to put up with government regulation, but its power base is in *public* schools, not private. As long as the best students pass through public schools, it still has some ability to use its teachers to influence the thinking of future generations. When those students start going to private schools, however, both the ministry and the union lose their power of influence. The positions of the ministry and the union, therefore, are not that different. Neither wants too much diversification if such change would result in too much inequality in the system or a loss in control.

The union's place in the process

Nikkyōso's exclusion from advisory councils

That the union shares certain common interests with the Ministry of Education, however, does not mean it is even close to being accepted as an inside player. Rather, *Nikkyōso* remains the classic case of an opposition interest group in Japan – not only limited to opposition but limited also in the means through which it can express that opposition. First, the union does not have the opportunity to communicate its views through representatives on government education councils. Even as the business community and local authorities have received consistent and broad representation on MOE councils, *Nikkyōso* has not had a single delegate selected. The 1971 CCE did not include a single teacher, much less a union member. While the Ad Hoc Council included one elementary-school teacher who happened to be a dues-paying member of *Nikkyōso*, she was chosen for her prior co-operation with an MOE moral education project rather than for her ability to represent the union.[21] Asked to what degree she represented union positions on the council, Tamaru Akiyo said that she read their literature and tried to talk to teachers in her own school. The union did not even contact her.[22]

Interestingly, this absence of union representatives on advisory councils is not simply due to government intransigence. In the most recent round of reform, there was actually a time in the period immediately after Nakasone announced his intention to establish a supra-cabinet council when the idea of including a union representative on the council was considered by both sides. While *Nikkyōso* leader Tanaka Ichirō was interested in the idea, however, he was eventually forced to close off the option when faced with a rebellion from the left-wing of his union.[23]

Meetings with the minister

Since 1971 the union has had slightly more access through a mechanism known as the *toppu kaidan* – top-level meetings between the minister of education and the leader of *Nikkyōso*.

157

While such meetings had been held only once in the preceding ten years, they have been held under virtually every minister since that time. Nevertheless, the same factors which have kept union representatives out of MOE councils militate to assure that these meetings never become too co-operative. In one case in the late 1970s, for example, the hawkish Minister of Education, Naitō Yosaburō, met with Makieda and worked out a last-minute agreement on the union's demand for a reduction in class size. With Naitō promising to make the achievement of a forty-member class size his personal responsibility, Makieda agreed to call off a threatened strike. Alarmed that Naitō was getting too close to the union, the *zoku* called a special meeting to demand that the minister cool his enthusiasm and cancel another scheduled meeting with the union leader.[24]

But again, the pressures work the other way as well. When union leader Tanaka attended a 1986 re-election party for LDP *zoku* leader Nishioka Takeo, the objections from the union side were greater than those from the party.[25] The whole question of co-operation versus non-co-operation has become one of the divisive factors in the leadership struggle which has paralysed the union since the summer of 1986.[26]

Strikes and 'movements'

Given that its access through advisory councils and even top-level meeting has been limited in these ways, *Nikkyōso* has been left with the option of expressing its positions through vocal 'movements' (*undō*) outside the regular political process. At a most basic level, it has the opportunity simply to state its positions in the mass media. Newspapers and television routinely seek to balance their coverage of government education initiatives with the almost always negative response of the teachers' union. While it can publicize its views in this way, however, publicity without a more serious 'movement' to back it up has little potency. That the union disagrees with the MOE is so predictable, its statements of opposition tend to be quickly dismissed unless accompanied by evidence of the *degree* to which the union disagrees.

One means by which the union demonstrates the degree of its opposition is the mass strike (*suto*). While all public employees – including teachers – are legally barred from striking, *Nikkyōso* has periodically resorted to this option to show its serious commitment to certain positions. Since 1970 it has struck or threatened to strike for reasons ranging from its opposition to the *shunin* system to its support for a reduction in class size. The strike weapon, however, is a two-edged sword. Due to its disruptive nature, it can often cost the union more in lost goodwill than it is worth in terms of demonstrating its solidarity. Particularly in the late 1950s and early 1960s, when the strike weapon was sometimes used for what were seen as blatantly political purposes, the union lost a great deal of public support.[27] More recently, *Nikkyōso* leaders have come to limit the use of this 'extreme' weapon to those cases which are most related to *labour* concerns.

As a result, the union has generally had to find other means of demonstrating its opposition to the government's political efforts to reform the education system. In 1971 the chief mechanism employed by *Nikkyōso* was the 'people's movement' – an effort to demonstrate broad-based opposition to the CCE proposals by bringing together many separate groups under one 'People's Coalition for the Promotion of Democratic Education' (*Minshu kyōiku o susumeru kokumin rengō*). The organization, set up in November 1971, included some sixteen groups including *Sōhyō* (The General Council of Trade Unions) and *Chūritsu rōren* (The Coalition of Independent Trade Unions) as well as *Nikkyōso*.[28]

In the more recent round, the union sought to revive the old 'people's coalition' (still officially in existence), but also tried to build a 'grass-roots' movement opposed to the AHCE line and in favour of 'democratic education reform'. The movement, led by a *Nikkyōso*-affiliated group called the 'Special Committee for Opposing the Ad Hoc Council and Promoting Education Reform in line with the People's Agreement', worked to establish education policy discussion groups at the level of individual school districts. The goal was to create a national bottom-up reform movement to contrast with the government's top-down AHCE-led effort.[29]

Strikes and 'movements' as part of a broader strategy

In many ways, *Nikkyōso*'s reliance on strikes and 'movements' seems to demonstrate the futility of its role in the policy-making process. How can the union expect such actions to have any effect when, in the end, the government retains majority voting power in the Diet? In fact, the union seeks to use these techniques despite the LDP's voting control by rejecting majority

159

rule as a legitimate way of making education policy. When examined in relation to this broader opposition strategy, *Nikkyōso*'s mass movements can be seen to have some influence.

The strategy can be seen as a three-step process. First, the union seeks to convince the public that education is a special, 'sensitive' issue requiring a higher standard of democracy than mere majority rule. This appeal is based partly on the general Japanese preference for at least the appearance of consensus (as discussed in Chapter 1). The union seeks to reinforce this preference with its interpretation of the FLE. According to the union, the various provisions of the FLE and the Constitution require that education policy-making be 'politically neutral'. To meet this condition, it argues, the government must demonstrate that it has support beyond the limits of the conservative camp. If it cannot, then such education policies must be seen as partisan and therefore illegitimate.

The second step in this opposition strategy follows logically from the first: *Nikkyōso* seeks to demonstrate that controversial policies do not meet its more-than-majority standard of democracy. As one *Nikkyōso* official explained:

> The key to the opposition is that if the *'hantai'* (cry of opposition) is strong enough and loud enough, then when the government tries to pass itself off as 'democratic', it can't. When all the voices outside government are crying out against their proposals, how can the government say it has a consensus?[30]

The official essentially assumes the first step: the government is expected to prove it has a consensus. He explains that the goal of *Nikkyōso*'s movements is simply to prove that the government has not met this standard. In 1971 the union sought to demonstrate the unanimity of outside opposition through its united organization of opposition groups. The CCE was seen by the public to be an MOE-dominated organ, so the mere show of opposition by groups left out of its narrow representation was enough to damage its democratic credentials. In the more recent round, while Nakasone worked harder to bring together a more broadly based council, *Nikkyōso* sought to damage the group's democratic credentials by focusing on its top–down approach: 'the people' were left out, it argued.

In the end, however, this *Nikkyōso* strategy depends on a more difficult third step: the union must scare the conservatives. It may convince the public and even the LDP that education requires a higher standard of democracy. It may convince some of the public that the government has failed to meet that standard. But the government will change its plans only if the union has convinced at least part of the conservative camp that a certain change creates unnecessary risks for maintaining conservative rule.

A comment by an LDP official reveals the challenge facing the union. Explaining LDP strategy in the area of education issues, Morita Tomio, the LDP Central Office official in charge of education issues, admitted that the party had to move carefully because 'the Constitution requires that education be politically neutral'. The party, he explained, is forced to create at least the surface appearance (*tatemae*) of wide support for its initiatives. If it were to push proposals through directly, it might succeed with regard to that particular issue, but in the long run its aggressive behaviour might 'become a wave' (*nami ni naru*) which could leave the LDP out of power.[31]

At one level, the official's comment demonstrates the power of the opposition strategy. The LDP seems to have accepted the higher standard of democracy for education. Comments made by Nakasone in the lead-up to the establishment of the AHCE indicate that he too recognized the need to respect the need for some degree of political neutrality and consensus rule in education policy-making.[32] They key word, however, is 'degree'. The government will seek to demonstrate wider support – but only to the degree necessary to avoid an issue becoming a 'wave'. In order to pursue this strategy successfully, the union must convince at least part of the conservative camp that a certain change or a certain Diet strategy creates unnecessary risks for continued LDP rule.

In the early 1970s there can be no doubt that the broad movement opposed to the 1971 CCE report served to convince less interested MOE bureaucrats and LDP members that the council's most controversial proposals were not worth the trouble. Little action was taken, therefore, on such ideas as pilot projects and the probationary year for new teachers. At other times, however, the union's movements have failed to gain public sympathy or have been ignored by LDP governments confident in their Diet majority. The opposition strategy based on strikes

161

and 'movements', therefore, offers only a limited avenue of influence at the national level.

Local non-co-operation as an opposition tactic

When opposition at the national level fails, *Nikkyōso* has one last line of defence: non-co-operation at the local level. In many ways this last weapon is the most effective. At the national level the union cannot even be sure that the government will talk to it. At the local level, school principals and prefectural administrators must work with and talk to union teachers every day. The post-war record of education policy-making contains several examples of policies which have been enforced at the national level against vocal opposition only to be largely neutralized at the local level.

In the case of the government's attempt to keep teachers in line through the use of efficiency ratings, for example, the union succeeded in rendering many prefectural programmes 'totally meaningless' through such local agreements as those which let teachers fill out their own forms.[33] More recently, *Nikkyōso* was able to limit the effect of the *shunin* reform in many areas through a similar process of local opposition. While the government sought to make teachers more compliant by making these administrative positions (with bonus) subject to promotion by local authorities, the union succeeded in undermining this purpose in many schools by convincing teachers receiving bonuses to 'pool' their funds and give them to the union, thereby removing the salary differential accompanying such positions (see Chapter 7).

This success of the union in altering certain policies at the local level points to the source of *Nikkyōso*'s strength. Not only can it neutralize some policies after the government has moved to implement them, it can also prevent national-level action by making its opposition known to the local administrators who will have to enforce those policies. Knowing what to expect, many of these officials are much more conservative in their willingness to support changes which might disrupt local schools. Many have developed working relationships with local unions and are aware of how certain national proposals might affect that relationship.[34] Local authorities in regions with strong unions are therefore often the first to question controversial central initiatives. As a recent survey of prefectural superintendents revealed, those policies which evoke the most divided responses are those which promise to spark the biggest local disruptions.[35] Uncertainty at the local level is then reflected in MOE uncertainty, and soon one has the beginnings of a breakdown in the internal consensus required to implement policy successfully.

The above analysis of *Nikkyōso* points to two basic characteristics of the opposition's role in education policy-making. First, the union's influence is almost entirely negative or reactive. As a force dedicated to maintaining the post-war system of 'democratic' and egalitarian education, its interest lies primarily in maintaining and 'substantializing' the status quo. Equally important, however, is the fact that its avenues of influence limit it to a role of *blocking* change. The demonstrations and strikes aimed at convincing conservatives that certain policy changes are too risky and the threats and use of local non-co-operation both are effective only at stopping change. The union has no significant means of contributing positively to the process of education reform – even if it wanted to.

Second, the analysis of the union reveals the degree to which its tactics depend on an indirect process of 'breaking the conservative consensus'. In the case of the union's strategy of local non-co-operation, *Nikkyōso*'s dependence on indirect influence is obvious. By making life difficult for school principals and local administrators, it initiates a process which it hopes will lead these actors (and possibly the MOE's more timid bureaucrats) to oppose change within the conservative camp. The direct cause of a policy being dropped may appear to be 'bureaucratic conservatism', but ultimately the union must be seen as having played an *indirect* role in encouraging that conservativism. Likewise, *Nikkyōso*'s three-step strategy aimed at convincing conservatives of the risks involved in aggressive education reform reveals a similar dependence on indirect influence. The direct cause of a policy not being pushed may appear to be 'a lack of interest on the part of many LDP members' while in fact the union may have played a part in convincing these elements to be disinterested.

UNIVERSITY GROUPS

Nikkyōso's opposition role in relation to elementary- and secondary-education policy has many parallels to the role of 'opposition interests' in the higher-education sector – such groups as *Nikkyōso*'s University Bureau; the Japan Scientists Association; the Japan Science Council; and the Association of National University Presidents (ANUP, *Kokudaikyō*). While these groups represent a broad range of ideologies, all are effectively conservative influences on the policy-making process. Concerned primarily with the goal of maintaining university autonomy, they tend to spend most of their energy defending the status quo and scuttling government attempts to give universities more 'leadership' and 'direction'. This section focuses on just one of these groups, the ANUP, examining how an organization seemingly so different from *Nikkyōso* plays a part in the process which is actually quite similar.

On first impressions, the ANUP seems hardly worthy of being called an 'opposition interest'. Composed of prestigious academic leaders recognized as having a role to play in formulating higher-education policy, it co-operates with the MOE to a degree which should exclude it from this category. Throughout the post-war period, leaders of the ANUP have been included in the policy-planning process while others have been excluded. In the latest round of education reform, one of the ANUP's former members served as the *chairman* of the AHCE while an active member served as the chairman of the council's subcommittee dealing with higher-education issues.[36]

Nevertheless, the group and individuals in it have played crucial roles in opposing government reform initiatives in the post-war period. Its opposition was particularly decisive in the first post-war decades as the government sought on several occasions to strengthen its control over the national universities. For example, when in the early 1960s the MOE attempted to introduce a comprehensive system of reforms aimed at centralizing power within universities and increasing the ministry's power over the selection of top administrators, the university presidents opposed *both* aspects of the initiative, rejecting even the proposals which would have strengthened their own authority within universities. Instead, they put forward their own plan proposing that prevailing, decentralized administrative procedures be largely maintained. The government was defeated.[37]

Since the mid-1960s, the opposition role of the ANUP has been much less direct. Many presidents have been sympathetic toward MOE views, and the ministry itself has sought to cultivate better relations with the ANUP. Still, the role presidents have played has had the effect of preventing significant university reform in either of the two recent initiatives. Perhaps the complex character of this opposition process can best be understood through an examination of the attitudes and role of one of its leaders: Nagoya University President Iijima Sōichi. An official of the left-leaning Japan Scientists Association as well as of the independent-minded Japan Science Council, Iijima is definitely not an MOE 'tool'. Although certainly more restrained than officials of the *Nikkyōso* University Bureau, he nevertheless speaks of the importance of university 'autonomy' and the need to reduce MOE control of national universities. The autonomy he seeks, he says, is 'real autonomy' – not the faculty idea of autonomy as 'having the faculty council decide everything' nor the 'outsider' idea of autonomy as having universities 'listen to society'. He wants universities to be able to make their own plans and carry them out without interference from the government.[38]

Despite this concern with increasing the independence of universities, however, Iijima served as one of the MOE's primary spokesmen on the AHCE. Concerned that the council might go too far with some of its ideas for university reform, the MOE actually *chose* Iijima and carefully arranged to have him named head of the higher-education subcommittee so that it would have a 'friend' in a crucial position.[39] The explanation for this paradoxical state of affairs lies in the subtle way in which the attitudes of MOE bureaucrats and university officials have converged in recent years. On the one hand, MOE officials and LDP *zoku* leaders, until recently intent on bringing the universities under tighter central control, have now come to accept that this is impossible. Some even speak of the need to *increase* university autonomy by allowing them more control over budget and planning decisions. Kida Hiroshi, representing the MOE line, and Kaifu Toshiki, representing the views of the LDP *zoku*, both express support for the idea of liberalized higher education.[40]

At the same time, university officials have come to realize that they do not want *too much* freedom. Faced with radical proposals for privatizing and incorporating public universities, university officials like Iijima have found themselves on the same side as the ministry in seeking to *maintain* government oversight. Not only the ANUP but also the more left-leaning university groups are opposed to this extent of liberalization. As

165

Iijima explained, 'I support the liberalization of universities, but not to the degree advocated by people like Amaya.'[41] Amaya Naohiro and a sector of the business community have been advocating the privatization (*mineika*) of national universities, a process which would involve the conversion of all university funding into block grants and the delegation of line item authority to individual universities. The MOE opposes the policy because it would be stripped of its control over national universities.[42] The ANUP and other opposition groups oppose it because they see it as a *zaikai* plot to reduce higher-education funding and increase business influence. Limited control by the government, they feel, is better than this proposed alternative. As in the case of the strange partnership between *Nikkyōso* and the ministry in opposition to the liberalization of compulsory education, therefore, academics and bureaucrats have become partners in favour of the status quo. The only difference is that this latter partnership, due to the prestige of organizations like the ANUP, has been officially recognized through such mechanisms as representation on the Ad Hoc Council.

Interestingly, this collusion in favour of the status quo – most visible in these groups' opposition to privatization proposals – recently seems to have grown to include a 'truce' in other areas of the administrative reform debate as well. Whereas the MOE until as recently as 1973 was vigorously pushing for reforms to centralize administrative control within universities, it recently seems to have limited its demands to rhetoric rather than action. Again, the crucial actor in this development has been the ANUP. On the one hand, its officials realize better than anyone the difficulty of managing universities given the current extent of fragmentation. Iijima, for example, complained that he faces limits on his authority from both sides: the MOE makes all of the money decisions and has to approve all plans while on the other side he must satisfy demands from numerous faculty blocks.[43] Still, these officials also realize the difficulty of changing the system. Knowing the opposition they would personally have to deal with were they to support real changes in the balance of administrative power, most are not willing to take the initiative. They will support the MOE position in principle but hesitate to put it into practice.

As noted above, the ANUP was actually forced to take sides in the 1960s debate over proposals to centralize administrative power within universities – and it came out in opposition. More recently, the group has succeeded in avoiding the question. Iijima, while speaking of the need for greater central authority, did not push any concrete proposals towards such an end in his capacity as head of the AHCE higher-education subcommittee. As will be seen in Chapter 8, the AHCE in the end decided merely to postpone the debate over university administration and delegated it to a new University Council. Once again, the status quo was the victor.

OPPOSITION PARTIES

Excluded from most of the policy-making process leading up to Diet deliberations and outnumbered by the LDP majority there, Japan's opposition parties play a relatively minor role in developing education policy. First, they are systematically excluded from the crucial early interaction between the MOE and LDP. They do not get seats on MOE advisory councils. Legislative proposals usually do not even arrive in the Diet until this entire process has been completed. Even in their role as representatives of the opposition, they have only a limited part. Much of what the opposition is able to accomplish is achieved through pressure at the site of implementation – through confrontations in the schools and universities rather than at the national level. Even at the national level, the central organizations of opposition groups such as *Nikkyōso* do most of their negotiating for themselves.

Nevertheless, the opposition parties do play a part in the overall opposition strategy. Basing their arguments and tactics on the assumption that education requires a higher standard of democracy than mere majority rule, the parties seek: (1) to show that the government does not meet it, and (2) to demand compromises when the government seeks to demonstrate broader support for its policies. Were such a standard not in place, the LDP could simply pass its policies through the Diet on majority votes and smoothly implement its complete education agenda. That it has not been able to do so is due partly to the role of the minor parties in *creating* and *taking advantage of* a more-than-majority standard of democracy for education policy.

Creating a higher standard of democracy

The important role of *Nikkyōso* in articulating the argument that education policies must meet a higher standard of democracy has already been described. The opposition parties – especially the Japan Socialist Party and the Japan Communist Party (JCP, *Nihon kyōsantō*) – work to dramatize that position. Facing unilateral attempts by the LDP to push through policies aimed at centralizing government control of the education system, both parties have been vocal and sometimes even violent in their opposition. At various times since the war – particularly in the late 1950s – they have employed almost all of the disruptive tactics at the disposal of opposition parties in Japan: boycotts of Diet deliberations, physical attempts to seize control of the speaker's chair and disruptions of Diet votes.[44] While these demonstrations do not prevent the LDP from 'forcing' a measure through the Diet on a majority vote, they make the LDP (and the public) realize that to 'force' a resolution would be an admission that the party was practising aggressive, 'tyranny of the majority'-style democracy. Combined with the argument that education is a special, 'sensitive' issue requiring 'the agreement of the whole people', these tactics have the effect of raising the standard of democracy with regard to the education issue.

Over the years, the way in which the opposition parties have repeatedly confronted the LDP on education issues has definitely affected the party's Diet strategy. After an initial period in the 1950s when several key education issues were 'forced', the LDP has by and large avoided direct clashes. As the comment of Morita Tomio above indicated, the party has learnt that it must create at least the surface appearance of wide support for its education policies. This attempt to create a broader base thus sets the stage for the second step in the opposition strategy.

Taking advantage of the higher standard

In a few cases, opposition party tactics have convinced the LDP to abandon its legislative proposals – usually because the party has higher legislative priorities which it does not want to jeopardize. More often, the tactics succeed in convincing the LDP to offer concessions in an effort to win multi-party support or just as the price for avoiding Diet disruption. Thus in 1973-4, for example, JSP opposition to the government's legislation designed to raise teachers' salaries and create a new five-grade scale eventually convinced the LDP to abandon the new salary scale. The amended law was passed with unanimous support (see Chapter 7).

In the more recent round of reform, legislative activity centred on the 1984 law establishing the AHCE. The JSP and JCP were strongly opposed to the bill's provision making the council an organ of the Prime Minister's Office. While the more moderate Democratic Socialist Party (DSP, *Minshatō*) and *Kōmeitō* ('the Clean Government Party') were willing to support the Prime Minister, they too demanded certain concessions. Nakasone, publicly committed to an education reform process which was 'politically neutral', was thus forced to compromise in order to meet the higher standard of democracy by the opposition. First and most significantly, he decided to insert a clause in the AHCE establishment legislation committing the council to 'respect the spirit of the Fundamental Law of Education'. Later, under continued pressure from the DSP and *Kōmeitō*, he agreed to accept two amendments to the law providing for Diet approval of his appointments of council members and requiring the council to submit its reports to the Diet as well as the Prime Minister. Particularly the FLE compromise represented a significant concession. Many in the party had hoped to avoid a commitment to the law since any such concession would seriously limit the council's ability to re-examine the post-war settlement.[45] In effect, the opposition had forced the LDP to abide by the basic document defining the status quo in post-war education.

CONCLUSIONS

In the final analysis, the influence of opposition interests in the education policy-making process presents a paradox. On the one hand, their formal and direct influence is very limited. Confined to permanent outsider status, they are excluded from almost all aspects of the regular policy-making process. They can demand 'consensus' and insist that their views be respected, but in the end the government can enact any policy to which it is strongly committed. As in the case of certain teacher-training programmes and the new bonus for *shunin* teacher-managers, the

169

recent rounds of reform have included several examples of the inability of opposition groups to prevent the government from implementing reform proposals to which the government was particularly committed.

On the other hand, this chapter has pointed to the important indirect and unofficial influence of opposition groups. They can raise the standard of democracy required to implement education reform policies and are able to prevent the implementation of at least some reforms by 'breaking the conservative consensus'. By using national 'movements' and Diet disruptions to make timid conservatives less interested in reform, by using local non-co-operation to convince local officials to convince MOE officials to oppose change, and by extracting compromises in the Diet, opposition groups have often been able to influence the outcomes of education reform debates. While each of these methods relies on indirect influence, it is influence nevertheless. As in the case of the government's failure to implement the CCE proposal on pilot projects and its inability to rewrite the FLE, the government's recent reform initiatives have included numerous cases in which opposition interests have made a difference.

In effect, opposition groups are both powerful and powerless. On their own, they can do virtually nothing. Thus, when the LDP and MOE can remain united on the need for some change, opposition interests are powerless to stop it. By preventing the MOE and LDP from agreeing on the need for change, however, they are sometimes able to block the most controversial government initiatives. *Through other actors*, they do play a part. The following two chapters – providing a comprehensive review of education reform between 1967 and 1987 – reveal numerous examples of both patterns.

7

Education reform in the 1970s

The key actors in Japan's education reform debate having all been introduced, the stage has finally been set for an examination of the actual drama of the policy-making process. Focusing respectively on the two major reform initiatives of the period under study, this chapter and the one which follows examine the complex interactions of the LDP, the MOE and the numerous interest groups concerned with education – illuminating the various policy-making patterns outlined in the previous chapters. The bureaucratic conservatism of the education *genba* and the MOE 'mainstream', the divisions within the LDP, and the process whereby 'opposition interests' help break the conservative consensus are all visible in the events of Japan's twenty-year debate over education reform. By finally bringing all of the actors together, these chapters reveal the full extent of the disagreement within the conservative camp. At the same time, by examining the education reform process in its full complexity – rather than in the actor-centred manner of the previous section – these chapters for the first time allow the reader to view the process as an integrated whole.

Both this chapter (focusing on the 1970s reform movement) and the following chapter (examining the Nakasone initiative) present a detailed chronology of the respective rounds of reform. Each begins with an examination of the way in which the reform processes were *initiated* and proceeds to follow their *deliberations and decisions* and the *implementation* of those decisions.

THE INITIATION OF REFORM

On 3 July 1967 the Minister of Education, Kennoki Toshihiro, issued a formal 'request for advice' (*shimon*) to the Central Council on Education, calling on the MOE's premier advisory organ to deliberate on 'basic guidelines for the development of an integrated educational system suited for contemporary society'. His action marked the formal initiation of the education reform process which culminated in the CCE's publication of a comprehensive set of reform proposals in 1971, a set of recommendations which effectively set the agenda for Japanese education policy-making in the 1970s and into the 1980s. While the events leading up to the CCE reform initiative and the issues which prompted it were surveyed in Chapter 2, the analysis of the previous set of chapters provides the basis for a more systematic evaluation in this chapter of the first stages of the reform process: what individuals and institutional actors were involved in initiating CCE deliberations and choosing the council's members in 1967, and how did these early steps help shape policy-making outcomes?

From the beginning the CCE reform initiative was an MOE project. The Minister of Education (Kennoki) officially issued the crucial 'request for advice' and appointed the council's members. The text of the *shimon* and other accompanying documents were drafted by bureaucrats in the MOE Planning Office and reflected the approval and input of all top officials in the ministry. These same officials also had a significant degree of input into the make-up of the council's membership. The LDP was only superficially involved at this stage. Kennoki confirmed in an interview that he had consulted with his colleagues in the LDP, but he could remember only that the chairman of the party's Education Division had cleared the text of the *shimon*.[1]

While the MOE as a whole was thus responsible for the CCE initiation, it was a smaller group within the MOE which was most active. According to accounts given in interviews, the men most involved in setting the council off on its reformist course were Morito Tatsuo, the reselected chairman of the CCE, and Amagi Isao, a top MOE bureaucrat long active in working with the CCE. Morito, a post-war moderate Socialist who had been minister of education under the Occupation at the time the 6−3−3−4 system reforms were introduced, had emerged from that experience convinced that the Occupation had gone too far in tampering with the Japanese education system. Feeling responsible for those 'excesses', he had devoted a great deal of time and energy since then in an effort to cleanse the system of Occupation influence. He was a 'specialist member' (*tokubetsu iin*) of the very first CCE (1953–5) and a full member of every council since that time – serving as chairman from 1963.[2] As a veteran of the struggle to right the perceived mistakes of the Occupation, he therefore had a great deal of influence on the MOE's education reform strategy. According to Kida Hiroshi (a senior bureaucrat at the time), it was Morito who was most responsible for the initiation of CCE deliberations in 1967.[3]

Also very involved, however, was Amagi Isao.[4] Up to this point, Amagi had served in a whole series of MOE posts in which he had worked with the CCE on education reform. As a young official, he was posted to the ministry's Research and Propagation Bureau where he worked with the council on some of its first attempts to rewrite the post-war reforms. He went on to serve as bureau chief of this bureau and, later, the University and Science Bureau. In each of these posts he had regular dealings with the council and developed a strong taste for education reform. Fluent in English and a regular participant in international conventions on education policy, he had a tendency to search the world for reform ideas which Japan could consider. As Kida described him, 'He looked at Japanese education with a knowledge of all sorts of things going on in the world.'[5] He was the central character of the MOE group known as the 'internationalists'.

It was these two men, then, who most significantly affected the tone of the CCE's deliberations through their active involvement in the initiation process. A close examination of the ministry's 'request for advice' and the membership of the council reveals the way in which they helped shape the course of the council's deliberations (and ultimately its recommendations). On the surface, the *shimon* was very open-ended: it called simply for a comprehensive review of the education system. A look at the fine print, however, reveals that it did point in a particular direction. In a section explaining the reason for the ministry's 'request for advice', the *shimon* gave specific guidance. The council, it suggested, should examine the structure and content of the entire education system from three perspectives:

173

1 The need for school education to meet the demands of society and the nation and provide equality of opportunity.
2 The need for education to be responsive to the stages of human development and the various abilities and aptitudes of individuals.
3 The need for an effective and proper allocation of responsibility for educational expenses.

While still not very specific, the text contained several phrases which held special significance in the Japanese education reform debate. The phrase 'demands of society' and the reference to the need for an education system capable of responding to 'the various abilities and aptitudes of individuals' both pointed in the direction of *diversification*: the need for changes in the single-track structure of the 6−3−3−4 system at a time when formerly elite upper secondary schools and universities were having to accommodate a widening ability range. At the same time, the reference to the need for an education system suited to the 'stages of human development' suggested that the 6−3−3 system was perhaps scientifically inappropriate in terms of the way in which it divided the years of school education.

An accompanying document issued by the MOE AVM, however, was even more to the point. This 'complementary explanation' (*hosoku setsumei*) issued along with the *shimon* identified several specific issues which it said were 'being raised by society': the idea of making kindergarten education compulsory, the lowering of the school starting age and steps to deal with the need for greater continuity between lower and upper secondary education. In addition, it suggested the possible need for changes in the system of higher education, notably the idea of 'dividing it into classes' (*shūbetsuka*).[6] It was therefore suggesting that the council consider changes in the structure of the entire education system. As will be seen in the following section, these ideas were each to become central elements of the CCE's reform recommendations.

The second important element of the initiation of CCE deliberations was the selection of the council's members. As in the case of other MOE advisory councils, the membership of the CCE was selected with an eye towards influencing the eventual outcome of its deliberation. First, the decision to keep Morito as chairman indicated a clear commitment to significant reform. The other veteran members selected in 1967 and remaining until

1971 (Hosokawa, Hiratsuka and Fujii) were also committed to reform. Hosokawa had been a member of the CCE since 1957 and was a vocal proponent of removing Occupation influence from the post-war system. Hiratsuka had acquired a reputation for being a rather outspoken advocate of education reform during his tenure as head of the National Institute for Educational Research, the research arm of the MOE. And Fujii, the chairman of the *Keizai dōyūkai* Education Committee, was associated with that organization's calls for radical changes. In addition, Ōizumi and Koga – both given key positions in the management of the council – were veterans of numerous MOE councils and thus were experienced in working with the ministry and specifically with Amagi. One will note that the bulk of the CCE members signing their names to the 1971 report only joined the deliberations at the half-way point. Clearly, this gave a large advantage to those veteran reform-minded members returning from the preliminary stage of the discussions. See Table 7.1 for a complete list of members.

All of these early manipulations – the choice of council members and the phrasing of the minister's *shimon* – thus contributed to the eventual shape of the 1971 CCE reform package. Given that it was composed of a group of men (and one woman) generally antipathetic towards the post-war 6–3–3–4 system, the council was predisposed to favour changes in the structure of the nation's education system. Given the *shimon's* emphasis on the need for education to respond to the diverse abilities of individuals, the council was destined to recommend changes in the structure of the system which would create alternatives to the single-track options at the secondary- and higher-education levels. Moreover, given the emphasis on matching the education system to 'the stages of human development', the council was bound to come out in favour of structural changes which would lower the school starting age (in recognition of the similar developmental needs of 5 year olds and 6 year olds) and join the lower and upper secondary schools (in recognition of the need for continuity in adolescent education). As the following section reveals, these ideas of system reform were to form the backbone of the CCE reform package.

Table 7.1 The membership of the Central Council on Education (1971)

Names	Appointed 1967–71*	Affiliations
Morito Tatsuo (Chairman)	Yes	Veteran CCE member (since 1955); former minister of education
Ōizumi Takashi (Vice-chairman)	Yes	Jōchi University professor with service on other MOE councils
Hiratsuka Masunori (Chair of the Elementary and Secondary Education Subcommittee)	Yes	Head of the National Institution for Educational Research – an MOE affiliate
Koga Issaku (Chair of the Higher Education Subcommittee)	Yes	Counsellor to KDD Corporation, former University of Tokyo professor, with service on other MOE councils
Hosokawa Ryūgen	Yes	Veteran CCE member (since 1957) and 'critic' (hyōronka)
Fujii Heigo	Yes	A top official of Keizai dōyūkai and vice-president of the New Japan Steel Corporation
Yorozu Naoji	Yes	Chairman of Nihon keizai shimbun Company
Sakamoto Hikotarō	Yes	A retired MOE official, and a professor at Aoyama Gakuin University
Abe Kenichi	No	Former president of Waseda University
Arimitsu Jirō	No	A retired top MOE official and president of Tokyo Kasei University
Kawamori Yoshizō	No	Critic and a former professor
Shinojima Hideo	No	President of Mitsubishi Chemical Company
Sōma Yukiko	No	Critic and the only woman
Takahashi Sanae	No	Ex-elementary school principal
Fukushima Tsuneharu	No	Ex-lower secondary school principal
Fujita Kenji	No	Former Ochanomizu University president
Horio Masao	No	Honorary professor of the University of Kyoto

Table 7.1 – *continued*

Names	Appointed 1967–71*	Affiliations
Yoshida Hisashi	No	Upper secondary school principal
Rōyama Masamichi	No	Chairman of the Tokyo Board of Education and former professor

* The work of the CCE leading to the 1971 report was divided into two parts: 1967–9 and 1969–71. Only some members were named to both phases – indicated by 'yes'. The remaining members only served for the latter part of the deliberations. Yoshida, in fact, only served the final seven months – replacing another upper secondary school principal.

Sources: Mombushō, *Chūō kyōiku shingikai yōran*, 8th edn, 1979; *AN*, 1972, p. 511; and various editions of *Jinji kōshinroku*.

DELIBERATIONS AND DECISIONS

For the next four years, between July 1967 and June 1971, the education reform process was centred on the deliberations of the CCE. A careful analysis of the developments in this period, however, reveals that much larger forces were involved: the CCE was merely the battleground. On the one hand, Amagi's group of 'internationalists' (commanded by Nishida Kikuo in his capacity as head of the CCE's MOE-run secretariat) sought to have their vision of education reform endorsed by the council – supported in this campaign by vocal elements in the business community and by some members of the LDP. On the other hand, MOE mainstream bureaucrats – urged on by the conservative education establishment – began their counter-attack. The aim of this latter group was to prevent disruptive changes in the established system.

The first two years: 1967–9

The first two years of the CCE's deliberations – overshadowed by the drama of student protests in the nation's universities – passed without significant controversy. While a subcommittee of the council was called on to produce an emergency recommendation regarding the government's plans for dealing with

177

the crisis in the universities, the rest of the CCE continued with its examination of the historical development of Japanese education in the 100 years since the Meiji Restoration. Its evaluation – contained in a 'mid-term report' published in June 1969 – sought to establish a base of 'facts' about the history and performance of Japanese education in an attempt to provide a firm foundation for its comprehensive reform programme still to come.[7]

Once again in this period, however, the council was subtly being led by the MOE 'internationalists'. The facts supplied by the council's secretariat were neatly arranged to support the type of reforms favoured by Amagi's group.[8] The central character in this process was Nishida Kikuo – the head of the CCE secretariat and a man committed to reforming the Japanese educational system on the basis of his theories about how the education system should work. (For a brief profile, see Chapter 4.) Suzuki Shigenobu, a 'specialist' member of the CCE, recalled how Nishida used his facts:

Nishida had this way of putting together all sorts of supporting documents and building his arguments from these. I don't think there was ever a CCE staff member who was as thorough in this way as Nishida. He didn't force his opinion on us but rather did an excellent job of putting forth his arguments. As a result, his contributions sparked no antipathy or ill feeling but instead led us to agree that there *was* a problem.[9]

The way in which Nishida guided the council was therefore very unobtrusive. Already sympathetic towards the reformism of Nishida and the other MOE 'internationalists', council members did not need very much convincing.[10]

The second two years: 1969–71

In July 1969 the CCE was convened with a new group of members, only eight of whom were returning (see Table 7.1). Divided into two subcommittees – one on elementary and secondary education and the other on higher education – its task was to devise a comprehensive programme for reform in each of these areas. Almost immediately there were signs that Nishida's task of guiding the council towards agreement on his favoured reform programme would not be easy. The Ministry of Education itself, it became clear, was not united on the question of whether significant education reform was necessary. Suzuki relates the following incident: on one occasion early in the third year of the council's deliberations, the issue of whether to change the structure of the 6–3–3 system was raised. An MOE official in attendance and the two former MOE bureaucrats among the council's membership (Arimitsu and Sakamoto) suggested that changes in the *structure* of the system were not necessary. The 6–3–3 system was fine, they said. The important thing was to increase the MOE budget. Hearing this, a more reformist member (Hosokawa) exploded: 'What are you saying! Look at the University of Tokyo, the *funsō*, the riot! *They* are the result of the post-war reforms. Who's responsible for that?' The MOE official and the two former officials reacted to this by becoming very quiet. The chairman Morito then broke the silence with what Suzuki described as one of his rare comments. Taking responsibility for his role in implementing the Occupation reforms, he blamed the 6–3–3 system for 'preventing Japan from becoming a spiritually strong nation again' and urged the council to address the 'problem' of the post-war system. The MOE representative and the two former officials were left speechless.[11]

If this episode reveals the strength of reformist sentiment within the council, it also reveals that the MOE mainstream was not in agreement. Whereas the council had been working towards reform under the influence of Nishida and Amagi, it would henceforth have to deal with a whole range of opinions within the MOE and in the education establishment. The final two years of the council's work would therefore be taken up in an effort to find common ground in a divided conservative camp. The course of this process with respect to several of the most contentious issues is summarized below.

Reform of the 6–3–3 system

In seeking to arrive at a recommendation on this most controversial issue, the reformists were handicapped by the fact that they could not agree on what division of years should replace the 6–3–3 structure. Among those recommended by various interest groups during this period were: 6–4–4, 5–4–4–4 and 6–3–5.[12] Amagi and Nishida, as was clear from their early manipulations of the council, were in favour of considering

179

changes in the system which would involve lowering the school starting age and joining lower and upper secondary schools. Nevertheless, they were not sure that such changes would produce the *best* system. The solution, they concluded, would be to initiate 'experiments' (*jikken*) aimed at determining which system would work best.

By May 1970 when the CCE's subcommittee on elementary and secondary education produced the first 'draft' of its 'basic course of reform', this idea had developed into a programme calling for the establishment of 'pilot projects' (*sendōteki shikō*) which would be 'the first step' in a process leading towards the total reform of the system in the near future. Specifically, this early draft suggested that pilot projects would be set up to examine the feasibility of the following alternatives to the 6−3−3 system: 4−4−4, 4−5−5, 4−4−6 and 5−4−4.[13] The idea of pilot projects − including the term itself − originated from within the CCE−Nishida−Amagi nexus. They decided that the best way to determine which system would be best for Japan would be to set up alternative school systems as part of a controlled experiment.[14] Sakata Michita, the Minister of Education (1968−71) and an influential LDP education activist, was persuaded to support the plan, but other party members were not significantly involved and seem to have wanted the CCE to endorse a particular structural change.[15] Active support for it was thus limited to two groups: the CCE and the MOE 'internationalists'.

In the period following the first announcement of the CCE's plan to set up 'pilot projects', the proposal encountered strong objections. Within the council, the elementary school principal (Takahashi) refused to support any plan which would reduce the number of years of primary schools.[16] His association − the National Association of Elementary School Principals − came out opposed to the idea, as did a number of other associations of educational administrators.[17] Most significantly, voices within the MOE began to express doubts. Because Amagi − the new AVM (1969−71) − was firmly in support of the pilot projects proposal, few officials spoke out openly against the proposal. A few, however, sent out signals indicating their opposition. Miyaji Shigeru − the chief of the Elementary and Secondary Education Bureau − stopped attending meetings on the subject, sending his deputy instead.[18]

The final recommendation of the CCE − contained in its report of 11 June 1971 − remained committed to the idea of pilot projects. Calling specifically for experimental schools to test the ideas of an earlier school-starting age and integrated secondary schools, it endorsed testing exactly those reforms which the MOE 'internationalists' had long envisaged. Even the arguments used in the report (the need 'to clarify on a scientific basis their relative effectiveness in promoting human development') echoed the wording of the 1967 *shimon*. Nevertheless, the proposal represented a slight retreat from the 'draft' of a year earlier. Rather than describing the projects as 'a first step' towards broader reform, it described them only as an exercise which would be evaluated after ten years to determine what (*if any*) permanent action would be taken.[19]

Kindergarten expansion

A related issue in CCE deliberations was that of kindergarten expansion. As noted above, the idea of making kindergarten compulsory had been put to the CCE as part of its original set of instructions. In its first draft in May 1970, the council – reporting that many localities did not have a single kindergarten – endorsed a bold policy calling for the government to require that all cities, towns and villages provide their residents with the opportunity to attend kindergarten.[20] When it released its 'basic course for reform' in November 1970, the council went even further: it proposed that nursery schools serving 4 and 5 year olds be allowed to qualify as kindergartens as part of a campaign to enrol all children of those ages in kindergartens.[21]

Both of these proposals, however, encountered objections from segments of the education 'establishment'. The association representing the 70 per cent of kindergartens which were private strongly objected to the government's plan to require localities to establish new institutions. These would be public and would thus take business away from the private sector.[22] In addition, the proposals were strongly attacked by the Ministry of Health and Welfare – representing the nursery schools under its jurisdiction. In Japan, nursery schools providing day-care services for the children of working mothers compete with kindergartens. Four and 5 year olds may attend either type of institution. The MOE was arguing at this time (and continues to argue) that 5 year olds in particular should attend education-orientated kindergartens. The MHW saw the MOE's proposals, however, as an invasion of its area of responsibility. In order to guarantee that its interests were considered, the MHW arranged to have its own advisory council (the Central Council on Child Welfare) publish a report on the exact day the CCE report was due.[23]

Though the CCE's final recommendations on kindergarten expansion was still ambitious, it represented something of a retreat from its earlier drafts. It no longer proposed to have nursery schools recognized as kindergartens, suggesting that 25 per cent of 4 and 5 year olds should attend the MHW institutions. It did propose, however, that children receiving MHW (nursery school) grants be allowed to attend kindergartens, and proposed to 'guarantee the opportunity of enrolment to all 5-year-old children who wish to go to kindergartens'. Although it still recommended that localities in areas with a shortage of kindergartens be required to establish such institutions, it put off any decision on whether to mandate attendance for 5 year olds.[24]

University reforms

When the CCE deliberations began in 1967 the structure of the university system was also a target for major reform. The council members of the pre-war generation (most of them) had grown up with a higher-education system which sharply differentiated between the elite national universities and lesser institutions. The Occupation reforms, however, had reorganized all institutions of higher education into four-year 'universities' and had reduced the ability of national universities to provide a high level of specialized training by requiring all students to spend their first two years taking 'general' courses. Given their background in the elite and specialized pre-war system, men like Morito saw the post-war system as inferior.

As in the case of the 6−3−3 reforms, however, the CCE could not agree on how to right the Occupation 'mistake'. One camp proposed that 'general' education be abolished and that the higher-education system be divided into 'diverse parallel tracks' (*tayō heiritsu gata*): two- or three-year institutions would provide courses in the humanities and the social sciences while elite five-year universities would provide scientists with specialized training up to Masters level. This idea was backed most notably by certain business interests and the more politically ideological CCE members. On the other hand, key academics on the council and the Nishida-run secretariat backed another proposal which called for the creation of a new class of graduate universities as a basis for recreating 'an elite course' (*besshu tsumiage gata*): the bulk of students would complete their studies at three-year 'general universities' while the best students would continue their education in graduate schools.[25] Either plan would have radically altered the nature of Japanese higher education.

In the event, neither plan gained enough support. The university 'establishment' opposed the plans, and they were not enthusiastically greeted by the section of the MOE dealing regularly with higher education – the University and Science Bureau. According to a journalist who covered the CCE process, the chief of the Bureau (Murayama Matsuo) opposed even the relatively innocuous final proposal.[26] The CCE's final report called for a policy of 'dividing into classes' (*shubetsuka*) the various institutions of higher education. Some would be classified as universities offering a relatively general education while others would be classed as specialized institutions. The most significant change provided for an increased emphasis on graduate schools – with these institutions being made more open to older students so as to allow retraining. There was no provision, however, for them to be made the focus of a new elite track.[27]

In addition to considering the proposals for the structural reform of higher education, the CCE also dealt with the issue of university administration. Particularly after the *funsō*, the council devoted a great deal of its time to the consideration of proposals aimed at ending the supposed insularity and immobilism of the universities. The CCE endorsed policies in both of these areas in its final report, recommending that universities should be made more open (through the participation of learned persons from outside the universities in their administration) and more rational (by strengthening central authorities).[28]

Once again, however, the council failed to line up firmly behind a specific plan. The business community and its supporters on the council backed a relatively radical plan calling for the government to transform all national universities into autonomous public corporations responsible for their own administration (*hōjinka*). Many in the MOE, however, favoured less drastic change. The end result was that the CCE came out with a fairly ambiguous recommendation: it suggested that the government rewrite its laws so that national universities would be able to 'choose' a new administrative structure. They could elect to become 'a new type of corporation' (much as business had proposed) or they could choose to adopt a 'new administrative organ' – a central administrative board including individuals from outside the university.[29] Clearly, this was a major retreat from what the reformers wanted to accomplish. It was unlikely that any established university would freely *choose* to accept the kinds of reforms the government was proposing.

Reforms concerning teachers

Another set of reforms which featured prominently in the final CCE report were those aimed at improving the quality of the teaching corps. There were four main proposals: (1) *salary reform*, a proposal that all starting salaries for teachers be increased by some 30 to 40 per cent while at the same time reforming the structure of the salary scale and providing certain bonuses (including the controversial bonus for *shunin*); (2) *master teachers*, a related reform calling for the creation of a new class of teachers having undergone retraining at new graduate teacher-training universities; (3) *teachers' colleges*, a plan to encourage more teachers (particularly at the elementary school level) to receive their original training at teachers' colleges rather than at regular universities or junior colleges; and (4) *the shiho proposal*, a plan calling for all teachers to be required to undergo a probationary year of on-the-job training.

Interestingly, such proposals had not been mentioned at the time the MOE set the council to work in 1967 and had not even been foreshadowed in the 1969 'mid-term report'. The reforms thus represented a relatively late addition to the CCE programme. This fact raises the question of where exactly they came from. It seems certain that the late interest in teacher reforms at least partly reflected the LDP's special concern with policies dealing with teachers. Nishioka Takeo, a young parliamentary vice-minister at the time, takes personal credit for one proposal in particular: the recommendation that teachers' salaries be increased by 30 to 40 per cent.[30] Nevertheless, the role of the LDP at this time was primarily indirect. The actual job of convincing the CCE to recommend various teacher reform policies was again undertaken by Nishida. It was he who convinced the council to back the *shiho* plan and again he who conceived of the plan to give *shunin* teacher-managers a special bonus.[31] The development of the reforms is outlined briefly in what follows.

The proposal for *salary reform* was added late in the reform process and attracted relatively little criticism. In fact, the *shunin* proposal which was to become one of the most controversial outgrowths of the CCE initiative was not even mentioned in newspaper articles reporting the publication of the final report.[32] The final plan called for starting salaries to be increased by 30 to 40 per cent and recommended that the salary scale be adjusted to recognize two new classes of teachers. Under the old system, the scale recognized only three classes: principals, regular teachers and assistant teachers. The reforms called for the creation of two new classes: a class for assistant principals (*kyōtō*) and a class of master teachers (*jōkyū kyōyu*). In addition, it recommended that schools be organized to recognize the special roles played by the chief instructor, the teachers in charge of each grade, the subject director, the chief counsellor and so on (a group collectively known as *shunin*). These middle managers, it suggested, should be given a bonus.[33]

One aspect of the salary reforms, as indicated, was the plan to provide extra remuneration for a new class of *master teachers*. Although this proposal – mooted first in the May 1970 draft – was criticized by the teachers' union as an attempt to create an elite corps of teachers sympathetic towards the government, it was included in the final report largely as it had been originally outlined. The final report spelled out the proposal in some detail, proposing that graduate universities capable of retraining 2,000 veteran teachers be established for the express purpose of training master teachers.[34]

The proposal to encourage teachers to be trained in *teachers' colleges* – first contained in the CCE's November 1970 draft – reflected government dissatisfaction with the post-war teacher-training system which allowed individuals to qualify as teachers with only a minimum of credits at a regular university. As noted in Chapter 2, teachers in the pre-war period were trained in 'normal schools' specializing in teacher-training. The CCE recommendations were an attempt to re-establish the emphasis on specialist training by re-emphasizing teachers' colleges. The teachers' union, however, considered the proposal too reminiscent of the pre-war system and thus strongly opposed it.[35] The council's final recommendation remained committed to the goal of having more teachers trained in teachers' colleges but was not specific in outlining how that goal was to be achieved.[36]

The November draft which first mentioned the council's plan to re-emphasize teachers' colleges also contained first mention of its plan to resurrect the old *shiho* proposal. The idea of requiring new teachers to undergo a probationary training year had been proposed several times previously in the immediate post-Occupation period but had been dropped after sparking strong opposition.[37] The teachers' union in particular saw the proposal as an attempt to brainwash new teachers and force them to stay out of the union. The MOE and the LDP, however, remained attached to the idea: the MOE emphasized the need for more on-the-job training while the LDP in particular saw the probationary year as a way of encouraging teachers to develop 'proper attitudes' towards their profession. In the lead-up to the final report, it seems that some ministry officials actually counselled against the probationary aspect of the training-year proposal. They considered the proposal that new teachers be given a 'special employment status' (*tokubetsu-na mibun*) during their training year inappropriate under the Japanese government's system of employment and worried that talented potential teachers would be deterred from joining the profession.[38] The final report reflected MOE worries. It endorsed the plan for a training year but suggested only that the government 'should consider' the idea of giving these trainee teachers a 'special status'. It also reflected MOE concern about the effect of the provision on hiring: the idea of probation, it said, should be studied while giving due consideration to recruitment.[39]

Other reforms

The above were the most controversial proposals contained in the CCE's 1971 report. They were the ones which dominated the headlines and preoccupied the editorial-writers. Nevertheless, there were several other significant proposals including the following: the council's commitment to diversification was reflected not only in its plans for structural changes but also in its plans for *curriculum reform*. Specifically, it proposed the introduction of ability- and interest-based streaming, grade-skipping, and the establishment of a wider selection of special-ized courses in academic upper secondary schools.[40] At the higher-education level, the proposal which in the end had more of an impact than any of the controversial reforms discussed above was the council's recommendation that the government greatly increase its financial support for private universities and that it include private universities in a new systematic programme of planning for higher education.[41] Neither of these reforms was the subject of significant conflict within the conservative camp in the CCE deliberative stage. Both are discussed in more detail in the following section.

IMPLEMENTATION

The analysis above revealed that the CCE's 1971 recommendations – while still far-reaching – had already been scaled back as a result of the interplay between the reformists and conservatives within the MOE and as a result of criticism from various interest groups. The university reforms had been greatly moderated, relying primarily on the willingness of universities themselves to initiate changes. The wording of recommendations on both pilot projects (they were no longer to be a definite 'first step' towards broader reform) and the *shiho* proposal (it was only to be 'considered') both represented a retreat from the bold endorsements reformers had been seeking. The proposal for an expansion of kindergartens had also been somewhat scaled back. These slight concessions, however, were insignificant compared to those which followed in the implementation period. In that stage – with the reform project no longer in the hands of Nishida and his MOE 'internationalists' – the cracks which had already been visible in the conservative consensus grew into gaping fissures which prevented reform across a whole range of issues.

Progressive camp opposition

Immediately upon its publication, the CCE's 1971 report encountered a storm of criticism. The most vocal attacks, as might be expected, came from the progressive camp. *Nikkyōso*, in its first formal response to the CCE plan, criticized the council's proposals as an attempt to 'revive pre-war governmental authority over education contrary to the Constitution and the Fundamental Law of Education'. Taking particular issue with the council's diversification proposals, the union repeatedly used terms like 'discriminatory' and 'against the idea of democratic education'.[42] Likewise, the president of the University of Tokyo, expressing the view of the Association of National University Presidents, attacked the CCE higher-education proposals for their continued emphasis on government-dominated solutions.[43]

The media sided with the opposition, publishing numerous editorials opposed to the implementation of the council's proposals. The *Mainichi*, for example, stressed the failure of the government to consider the opinions of those most involved in education and concluded that education reform can only be built on 'the complete understanding and consent of the people' (*kokumin no zenpantekina rikai to nattoku*).[44] The rhetoric of the opposition is interesting because it followed the general pattern outlined in Chapter 6: an insistence that education reform must meet a higher standard of democracy (a 'consensus') followed by an attempt to illustrate how the government failed to meet that standard. By demanding consideration of their views and at the same time making those views totally incompatible with the reform plan, the opposition sought to discredit the entire CCE project.

Opposition within the conservative camp

Opposition to CCE proposals, however, also came from within the conservative camp. The MHW advisory council, asserting that nursery schools had an important role to play in caring for pre-school children, demanded that the MOE consult with it before instituting a major programme of kindergarten expansion.[45] The Japan Private Kindergarten Coalition was more direct, arguing that the council's proposals would 'cause chaos' in the kindergartens.[46] It was the pilot project proposal, however, which aroused the most opposition among conservative groups. The three national associations of school principals (elementary, lower secondary and upper secondary) all testified against the MOE's decision to concentrate on projects structured on a 4−4−6 basis. The elementary school principals in particular insisted that the 6−3−3 system should be maintained.[47]

Despite the protests, the government showed signs of actual commitment to the CCE reform programme in the early days following publication of the council's final report. Prime Minister Satō, speaking on behalf of the LDP, declared that 'the government is committed to endeavouring with its utmost effort to achieve education reform in accordance with the aspirations of the people'.[48] Towards such an end, the Ministry of Education on the very day it received the CCE report announced a

seven-point plan for implementing the council's reform programme and set up an Education Reform Promotion Bureau
(*Kyōiku kaikaku suishin hombu*) under the leadership of the
vice-minister.[49]

It was not long, however, before it became apparent that
much of the early enthusiasm may have been just a façade
designed to mask a less committed reality. As the journalist Yagi
Atsushi writes, 'The party – while pledging to respect the report
– never seriously intended to implement the reforms.'[50] Sakata
Michita, the party's Minister of Education through the final
three years of the CCE's deliberations and a firm supporter of
the CCE line, was replaced less than a month after the council
issued its final report. The new minister, Takami Saburō
(1971–2), was much less committed to the council's proposals.[51]
As Suzuki put it, 'He seemed to go senile upon taking his cabinet
post. All he would do was read the statements prepared for him
by his ministry staff.'[52]

And that ministry staff – as Suzuki was eager to point out –
was also no longer very committed to the reforms. Nishida, the
ministry official who had worked hand-in-hand with the council
and actually developed many of its proposals, was assigned to
head the Japanese office of UNESCO, a position totally
unrelated to the implementation of education reform. Even
more damaging, however, was the retirement of Amagi just
eleven days after the CCE issued its report. He was replaced by
Murayama Matsuo (AVM, 1971–4), one of the 'mainstream'
MOE officials who had been unenthusiastic about Amagi's
reformism while the CCE was still at work. At the same time,
another 'mainstreamer' – Iwama Eitarō – took over as bureau
chief of the Elementary and Secondary Education Bureau. With
the personnel shifts, it was soon apparent how many MOE
officials were cool towards the CCE's reform proposals. Amagi
described the effect of his departure in this way: 'Even at the
ministry, some people were less supportive. As long as I was
vice-minister, I could keep things going. But when I had to step
down . . .' The implication was that when he left, the whole CCE
reform movement fell apart.[53]

The lack of MOE interest in implementing many of the CCE
proposals first emerged in public on 19 August, just two months
after the council had issued its report. The Education Committee of the Upper House was holding hearings and had invited
MOE officials to testify. One of those being examined was

Okuda Shinjō, the man who had replaced Nishida and was thus in charge of co-ordinating the implementation of the CCE reforms. Asked what the MOE was doing to implement the proposals, he answered that it was seeking to decide various details of the pilot projects which it planned to initiate in 1974. He had hardly taken his seat, however, when Iwama – the new bureau chief – rose to contradict him: as far as the projects were within his area of responsibility, he began, he wanted to point out that no firm decision had yet been taken on whether to initiate any pilot projects at all.[54] It was an unprecedented public display of inter-ministerial conflict, and the media – which promptly began investigating the story – discovered that indeed many officials in the ministry were not fully behind the CCE reform proposals. The main area of disagreement, as before the report was issued, concerned the pilot projects. Many officials felt system reform was unnecessary, and many felt that the idea of *testing* new systems in particular was an improper way to go about it.[55]

By the time the first post-CCE budget season came to a conclusion, the government's lack of commitment to the CCE reform programme was apparent. First, in its budget request, the MOE revealed its sense of priorities by choosing to emphasize expansion programmes rather than substantive reform. It requested a 25 per cent increase in its budget, but almost all of the new money was to go to three programmes: aid to kindergartens, aid to education for the handicapped and aid to private universities – all relatively non-controversial expansion projects. The ministry did request some ¥600 million (US$1.6 million) to cover various costs involved in planning for substantive reforms in elementary, secondary and higher education, but this request was ultimately cut back to just ¥150 million (US$400,000).[56]

Most significant was the Ministry of Finance's refusal to provide the funds the ministry had requested to cover the cost of preliminary research at fifty-six schools which was meant to lay the groundwork for the pilot projects; instead, it agreed to provide only a token amount to allow the ministry to set up a committee of experts to undertake the planning. In addition, the MOF drastically cut back the MOE's request for new personnel. Where the ministry had requested a 31-man Research and Development Department, the MOF agreed to fund only a four-man R & D 'Room'. Interestingly, the LDP did not place a priority on restoring these cuts in the final renegotiation (*fukkatsu*) stage of the budget process. Instead it sought and won restoration of funds for kindergartens and private universities.[57]

The 1972 budget effectively killed the centrepiece of the CCE reform programme – the pilot projects. Later that year the ministry decided to postpone any decision on whether to set up the projects until its Educational Research and Development Co-operative Council completed further preliminary studies.[58] The council eventually issued a report, but the projects were never set up.[59] With the demise of that programme, however, more was lost than just that one CCE proposal. The momentum of the CCE reform movement in general seemed to slow down. The ministry had devoted much of its energy in the first year after publication of the CCE report to this single proposal, and as a result it was hesitant to push forward with any other controversial changes.

Nevertheless, many of the CCE's other proposals were eventually revived. Especially as the new, younger generation of LDP education Dietmen began asserting itself, it looked to the CCE report for inspiration and ideas. In the decade which followed, therefore, the council's other reform recommendations remained the focus of policy-making activity. The following section reviews the record of implementation of those other proposals.

Kindergarten expansion

Even as the MOE was backing away from the CCE's pilot projects proposal in that first year, it was vigorously pushing ahead with its plan for kindergarten expansion. In August the ministry announced a ten-year plan aimed at increasing the number of kindergartens such that by 1982 all 4 and 5 year olds would be able to attend. Its first-year request called for a large increase in the government's support for the establishment of public and private kindergartens, subsidies for lower-income parents and grants to help kindergartens cover the cost of teachers' salaries.[60] In the end, although the MOE request was reduced by the MOF, the budgets for assisting the establishment of kindergartens were increased in that first year by ¥1.2 billion (US$3.3 million) – double the previous year's allocation. In addition, after LDP education Dietmen intervened, a new budget for assisting low-income parents was established at a level of ¥1 billion (US$2.8 million).[61] In the years which followed, all of these allocations were increased yearly at a rapid rate until, by 1980, these kindergarten-expansion programmes were receiving twenty times the 1971 levels of allocation.[62]

The success of the ministry in having its kindergarten budget increased, however, contrasted with its failure to win MHW co-operation in its effort to bring all 4 and 5 year olds into the kindergartens. Shortly after the CCE issued its report, the MOE sought to work out a settlement in its conflict with its fellow ministry by inviting numerous nursery school and MHW representatives to be part of an MOE 'discussion group'. Although the group never published its conclusions, it seems that the two parties agreed to disagree: the MOE agreed not to seek to push nursery schools out of pre-school education and agreed not to attempt to turn its kindergartens into prep-schools for elementary schools – a trend which the MHW and the kindergarten associations saw as contrary to the needs of pre-schoolers. The MHW gave its final verdict on the MOE's goal of 'unifying the kindergarten and nursery school systems' (yō-ho ikkanka) when its advisory council came out expressly against the concept in October 1971.[63] Having failed to win MHW co-operation, the MOE was never able to push forward with its plan to mandate kindergarten attendance and was not even able to implement the CCE-recommended policy of requiring localities in areas with a shortage of kindergartens to establish such institutions.

Aid to private universities

Of all of the CCE recommendations, the one which was most quickly and completely implemented was its proposal for increased aid to private universities. In fact, that CCE recommendation was actually being implemented even before the council issued its final report. It was still only 1970 when the government initiated the System for the Provision of Aid for Private University Operating Expenses (Shiritsu daigakura keijōhi hojokin seido) with an initial allocation of ¥13.2 billion (US$37 million). Legislation passed that year and another law passed in 1975 gave the system legal basis. Funding under the programme was increased at an annual rate averaging 25 per cent through the 1970s and had grown to cover almost 30 per cent of private university expenses by 1980.[64]

Behind this rapid implementation was an unusual degree of consensus among concerned actors about the need for the government to increase its support for private universities. These universities – which by 1970 admitted 70 per cent of university students – had been treated by the government with benign neglect through much of the post-war period. Even as the demand for places in universities expanded rapidly in the 1960s, the government chose to let private universities find their own resources to finance their expansion.[65] The university disturbances of the late 1960s, however, had revealed the weakness of this policy: among the factors causing students to protest was the overcrowded state of the private universities.[66] By the late 1960s, therefore, most actors concerned with education policy were starting to recognize that the government needed to begin providing private universities with a standard share of their expenses. While there was still some resistance to this proposal when an MOE council first considered it in 1965–7, the objections had largely disappeared by the time the CCE took up the issue in the course of its deliberations.[67]

Particularly significant in explaining the rapid introduction of aid to private universities was the active support for the policy given by the LDP *zoku*. In 1968 the *zoku* set up its own Subcommittee on the Private Education Problem, concluding a year later that the government should begin providing grants to cover half of private university operating expenses. Sakata Michita was especially active, as were the younger Dietmen of Nishioka's group. Despite the MOE's initial desire to delay implementing any new aid programme for private universities until the CCE completed its review, the *zoku* convinced the ministry to support its accelerated schedule. Quickly winning the support of the opposition parties and the MOF, the Dietmen were able to have an initial allocation of funds inserted in the 1970 budget.[68] The *zoku* was similarly active in pushing through related legislation later that year and again in 1975. The Dietmen's role was particularly noteworthy in the case of the 1975 legislation, a law which confirmed the government's commitment to private universities and expanded its aid programme to include private upper and lower secondary schools, elementary schools and kindergartens. Breaking all the established norms of law-making, the *zoku* inserted greatly increased allocations for private universities and a first-ever allocation for private schools in the 1975 budget and only afterwards introduced the authorizing legislation. The legislation was introduced as a private member's bill less than ten days before the end of the legislative session but was rushed through the entire process in that short time.[69]

The case of aid to private universities thus illustrates the ability of the Japanese policy-making process to work smoothly when the various parts of the government are not working against each other. The *zoku* played the most active role, but its initiatives were fully supported by the MOE and encountered little opposition from concerned interest groups or the progressive camp. While the Ministry of Finance was not always willing to accept the levels of spending advocated by the education *zoku* and the MOE, these disagreements were usually resolved simply by compromising on the levels of allocation. A similar process of smooth implementation characterized several other CCE recommendations not treated in detail here: the initiation of aid to private schools below the university level (noted above in the discussion of the 1975 legislation) and the expansion of education programmes for handicapped students.[70]

Higher-education reforms

Unlike the CCE's recommendation calling for aid to private universities, the council's more controversial proposals dealing with the 'division into classes' (*shubetsuka*) and administrative reform of higher education were not smoothly implemented. In fact, while the government succeeded in convincing one national university (Tsukuba University) to accept some of its reforms, its higher-education reform efforts in general were almost as much of a non-starter as its pilot projects. From the beginning the CCE's reform proposals for higher education encountered strong objections not only from the usual progressive opposition but also from such respected bodies as the Association of National University Presidents. Rather than bend when faced with government efforts to promote its reforms, the opposition to the CCE line actually grew in its vehemence in the months following the issuance of the council's report. While the ANUP had agreed at least on the need for reform in its initial statements in 1971, by December 1973 it had returned to its old emphasis on the inviolability of 'university freedom' in firmly opposing the CCE line.[71]

The first casualty of the anti-CCE movement was the council's *shubetsuka* proposal. As noted above in the section on CCE deliberations, this proposal was already a largely watered-down version of what the council's reformers had originally intended. In the end, however, even this weakened plan was not implemented. No legislation to classify the institutions of higher education was introduced, and universities in particular remained a largely homogeneous group of institutions. The goal of having some offer a general education while others offered more specialized courses was not achieved. The single notable outgrowth of the council's diversification efforts was a legislative change in 1975 establishing 'specialized schools' (*senshū gakkō*) as a new category of educational institution offering secondary and post-secondary education.[72] While advertised as a major step towards the diversification of higher education, most of the (predominantly private) institutions which appeared under the new label were actually already established schools operating under the label 'miscellaneous schools' (*kakushu gakkō*).[73]

The government was not much more successful in its campaign to make the administration of universities 'rational' and 'open'. While it originally sought to establish a University Reform Promotion Council (*Daigaku kaikaku suishin kaigi*) as a means of 'working with' universities to encourage administrative reform, it was finally forced to give up on the idea in the face of continued protests from university officials who insisted that they should be totally free to develop their own reform plans. The ministry did set up a Higher Education Discussion Group (*Kōtō kyōiku sōdankai*) in June 1972, but the mandate of this council did not emphasize administrative reform issues.[74]

The government's entire effort aimed at university administrative reform thus came to be concentrated on its ongoing campaign to establish a single 'model university' which it hoped would serve as an example for other universities. In September 1973, after many years of heated debate and discussion, the government finally succeeded in pushing the required legislation through the Diet enabling the old Tokyo Education University (TEU, *Tokyo kyōiku daigaku*) to transform itself into a 'new course' university incorporating many of the reforms suggested by the CCE. Located at a new, much more spacious campus, the reorganized and renamed Tsukuba University was to be administered by a strengthened executive composed not only of the president but also five vice-presidents; personnel decisions were to be made not by the faculties but by a central Personnel

195

Committee; the president was to be advised by a University Advisory Body (*Sanyōkai*) composed of individuals from outside the university; and the whole organization of the university's staff was to be restructured based not on the traditional faculty (*gakubu*) system but on a dual system with separate organizations for teaching and research. In short, Tsukuba University was to be much more 'open' (advised by a board) and 'rational' (run by a central executive without competition from the faculties).[75]

On the surface, the government's success in pushing through the Tsukuba legislation over vehement protests from the progressive camp (including the ANUP) was evidence of its potential to implement education reform. The Tsukuba legislation had been strongly supported by the MOE and a number of influential figures in the LDP, and it had also been supported by a core group of faculty in the old TEU. Together, the three groups formed an unbeatable coalition. On another level, however, the legislation illustrated the *limits* of the Japanese system's ability to change. The legislation which was passed, while seemingly ground-breaking, actually represented the lowest common denominator which the three parties could agree upon. As a result, the new board – while including outsiders – was limited to an advisory role. Likewise, the new administrative system – though somewhat more centralized – remained subject to the sectoral claims of teaching and research subunits. A look at what Tsukuba had become by the 1980s reveals the limits of what was accomplished in 1973.

The following brief survey of the Tsukuba reform movement illustrates the effect of 'lowest common denominator politics'. The movement actually began in 1963 as a discussion within the TEU as to whether or not the university should move from its scattered Tokyo campuses to a newly developed site at Tsukuba. The simple question of whether or not to move was already causing some controversy when, in 1967, those opposing the move walked out of the discussions charging that a decision to move had been made without the consent of all the departments. Shortly afterwards, the issue became a subject of student protests.[76] It was in this turbulent atmosphere (on 24 July 1969) that the pro-move faction decided that the university should adopt a set of administrative reforms to accompany the move. Concurrently, the MOE and the LDP, both worried about the university disturbances, were also considering various ideas for reforming the administration of universities. As early as 1965, the MOE had brought together a group of reform-minded faculty from several leading universities, including three key pro-move faculty from TEU, for the purpose of 'studying' university reform.[77] Certain LDP Dietmen – notably Hashimoto Tomisaburō, a close associate of Prime Minister Satō – also had a significant influence on the course of the movement. Hashimoto's Model University Discussion Group, meeting from July 1969, outlined exactly what a 'new course' university ought to look like and advocated the establishment of such a university at Tsukuba.[78]

A great deal of controversy surrounded the question of who influenced whom in this process. The opposition was eager to prove that the pro-move faction was merely being manipulated by government forces. What is most interesting, however, is the fact that all three parties in favour of the Tsukuba reforms were forced to argue that the pro-move faction's reform plan was purely its own idea. As one pro-move leader put it, 'If the MOE had put the idea out first, the anti-move group would have soon crushed it.'[79] The necessity of respecting university autonomy thus meant that neither the MOE nor the LDP could force the pro-move faction to accept any reforms the faction did not want. The LDP and the ministry definitely had their own ideas about what Tsukuba should look like, but to see them implemented they had first to convince the pro-move leaders and then help them persuade the rest of their university.

The result was that the Tsukuba reform package arising out of negotiations between the pro-move leaders and the government was much weaker than Hashimoto's original conception. Two reforms in particular were left out of the final plan: (1) the introduction of a contract system for a large share of the faculty, and (2) 'the reorganization of university management under an independent public corporation' (hōjinka). These proposals were opposed as too radical both by the MOE and the university.[80] The ministry favoured a slightly more moderate structure which would have kept Tsukuba as a national university while establishing a strong advisory body of outsiders given ultimate responsibility for administration and planning. The university, however, opposed the idea of a powerful board as well, arguing that a group of outsiders should not be allowed to participate in the management of the university and insisting that the board be limited to a purely advisory role.[81] Confirming the dependence of the ministry and the LDP on the university's support, the final Tsukuba law passed in 1973 settled for the university's version of an advisory body – the lowest common denominator.

Although the government finally succeeded in pushing through the Tsukuba legislation in 1973, the limited nature of that victory had become clear by the time the Ad Hoc Council began looking again at university administration a decade later. Even MOE officials admitted that Tsukuba's advisory board had turned out to be 'totally powerless'.[82] The centralization of personnel management was also failing to develop as planned. One of the first decisions made by the new university was to keep the president off the Personnel Committee, substituting a vice-president in his place. According to one top administrator there, the Personnel Committee had been effectively emasculated since that time by the faculty's continued insistence that 'it takes one to know one'. Personnel decisions are therefore only made when the parties concerned with individual decisions can agree – that is, when the teaching organization and the research organization agree about the quality of a particular applicant. When they cannot agree (apparently quite often), no decision is made and promotions are simply frozen. 'There is no central initiative on this issue', complained the administrator.[83]

While the reforms thus had a limited impact on Tsukuba, what was more striking a decade after the controversy was the fact that no other established national university had adopted even a single feature of the Tsukuba model: all remained faculty-dominated, centrally-weak institutions without advisory boards for input from outside the universities. Furthermore, while many had been considering their own administrative reform plans in the early 1970s, most abandoned their efforts before implementing significant changes.[84] A measure of the failure of the government's effort to encourage administrative reform in the post-CCE period was the frustration in the voice of Kida Hiroshi (AVM, 1976–8) as he expressed resignation that Japan's universities would continue to be dominated by their faculties until they themselves decided to change.[85]

Reforms concerning teachers

The government was somewhat more successful in implementing its reforms aimed at 'improving the quality of teachers'. Going back to the four main policies recommended by the CCE, the results can be summarized as follows:

1 *Salary reform*: the recommended salary increase was fully implemented and the salary structure was partially reformed through the establishment of the position of assistant principal (*kyōtō*) as an official administrative position and through the establishment of a system of bonuses for teachers with management responsibilities (*shunin*).

2 *Master teachers*: the government succeeded in setting up several graduate teacher-training universities, but its efforts to have 'master teachers' rewarded through changes in the salary scale failed.

3 *Teachers' colleges*: the government established several new teachers' colleges, but it failed to establish any incentives to encourage more teachers to be trained in such institutions. Its attempt to strengthen the teacher-training courses at regular universities through licensing reform failed to win Diet approval.

4 *The shiho system*: although the training requirement for new teachers was increased to twenty days, no attempt was made to create a one-year probationary training programme.[86]

In its efforts to change policies concerned with teachers as well, therefore, the government was only partially successful in seeing its proposals implemented. Particularly in the area of salary reform, however, it was more successful than in many of the other ventures arising out of the 1971 CCE report. The following section thus focuses in detail on the process through which the government worked to implement its salary reform proposals.

In 1971 the MOE was largely unified in its support for the CCE salary proposals. It has long been committed to the goal of strengthening the authority of management through changes in the salary scale, and by that year it was becoming concerned as well about the general decline of teachers' salaries relative to other professions.[87] In the months following the publication of the CCE report, however, the ministry did not immediately push ahead in an effort to implement those proposals. In 1971 its only action was to request funds for a research council to study the salary system. It was hesitant partly because it was overwhelmed with the other CCE proposals, but also because the salary reform proposals were being strongly attacked by *Nikkyōso*. The research council finally began work in August 1972.[88]

The LDP *zoku* was much quicker off the mark. It had been a major force behind the original CCE recommendation calling for a salary rise, and so it naturally made the salary proposals a leading priority of its reform campaign. In the spring of 1972, during a heated leadership struggle within the LDP, the *zoku* brought together concerned members on both sides to endorse a bold plan for implementing the CCE's recommendations concerning teachers. Its report, released on 1 July, was published in time to influence the budget deliberations for fiscal year 1973.[89]

Although the MOE had only just put its own research council to work, it was soon swept along at the LDP pace. Elementary and Secondary Education Bureau Chief Iwama, meeting with Prime Minister Tanaka soon after he was installed, was surprised when the new leader greeted his plea for a large allocation of funds for a teachers' salary rise with a simple reply: 'Do it.' Prodded along as well by further *zoku* pressure, the ministry worked furiously to prepare its request for funds, presenting the demand in September as a late addition to its original set of requests. When the MOF turned down the MOE request later in the budget season, the *zoku* worked behind the scenes to have it restored. Although the final budget provided the MOE with less than it originally requested, it nevertheless included the funds necessary to cover a 10 per cent salary rise for all teachers of the compulsory education level – with a MOE–MOF memo committing the government to further increases in the future.[90]

Despite agreement on the budget, however, the issue was not yet settled. Due to the rapid pace at which the salary rise had suddenly been pushed forward, the budget allocation (for the rise) had actually been agreed before its legal basis could be decided. Legislation was not absolutely necessary. Several ministries (Finance, Labour, and Home Affairs) in fact supported the non-legislative option of simply asking the Personnel Commission (PC, *Jinjiin*) to recommend the teachers' salary rise. They opposed formal legislation *forcing* the PC to endorse the salary rise as an affront to the PC's neutrality. The *zoku*, however, insisted on the legislative course. It wanted the government to commit itself formally to a salary rise, and it also wanted to use such legislation to initiate a more comprehensive reform of the salary structure. Despite the opposition from within the government – and criticism from *Nikkyōso* as well – the *zoku* once again succeeded in mobilizing the necessary support. Tanaka was induced to change his mind and support the *zoku* strategy, and 'The Law to Guarantee the Quality of Teaching Personnel' (*Jinkakuhō*) was sent to the Diet on 20 February 1973.[91]

As originally drafted the *Jinkakuhō* committed the government to two basic policies, one much more controversial than the other. While the teachers' salary rise was supported by a broad spectrum of opinion, the bill's provision for the introduction of a five-grade salary scale (two new grades: one for assistant principals and one for master teachers) was strongly opposed by the progressive camp as an attempt to divide the teaching corps and increase the power of 'the administration' in the management of schools. *Nikkyōso*, calling an emergency conference shortly after the legislation was sent to the Diet, decided to conduct a half-day strike in protest. It was willing to take the salary rise, but it strongly opposed the rest of the bill.[92] In the end, a surplus of controversial legislation in that session forced the government to resubmit the bill the following session. Facing the prospect of losing the budget allocation for the salary rise altogether, the government finally agreed to negotiate with the opposition. *Zoku* leaders met with Japan Socialist Party Dietmen, the Minister of Education met with the *Nikkyōso* leader, and finally an agreement was reached: if the salary-scale reform provisions were removed, the union and the opposition parties would support the bill. After amendment, the bill won the unanimous support of the Diet on 22 February 1974.[93]

The first round of the salary reform process thus ended on an amicable note: the various concerned parties had managed to put aside their disagreements in order to assure that the part of the reform they all supported (the salary rise) was fully implemented. It soon became clear, however, that amicable relations would not last. The year 1974 saw the government finally succeed in winning Diet approval of a separate law establishing the assistant principal as an official administrative position. Once again, the aggressiveness of *zoku* Dietmen (notably Inaba Osamu) had been critical.[94] The next year, the government's attempt to recognize those teachers with special responsibilities in the management of schools (*shunin*) as official 'middle management workers' (*chūkan kanri shoku*) brought the conflict to a head.

Under the system in place in 1975, teachers with special responsibilities – the chief of instruction, the various heads of grade, the department heads, the chief counsellor and others – were not officially recognized. Such positions existed in many schools but were not prescribed by MOE regulations. This unofficial status meant that those teacher-managers (*shunin*) were chosen within individual schools by their fellow teachers and that they received no extra remuneration. In early 1975, under pressure particularly from the *zoku*, the MOE began to plan for the conversion of these positions into official posts prescribed by MOE regulations. Concurrently, it approached the Personnel Commission in order to get its authorization to devote some of the *Jinkakuhō* funds to the creation of a salary bonus for these newly recognized teacher-managers.[95]

It was not until October, however, that the issue emerged as the focus of a major policy dispute involving the *zoku*, the MOE and the teachers' union. While the *zoku* was intent on seeing teacher-managers given official status and a bonus, *Nikkyōso* was totally opposed. Caught in the middle was the Ministry of Education. It agreed with the *zoku* in principle but wanted to prevent the disruption of schools which the politicians' confrontational approach threatened to unleash. Among the most vulnerable was the newly appointed chief of the Elementary and Secondary Education Bureau, Imamura Taketoshi. It was he who in October discussed his plans for giving *shunin* official status with union leaders in the course of his planning efforts. When *Nikkyōso* went public with an attack on Imamura's proposal, the battle lines were drawn. Nishioka (the *zoku* Dietman in charge of the teacher reforms) was furious with Imamura for contacting the union without his consent and vowed to take personal responsibility for the implementation of the *shunin* reforms. *Nikkyōso* announced its intention to conduct another half-day strike in opposition to the government's plan. Imamura, seeking to find a compromise, only succeeded in stoking Nishioka's anger when – again without *zoku* consent – he agreed to delay the implementation of the *shunin* reforms and assured union leaders that the MOE would consult with the union before making a final decision.[96]

These developments put the Minister of Education, Nagai Michio, in a particularly sensitive position. The first layman to be named minister since the immediate post-war period and a man politically close to the progressive camp, Nagai was personally opposed to the *shunin* reforms.[97] The *zoku*, however, was insisting that he fire Imamura and implement the changes. On

18 November he succumbed to the pressure and transferred the bureau chief to an end-of-career position as Head of the Culture Agency (*Bunkachō*). On 6 December he announced the ministry's decision to implement the regulatory changes necessary to turn *shunin* positions into officially prescribed posts. The decision announced that day also committed the MOE to seeking Diet approval of its plans to use *Jinkakuhō* funds to establish a ¥5,000 (US$16) per month *shunin* bonus. Although Nagai sought to portray his decision as a compromise by describing the positions as 'leadership positions' rather than 'middle management positions', it was clear to all observers that the *zoku* had forced his hand. The regulatory changes establishing the *shunin* system were issued in January 1976, and Diet approval − though delayed by strong opposition − was finally granted in December 1977.[98]

The *zoku*'s victory at the national level was a major defeat for the union. The final battles, however, would take place at the local level where the union was strongest. In many prefectures (particularly the large urban ones) and in many schools, union opposition forced local officials and principals to modify the way in which the *shunin* system was implemented. In some areas the number of *shunin* posts was expanded to include up to half of the teachers − undermining the government's attempt to use the *shunin* system to create an elite consciousness among those receiving the bonus. In schools where the union was strong, the system was implemented according to union rules: *shunin* teachers donated their bonuses (which were not very large anyway) directly to a special union 'pool' which was spent on special educational projects.[99] Suzuki Isao, the Elementary and Secondary Education Bureau Chief who oversaw much of the implementation process, admitted that the union's tactics had been (and continued to be) successful in many schools. In the case of schools where the union was strong, he said, the *shunin* bonus money was going directly to the union; the teachers did not even see the money. Furthermore, the *shunin* positions had failed to become established as a step in the elite career route leading to the position of principal; there were too many posts. Perhaps, he speculated, the government should simply cancel the bonus.[100] Despite the implementation of this reform at the national level, therefore, its impact at the individual school level was in many cases limited.

Diversification of secondary education

The final CCE reforms to reach the agenda – with no change in policy implemented until the late 1970s – were the council's proposals calling for the diversification of secondary education. In contrast to the process leading to the partial implementation of the teacher reforms, no dramatic confrontations marked the reform process in this sphere. The lack of confrontation did not mean, however, that the original CCE reforms were not altered during the long implementation process. On the contrary, the reforms in this area were transformed by a subtle process involving an interesting degree of co-operation between the teachers' union and the MOE. Whereas one of the original goals of the CCE diversification proposals had been to provide greater opportunities for 'gifted education' (*eisai kyōiku*) in the upper secondary schools, the reforms which emerged at the end of the implementation period were focused much more on the needs of those who were falling behind at that level.

The CCE, in its original diversification proposals, had put forward several blatantly 'gifted education' proposals. It had proposed that the rigid grade-based system of school organization be replaced by a 'non-graded system' (a module- or credit-based system) to allow bright students to advance more quickly, and it had suggested that the brightest students be allowed actually to skip grades. Two other CCE proposals also contained 'gifted education' aspects. The proposal that streaming by ability be introduced within *kōtōgakkō* (students at this level were already streamed *between* schools) was at least partly motivated by the council's desire to allow bright students to be grouped together. The recommendation that academic *kōtōgakkō* students be allowed to 'choose' from a wide selection of courses matched to their abilities and interests was also viewed by many as an elitist proposal. While the council had proposed that students be allowed to 'choose', many progressive observers suspected that students would inevitably be 'guided' into courses by ability so that the result would still be elitist.

In the period immediately following the publication of the CCE report, these 'elitist' proposals were strongly attacked by the progressive camp. In a 1971 statement, for example, *Nikkyōso* accused the CCE of planning to 'discriminate by ability' (*nōryokushugi sabetsu*).[101] Some non-progressive education groups and local authority organizations also urged the government to be cautious in its diversification efforts. They did not want it to devise too many narrowly specialized courses.[102] MOE officials too were not eager to take the initiative in pursuing the 'gifted education' aspects of the proposals on their own (see Chapter 4 above). As a result, the proposals were gradually transformed as they were taken through a series of reviews. First, they were considered over a several year period starting in 1973 by the ministry's Educational Curriculum Council (ECC, *Kyōiku katei shingikai*) which examined the CCE proposals in the course of its regular review of the curriculum. After the ECC issued its final report in 1976, the MOE itself took another few years before issuing the final curriculum guidelines in 1977 and 1978.

The final reforms, introduced in the form of a series of alterations in the curriculum guidelines, emerged from this extended process stripped of the 'gifted education' emphasis which had caused the original CCE proposals to be attacked. The reforms did not introduce a non-graded organization of schools nor grade-skipping. While the reforms did allow for streaming by ability and a greater diversity of courses (both only at the *kōtōgakkō* level), the emphasis in both cases had been subtly shifted from bright students to those students who were falling behind (the *ochikobore*). The shift was most visible in the MOE's use of the slogan *'yutori no aru kyōiku'* to promote the changes. This emphasis on 'education with room to enjoy it' actually reflected the teachers' union's concerns about the pressures of 'examination hell'. The bulk of changes introduced in the new curriculum were designed to lessen these pressures by reducing the amount of material students were forced to learn under curricular guidelines. The final curriculum package provided for a 20 to 30 per cent reduction in curriculum and a 10 per cent cut in the hours of academic instruction.[103]

With this new emphasis, the curriculum reform was widely supported. It was in fact a priority policy of Education Minister Nagai, an original critic of the CCE.[104] Seeking to 'take education out of the political battlefield', Nagai concentrated his efforts on achieving what he called his policy of a 'cart drawn by four horses', a set of four policies aimed at addressing what he saw as the major problem in education: excessive examination competition and exam-orientated education. One of the four horses was to be curriculum reform of the type the MOE finally put forward.[105] The curriculum reform was thus wrapped in a largely uncontroversial package which everyone could endorse: *Nikkyōso* supported it, the ministry supported it, and the party did not object.

The final curriculum package, while stripped of its 'gifted education' aspects, was still meant to provide greater *flexibility* at the upper secondary level. Most importantly, the reduction in the amount of material and number of courses *kōtōgakkō* students were required to study was supposed to provide them with the flexibility to pursue a greater diversity of specialized courses. In fact, the curriculum did significantly increase the latitude for specialization: where previously students were forced to take forty-seven units of 'required courses' (out of ninety-odd units needed to graduate in most schools), the new curriculum guidelines required only thirty-two units.[106] Although this relaxation in rules did lead to some increase in choice in upper secondary schools, however, the level of specialization actually achieved in the schools was not greatly enhanced. The large majority of academic *kōtōgakkō* continued to list more than thirty-two credits as required.[107] More significant, however, was the fact that many subjects not listed as required were effectively mandatory. English, for example, was not listed as required. Nevertheless, because it was on the university entrance exam, virtually every *kōtōgakkō* student continued to study it – most for three years.

Ironically, the major factor limiting the degree to which schools and students took advantage of the greater opportunity for specialization available under the new curriculum guidelines was another education reform introduced at the same time: the new Unified First-stage University Entrance Examination (*Kyōtsūichiji*). Whereas previously national universities had selected students with their own (albeit similar) examinations, the reform established a single first-stage exam in order to simplify and rationalize the selection system.[108] A side-effect of the change, however, was that it provided all upper secondary school students aiming for a national university with a broad, uniform and very rigorous standard by which they would be judged. The new examination required all such students to be examined in seven subjects from five subject areas (maths, science, Japanese, social studies and a foreign language). To prepare for rigorous exams in all of these areas forced these students to fill virtually all of the ninety-odd units of their upper secondary course with the same broad selection of courses they had studied before the 1978 curriculm reforms. Once again, therefore, the government's reform effort, although implemented, had only a limited effect in the schools.[109]

CONCLUSIONS

The preceding account of the education reforms arising out of the CCE initiative presented the story in its full complexity. Clearly the record demonstrates the folly of any attempt to point to any single variable as the driving force (or limiting force) in Japanese policy-making. Nevertheless, it is the goal of this book – and this chapter – to identify some patterns in this tale of a few successes and many failures in the government's attempt to achieve a far-reaching set of education reforms. The results of the initiative are summarized briefly in Figure 7.1. The following are some of the lessons which can be drawn from this record.

Figure 7.1 Results of the CCE initiative

Totally stymied
  'Pilot projects' (*sendōteki shikō*)
  Kindergarten – nursery school unification (*yō-ho ikkanka*)
  Higher-education system reform (*shubetsuka*)
  University administrative reform (centralization and *hōjinka*)
  Probationary training year for new teachers (*shiho* system)
  Licensing reform to upgrade university training of teachers
  Salary-scale reform to create a new grade of 'master teachers'
  Non-graded schools and grade-skipping

Partially implemented
  The *shunin* reforms
  Diversification of upper secondary schools

Largely implemented
  Aid to private universities
  Aid to private schools
  Expansion of kindergartens
  Expansion of education for the handicapped
  Teachers' salary rise
  Formal recognition of assistant principals
  Establishment of graduate teacher-training universities

1. *Programmes supported by a broad consensus of political actors are more easily implemented.* Of the seven education policies listed as 'largely implemented', five were supported by virtually all concerned actors: aid to private universities, aid to private schools, expansion of kindergartens and education for the handicapped and the teachers' salary rise. All of these policies – each involving an expansion of the education budget – enjoyed the active support of the education subgovernment. Both the MOE and the LDP *zoku* saw the policies as a means of increasing 'their' budget and 'their' influence. Also significant, however, was the lack of any progressive camp opposition to these policies. In fact, the teachers' union and other progressive elements actually campaigned for several of the changes: they had long called for a teachers' salary rise and increased aid to education for the handicapped, and they became leading advocates of aid to private education. While the Ministry of Finance and in some cases the LDP 'centre' were sometimes opposed to the size of the budgetary allocations requested by the LDP *zoku* and the MOE, these differences were generally resolved through compromises which – at least in days of less financial stringency – allowed substantial room for new expansion programmes.

2. *Conflict between subgovernments makes change difficult.* The record of the MOE–MHW conflict over pre-school policy offers a clear example of the immobilism arising from conflict between subgovernments. Unable to resolve their jurisdictional dispute, the two ministries decided to maintain the uncoordinated status quo rather than integrate their nursery school and kindergarten policies.

3. *Conflict within the education subgovernment makes change difficult.* The list of 'totally stymied' policies includes a whole range of reform proposals which failed primarily due to the inability of the education subgovernment to agree on the direction of change. While the CCE initiative began as the province of reform-minded MOE officials, many of the proposals advocated by this group were opposed by other elements in the MOE and by influential education interest groups. The pilot projects proposal, the university *shubetsuka* plan and the elite education aspects of the CCE's diversification programme were all opposed by at least part of the education subgovernment. In the end, it was the absence of a conservative consensus in these areas

which prevented the implementation of these and other CCE proposals.

4. *Opposition from the progressive camp makes change more difficult.* While it was opposition within the conservative camp which ultimately decided the fate of the above programmes, the role of the progressive opposition in encouraging the conservative failure of will cannot be ignored. In the case of the pilot projects, *shubetsuka* and elite education, the teachers' union and independently minded university authorities had made clear their strong opposition. When elements within the MOE failed to act to implement these changes, they were failing to act at least partly in order to avoid disruptive conflict with progressive forces.

The role of the progressives was even clearer in the case of several other initiatives. Most conservatives supported the CCE proposals calling for a probationary teacher-training year, teachers' salary reform and university administrative reform. The LDP *zoku* considered all of these policies to be high priorities, and many MOE officials were sympathetic at least in principle. In all three cases, however, progressive opposition prevented the conservatives from achieving their objectives. The *shiho* system was made one of the first casualties of the progressive onslaught when it became clear that the MOE was not willing to face the *Nikkyōso* backlash. In the case of salary reform, the teachers' union forced the government to abandon its five-grade salary scale in 1974. While the union eventually failed to stop the government from recognizing assistant principals and implementing the *shunin* bonus, it prevented the creation of a new grade for master teachers and reduced the impact of the *shunin* reforms through continued opposition in individual schools. In the case of university administrative reform, the progressives' position was the strongest: the government could not implement changes without the co-operation of the universities themselves. In most cases no co-operation was given and no changes were implemented. While some TEU faculty worked with the MOE, the reforms which they agreed to accept were the 'lowest common denominator' and were eventually subverted by traditional faculty sectionalism which re-emerged at the new Tsukuba campus. In all of these cases the progressives used the type of tactics described in Chapter 6. They appealed to a 'higher standard of democracy' for education issues in arguing that the

209

conservatives should only be allowed to implement education reforms based on broader-than-majority support.

The record of education reform in the 1970s contains many other important insights into the workings of Japan's policy-making system. The Central Council on Education (1967–71) serves as a case study in the function of advisory councils in the policy process. The way in which it was initially manipulated by MOE internationalists and later served as a forum for the battle within the MOE reveals the falsity of claims that such councils actually provide independent input into the system. Similarly, the record of education policy-making in the 1970s would serve as an excellent case study illustrating the rise in the influence of LDP policy groups (the *zoku*). By the mid-1970s the education *zoku* was playing a much more active role in the policy-making process – pushing through controversial legislation and large budget increases.

The primary lessons of the CCE initiative for this study, however, were those enumerated above – the insights into the limits of change in the Japanese political system. Aside from the expansion programmes and a few teacher reforms which were pushed through over progressive opposition, the government was unable to implement significant change. Reform of the 6–3–3 system and university administrative reform – both early priorities of the CCE – as well as many of the council's other controversial proposals were completely blocked by a combination of progressive opposition and conservative attachment to the status quo. The significance of these insights for an understanding of the limits of Japanese policy-making in general will be explored in Chapter 9.

8

Education reform under Nakasone

The second of the two recent education reform initiatives had several advantages over the first. Built around a cabinet-level council rather than just an MOE council, it began with a much greater opportunity to build government-wide support for education reform: the council was authorized to make policy recommendations on behalf of the entire government rather than just a single ministry. Equally important, the council had been established through a process which gave it a clear mandate to reform the education system. Prime Minister Nakasone had campaigned in the December 1983 general election on a platform of education reform and had received multi-party Diet endorsement of reform through the process leading to the legal establishment of the AHCE in August 1984. Finally, the great publicity surrounding the activities of the council gave it the chance to build broad public support for its reform proposals.

Nevertheless, the second initiative was not any more successful than the first. In fact, where the CCE was able at least to put together a substantive reform package – failing mostly in the implementation stage – the Ad Hoc Council did not even get that far. The concrete proposals it produced included a few recycled recommendations from earlier reform initiatives, a few proposals to expand education programmes and little else. Most of its more far-reaching ideas died inside the council. The aim of this final chapter is to determine the reasons for this failure. As in the previous chapter, the analysis focuses on the three stages of the reform process: initiation, deliberations and implementation.

THE INITIATION OF REFORM

On 5 September 1984 the Ad Hoc Council on Education began its deliberations, charged by the Prime Minister and the Diet with the task of advising the government on 'basic strategies for necessary reforms with regard to governmental policies and measures in various aspects, so as to secure such education as will be compatible with the social changes and cultural developments of our country'. As in the case of the CCE, however, the broad mandate and seemingly diverse make-up of the council's membership concealed the fact that the direction the council would take had already been largely determined through the process which led to its establishment. This section surveys that process.

While the initiation processes of the CCE and AHCE were alike in the degree to which they influenced the councils' subsequent deliberations, they differed in one significant respect. Whereas the CCE initiation had been largely dominated by a small group of like-thinking CCE veterans and MOE 'internationalists', the establishment of the AHCE involved a much wider range of actors: the LDP education *zoku* was much more active than in the previous initiative; the Prime Minister was a central character; the entire MOE was mobilized to assure that its interests were respected; other government ministries were involved; and even the opposition parties played a role. While this broader involvement ensured that the AHCE would have a much wider foundation upon which to build its education reform proposals, it also meant that the differences in attitudes among these diverse actors would have to be dealt with even before the council began its work.

The build-up to reform within the education subgovernment

The actor initially most active in urging a new education reform offensive was the LDP education *zoku*. As early as December 1980 the party's Education Division and Education System Research Council had established five subcommittees to examine various education 'problems': the teacher problem, the higher-education problem, the textbook problem, the school-system problem and the 'fundamental problems of education'.[1] Through these committees the *zoku* established its positions on the major education reform issues, endorsing proposals such as a probationary training year for teachers and reforms in the teacher licensing system to create a new grade of master teachers (both unimplemented ideas inherited from the CCE).[2] Although the *zoku* as a whole was not able to agree on a specific plan for the reform of the 6−3−3 school system, it was clear that a vocal sub-group considered changes in this area to be a priority as well. A draft of the School System Problem Subcommittee report published independently by the subcommittee chairman, Kondō Tetsuo, called for the laws governing the school system to be made more flexible to allow alternatives to the 6−3−3 division of years as well as 'grade-skipping' for bright students and 'holding back' for slow ones.[3] Subsequent comments by leading *zoku* Dietmen such as Nishioka Takeo, Ishibashi Kazuya and Fujinami Takao indicated that Kondō was not alone in calling for system reform.[4]

Largely in response to the *zoku*'s activism, the MOE as well used its advisory councils to establish its positions on pending reform issues. The Teacher Training Council, in its November 1983 report, recommended changes in the teacher licensing system, university training courses and practice teaching along the lines recommended by the *zoku* several months earlier.[5] Also that November, the CCE Subcommittee on Educational Content issued a report which dealt with several significant reform issues. It proposed that streaming by ability within schools be introduced in lower secondary schools and that third-year *chūgakkō* students as well as all *kōtōgakkō* students be given greater latitude to choose more of their classes from a selection of optional courses. Regarding the controversial issue of whether or not to reform the 6−3−3 division of years, the council recommended that the question be examined further by the next session of the CCE.[6] Although this last recommendation was preceded by a period of argument between the *zoku* and the MOE over whether or not system reform was necessary, the final proposal indicated that they had finally come to an uneasy agreement.[7] As the year 1983 came to a close, the two actors of the education subgovernment were therefore ready to proceed with a full review of the education system under the leadership of a new session of the CCE.

The build-up to reform outside the education subgovernment

Even as the *zoku* and MOE were preparing for a new CCE-led reform initiative, actors outside the subgovernment were also beginning to take a greater interest in education reform. Among the newcomers was the Ministry of International Trade and Industry whose Industrial Structure Council issued a report in March 1980 calling for radical education reform. Charging that the established uniform and exam-orientated system was failing to produce the creative, diversely talented and internationalist workers needed to meet the nation's new economic needs, it argued for the introduction of greater flexibility into the system, specifically proposing the abolition of upper-secondary-school entrance examinations and the merging of lower and upper secondary schools.[8] Also newly active were the various business organizations on the *Keizai dōyūkai* wing of the business community. The *Dōyūkai* itself produced a report which echoed the MITI recommendations in July 1984.[9] The Kyoto Group for the Study of Global Issues published its radical proposals for liberalizing the education system in March of that same year.[10]

The most important newcomer, however, was the Prime Minister. Nakasone had long been interested in education from a nationalist perspective. He felt that the post-war education system was failing to teach the new generation to accept traditional Japanese values, and he saw the 'Occupation-imposed' 6−3−3 system as a symbol of Japan's defeat. When he became prime minister in 1982, therefore, Nakasone soon began speaking of the need for education reform as part of a 'total clearance of the post-war political accounts'. In February 1983, after several particularly violent incidents of juvenile delinquency focused national attention on the issue of school violence, the Prime Minister spoke for the first time about the need for a 'radical solution' to the nation's education problems.[11] In June he appointed a personal advisory council − the Group for Discussing Education and Culture − to examine the problems of the education system. Finally, during the December general election campaign, he issued his own 'Seven Point Proposal for Education Reform'.

The seven points may be summarized as follows:

1 Reform of the 6−3−3−4 school system.
2 An improvement in the system of high school entrance examinations.

3 Improvement of the university entrance examination system
– including reform of the *Kyōtsūichiji* entrance examination.
4 Incorporation of work-experience activities and overnight
camps into the education system.
5 An increased emphasis on moral and physical education.
6 Continued promotion of the internationalization of education.
7 An improvement in the quality of teachers.[12]

Nakasone also had his own proposal regarding the mechanism
through which his education reform ideas should be developed.
While the MOE and *zoku* were seeking to refer the task to a new
session of the CCE, he had on several occasions expressed his
desire to refer the job to a supra-cabinet advisory council based
on the model of the Provisional Commission for Administrative
Reform (*Rinchō*).[13] Having worked with *Rinchō* as Director
General of the Administrative Management Agency, Nakasone
had learnt to appreciate the way in which such councils could be
used to overcome bureaucratic conservatism. Fearing that the
CCE – operating within limits imposed by the MOE – would
fail to endorse the radical reforms he envisaged, the Prime
Minister therefore proposed that an 'Education *Rinchō*' was
required.[14]

Confrontation and compromise

As the calendar year 1984 began, developments both inside and
outside the education subgovernment were thus pointing
towards a major education reform initiative. A major disagreement existed, however, over the forum in which the reform
issues would be discussed: while the MOE and *zoku* favoured
using the CCE, Nakasone wanted to use a supra-cabinet council
directly under his office. For a few weeks following the December elections, the issue seemed to be settled. The party's substantial losses having left Nakasone in a weakened position, the
Prime Minister had on several occasions expressed his intention
of letting the MOE lead the reform with its Central Council.[15] In
mid-January, however, he changed his mind – at first privately
and then publicly. He would insist on the establishment of an
Education *Rinchō*.[16]

Nakasone's decision to opt for his original plan – despite

opposition from the MOE and *zoku* – ushered in a period of heated confrontation between the two sides. The confrontation reflected first their conflicting territorial interests. The subgovernment insisted that it should control policy-making in its sphere, while Nakasone argued that the issue was broader and required top-level leadership. The territorial conflict was aggravated by the fact that many members of the education *zoku* were leading Dietmen of factions opposed to Nakasone's leadership of the party. Their natural opposition to prime ministerial intervention in their sphere was thus compounded by their desire to prevent Nakasone from 'taking away their issue' and using it to extend his tenure.

The subgovernment's opposition was also aggravated, however, by underlying differences of opinion about education reform issues. First, none of the education actors was confident that Nakasone was willing to devote financial resources to education reform. Remembering the Prime Minister's close association with the budget-cutting *Rinchō*, some even feared that he might seek reforms which would result in further budget reductions. Both the MOE and the *zoku* were also concerned about Nakasone's tendency to embrace radical reform ideas. Some of the Prime Minister's advisors were known to be advocates of the total liberalization of the education system. The MOE in particular was afraid that a politicized council might propose too many disruptive changes. Officials worried especially about the Prime Minister's commitment to the reform of the 6–3–3 system and major changes in the university entrance examination. These conflicts have been discussed in great detail in previous chapters. It was at this point, however, that all of them came to a head.

The Prime Minister was fully aware of these concerns. He was also aware that he would need the support of the subgovernment – especially that of the *zoku* – if he were to succeed in setting up an Education *Rinchō*. Such a council could only be established through Diet legislation, and such legislative action could only be taken if the *zoku* consented. Immediately upon making his decision to seek the establishment of a supra-cabinet education reform council, therefore, Nakasone began a process of compromise. He had to convince the actors of the education subgovernment that they would have a major role in his reform campaign.

The Prime Minister's first task was to build support for the idea of a supra-cabinet council within his own party. His most important allies in this campaign would be the education *zoku* members of his own faction, most notably Inaba Osamu and Sunada Shigetami (both former ministers of education) and Fujinami Takao (a former chairman of the party's Education Division and at the time his chief cabinet secretary). At a meeting in mid-January Nakasone instructed all three to begin quietly canvassing their fellow *zoku* members.[17] The Education Minister, Mori Yoshirō, was another key ally. Despite being a member of the 'opposition' Fukuda faction, he was obliged as a cabinet member to support the Prime Minister's position. He had in fact promised his co-operation at the time he was brought into Nakasone's new post-election cabinet.[18]

Building on this base, Nakasone was gradually able to win the support of the LDP *zoku*. On 22 January, still before the public announcement of the Prime Minister's intention to set up a council, Mori and Fujinami met with two 'opposition' leaders of the *zoku* – Kaifu Toshiki of the Kōmoto faction and Mitsuzuka Hiroshi of the Fukuda faction. Based on Fujinami's argument that only a top-level council could implement reforms and Mori's argument that even a supra-cabinet council could involve the Ministry of Education in a leadership capacity, Kaifu and Mitsuzuka agreed to support the Prime Minister – conditionally. As Kaifu told Nakasone the next day, he could support the idea of a supra-cabinet council 'as long as the responsibility of the MOE and past reports of the CCE are respected'.[19] A few days later *zoku* veteran Sakata Michita accepted a similar deal with the Prime Minister on behalf of the *zoku* as a whole. Sakata was particularly insistent that the 1971 CCE report serve as the basis for the new council's deliberations. 'There is no need,' he said, 'for the council to start from scratch in reviewing the basic philosophy of reform.'[20] On 31 January, Nakasone finally made a public announcement of his decision to seek the establishment of a *Rinchō*-type education reform council.[21]

Up to this point, the compromise process had involved only two actors: the Prime Minister and the *zoku*. The Ministry of Education had been almost totally excluded.[22] In the next stage, however, the MOE and *zoku* worked together to assure that the Prime Minister's promises to Kaifu and Sakata were respected. Thus, when the Ad Hoc Council Establishment Law was finally sent to the Diet on 27 March, it included express stipulations regarding the role to be played by the MOE. First, the council's members and expert members, though to be chosen by the Prime Minister, were to reflect the advice of the Minister of Education. Second, the council's secretariat was to be headed by the MOE AVM.[23] In addition, Nakasone announced on the day of the cabinet decision sending the law to the Diet that the Minister of Education, Mori, would serve as the cabinet member in charge of the council and that the office working on the Establishment Law would be set up within the MOE rather than in the Prime Minister's Office.[24] Through these concessions guaranteeing the Ministry of Education's special place in the management of the Ad Hoc Council, Nakasone was able to gain the tentative support of the education bureaucracy and the MOE's allies in the LDP.

The Prime Minister faced another hurdle, however, before he could see his council established. In order to win prompt Diet approval of the AHCE establishment legislation, he had to avoid a confrontation with the opposition parties. Once again, Nakasone faced strong resistance when he first proposed a supra-cabinet council. His nationalist rhetoric about 'a total clearance of the post-war political accounts' had convinced the Japan Socialist Party, the Japan Communist Party and *Komeito* that he planned to reform even the basic ideology of the post-war education system. If his council was meant as a means to achieve such a reform, the three parties stood ready to obstruct Diet procedings. Even if they failed, such resistance threatened to turn the public against his reform initiative.

Facing this challenge, Nakasone again decided to compromise. As described in Chapter 6, he agreed, first, that the council would abide by the 'spirit' of the Fundamental Law of Education. Then, in later stages of Diet deliberations, he went on to accept two amendments which limited the Prime Minister's personal control over the council by providing for some Diet oversight. While the JSP and JCP continued to refuse to support the Prime Minister, the Democratic Socialist Party and *Komeito* joined the LDP in voting for the law when it finally received Diet approval on 7 August 1984.[25]

The legacy of the initiation process

Although Nakasone finally succeeded in establishing the Ad Hoc Council, he had been forced to make significant concessions both to the education subgovernment and to the progressive camp. He had agreed to give the Minister of Education a special role in the selection of the AHCE's membership, and he had agreed to let the MOE direct the council's secretariat. He had also agreed to some Diet oversight of the council. All of these were concessions of *power*: Nakasone had won the support of his opponents by agreeing to share control of the council.

The underlying differences of opinion about education reform *issues*, however, had not been resolved. The Prime Minister was still hoping for radical reform without higher education expenditure while the MOE was hoping for higher expenditure without radical reform. Furthermore, while Nakasone's decision to abide by the spirit of the FLE seemed to be a compromise on the main issue dividing the conservatives and the progressives, here again the *underlying* issue had not been truly resolved. The Prime Minister remained committed to a programme of nationalist reform – perhaps through a reinterpretation of the FLE – while the progressives intended to prevent any changes in the ideology of post-war education. That the basic conflicts underlying the Prime Minister's education reform initiative had not been resolved – despite the compromises – was soon painfully clear.

The first sign of the divisive struggle ahead came even before the council held its first meeting. Seeking to come to an agreement on the council's membership, the Prime Minister and the education subgovernment were soon at loggerheads over the question of who should be named chairman. Nakasone wanted to name a leader of the business community to establish from the beginning that the Ad Hoc Council would be different from MOE councils of the past. His preference was Nakayama Sohei, a businessman long concerned about education policy. The *zoku* and the ministry, on the other hand, remembered that a business-man had been in charge of the budget-cutting *Rinchō* and there-fore strongly resisted the idea of naming a *zaikai* man to head the AHCE. They insisted that the Prime Minister should choose an established figure from the 'education world': either Ishikawa Tadao, the president of Keiō University and a regular member of MOE advisory councils, or Okamoto Michio, the former presi-dent of Kyoto University and a man who had worked closely with the ministry on its reform of the university entrance examination in the 1970s. In the end Nakayama declined to serve as chairman, leaving the Prime Minister with little choice but to accept one of the subgovernment's choices: he named Okamoto chairman and appointed Ishikawa and Nakayama as vice-chairmen.[26]

Table 8.1 Membership of the Ad Hoc Council on Education

Name	Affiliations
Okamoto Michio (Chairman)	Former president of Kyoto University; worked closely with the MOE on examination reform but also worked with Nakasone through his capacity as head of the Japan Science Council policy unit.
Nakayama Sohei (Vice-chairman)	Former president of the Industrial Bank of Japan; former secretary of *Keizai dōyūkai*; served on Nakasone's private advisory council (PAC) on the 'peace problem'.
Ishikawa Tadao (Vice-chairman)	The president of Keiō University; head of Private University Federation and member of three different MOE advisory councils; also served on Nakasone's PAC on education.
Amaya Naohiro (Chairman of the No. 1 Subcommittee)	Former MITI senior official; president of Japan Economic Foundation; member of the Kyoto Group; served on LDP think-tank closely associated with *Rinchō*'s privatizing ideas.
Ishii Takemochi (Chairman of the No. 2 Subcommittee)	Tokyo University professor; member of the Kyoto Group; an advisor to Prime Minister Ōhira on technical/economic policy who went on to advise Nakasone; chaired one of Nakasone's PACs.
Arita Kazuhisa (Chairman of the No. 3 Subcommittee)	Former LDP and New Liberal Club member of the Diet Upper House – active member of the *zoku*; a former member of the MOE's CCE; a former president of various companies, he was once chair of *Nikkeiren*'s Education Committee.
Iijima Sōichi (Chairman of the No. 4 Subcommittee)	President of Nagoya University; a former member of the CCE and other MOE advisory councils; member of ANUP and JSC.
Sejima Ryūzō (Final member of Executive Committee; No. 4 Subcommittee)	Counsellor, C. Itoh & Company; *zaikai* activist; a member of *Rinchō*, he went on to become a close advisor of Nakasone; member of his PAC on the 'peace problem'; was brought onto a CCE subcommittee despite lack of connections with MOE in order to provide link to *Rinchō*.

Table 8.1 – *continued*

Name	Affiliations
Uchida Kenzō (No. 1 Subcommittee)	A long-time journalist of Kyōdō Press Service; was chief of editorial committee; retired to become Hōsei University professor.
Kanasugi Hidenobu (No. 1 Subcommittee)	Advisor of *Dōmei* Labour Confederation; close links to the Democratic Socialist Party; was a member of *Rinchō*.
Kōyama Kenichi (No. 1 Subcommittee)	Gakushūin University professor; a former advisor to Prime Minister Ōhira, he became one of Nakasone's chief 'brains'.
Nakauchi Isao (No. 1 Subcommittee)	President of Daiei, Inc.; member of the *Keidanren* standing committee; member of *zaikai* group supporting Nakasone.
Minakami Tadashi (No. 1 Subcommittee)	Tokyo education superintendent; a long-time local education administrator in Tokyo.
Kimura Harumi (No. 2 Subcommittee)	Chiba Institute of Technology professor; an essayist known for her view that Japanese have gone soft; member of Kyoto Group.
Saitō Toshitsugu (No. 2 Subcommittee)	Executive director, Daishōwa Paper Manufacturing; past president of Junior Chamber; Nakasone's 'relative' (PM's niece married his brother).
Dōgakinai Naohiro (No. 2 Subcommittee)	Former governor of Hokkaidō; given AHCE place after failing to win LDP Upper House seat.
Sono Ayako (No. 2 Subcommittee)	Author; another of Ōhira's brain-trust who went on to advise Nakasone; member of two of the PM's PACs – including the one on education.
Miyata Yoshiji (No. 2 Subcommittee)	Senior advisor of a *Sōhyō*-affiliated labour union; member of PM's PAC on 'peace problem'.
Okano Shunichirō (No. 3 Subcommittee)	Former football (soccer) player; head of the Japan Olympic Committee; was member of CCE.
Kobayashi Noboru (No. 3 Subcommittee)	General director of Children's Medical Research Centre, National Children's Hospital; member of MHW advisory councils; a former Ōhira 'brain'.

continued overleaf

Table 8.1 – *continued*

Name	Affiliations
Saitō Sei (No. 3 Subcommittee)	Former MOE AVM; president, National Theatre; member of MOE advisory councils, including CCE.
Tamaru Akiyo (No. 3 Subcommittee)	Elementary school teacher; participated in MOE moral education project.
Tobari Atsuo (No. 3 Subcommittee)	Lower-secondary-school principal; head of the Tokyo association of LSS principals.
Sunobe Ryōzō (No. 4 Subcommittee)	Former Ministry of Foreign Affairs AVM; Kyōrin University professor.
Hosomi Takashi (No. 4 Subcommittee)	Former Ministry of Finance senior official; member of LDP think-tank and Nakasone 'brain'; member of Nakasone PACs.

Sources: *NKS*, 27 August and 3 September 1984; Aoki Satoshi *Rinkyōshin kaitai* (Akebi shotoku, Tokyo, 1986), pp. 289–323.

A similar, if less heated, struggle characterized the rest of the membership selection process. While the ministry and *zoku* sought to secure as many places as possible for members of the 'education world' through their role in preparing the list of potential appointees, Nakasone made sure that at least some positions went to more independent-minded men and women willing to fight the conservatism of the MOE. The final membership was in effect another compromise: some members were sympathetic towards the ministry while others were close to Nakasone (Table 8.1). To anyone familiar with the backgrounds of the various members, the outlines of the two camps which were to emerge in the course of the council's deliberations were already visible. The 'MOE Camp', including leaders of the 'education world' and others with close ties to the ministry and *zoku*, included Ishikawa, Arita, Iijima, Saitō Sei, Minakami, Tobari and Tamaru.[27] The 'Nakasone Camp', composed of men and women closer to the Prime Minister, included Nakayama, Amaya, Ishii, Sejima, Kōyama, Nakauchi, Saitō Toshitsugu, Miyata, Sono and Hosomi.[28] The two sides could agree on a membership list only by dividing the council.

DELIBERATIONS AND DECISIONS

Meeting for the first time on 5 September 1984 the Ad Hoc Council began its deliberations with several potential advantages over predecessors such as the CCE. Having received the endorsement of the entire cabinet and the Diet in the initiation process, the AHCE would be able to point back to this mandate when it came to seek the implementation of its proposals. In fact, the AHCE Law actually obliged the Prime Minister to 'respect' the council's advice.[29] Even its diverse membership was a potential advantage. With representatives of the Prime Minister, the 'education world', the LDP education *zoku*, the Ministry of Education, as well as four other ministries (Finance, Health and Welfare, International Trade and Industry, and Foreign Affairs) all sitting on the council, the AHCE would be able to describe anything it could agree upon as a true conservative consensus. If it could agree on a set of education reform proposals, therefore, the council was in an excellent position to assure that these ideas were implemented.

In the end, however, 'if it could agree' turned out to be a crucial qualifying statement. As the analysis of the 1971 CCE-led initiative revealed, the MOE had trouble arriving at a consensus even within the narrower ranks involved in drafting that set of recommendations. With the inclusion of the reformist friends of the Prime Minister, the Ad Hoc Council found it even more difficult to come to an agreement on reform proposals. Whereas previously the main battle was between internationalists and bureaucratic conservatives within the MOE, the AHCE brought in a whole new group of members approaching education reform from a position hostile to the ministry's domination of the education system. Therefore, while the Prime Minister's council did succeed in bringing more concerned parties into the policy-making process at an earlier stage, it did not succeed in altering the basic pattern of conservative division and disagreement which had limited the success of earlier reform initiatives. Whereas the CCE initiative had encountered this problem and foundered in the implementation stage, the new policy-making structure merely forced the AHCE to confront the persistent divisions in the conservative camp at the stage of its deliberations and decisions.

The first year

Early radicalism

Despite the balance of MOE and Nakasone forces in the membership of the Ad Hoc Council, it was the Prime Minister's men who took the initiative in the early months of the council's deliberations. The first to act was Kōyama. Seeking to make 'liberalization' (jiyūka) the council's guiding philosophy, he presented a plan for radical reform at the council's third general meeting. 'It is essential,' he said, 'that we carry out a general re-examination of the bureaucracy's policies of authorization, regulation and aid.' Arguing that the council should 'take decisive action to introduce private-sector vitality into the sphere of education', he proposed more specifically that the establishment of private schools be encouraged at the compulsory school level and that private cram schools (juku) be officially recognized as alternatives to the established schools. The council should pursue such a course, he said 'even to the point of reforming Articles IV and VI of the FLE'.[30]

The nationalist reformers were equally quick off the mark. Speaking at a convention of the alternative (conservative) teachers' union in October, Kanasugi Hidenobu and Arita Kazuhisa both spoke out in favour of taking another look at the FLE. As Kanasugi said:

> While the FLE emphasizes the need to create a 'democratic country', even totalitarian countries like the Soviet Union have education systems centred on the idea of a 'democratic country'. Furthermore, the law's statement that the purpose of education should be the creation of 'complete persons' is vague as to what kind of person should be completed. Clearly, the idea that a person should be raised in the culture and traditions of the country where he was born is connected to this idea of 'complete persons'. Given these considerations, the FLE must be re-examined.[31]

With such statements as this one coming on top of an NHK poll which revealed that only seven of the council's members felt committed to the FLE, the news media were quick to attach a 'reactionary' label to the newly formed Ad Hoc Council.[32] Responding to the uproar, Nakasone and the Education Minister, Mori, did nothing to deter the council from its apparent radicalism, stating that members of the council were perfectly free to express their opinions.[33]

The internal debate

While the reformists were making the headlines in this early period, however, the council was in fact already divided regarding the direction and degree of reform. Council members reluctant to discuss the issue of the FLE before the uproar over the Kanasugi and Arita statements were even more sensitive after experiencing the media criticism which followed that episode. Despite his own statements regarding the need to revise certain restrictive parts of the law, it was Kōyama who finally convinced the council that it should turn away from 'unproductive ideological arguments' and concentrate more on concrete plans for reform, that is his liberalization ideas.[34]

Kōyama himself, however, was not without opponents. By the beginning of November when the council split up into four subcommittees, the battle lines over *jiyūka* were already drawn. The First Subcommittee, charged with developing the basic philosophy of the reform, was to be headed by Amaya Naohiro (chairman) and Kōyama (vice-chairman) – both strong advocates of *jiyūka* – and was to include several other members close to the Prime Minister. On the other hand, the Third and Fourth Subcommittees, charged with developing more concrete reform proposals for elementary and secondary education (Third) and higher education (Fourth) were to be dominated by the MOE camp. Arita, an avid defender of maintaining government control over compulsory education, was given charge of the Third Subcommittee – also to include Saitō Sei, Tamaru Akiyo and Tobari Atsuo from the MOE side – while the Fourth Subcommittee was placed under the leadership of Iijima Sōichi, the Nagoya University President closely associated with the MOE position (see Table 8.1).

According to Ōmori Kazuo, the *Asahi Shimbun* journalist covering the council, this division of membership reflected the conscious strategy of the MOE secretariat. Recognizing the challenge posed by liberalizationists, it decided that the best way to limit the damage would be to put the reformist leaders in charge of philosophy while making sure its own members were firmly in control of the subcommittee dealing with concrete reform, thereby putting them in a position to block First

Subcommittee ideas when it got to the stage of drawing up actual recommendations.[35]

Disagreement finally broke out into the open in January 1985. First Arita, speaking at a press conference following a subcommittee meeting, attacked the idea that schools could be improved through free competition. 'Children are not consumers and compulsory education is not a service,' he argued. 'For example, suppose you teach children Japan's cultural tradition. You have to teach it to them whether they like it or not.'[36] Just a few days later, Kōyama responded by attacking his attackers, charging the Ministry of Education with attempting to maintain the uniformity and standardization of the status quo in the face of the educational crisis.[37]

By this time, the MOE had in fact weighed in with an official statement against the First Subcommittee's *jiyūka* plans. Nothing could better illustrate the degree to which the ministry had been excluded from the new policy-making process than this unusual sight of ministry officials publicly appealing to the council to modify its views.[38] A few days later, the LDP *zoku* joined the debate. Inviting several council leaders to an unofficial meeting at a Tokyo hotel, six former education ministers criticized the council for its advocacy of *jiyūka* at the compulsory level.[39] Over the next few weeks, as the council held hearings to obtain the opinions of various groups concerned with education issues, group after group expressed opposition to the *jiyūka* line, criticizing in particular the Kōyama plan to introduce free competition into the compulsory education sector through the abolition of school zones and the relaxation of school establishment regulations.[40]

By the time the council finally got together and published an official 'Summary of Deliberative Progress' in April, the reformist First Subcommittee had agreed to reduce its emphasis on *jiyūka* and accept a new phrase to describe the council's guiding philosophy: the goal of education for the twenty-first century was to be 'the promotion of *koseishugi* (individuality-ism)'. *Jiyūka*, the council decided, was too vague a term and tended to confuse ends with means. While still disagreeing on the means, the council could agree that the aim of education in Japan should be 'individuality-ism'. A system 'emphasizing individuality, individual dignity, freedom, autonomy and self-responsibility' was portrayed as the necessary alternative to the uniformity and standardization of the status quo.[41] Such a change in emphasis, however, still looked extremely radical to many in the 'education world'. Critics were particularly concerned with the similarity between the council's key word *koseishugi* – a non-standard term – and the more common '*kojinshugi*' (individualism), a term with certain negative connotations not unlike, for example, the term 'self-centred' in the English language. The Ad Hoc Council seemed to be committing itself to introducing 'Western-style' egoism at the expense of the 'Japanese' emphasis on social harmony.[42]

Intervention

Until this point, all of the main government actors – the *zoku*, the MOE and Nakasone – had been generally content to let the council find its own way. After the AHCE issued its April interim report, however, each decided it could not afford to remain passive. The *zoku* and the MOE were worried about the AHCE's individualist ideology and its failure to call for higher education spending. Nakasone was concerned that the council had not endorsed any of the high-profile radical reforms he favoured.

The *zoku* responded first. Calling AHCE Chairman Okamoto before the party's Special Research Council on Education Reform on the day after the publication of the interim report, the Dietmen attacked the council for failing to understand the nature of educational problems: Okamoto and his fellow members did not seem to see the importance of increased public funding; they seemed to be ignoring the importance of tradition and social harmony in the Japanese education system.[43] The forum for this exchange – the Special Research Council – had been set up within PARC by *zoku* leaders at the time the AHCE started its deliberations. While it had been largely inactive since that time, the *zoku* moved with this episode to bring it into the game.

The *zoku*'s most concerted attempt to influence the council came more than a month later, on 3 June 1985. At an unofficial meeting between key *zoku* politicians and several AHCE leaders, the Dietmen were discussing some of the issues they had raised with Okamoto – focusing particularly on their concerns about *jiyūka*. It was at that point that one of the AHCE members responded by revealing that he was being thwarted in his attempt to steer the council away from *jiyūka* by another council member's claims that he was representing the Prime

Minister's point of view. The disagreement over liberalization would not be resolved, he said, as long as the party itself remained divided on the issue. The stage was finally set for the *zoku* to confront the Prime Minister.[44]

That evening *zoku* representative Sunada Shigetami went to call on the Prime Minister. Hearing about the claims being made by one of his advisors on the council, Nakasone responded by making it clear that the man was not working on his behalf.[45] The next day, he took a firm stand on the liberalization issue. Calling Sunada back to his office, he came down firmly on the side of the argument that 'compulsory education is the government's responsibility', adding that talk of *jiyūka* of that sector was 'frivolous'.[46] Given that Nakasone had until this point steadfastly refused to speak out against *jiyūka* – once going so far as to describe himself as a 'liberalizationist' – this announcement marked a significant victory for the *zoku*. Nakasone had endorsed its position against any *jiyūka* of the compulsory sector.[47]

While the *zoku* had been successful in blocking Nakasone on *jiyūka*, the subgovernmental forces were not so successful in their efforts to convince the AHCE to support their own reform goals – particularly on the issue of public finance. The MOE, seeking to play a more active role through its part in providing staff assistance to the council, had tried to have a clause inserted into the AHCE's First Report endorsing increased funds for education. The clause was to read: 'consideration must be given to the financial measures required (to pay for reforms)'. In the final version of the First Report, however, fiscal conservatives on the council effectively neutralized the recommendation by adding a qualifying statement. Funding should be provided, the council recommended, 'in the context of the overall financial situation of the government'.[48]

The final actor to intervene in the course of AHCE deliberations was the Prime Minister. Having expended so much political energy on bringing about the establishment of the Ad Hoc Council, he was concerned at the lack of substance in the April interim report. He needed the council to propose *some* radical reforms so that he could portray his initiative as a success. With both the nationalists and the liberalizationists unable to build support for their far-reaching proposals, he turned his attention to two less ideologically divisive but nevertheless 'radical' ideas.

In the end, however, he could not win the council's endorsement of even these less controversial ideas.

His first target was the school calendar: a change in the school starting date from April to September. The idea was not in fact a new one. Long advocated by the business community and the LDP education *zoku*, the switchover to a September start was defended both in terms of 'internationalization' and 'examination relief'. Such a change, it was argued, would bring Japan into line with the school calendar most commonly employed in 'western' nations, thereby making it easier for Japanese universities and other educational institutions to participate in international exchanges. In addition, by allowing university entrance examinations to be scheduled during the summer *after* the end of the school year, the switch would also end the disruptive effect of the April start which forced examinations to be conducted in the middle of the final term.[49]

This reform proposal, having been backed by a special *zoku* study group in 1983, enjoyed support among that group of Dietmen and also seemed to appeal to many AHCE members.[50] When Nakasone put it on the council's agenda, therefore, he had reason to hope that it would serve as a visible sign of progress in his reform campaign. Even in this case, however, the reformists ran into opposition. The Third Subcommittee, under Arita, was firmly opposed to the establishment of a September start for elementary and secondary schools. Such a switch, the committee argued, would leave students between school years (summer vacation) without supervision from school teachers. The 1 April to 31 March school year left all vacations covered.[51] As for the more widely supported idea of changing the school year only for universities, the idea was opposed by some university officials as unnecessary. The Ministry of Education, they pointed out, changed its regulations in 1976 to allow universities – if they wished – to admit students outside the otherwise strict April to March school schedule. A forced changeover on the part of all universities was unnecessary when institutions could gradually change over under existing regulations.[52] With several university organization's taking this position, the council eventually decided to put off a decision on the school year reform, despite Nakasone's efforts.

Having failed to elicit quick action on this issue, Nakasone focused all of his efforts on his second 'radical' reform: his vow to abolish the *Kyōtsū-ichiji* university entrance examination.[53] That the university entrance examination system required reform was one issue on which virtually all parties concerned with education reform could agree. The Ad Hoc Council, therefore, did not need much prodding from Nakasone to set it on its way to drafting a reform plan. Paying close attention to the opinions of such concerned parties as the National Association of University Presidents and the Private Universities Association, the council's Fourth Subcommittee led by Iijima Sōichi quickly arrived at a strategy for reform. The plan was to 'reform' the *Kyōtsū-ichiji* examination system – limited to national and a few local public universities – so that all universities (including private) would be able to participate in a flexible manner. The new test was to be called the '*Kyōtsū Tesuto*'.[54]

This plan, however, did not go far enough for Nakasone. He had vowed to 'abolish' the *Kyōtsū-ichiji* while this plan only 'reformed' it. Based on various Nakasone statements made after the publication of the AHCE's First Report, it seems that the Prime Minister's primary concern – in seeking the 'abolition' of the *Kyōtsū-ichiji* exam – was with the examination's role in limiting the creativity and diversity of Japanese students. He objected to the way in which the single, uniform examination played such a large role in determining an individual's future and disliked its insistence on success across the whole range of academic disciplines. The exam, he believed, was at the root of the standardization of Japanese education.[55] The course he favoured was the outright abolition of the standard university entrance examination. With each university thereby forced to develop its own test, the standardizing influence of the exam system would be mitigated.[56]

Iijima could not accept Nakasone's proposal for several reasons. First, as a university official, he represented an academic community which prized the ideal of a student trained in a broad range of school subjects – encouraged by the existing *Kyōtsū-ichiji*. He could see the need for some flexibility, but was not willing to abandon the ideal altogether. Second, he argued that neither students nor universities could deal with the workload required by a totally unstructured system of examinations. Students would not know what to study for, and university officials would have to go through the time-consuming process of drafting their own examinations. Most importantly, however, he represented the view that university officials ought to be able to determine their admission procedures themselves.[57] His own plan had been worked out in detail with various university organizations and was purposely vague in order to leave the universities with some latitude to deal with the issue on their own.[58]

On 5 June the Prime Minister made one last attempt to convince the council to 'abolish' the examination. Following an AHCE meeting at which Kanasugi had proposed a radical plan to abolish totally the system of standard university entrance examinations, Nakasone called Okamoto, Ishikawa and Nakayama to an Akasaka restaurant and demanded that they at least change the wording of the recommendation on *Kyōtsū-ichiji* to read 'abolish'. The next day, at a meeting of the council's executive committee, the wording of the AHCE recommendation was changed to read that the *Kyōtsū Tesuto* should 'replace' the *Kyōtsū-ichiji*. In addition, a clause was added specifying that the new test should be structured to allow universities to choose 'as few as one subject'.[59] While this last provision held the potential to serve as a means of reducing the uniformity of the examination system, the recommendation as a whole fell short of what Nakasone had hoped to achieve.

The First Report

On 26 June 1985 the AHCE issued its First Report, a document combining a discussion of the reform's basic philosophy with a section outlining its first concrete reform proposals. Virtually every section testified to the heated battles of the council's first year. The section on the council's philosophy – originally centred on the idea of *jiyūka* and then on *koseishugi* – had been further softened in recognition of continued opposition from the Third Subcommittee and the *zoku*: the new key word was *kosei-jūshi* (an emphasis on individuality). This new phrase was also qualified by several statements describing the need for students to learn about their social responsibilities in an interdependent society. Symptomatic of the inability of the council to agree on a clear direction for the reform was a paragraph in which the council began by describing the problems of an overly standardized education system and followed this with a passage mourning the loss of tradition, morals and 'a consciousness of responsibilities' to balance the post-war emphasis on 'rights'.[60] The council seemed to be trying to seek both greater diversity and greater conformity at the same time.

The concrete reform proposals of the First Report were also less bold than they might have been because of lack of agreement on crucial issues. As noted, the proposal on examination reform, while reworded to provide for the 'replacement' of the *Kyōtsū-ichiji* exam, still fell short of Nakasone's goal of abolition. The council's recommendation calling for the establishment of a parallel track of six-year secondary schools also did not provide what certain reformists had hoped to achieve. Whereas Nakasone and several *zoku* members had hoped that such schools might serve as a new elite track (used, for example, to train creative scientists), the council specified that they were to concentrate on such subjects as art, foreign languages and physical education. They were not to become exam-preparation schools. Likewise, the AHCE's proposal calling for the establishment of 'credit system' (or module-based) upper secondary schools failed to specify the purposes such schools might serve. The advocates of elite education were hoping the council would endorse them as a means of letting talented students break out of the rigid school-year structure and pursue their studies at a faster pace. Finally, the recommendation concerning the need for society to relax its emphasis on school background contained few specific reform ideas.[61]

The effect of the first-year battles was most visible, however, in what the council did *not* recommend. It did not recommend the rewriting or reinterpretation of the FLE − a goal of Nakasone's nationalist supporters on the council. It did not, as noted above, give a clear call for increased education funding − a goal of the MOE representatives on the council. It expressly declined to make a recommendation on the lowering of the school starting age or the unification of nursery school and kindergarten administration − goals of certain *zoku* politicians. It put off a recommendation on whether or not to move the school starting date to September. It also put off decisions on all of Kōyama's concrete liberalization proposals. All of these issues were discussed further in the following two years. The battle lines, however, had already been drawn, and as it turned out, the decisive battles had already been fought.

The second and third years

In retrospect, it is clear that the first year of the AHCE was Nakasone's only chance to establish a bold direction for his reform initiative. Having won Diet approval of his plan to establish a supra-cabinet council in 1984 largely through his personal intervention and having convinced the MOE and *zoku* to give the new council some room in which to work, he had begun the first year with the 'momentum' necessary to set the council on the road to significant reform. By the end of that year, he had lost that momentum. In part, this reverse reflected the fact that the Prime Minister (and his 'brains') had chosen the wrong policies on which to fight. Rather than focusing their attack on the overly standardized nature of the education system and building support for 'flexibilization', they had concentrated on promoting 'liberalization' – a catchword associated with a radical set of proposals for introducing market competition into the education system. When this idea turned out to be too radical for most members of the council and the public, Nakasone's entire attack on the over-regulation of the system lost its appeal. The miscalculation having given the MOE and the *zoku* a chance to regroup, the two actors of the education subgovernment quickly worked to take control of the council.

In the aftermath of the First Report, both the MOE and *zoku* permanently cast aside their 'wait and see' approach and moved to intervene more directly. Expanding its Special Research Council on Education Reform, the *zoku* established two new subgroups with a total of six working subcommittees. Each was to conduct its own studies of education reform issues, providing information and a forum from which to influence the AHCE.[62] At about the same time, the MOE began feeding the council increasing quantities of information and ideas, once again using its role in providing staff assistance to help turn deliberations more towards the MOE line. Whereas both the ministry and the *zoku* had been forced to respond to events in the first year, they were able to use the next year to help shape the debate as it was progressing.

Using this expanded role, the two subgovernmental partners made the second year 'their' year. When the council's Second Report was issued on 23 April 1986, it was full of long-standing MOE ideas, most of them relatively non-controversial and few of them very far-reaching. Large sections were devoted, for example, to the need for new education programmes to respond to the internationalization and 'information-ization' of society. The section on curriculum reform virtually repeated the 1983 proposals of the CCE Subcommittee on Educational Content. The single controversial reform proposal was that calling for the establishment of a training year for new teachers. Even this was a somewhat softer version of the 1971 *shiho* proposal.

The influence of the subgovernment was also visible in the *absence* of certain proposals in the Second Report. Decisions on virtually all liberalizationist ideas – the deregulation of textbooks, the abolition of school zones, the incorporation (*hōjinka*) of the national universities – were put off to the third and final year, as was the decision on whether or not to move the school starting date to September. These were the proposals which Nakasone's supporters on the council steadfastly refused to abandon but which the MOE and *zoku* opposed. Interestingly, about the time the AHCE was starting to work towards its Third Report, newspapers began to report that the council had effectively reached the end of its usefulness. Both LDP *zoku* politicians and MOE bureaucrats were quoted suggesting that they had already heard all that they needed to hear from the council and that henceforth they would pursue the education reform process on their own.[63] It was a blatant attempt to end the game while they were ahead. While the council did continue its deliberations until August 1987, for all practical purposes it could have stopped its work after the second year. The Third Report issued on 1 April 1987 and the Final Report issued on 7 August 1987 contained few significant new proposals. The pattern of deliberations over those final two years with respect to the most important reform issues is summarized below.

Liberalization reforms

The ability of the education subgovernment to prevent the council from recommending policies it opposed was most vividly demonstrated in the case of the *jiyūka* proposals – narrowly defined here as those policies aimed at introducing a 'competitive mechanism' into the education system. As articulated by First Subcommittee member Kōyama, the *jiyūka* argument blamed the uniformity of the education system on its domination by the MOE and proposed that the introduction of competition would give the system more 'vitality'. A particular concern was the lack of competition at the elementary and *chūgakkō* levels where the large majority of students (99 per cent at the elementary level) attended state schools organized on a strict neighbourhood basis with no provision for choice. Kōyama therefore proposed: (1) that the establishment of private schools at this level be encouraged, and (2) that school-choice restrictions be eliminated to give parents a choice of local schools. In addition, he proposed that the government allow the informal private sector – cram schools (*juku*) and special training schools (*senshū gakkō*) – to play a more important role in the school system.

The 'MOE Camp' on the council succeeded in keeping virtually all of these ideas out of the Second Report. The only concession was a paragraph recommending that measures to facilitate the establishment of private elementary and lower secondary schools 'should be studied' – a proposal vague enough to allow the MOE substantial room for non-implementation.[64] The other two ideas received equally half-hearted support in the Third Report. Responding to Kōyama's call for a relaxation of restrictions on school choice, the council did suggest that localities create *some* means by which to respect the wishes of parents. It also specified, however, that such changes should only be introduced such that they would not create inequality or administrative problems. Localities would not have to do anything if they did not want to. Finally, the council proposed that the government should 'reflect' on the new role of the informal private education sector and 'study' new ways in which it might be incorporated into 'a flexible education network'.[65] It was the vaguest of three vague recommendations.

'Flexibilization' reforms

In principle the AHCE was totally committed to 'flexibilization' (*jūnanka*), defined here as policies aimed at ending the uniformity of the content of Japanese education. The idea was central to the council's guiding philosophy of 'an emphasis on individuality' and was repeatedly employed to explain its general aims in various areas. In most cases, however, the subgovernment and its representatives on the council succeeded in blocking or at least rendering impotent the attempts of 'Nakasone Camp' members to endorse specific *jūnanka* proposals.

Symbolic of this struggle was the debate over 'regulatory relief' (*kisei kanwa*) in the lead-up to the Second Report. The First Subcommittee had succeeded in inserting a strong endorsement of this principle in an early draft of the council's recommendations.[66] In the final version of the Second Report, however, the proposal was qualified with the stipulation that changes should be introduced while recognizing that the government retained the responsibility to 'ensure certain standards and maintain the quality of education'.[67] It would be left to the MOE to determine which standards were necessary to maintain the quality of education.

A specific set of regulations targeted for 'relief' were the MOE's curriculum guidelines. The Second Report recommended that the government 'rewrite its specifications in a broader, outline form' (*taikōka*) and suggested that it allow more room for students to select courses in the final year of *chūgakkō* and at the *kōtōgakkō* level.[68] Once again, however, it would be the MOE which decided how 'broad' to make its guidelines and how many electives to allow. The ministry's own CCE had made similar recommendations in 1983, and the MOE had been moving slowly in that direction since the 1970s.[69] Nothing in the AHCE recommendations would force it to move at a faster pace.

Another aspect of the AHCE's flexibilization campaign was its recommendation calling for greater decentralization (*chihō bunken*). Paradoxically, despite the MOE's long history of building up its central power, the MOE Camp co-operated with the liberalizationists in developing the council's recommendations in this area. The two sides agreed that local authorities should be encouraged to develop diverse and innovative programmes. The ministry pointed out, however, that such innovation could take place only if local boards of education were made stronger. In the end, most of the AHCE's specific recommendations were in the latter area: board members were to be 'better trained', city-town-and-village superintendents were to be made full-time professional positions, and the means by which local boards dealt with 'problem teachers' were to be improved. The council's proposals in the first area were much less specific: localities were to be allowed to 'develop fully their diverse identities' and were to be 'actively encouraged to adopt new innovations'.[70] The council did not propose that the ministry give up any specific powers: it was still to be responsible for maintaining 'certain minimum standards'. This imbalance explained why the MOE had been so eager to endorse decentralization. In the name of 'revitalizing' local school boards to enable them to develop local innovations, it had succeeded in getting the council to endorse several of its long-standing proposals for strengthening the ability of local authorities to deal with local teachers' unions. It won this support, furthermore, without committing itself to any actual delegation of its powers. With its local boards more able to deal with local unions, it would actually be left in a stronger position for imposing its decisions on localities if it so chose.

Most indicative of the council's ambivalent attitude towards *jūnanka*, however, were its recommendations in the areas of examination and textbook reform. Unless the education system's emphasis on broad-based examinations and uniform textbooks were changed, the content of what was taught in schools would not in the end be any more diverse. Nakasone's inability to convince the council to propose radical examination reform in the first year was discussed above. In the end this failure to take a strong position guaranteed that most universities would continue to require a broad range of examinations. In recommending that private universities be invited to participate in the *Kyōtsū Tesuto*, the council actually threatened to extend the standardizing influence of exams.

The textbook issue was not decided until the final year of the council. Even in January 1987, when the AHCE issued its last 'summary of deliberations', the issue was not settled. While Kōyama and his allies on the First Subcommittee argued for a significant reduction in ministry control over textbooks and 'free publication, free selection' by the end of the century, the Third Subcommittee insisted on maintaining the established system.[71] The final recommendation was thus an artificial compromise. Although it let Kōyama claim some credit for achieving reform by endorsing the idea of diverse texts in principle, it actually left the ministry fully in control. The textbook review process was to be simplified and made more public, but the MOE was to retain final authority to insist on changes in textbooks.[72]

Gifted education reforms

One of the leading priorities of conservative reformers throughout the period under study was that of recreating an elite track of high-quality education or at least providing education better matched to the abilities of individual students. In the end, however, the AHCE produced virtually no reform proposals in this area. As noted in the discussion of the First Report, neither the six-year secondary-school proposal or the credit-system upper-secondary-school proposal was presented as a means of gifted education. The council also did not call for streaming by ability within *chūgakkō* – a proposal which had actually been supported by the 1983 CCE Subcommittee. Likewise, the 'grade-skipping' proposal included in the LDP *zoku*'s 'Kondō Plan' was not endorsed. There was very little in the AHCE reports, therefore, for the advocates of gifted education.

University reforms

Virtually all of the reform proposals raised during the 1970s reform initiative were subjects of debate within the AHCE: stronger central administration, greater input from outside universities, reform of the system of general studies, the incorporation (*hōjinka*) of the national universities and the conversion of lifetime faculty positions to contracted posts. In addition, the liberalizationists on the council raised a new issue, a proposal that national universities be encouraged to rely on private endowments to provide extra support for their operations. As in most of the cases above, however, the council was not able to endorse firmly any of these changes. The proposals on a stronger central administration, input from outside universities, and reform of the general studies system were all worded in very vague terms. The recommendation on general studies, for example, pointed to various problems with the system and concluded that 'it is necessary to enter into serious research into the way general studies ought to be organized'.[73] The council expressly endorsed the idea that faculty-employment regulations ought to be changed to allow employment on a termly basis. It went on to say, however, that such a system should apply primarily to young assistants and lecturers – not necessarily to assistant professors or professors.[74] Finally unable to arrive at concrete positions on these issues, the council called for the establishment of a new MOE 'University Council' to discuss them further.[75]

The most vocal disputes over university reform, however, were again those which matched the MOE Camp against the liberalizationists. Kōyama and Kanasugi, both First Subcommitee members, were strong advocates of *hōjinka* and the proposal that universities seek to increase their funding through the solicitation of private funds. Both changes promised to force universities to listen more closely to the needs of the business community while the second also promised to save the government money in the long term. The MOE Camp – represented by the Fourth Subcommittee Chairman, Iijima – fiercely resisted both of these ideas.[76] In the final report, the AHCE noted only that it had discussed *hōjinka* and failed to come to an agreement. On the issue of private funds, it urged national universities to establish endowments but stopped short of recommending that the government take any steps to encourage such forms of finance. The establishment of tax incentives, it said, 'should be studied'.[77]

Pre-school reform

As in 1971, the question of whether to unify the administration of kindergartens and nursery schools was an issue. After delaying its recommendation until the final year, the council finally decided to propose only that the respective institutions be separately expanded and improved. It did not endorse unification or even any specific steps toward co-ordination.[78]

September school-start

The debate over whether or not to move the school starting date to September was outlined above. The council put off its decision until the very end of its deliberations, but still could not agree. It finally decided to endorse the *concept* of eventually converting to a September start while noting that such a change should only be attempted when national public opinion was ready. 'At present,' it went on, 'one cannot say that the general public has accepted the need for a switch to an autumn start.'[79]

Expansion programmes

A large number of the AHCE's proposals fell into the category of 'expansion programmes'. Just as the 1970 reform initiative had targeted kindergartens, private universities and education for the handicapped for additional aid, the AHCE focused on graduate education, scientific research and programmes to internationalize and 'informationize' the schools. Among the projects supported were the rapid expansion and improvement of graduate schools; the promotion of basic research in universities; the incorporation of new information technology into schools and other buildings to create 'intelligent schools' and 'intelligent' public buildings for use by all age groups and local businesses; the improvement of 'educational conditions' (e.g.

reducing the number of students in classes); further expansion and improvement of education and training programmes for the handicapped; the establishment of 'nature schools' to allow urban-area students to be exposed to nature; new programmes for 'returnee children' – the children of parents returning from abroad – including the establishment of 'new international schools'; the rapid expansion of programmes bringing foreign students to Japanese universities; and the expansion of programmes for training teachers of the Japanese language.[80]

As in the case of the CCE, this proliferation of expansion projects was a natural result of the desire of the MOE and the LDP *zoku* to increase 'their' share of the budget. It also reflected the lack of opposition to such programmes relative to issues involving reform of existing structures and institutions. Whereas the MOE had easily won CCE endorsement of its expansion programmes, however, the ministry and its allies on the AHCE were forced to contend with objections from fiscal conservatives also sitting on the council. Just as the MOE Camp had blocked many of the liberalizationists' structural reform proposals, Kōyama and his First Subcommittee allies stood in the way of the MOE's expansion efforts. The MOE's first failed effort to win support for an unqualified statement endorsing full funding of the council's reform programmes was described above. Although the ministry, the *zoku*, and their supporters on the AHCE, persisted in trying to get the AHCE to include such a statement in its Second and Third Reports, they continued to be unsuccessful. The statement in the Final Report was a major disappointment. It called on the government to 'endeavour to its utmost to achieve the smooth implementation of this council's recommendations while giving heed to the relationship between this goal and that of budgetary restraint (*gyōzaisei kaikaku*). The Final Report also called for the government to consider private funding for the reforms rather than just public funding.[81] Despite the large number of expansion programmes included in the AHCE reports, therefore, funding for them was not assured.

Nationalist reforms

While AHCE members took totally opposite views on many of the issues described above, they were at least in agreement about the direction of change in the case of most 'nationalist' reform issues. They agreed that Japanese values needed to be taught; they agreed that more moral education was necessary; and they agreed that teachers needed to be better trained. The AHCE was always likely to produce some 'nationalist' recommendations. After the council failed to establish a clear direction for its reform initiative in the first year, however, the MOE and *zoku* were able to make their 'nationalist' proposals the centre of the council's reform programme.

The emphasis on Japanese values, moral education and teacher training was particularly visible in the council's Second Report. The philosophical section of the report – aimed at establishing a foundation for Japanese education by exploring the meaning of the FLE – concluded that education in Japan should play a special role in cultivating 'a proper national awareness', teaching students about social responsibilities and preserving 'the unique culture and traditions of Japan'. It went on to assert, in a particularly controversial section, that the new international era made it ever more important for education to foster the 'patriotism' (*kuni o aisuru kokoro*) required to enable one to come to a true understanding of foreign cultures.[82] This argument was taken a step further in the Final Report with the inclusion in this section of the council's recommendation calling on schools to train students to respect and understand the national flag and anthem.[83]

The Second Report also prominently featured recommendations for the expansion and improvement of moral education and the establishment of a year-long training programme for new teachers. Among the more specific moral education proposals were a recommendation that the use of supplementary readers be encouraged and a proposal that programmes such as overnight excursions to nature camps be expanded.[84] The teacher-training proposal called on the government to require all new teachers to undergo a full year of on-the-job training (*shoninsha kenshū*) under the supervision of experienced teachers. It also called for the 'conditional employment period' of newly employed teachers (originally six months as in the case of all public employees) to be extended to a full year in recognition of their trainee status.[85]

While these reform proposals represented significant progress for advocates of 'nationalist' education reform, they were not total victories. They were the result of a process of give-and-take between the most 'hawkish' nationalists and those more concerned about the disruptive effects of such proposals on the education system. As a result, the philosophical section, for

241

example, did not accomplish the revision of the FLE long sought by the hawks. Although it contained some nationalist rhetoric, the final version of the text was actually a much-moderated version of the 'reinterpretation' proposed by AHCE members such as Kanasugi and specialist member Takahashi Shirō.[86] Similarly, the moral education proposal did not call, as some had urged, for the initiation of a morals textbook. It only suggested that the use of a supplementary reader be 'encouraged'.

Finally, the moderation was apparent even in the case of the centrepiece nationalist reform, the *shoninsha kenshū* proposal. The *zoku* had originally urged the council simply to endorse the old *shiho* proposal as articulated by the CCE in 1971. The final version of the plan, however, was somewhat more moderate – reflecting MOE concerns about the disruptive effects of a strict system of 'probation'. Most significantly, the AHCE proposal did not propose that new teachers be given a 'special status' (*tokubetsu na mibun*). It simply suggested that the established 'conditional employment period' (usually a mere formality) be extended. It urged, furthermore, that 'consideration be given in order to avoid causing new or prospective teachers to feel anxiety'. The emphasis in the report was on the training aspect of the proposal.[87] In the case of the nationalist proposals as well as in other areas, therefore, the bargaining process within the conservative camp led to a clear softening of reform proposals.

The above summary of the AHCE's deliberations and decisions has necessarily left out some reform proposals.[88] What it reveals, however, is the way in which internal conflict – particularly that between the First and Third Subcommittees as representatives on the education subgovernment on the one hand and Nakasone on the other – made it impossible for the council to make a strong commitment to reform across the range of issues. The Third Subcommittee blocked the *jiyūka* proposals and succeeded in having the *jūnanka* recommendations worded in very vague terms. It also kept the council from endorsing a switch to a September school-starting date. On the other hand, the First Subcommittee prevented the council from endorsing the MOE's statement calling for increased educational finance and thereby put a whole range of expansion programmes in jeopardy. In the case of the nationalist reforms, the disagreement was less a First versus Third battle. Nevertheless, differences between hawks and doves on the council and in the government resulted in the softening of key reform proposals.

IMPLEMENTATION

On 20 August 1987, in a ceremony marking the end of the AHCE's existence, the Council Chairman, Okamoto, removed the sign marking the council's rooms in the Prime Minister's Office and handed it to the MOE AVM, Takaishi Kunio.[89] The transfer was symbolic: Nakasone's council, originally conceived by the Prime Minister as a means of breaking the MOE's conservative hold on the education system and radically transforming Japanese education, was leaving the implementation of its recommendations to that same ministry. Nakasone, in his final months as prime minister, tried to convince his party that the AHCE needed a strong supra-cabinet 'post-AHCE' council to oversee the implementation of its recommendations. Such a follow-up body had played a crucial role in the case of the *Rinchō* administrative reform council. This time, however, he faced unbending opposition from the MOE and the education *zoku* – and he was running out of time. With his departure from the prime ministership on 6 November 1987, the task of implementing the Ad Hoc Council's reform proposals was essentially left to the MOE.[90]

The fact that the MOE was left in charge of implementation had immediate significance for the prospects of several reform proposals. As 1987 came to a close, the MOE was still committed to 'studying' the proposals for six-year secondary schools and a switch to a September school starting date. The ministry's opposition to both ideas was well known, however, and its decision to refer them to further study did not disguise the fact that neither of these specific AHCE proposals was likely to be implemented in the near future, if at all.[91]

Equally significant was the effect of the MOE-dominated implementation process on the way in which the vaguer AHCE recommendations on *jiyūka* and *jūnanka* were to be put into practice. In response to the AHCE's proposal on increasing parent choice of schools, for example, the ministry did issue a communication (*tsūchi*) to all local authorities. The text of its directive, however, suggested only that localities 'study' how they might go about responding more flexibly to parental requests and emphasized their right to determine their own policies.[92] Similarly, in response to the AHCE proposal that curriculum regulations be made 'broader' – a proposal central to 'flexibilization' – the MOE Curriculum Council did endorse the idea in principle. In its detailed recommendations, however, it did not seem to give much attention to this goal and actually recommended more detailed regulatory specification in several areas.[93] Finally, while the MOE moved quickly to reform its textbook review process in response to the AHCE recommendations in that area, it was putting much less emphasis on the AHCE goal of diversifying textbook content than it was on the council's suggestions for simplifying the process.[94] In all of these areas, therefore, the MOE's actions were far removed from the original goals of *jūnanka* and *jiyūka*.

While the MOE's control over regulatory aspects of the implementation process was limiting change in areas such as those outlined above, its lack of control over one crucial aspect – its budget – was limiting its ability to implement even those reforms which it favoured. Despite repeated pleas from the *zoku* and the MOE, Nakasone refused to exempt the education budget from restrictive budget ceilings.[95] Thus forced to find funds for expensive reforms from within their own budget, the MOE and *zoku* had to scale back some of their plans for expensive expansion programmes. The rapid expansion of graduate universities, the grand scheme for incorporating technology into the schools, and even long-standing priorities like reducing the size of school classes would have to await the availability of funds.[96]

The status of the other major AHCE reform recommendations at the end of 1987 could be summarized as follows.

(1) *Teacher training.* The MOE's Teacher Training Council issued its final recommendations on the *shoninsha kenshū* programme and other teacher reforms in December 1987, in time to allow legislation to be submitted to the next session of the Diet. Pilot *shoninsha kenshū* projects were set up in thirty-six prefectures and cities in 1987 and were scheduled for further expansion in 1988.[97] While it thus looked likely (pending the availability of finance) that this programme would be fully implemented, it was also clear that the system put in place would not be as strict as the *shiho* proposal advocated by LDP hawks. The MOE council's report recommended that the 'conditional year' provision be applied 'cautiously and appropriately'. The goal was

merely to assure that teachers came out of the training having acquired the personal qualities and abilities appropriate for teaching.[98]

(2) *University reform.* Through Diet action in September 1987, the government won passage of a law establishing the University Council as a new MOE advisory body, and on 29 October the MOE referred most of the AHCE proposals on higher education to the new body. The members appointed to the council included several outspoken *zaikai* advocates of university reform but also featured several former MOE bureaucrats and figures from the university establishment – suggesting that indecision on these issues would probably continue.[99]

(3) *Examination reform.* The AHCE proposal had three main parts: that the test should be offered more than once a year; that it should include private universities; and that it should be more flexible – the last point being the only one which held any promise of reducing the degree to which Japanese education was exam-orientated. It was the first two, however, which were emphasized in the implementation process. The test was offered twice a year starting in 1987. Despite early efforts to introduce quickly a 'new' more flexible test, the target date was postponed to 1990 under MOE pressure due to its overriding goal of using the reform process to bring private universities into the exam system. No private university seemed interested. In November 1987 the new Minister of Education was quoted as saying that examination reform was not worth undertaking if private universities could not be brought into the system.[100] While discussions on the new test continued as 1987 came to a close, the chances that a significantly more flexible and diverse exam system would emerge seemed slim.

(4) *Curriculum reform.* In December 1987 the MOE's Curriculum Council completed the first stage of the curriculum reform process by issuing its report setting out more detailed proposals on a number of AHCE recommendations. The council basically endorsed the AHCE's moral education recommendations and repeated its exhortations regarding the teaching of respect for the national flag and anthem. It also proposed that 'teaching-based-on-ability' (*shūjukudo betso shidō*) be allowed at the *chūgakkō* level in principle and suggested that final-year lower secondary school courses be optional.[101] It remained unclear,

however, to what degree these curriculum changes would actually result in diversity in the schools. If entrance exams continued to require a broad knowledge, *chūgakkō* students would probably continue to take the same courses. Furthermore, given that the council expressly ruled out organizing classes based on ability and urged caution in how ability-based-teaching was to be introduced, it was unclear what exactly would change in the way ability differences were handled.

(5) *Credit-system upper secondary schools.* As noted above, these schools had the potential for being used to provide talented academic *kōtōgakkō* students with the opportunity to proceed at a more rapid pace. It was clear by the end of 1987, however, that the MOE and local authorities only planned to use them to provide for students at the very bottom of the ability range.[102]

(6) *Strengthening of local authorities.* An official communication implementing several of the AHCE recommendations was issued in December 1987, and legislation to implement several other changes was due to be submitted to the Diet in 1988.[103] It remained unclear, however, whether these changes would result in greater local diversity or actually increase the central control of the MOE.

CONCLUSIONS

According to newspaper reports, the AHCE's four reports contained a total of some 500 separate recommendations for education reform.[104] If the Nakasone reform initiative was judged by the sheer volume of changes proposed, then it would certainly have to be considered ground-breaking. In many cases, however, the proposals were either vague or heavily qualified. Some were addressed to 'society' and did not provide for a government role. Others were referred for endless study by the Ministry of Education at the implementation stage. Apart from a few exceptions, most of the proposals implemented provided for minor adjustments to the established system. The 6−3−3 system, the university entrance exams, the strict egalitarianism of the system and the Ministry of Education's regulatory control over virtually all aspects of school education − all targeted for 'radical' reform by the Prime Minister − remained essentially unchanged (Figure 8.1). In the final analysis, Nakasone's bold reform efforts had produced little more in the way of significant 'change' than had the 1970s initiative. Again, the question arises: why had education reform been blocked?

Figure 8.1 Results of the Nakasone initiative

Totally stymied or likely to be stymied
Jiyūka (market competition) reforms
Textbook deregulation
University entrance examination 'flexibilization'
Six-year secondary schools
Gifted education reforms
Unification of kindergarten and nursery school administration
University administrative reform (including hōjinka)
Switch to September school start
Revision of the FLE

Partially implemented or too early to judge
Credit-system upper secondary schools
Curriculum 'flexibilization'
Expensive expansion programmes
Probationary teacher-training year: somewhat more moderate
    shoninsha kenshū proposal likely to be implemented

Largely implemented or likely to be implemented
Moral education expansion and improvement
The teaching of respectful attitudes towards the national flag and
    anthem
A new 'University Council'
Various internationalization proposals

Building on the explanations suggested in the previous chapter, the following section summarizes the lessons which can be drawn from the record of Nakasone's reform campaign.

(1) *Programmes supported by a broad consensus of political actors are more easily implemented.* The record of the Nakasone initiative did not contain anything to disprove this assertion. The fact was, however, that there were not very many education proposals supported by a broad consensus in the 1980s. In the 1970s, all of the expansion programmes fell into this category. In the fiscally restrained Nakasone years, however, even such ideas as higher levels of public support for universities aroused opposition in certain conservative circles for fiscal reasons.

247

The proposals enjoying fairly broad support (if not a consensus) were those calling for the internationalization of Japanese education: communicative language education, programmes for returnee children, expanded international student exchanges, and so on. These were all relatively inexpensive programmes and were supported across the political spectrum. An additional category of 'largely implemented' proposals were those supported merely by a *conservative* consensus. Expanded moral education, the teaching of respect for the flag and anthem and the moderate version of the *shoninsha kenshū* programme, were all supported widely in the LDP and among conservatives in general.

(2) *Conflict between subgovernments makes change difficult.* In the 1970s the primary case of subgovernmental conflict was that matching the MOE against the MHW over the issue of kindergartens and nursery schools. It is testimony to the intractability of such disputes that this issue was still not resolved after another three years of reform deliberations. The primary subgovernmental conflict hampering reform in the 1980s, however, was that pitting the actors of the education subgovernment against Nakasone and the 'centre' ministries – the MOF and MITI. The former wanted to maintain their control over the education system and wanted more funds for the MOE budget. The latter sought a leaner, less-regulated and more economically-responsive education system. It was this fundamental clash of interests which divided the First and Third Subcommittees of the AHCE and prevented change across a range of issues.

The story of the Nakasone reform initiative was largely the story of the battle between these two conservative groups. It began before the establishment of the AHCE with two different visions of what the reform ought to accomplish and how the reform ought to be conducted. While Nakasone compromised sufficiently to win the subgovernment's support for the establishment of a supra-cabinet council, he paid a heavy price. The two sides had merely managed to replicate their divisions within the council. By the time the actual deliberations began, therefore, the final stalemate was already foreseeable. While the subgovernment forces blocked such proposals as *jiyūka*, textbook deregulation, examination reform, a switch to a September school starting date and many 'flexibilization' programmes, Nakasone's supporters prevented an endorsement of education finances.

(3) *Conflict within the education subgovernment makes change difficult*. Interestingly, whereas the 1970s reform initiative saw significant conflict within the subgovernment, the education actors had generally co-operative relations during the course of the Nakasone initiative. They worked together to block the Prime Minister's offensive. Nevertheless, the failure of certain reform proposals may be partly attributed to a lack of agreement within the education establishment: while some *zoku* members advocated elite education, six-year secondary schools and an autumn school start, other *zoku* members and most MOE officials preferred the status quo. Had the education subgovernment been in charge of the 1980s reform initiative, these divisions would probably have been very significant. In the event, the subgovernment was too concerned with defending itself against Nakasone's reformism to worry about its own divisions.

(4) *Opposition from the progressive camp makes change more difficult*. Perhaps because of a decline in teachers' union power, or perhaps because the conservatives were so busy fighting among themselves, the progressive camp did not play as large a role in blocking reforms as it had in the 1970s. Nevertheless, it is possible to identify areas in which the progressives were effective. Nakasone was forced to accept the opposition's 'higher standard of democracy' for education in order to win passage of his AHCE Establishment Law. As a result, he had to give up his aim of revising the FLE before he could even begin his reform initiative. The threat of teachers' union opposition was also a significant factor in causing the MOE to work for a somewhat more moderate version of the probationary training-year proposal and probably also influenced the ministry's decision not to work for gifted education reforms.

The record of the Nakasone reform initiative, like the 1970s CCE campaign, has other lessons for students of Japanese politics. It would be an interesting case study, again, of Japanese advisory councils: even more than in the case of the CCE, the AHCE and its members served as proxies for a much broader political battle. It would also stand as a good illustration of Nakasone's 'presidential' leadership style and the entrenchment of *zoku* politics in the LDP. The main interest of this chapter, however, has been to examine the record of the latest reform initiative for further clues as to why the government has been consistently unable to achieve reform in the education sphere. While the reasons in the case of the 1980s initiative were somewhat different from those advanced in the previous chapter as explanations for the failure of the CCE initiative, the main lessons have been confirmed: reform has been prevented by the absence of a conservative consensus and by the progressive camp's ability to block (or at least moderate) the most controversial changes.

9

Final conclusions

This book began with a single central question: why did the Japanese government fail to achieve its reform objectives in the sphere of education? The previous two chapters identified the *immediate* factors responsible for this failure. It was demonstrated that conflict within the conservative camp and opposition aggravation of that conflict were primarily to blame for the lack of progress in the government's two recent initiatives. Chapters 2 to 6 complemented this analysis by identifying the sources of these conflicts. It is the aim of this final chapter to review the findings of these two sections in tandem in an effort to provide a more complete examination for the failure of education reform. Based on this analysis, the second part of the chapter will seek to determine what insights this case study provides for the broader question of the Japanese system's more general ability to adapt to new policy challenges.

REASONS FOR THE FAILURE OF EDUCATION REFORM

The absence of a conservative consensus

The concluding sections of Chapters 7 and 8 made it clear that disagreements among conservatives were directly responsible for the failure of the two recent education reform initiatives. In the first round of reform in the 1970s, it was primarily divisions within the MOE which led to the ministry's failure to implement key CCE reform proposals. Likewise, the persistent conflict between Prime Minister Nakasone and the LDP education *zoku* contributed greatly to the AHCE's inability to agree on significant reforms. To say that conservative disagreement caused the failure of education reform, however, does not provide the full answer to the question at hand. In order to understand why the government had such difficulty achieving its objectives in the education sphere, one must ask *why* the conservatives did not agree. By drawing on the analyses of Chapters 2 to 6 and exploring the reasons for conservative disagreement, it is possible to identify several underlying causes of the failure of education reform.

The impact of one-party dominance

In each of the two recent rounds of reform, the lack of agreement among conservatives resulted at least partly from the status quo orientation of key institutions. In 1971 it was the bureaucratic conservatism of MOE 'mainstream' officials which prevented the implementation of many CCE proposals. In the more recent round, the LDP education *zoku* joined forces with the MOE to defend the established system. While the analyses of LDP and MOE attitudes in Chapters 3 and 4 pointed to multiple reasons for this *genjō iji* orientation, part of the explanation can be traced to the one-party dominant nature of the Japanese system.

There is clearly no simple relationship between one-party dominance and a status quo orientation. The LDP includes reform-minded leaders such as Nakasone and Nishioka as well as defenders of the established system. Nevertheless, as the analysis of LDP education *zoku* attitudes in Chapter 3 illustrated, many of those most involved in the education sphere have come to be committed to the existing way of doing things. They tend to be more interested in praising the system they helped build than in offering constructive criticism. Their influence depends on strengthening and expanding the present system rather than reducing the governmental role and allowing greater diversity and choice. Most are interested primarily in obtaining a larger share of the budget. Particularly in the latest round of reform, these tendencies made the *zoku* one of the leading forces opposed to change.

The link between one-party dominance and the conservatism of MOE officials is less obvious but nevertheless discernible. If Japan had experienced party alternation, it is conceivable that officials would still have developed an attachment to the established system. As the analysis of MOE conservatism in Chapter 4 revealed, however, this attachment has been strengthened by the stability of LDP rule. Most interesting were the comments by Kida Hiroshi noting the change in the attitudes of MOE officials as the post-war period progressed. While those of his generation, having entered the ministry at a time of reform, were relatively willing to consider changing the system, those reaching senior positions after the early 1970s were inclined to defend the system they had spent their entire careers building. Working closely with *zoku* Dietmen over the long period of LDP rule along a fairly consistent line of educational policies, MOE officials have come to develop proprietary attitudes similar to those of the *zoku*: they are unable to criticize the existing system without criticizing themselves; their influence depends on maintaining the status quo. Especially in the CCE round of reform, such tendencies on the part of MOE 'mainstream' officials played a critical role in contributing to the limited success of the initiative.

The narrow segmentation of the education sphere

Despite the LDP's continuing rule, the mere fact that there were two recent reform initiatives indicates that the system is not without its reformers. In the first round, the reform advocates were led by Amagi and Nishida of the MOE 'internationalist' faction. In the more recent round, the reformist lead was taken by Nakasone. In both cases, however, the reformers were unable to overcome the resistance of the status quo orientated education establishment. While it is possible to blame this failure simply on the conservatism of the education subgovernment (as argued above), it can also be attributed to the inability of 'outside' supporters of education reform to bring their influence to bear on the narrowly segmented education sphere.

The significance of 'outside' forces becomes particularly clear when one contrasts Nakasone's reform efforts in the education sphere with his efforts in other areas. In the case of his campaign to achieve 'administrative reform' objectives such as the privatization of the national railways, for example, Nakasone was able to build reformist alliances with the MOF and the business community in order to strengthen his 'centre' coalition against resistance from the transportation subgovernment. This was made possible by the fact that the need to save budgetary funds rendered issues normally within the realm of a single subgovernment a legitimate matter of concern for outside interests. A similar reliance on outside interests characterized the Prime Minister's efforts to overcome opposition to market liberalization measures from ministries such as Agriculture. He was able to appeal again to support from economic ministries (in this case MITI) and was also strengthened by his ability to point to foreign pressures for reform. The appeal to broader forces was made possible by the internationalization of what had been largely domestic concerns.[1]

In contrast, this analysis of education reform has described the inability of Nakasone to bring such outside pressures to bear on the education subgovernment. He sought to involve the *zaikai* in his education reform efforts – even trying to make a businessman head of his Ad Hoc Council. The education subgovernment blocked this attempt, however, and the business representatives on the council (and outside it) were ultimately too divided and lacking in expertise to have an impact. Nakasone also sought to draw on MOF and MITI support for reform, including men like Amaya Naohira (a retired senior MITI official) on his council. Amaya himself had been involved in other reform initiatives in which he had helped mobilize outside interests against resistance to change. In this case, however, he and the other 'outsiders' were unsuccessful.

Amaya's own explanation for their failure is worth quoting. In an interview which the writer conducted for this study, Amaya reflected on the frustrating experience of seeking to achieve education reform:

Major reform takes place in Japan only when there is strong pressure from the outside. The inside has virtually no initiative – it's all *genjō iji*. With economics, Japan has been fairly successful since the outside is so strong that it can force reform. But with education there simply is not any outside.[2]

Amaya's argument is that all policy spheres in Japan are characterized by conservatism 'inside' the immediate area concerned. The difference is that the education sphere lacks the so-called outside interest necessary to force reform. There is no international dimension. Business is not closely involved. Other ministries are excluded. The entire issue is narrowly contained within the education subgovernment. Particularly in the latest round of reform, this structural characteristic of the education issue can be seen to have played a critical role in contributing to the failure of reform in that sphere.

The role of public opinion

This study has not dealt directly with the role of public opinion in the education debate, primarily because of the difficulty of determining what 'the public' think and because of the indirect and informal nature of their influence. Public opinion polls conducted at the time Nakasone set off on his reform initiative actually indicated that 80 per cent of the public supported the idea of 'education reform'.[3] Nevertheless, the analysis in various chapters of this book has indicated that various actors have often *perceived* the public to be opposed to specific changes. It was noted, for example, that many MOE officials have perceived the public to be unwilling to accept any significant departure from the egalitarianism of post-war education. Chapter 8 noted that the AHCE perceived the public to be not yet ready for a switch to a September school starting date.

Interestingly, in interviews conducted by the writer for this study, the lack of public support for education reform was one of the factors most often cited to explain the limited success of the government's recent initiatives. Amagi blamed the failure of the CCE initiative on what he perceived to be a decline in public support for education reform after the university disturbances quietened down.[4] Amaya, expanding on his point about the lack of outside involvement in the education sphere, attributed the lack of progress on university reform in particular to what he described as the public's lack of knowledge or concern about what was going on inside the universities.[5] Kida Hiroshi pointed to the lack of any parent movement working constructively for reform; most parents were concerned only with the progress of their own children.[6] While opinion polls thus indicated broad support for 'education reform' in general, it seems that public opinion (at least in the way in which it was perceived) may in the end have served as another factor limiting the government's ability to achieve change.

The impact of history

It was not by accident that the analysis of this case study began in Chapter 2 with a review of the historical background to the recent education reform debate. The history of pre-war militarism, Occupation reform and post-Occupation revisionism in the education sphere has had an all-pervasive impact on the way policy is made in that area. It has shaped the lines of cleavage which separate the progressive camp from the conservative camp across the range of reform issues, and it has shaped the way these conflicts are dealt with in the policy process. In analysing the reasons for the failure of the government's reform initiatives, therefore, the impact of this turbulent history cannot be ignored.

First, it is significant that the history of post-war education politics has made the progressive opposition one of the leading forces defending the status quo. The Occupation left Japan with an education system favoured by the progressives, creating a situation in which the progressives sought to defend that system from conservative camp attempts to reintroduce earlier specialization and nationalism. As described in Chapter 6, the opposition has thus emerged as an extremely 'conservative' (status quo conservative) force. The opposition's conservatism on the education issue contrasts, for example, with its advocacy of reform in areas such as the environment. In that case, reformists within the conservative camp were able to ally themselves with opposition interests in order to force opponents of change within the conservative camp to accept some reforms. Even in the education sphere, the analyses in Chapters 7 and 8 pointed to several cases in which opposition support for expansion projects led to smooth implementation of changes. In the case of most reforms, however, history has left the opposition in the position of opposing change – preventing the formation of the type of reformist alliance which led to environmental reform.

Second, history has also made the education subgovernment (particularly the MOE) more conservative. As argued in Chapters 4 and 5, the long history of polarized relations between the teachers' union and other progressives on the one hand, and local authorities and the MOE on the other, has created a situation in which the latter have come to be very careful in their approach to any reform proposals which might disrupt their administration of the schools. Typically, a controversial proposal prompts concern from local authorities in areas with strong unions. These local officials then communicate their concerns to the relevant MOE bureaucrats who in turn represent them to their superiors. History has thus made it more difficult for the conservative camp to agree on controversial reforms.

Finally, the history of the education sphere has left the opposition with the ability to appeal to a 'higher standard of democracy' in dealing with proposals for change. Chapter 6 described how *Nikkyōso* and other groups pointed to the sensitive nature of the education area in calling for reform proposals to be based on a consensus of the whole nation. Chapters 7 and 8 illustrated how these campaigns actually convinced conservative camp actors in many cases to accept a higher standard and refrain from 'forcing' change on a majority vote of the LDP's Diet members. In the most recent round, Nakasone expressly accepted the need to respect certain opposition demands when he agreed to have his Ad Hoc Council respect 'the spirit of the Fundamental Law of Education'. In all of the above ways, the history of Japanese education has worked to limit the ability of the government to achieve education reform.

Given the sum of these varied factors limiting its ability to achieve reform, it is perhaps surprising that the government even set out on two reform initiatives. In each case, the reformists faced conservative disagreement, an education establishment tied to the status quo by prolonged LDP rule, an inability to bring outside support for reform to bear on the narrow education sphere, a public which was perceived by various actors to be opposed to specific changes and a progressive opposition strongly committed to the post-war system. It should be noted, however, that this list of explanatory factors is not meant to imply that all of these factors limited the government's ability to achieve reform in all cases. Depending on the specific education reform issue, certain factors were clearly more relevant than others. Thus while public opinion may have been the most important barrier preventing a switch to a September school-start, for example, the history of conflict in the education sphere was probably the leading factor contributing to the MOE's decision not to implement the 1971 CCE probationary teacher-training year proposal.

IMPLICATIONS FOR THE GENERAL ADAPTABILITY OF JAPANESE POLICY-MAKING

Judging from this case study of the government's education reform attempts, it may seem to a reader that Japanese policy-making is doomed to immobilism. In fact, while the study has identified specific factors contributing to immobilism in Japanese policy-making, it has not claimed that these factors are somehow common to all policy challenges facing the Japanese government. Some limiting factors may apply to broad areas of policy, but others are clearly specific only to certain kinds of issues. Based on the case of education reform, this final section seeks to determine the answer to the other broader question with which the study began: to what extent are Japanese leaders able to achieve the policy changes they see as necessary?

The lessons of the Pempel–Campbell model

In confirming the central role of 'conservative consensus' in the Japanese policy-making system, this case study of education reform essentially reinforces the modified Pempel–Campbell model constructed in Chapter 1. As predicted, it found that education issues characterized by certain conflict patterns resulted in certain patterns of policy-making – all centring on the question of whether or not the conservatives were in agreement (Table 9.1). This finding implies that the general adaptability of the Japanese policy-making system could be seen as a function of this threefold classification of conflict patterns. Given adequate information about the types of conflict characterizing other policy challenges, one could calculate the degree to which other issues and the system as a whole would be marked by 'dynamism' or 'immobilism'.

While such an approach promises a theoretical answer to the broad question of Japan's adaptability, it would require studies of conflict patterns on the scale of this one to be conducted of each policy challenge facing the government. Fortunately, the above analysis of the factors underlying conflict in the education sphere provides an easier way of obtaining at least some idea of the limits of change in Japanese politics. By considering whether or not these factors are likely to characterize broad areas of Japanese policy or only certain types of issues, it is possible to predict overall patterns of adaptability.

Table 9.1 Education reform and the Pempel – Campbell model

Classification	Examples
Issue type no. 1: 　Low conflict disputes 　Incremental change or pressure 　group pluralism involving 　contrived consensus-type 　decision-making	1970s expansion projects Various internationalization 　programmes under Nakasone
Issue type no. 2a: 　High conflict dispute involving 　outside forces 　Camp conflict and forced 　resolution by the government	*Shunin* programme in 1970s *Shoninsha kenshū* programme 　under Nakasone Moral education expansion
Issue type no. 2b: 　Again, high conflict dispute 　involving outside forces 　Camp conflict followed by 　opposition success in 　convincing some conserva- 　tives to back down, 　resulting in inaction as in 　no. 3	Elite education reforms Revision of FLE *Shiho* proposal in 1970s
Issue type no. 3: 　High conflict dispute involving 　conservative camp actors 　Conflict avoidance and little 　change	Pilot projects proposal Six-year secondary schools *Jiyūka* Unification of nursery schools 　and kindergartens

The broad factors

Of the limiting factors identified in this case study, the one with the broadest applicability is the 'one-party dominance' factor. Just as the LDP education *zoku* and the MOE have come to identify with and defend the established system in the area of education, it is likely that corresponding groups in other policy spheres have come to identify with the status quo in their areas. Thus, for example, it is likely that the agriculture *zoku* and the relevant sections of the Ministry of Agriculture, Forestry and Fisheries would defend established agricultural subsidies, and the Dietmen tied to heavy industries and the MITI officials in charge of heavy industry would seek to prevent efforts to reform industrial policy in a way which would threaten their interests. It

259

is likely, in other words, that within most subgovernments, one-party dominance will have created a situation in which stable alliances built up over the years of LDP rule will seek to prevent change. It is important to note, however, that nothing in this education case study suggested that one-party dominance has produced a situation in which the *entire* Japanese system is tied to the status quo. The effect was found to be concentrated within subgovernments most closely concerned with given issues.

The issue-specific factors

All of the other factors found to limit adaptability in the case of education were discovered to have a more issue-specific applicability. First, the study found that the inability of 'outside' supporters of change to influence education policy-making limited the government's capacity to achieve reform in that sphere – suggesting that the narrowness of a policy sphere is one issue-specific factor preventing change. This finding is particularly interesting in relation to the above conclusion about the conservatism of subgovernments. It indicates that policy spheres which are broader (of concern to more than one ministry and *zoku*, of concern to foreign governments) may not be as locked into the status quo as the case of education. Thus, for example, the Ministry of Foreign Affairs' concern about the effect of agricultural subsidies on US–Japanese relations might bring it directly into the policy-making process as an advocate of reform, and Dietmen and MITI officials in charge of newly-emerging growth industries might urge changes in Japan's industrial policy designed to shed declining industries. Of course, these speculations should not be taken to imply that the mere presence of 'outside' supporters of change would be likely to produce reform; the Pempel–Campbell model predicts that in cases of serious disagreement, inaction is a likely result. Nevertheless, the lesson of this study of education reform is that one would expect less change in the case of issues which, like education, were purely domestic concerns under the jurisdiction of a single ministry.

Similar lessons can be drawn regarding the other issue-specific factors found to limit change in the case of education. One would expect adaptation to be more difficult in the case of issues characterized by a lack of public support for change, whereas, conversely, change would be more likely in those areas in which the public perceived some 'crisis' and demanded action. Likewise, one would expect 'immobilism' to be more likely in the case of issues which, like education, were burdened with a history of pre-war militarism and post-war polarized politics. Thus, for example, the progressives play a role similar to that seen in the education sphere in defending the Occupation settlement in areas such as defence. They seek to define the issue as 'sensitive' and demand that a 'higher standard of democracy' be applied. Moreover, they seek to appeal to moderate conservatives in an attempt to break the conservative consensus and prevent change. Were it not for the demands from the US calling for higher defence expenditure (making it a broader issue than education), it would be an issue almost exactly like education in its tendency toward immobilism.

Chapter 1 posed a final question: to what degree can a system firmly set in patterns of one-party dominance and consensus rule, maintain the vitality needed to meet new policy challenges? In the case of education reform, for various reasons identified in this conclusion, the government was found to be very limited in its ability to achieve its objectives. Were one to accept Nakasone's argument that change was 'necessary' in order to maintain Japan's economic advance into the twenty-first century, one would have to be concerned about the 'limits to change' in this case.[7] The expanded analysis which followed, however, made it clear that education reform represented an extreme example. The narrow segmentation of the sphere, the lack of active public support for change, and the position of the progressive opposition as an active defender of the status quo were found to be issue-specific factors not necessarily affecting all areas of Japanese policy. By identifying the factors limiting the degree to which Japan's government is able to achieve its reform objectives, therefore, it also made it clear the system is not doomed to immobilism: the one-party dominant system *per se* does not prevent change. In cases where the nature of the issue allows broader forces to become involved, where the public perceives more of a need for change and where the opposition is less active in defence of the post-war settlement, one might find much greater dynamism.

Notes

CHAPTER 1
INTRODUCTION AND THEORETICAL BACKGROUND

1 Rinkyōshin, *Kyōiku kaikaku ni kansuru daiichiji tōshin*, 26 June 1986, in *RD*, special editions 2–3 (June 1985): 9.

2 Chalmers Johnson, *MITI and the Japanese Miracle: The Growth of Industrial Policy, 1925–1975* (Stanford University Press, Stanford, 1982), describes how advocates of change won out over advocates of maintaining old industries in the crucial debate within MITI in the late 1960s and early 1970s; see especially pp. 275–304.

3 Margaret McKean, *Environmental Protest and Citizens Movements in Japan* (University of California Press, Berkeley, 1981); also 'Pollution and policymaking', in T.J. Pempel (ed.), *Policymaking in Contemporary Japan* (Cornell University Press, Ithaca, 1977), pp. 201–38.

4 For the view that Japan's approach to market opening in the area of trade has been dynamic, see Alan Rix, 'Dynamism, foreign policy and trade policy', in J.A.A. Stockwin *et al.* (eds), *Dynamic and Immobilist Politics in Japan* (Macmillan, London, 1988), pp. 297–324. This adaptability was evident most recently in the government's achievement of an agreement on citrus and beef: *Nihon keizai shimbun*, 21 June 1988.

5 Aurelia George, 'Japan and the United States: dependent ally or equal partner?', in Stockwin *et al.* (eds), *Dynamic and Immobilist Politics*, pp. 237–96, describes the immobilist forces limiting change in Japanese defence policy, particularly in the area of defence spending. She finds, however, that Japan in the 1980s has gradually begun to play a more active role in western defence strategy. For the view that Japan's approach to market opening remains immobilist in many areas, see Karel G. van Wolferen, 'The Japan problem', *Foreign Affairs* 65/2 (Winter 1986/87): 288–303.

6 Nakasone Yasuhiro, *Atarashii hoshu no ronri* (Kōdansha, Tokyo, 1983), quoted in *NKS*, 14 May 1984.

7 Nakasone Yasuhiro, 'Speech made at the first meeting of the Provisional Council on Education Reform', translated in Provisional Council on Educational Reform, *First Report on Educational Reform*, 26 June 1985, pp. 68–9.

8 J.A.A. Stockwin, 'Dynamic and immobilist aspects of Japanese politics', in Stockwin *et al.* (eds), *Dynamic and Immobilist Politics*, p. 2.

9 Yanaga Chitoshi, *Big Business in Japanese Politics* (Yale University Press, New Haven, 1968), pp. 28–9.

10 In addition to Yanaga's work, see Misawa Shigeo, 'An outline of the policy-making process in Japan', in Itoh Hiroshi (ed.), *Japanese*

Politics: An Inside View (Cornell University Press, Ithaca, 1973), pp. 12–48; Robert A. Scalapino and Masumi Junnosuke, *Parties and Politics in Contemporary Japan* (University of California Press, Berkeley, 1962); Fukui Haruhiro, 'Economic planning in postwar Japan: a case study in policy making', *Asian Survey* 12/4 (April 1972): 238–47. Among more recent studies which subscribe to the 'power elite model' is that of Gavan McCormack and Sugimoto Yoshio (eds), *Democracy in Contemporary Japan* (M.E. Sharpe, Armonk, New York, 1986), see p. 12.

11 For a summary of this literature, see Fukui Haruhiro, 'Studies in policymaking: a review of the literature', in Pempel (ed.), *Policymaking*, pp. 22–59. Among the case studies which have focused on the pluralism of the conservative camp are several studies in the volume edited by Pempel: Fukui Haruhiro, 'Tanaka goes to Peking: a case study in foreign policymaking', pp. 60–102; John C. Campbell, 'Compensation for repatriates: a case study of interest group politics and party–government negotiations in Japan', pp. 103–42; and Michael W. Donnelly, 'Setting the price of rice: a study in political decisionmaking', pp. 143–200. See also Donnelly's 'Conflict over government authority and markets: Japan's rice economy', in E.S. Krauss, T.P. Rohlen and P.G. Steinhoff (eds), *Conflict in Japan* (University of Hawaii Press, Honolulu, 1984), pp. 335–74; William Steslicke, *Doctors in Politics: The Political Life of the Japan Medical Association* (Praeger, New York, 1973); Gerald L. Curtis, 'Big Business and Political Influence', in Ezra F. Vogel (ed.), *Modern Japanese Organization and Decision-making* (University of California Press, Berkeley, 1975); John C. Campbell, *Contemporary Japanese Budget Politics* (University of California Press, Berkeley, 1977). Recent studies of the Japanese system in general which have emphasized the pluralist view have included: John C. Campbell, 'Policy conflict and its resolution within the governmental system', in Krauss *et al.* (eds), *Conflict*, pp. 294–334; and T.J. Pempel, 'The unbundling of "Japan, Inc.": the changing dynamics of Japanese policy formation', *Journal of Japanese Studies* 13/2 (Summer 1987): 271–306; and Muramatsu Michio and Ellis Krauss, 'The conservative policy line and the development of patterned pluralism', in Yamamura Kōzō and Yasuba Yasukichi (eds), *The Political Economy of Japan, Vol. 1: The Domestic Transformation* (Stanford University Press, Stanford, 1987), pp. 516–54.

12 The case studies in this group include two on the sphere of education: Benjamin Duke, *Japan's Militant Teachers* (University Press of Hawaii, Honolulu, 1973) and Donald Thurston, *Teachers and Politics in Japan* (Princeton University Press, Princeton, 1973). See also Mike Mochizuki, 'Managing and influencing the Japanese legislative process: the role of parties and the National Diet', unpublished PhD dissertation, Harvard University, 1982; Satō Seizaburō and Matsuzaki Tetsuhisa, 'The Liberal Democrats' conciliatory reign', *Economic Eye* 6/4 (December 1985): 27–32; Ellis Krauss, 'Conflict in the Diet: toward conflict management in parliamentary politics', in Krauss *et al.* (eds), *Conflict*, pp. 243–93;

and Muramatsu and Krauss, 'The conservative policy line', pp. 533–5, 538.

13 The term was coined by Muramatsu and Krauss, in 'The conservative policy line', pp. 536–48.

14 This was the emphasis, for example, of Chalmers Johnson in his article 'Japan: who governs? An essay on official bureaucracy', *Journal of Japanese Studies* 2/1 (Autumn 1975): 1–28.

15 Muramatsu and Krauss, 'The conservative policy line', write: 'The bureaucracy is the pivot around which policymaking alliances are formed on particular issues' (p. 542). Inoguchi Takashi describes Japanese pluralism as 'bureaucracy-led mass-inclusionary pluralism' (*kanryō shudo taishū hōkatsu gata tagenshugi*) – *Gendai nihon seiji keizai no kōzo* (Tōyō keizai shimpōsha, Tokyo, 1983). See also Campbell's discussion of subgovernments as outlined below.

16 Satō Seizaburō and Matsuzaki Tetsuhisa note, for example, that the LDP organ responsible for policy analysis – the Policy Affairs Research Council (PARC) – has a staff of only thirty-four. Similarly, Dietmen in Japan have at their disposal a total of only 1,526 secretaries compared to the 11,125 available to help US congressmen develop their own sources of information: *Jimintō seiken* (Chūō kōronsha, Tokyo, 1986), p. 83.

17 T.J. Pempel, 'The bureaucratization of policymaking in post-war Japan', *American Journal of Political Science* 18/4 (November 1974): 654–6. Johnson, *MITI*, also puts emphasis on the bureaucrats' use of administrative guidance (pp. 264–74). Others have disputed the significance of these powers however: see John O. Haley, 'Governance by negotiation: a reappraisal of bureaucratic power in Japan', *Journal of Japanese Studies* 13/2 (Summer 1987): 343–57.

18 Pempel, 'The bureaucratization', pp. 656–63; Yung H. Park, 'The governmental advisory system in Japan', *Journal of Comparative Administration* 3 (February 1972): 435–67.

19 Kubota Akira and Tomita Nobuo report survey results which indicate that Japanese bureaucrats (by large margins) continue to view themselves as the protectors of rational public policy while seeing the role of political parties as one of exacerbating political conflict – 'Nihon seifu kōkan no ishiki kōzo', *Chūō kōron* 92/2 (February 1977): 190–6; Muramatsu Michio and Ellis Krauss, 'Bureaucrats and politicians in policymaking: the case of Japan', *American Political Science Review* 78/1 (March 1984): 131–3. The latter puts the Kubota and Tomita figures in a comparative context. Most studies have attributed this attitude to the fact that Japan's bureaucrats were until recently (1945) directly responsible to the emperor: see Tsuji Kiyoaki, 'Public administration in Japan: an overview', in Tsuji (ed.), *Public Administration in Japan* (Tokyo University Press, Tokyo, 1984), pp. 3–4. Johnson emphasizes the particular role of the post-war occupation in leaving this power relatively intact and even strengthened – 'Who governs?', pp. 12–22.

20 Johnson, *MITI*, pp. 47–8; See also Pempel, 'The bureaucratization', p. 653.

21 Muramatsu Michio, *Sengo nihon no kanryōsei* (Tōyō keizai shinpōsha, Tokyo, 1981); Muramatsu and Krauss, 'Bureaucrats and politicians'; Satō and Matsuzaki, *Jimintō seiken*; Inoguchi Takashi and Iwai Tomoaki, *'Zoku ginn' no kenkyū: jimintō seiken o gyūjiru shuyakutachi* (Nihon keizai shimbunsha, Tokyo, 1987); and Yung H. Park, *Bureaucrats and Ministers in Contemporary Japanese Government* (University of California Press, Berkeley, 1986).

22 Satō and Matsuzaki, though emphasizing the emergence of LDP power in recent years, note that the LDP review of legislation was not always as stringent as it is today – *Jimintō seiken*, pp. 84–5.

23 All of the recent studies of the LDP have emphasized the power of PARC. See in particular Satō and Matsuzaki, *Jimintō seiken*; Inoguchi and Iwai, 'Zoku giin'; and Park, *Bureaucrats and Ministers*. See also Yuasa Hiroshi, *Kokkai 'zoku ginn'* (Kyōikusha, Tokyo, 1986).

24 Inoguchi and Iwai use several case studies to illustrate the specialized career paths of LDP Diet members – *'Zoku ginn'*, pp. 41–53. See also Park, *Bureaucrats and Ministers*, pp. 34–9, and Satō and Matsuzaki, *Jimintō seiken*, pp. 32–51. Muramatsu and Krauss, 'The conservative policy line', offer a concise definition and explanation (pp. 540–1).

25 Muramatsu and Krauss find that the top two grades of ministry officials, despite generally negative attitudes towards political party intervention, see one of their primary roles as that of 'aiding politicians in decision-making' – 'Bureaucrats and politicians', p. 134. According to Park, the increasing tendency for higher-ranking officials to be involved in earlier stages of decision-making (rather than delegating to subordinates) reflects the role such officials play in assuring that LDP demands are met: *Bureaucrats and Ministers*, pp. 14–17.

26 Park, *Bureaucrats and Ministers*, pp. 55–77.

27 Inoguchi and Iwai, *'Zoku giin'*, pp. 21–2.

28 Many recent studies have noted how the increasing complexity of issues has led to a stronger party role. See Satō and Matsuzaki, *Jimintō seiken*, pp. 96–9. Muramatsu Michio takes a close look at how Nakasone sought to assert central leadership in such circumstances – 'In search of national identity: the politics and policies of the Nakasone administration', *Journal of Japanese Studies* 13/2 (Summer 1987): 307–42.

29 The broad studies emphasizing these cross-cutting cleavages include the works by Campbell cited below as well as Pempel, 'The unbundling of "Japan Inc." ', pp. 287–91; Satō and Matsuzaki, *Jimintō seiken*, pp. 158–72; and Muramatsu and Krauss, 'The conservative policy line', pp. 536–43. The case studies include those included in the Muramatsu and Krauss article, pp. 543–8; as well as many of those cited in note 11 above.

30 Campbell, *Contemporary Japanese Budget Politics*, pp. 38–42. Campbell takes the expression 'subgovernments' from R.B. Ripley and G.A. Franklin's study of US politics, *Congress, the Bureaucracy, and Public Policy* (The Dorsey Press, Homewood, Ill., 1976), pp. 5–7.

31 Campbell, *Contemporary Japanese Budget Politics*, p. 41.
32 For Campbell's discussion of 'balance', see his 'Japanese budget *baransu*' in Vogel (ed.), *Modern Japanese Organization*, pp. 71–100. The broader MOF role is described in Campbell, *Contemporary Japanese Budget Politics*, pp. 43–114.
33 Campbell argues that the LDP central leadership largely fails to define clear priorities and therefore leaves the bulk of the co-ordinating role to the MOF – *Contemporary Japanese budget politics*, pp. 128–33. Since the early 1980s, however, the LDP has taken a much more active role in defining budgetary priorities earlier in the process. Muramatsu Michio emphasizes the role of the prime minister in his discussion of the 'centre' concept, but he too includes the MOF and the other economic ministries: see 'In search of national identity', p. 326.
34 Campbell, 'Policy conflict', p. 301.
35 Muramatsu and Krauss, 'The conservative policy line', p. 537; Aurelia George, 'Japanese interest group behaviour: an institutional approach', in Stockwin *et al.* (eds), *Dynamic and Immobilist Politics*, pp. 106–40.
36 For a comparative discussion of 'hybridization', see J.D. Aberbach, R.D. Putnam and B.A. Rockman, *Bureaucrats and Politicians in Western Democracies* (Harvard University Press, Cambridge, Mass., 1981). Several studies of Japanese policy have argued that 'hybridization' has gone particularly far due to the unusual stability of their interactions under continuing LDP rule. Within subgovernments, they point out, bureaucrats play such political roles as the management of interest group conflict while LDP politicians use their growing experience and expertise to approach problems in a more bureaucratic fashion: see Muramatsu and Krauss, 'Bureaucrats and politicians', pp. 133–5, and Satō and Matsuzaki, *Jimintō seiken*, pp. 79–81.
37 See J.A.A. Stockwin, *Japan: Divided Politics in a Growth Economy*, 2nd edn (Weidenfeld & Nicolson, London, 1982), p. 161, 163–93; T.J. Pempel and Keiichi Tsunekawa, 'Corporatism without labor? The Japanese anomaly', in P.C. Schmitter and G. Lehmbruch (eds), *Trends Toward Corporatist Intermediation* (Sage, London, 1979).
38 See references in note 12 above.
39 Muramatsu and Krauss, 'The conservative policy line', pp. 542–3.
40 Satō and Matsuzaki call it 'compartmentalized pluralism' (*shikirareta tagenshugi*): *Jimintō seiken*, pp. 163–172. Inoguchi, as noted above, calls it 'bureaucracy-led mass-inclusionary pluralism'.
41 Muramatsu and Krauss, 'The conservative policy line', p. 532; Stockwin discusses how the one-party dominant system has encouraged this tendency: 'Dynamic and immobilist aspects', pp. 15–17.
42 Many such case studies have been cited above, particularly in note 11. In addition, see the collection of cases in Bradley M. Richardson, 'Policymaking in Japan: an organising perspective', in Pempel (ed.), *Policymaking*, pp. 239–68.

43 T.J. Pempel, *Patterns of Japanese Policymaking: Experiences from Higher Education* (Westview Press, Boulder, Colorado, 1978), pp. 14–20.

44 ibid., pp. 22–5.

45 T.J. Pempel, *Policy and Politics in Japan: Creative Conservatism* (Temple University Press, Philadelphia, 1982), p. 42.

46 Many of these issues have involved outside opposition as well, but in each of these cases I believe it is fair to argue that it has been disagreement among conservatives which has caused the most difficulty. On the rice price issue, see Donnelly, 'Conflict over government authority and markets'; on administrative reform, see Itō Daiichi, 'Policy implications of administrative reform', in Stockwin *et al.* (eds), *Dynamic and Immobilist Politics*, pp. 77–105.

47 Pempel, 'The unbundling of "Japan, Inc." ', pp. 279–94.

48 Other studies have noted the consensual nature of Japanese policymaking, but none has focused on the consensual dynamics as closely as Campbell. See Pempel, *Policy and Politics in Japan*; and Pempel and Tsunekawa, 'Corporatism without labor?'.

49 Campbell, 'Policy conflict', p. 311.

50 See, for example, Nakane Chie, *Japanese Society* (Wiedenfeld & Nicolson, London, 1970), pp. 144–5; and Ishida Takeshi, 'Conflict and its accommodation: *omote–ura* and *uchi–soto* relations', in Krauss *et al.* (eds), *Conflict in Japan*, pp. 16–38.

51 Campbell, 'Policy conflict', pp. 313–20.

52 ibid., p. 320. See, for example, the case studies on environmental assessment and administrative reform in Muramatsu and Krauss, 'The conservative policy line', pp. 544–5, 546–8.

53 Campbell, 'Policy conflict', p. 296.

54 Such an assumption seems built into the theories of both Campbell and Pempel. See also Pempel and Tsunekawa, 'Corporatism without labor?'.

CHAPTER 2   BACKGROUND TO THE RECENT DEBATE

1 Ronald Dore, 'The legacy of Tokugawa education', in Marius Jansen (ed.), *Changing Japanese Attitudes toward Modernization* (Princeton University Press, Princeton, 1969), p. 100.

2 Ronald Dore, *Education in Tokugawa Japan* (University of California Press, Berkeley, 1965), pp. 252–90.

3 ibid., pp. 33–64. See also Thomas Rohlen, *Japan's High Schools* (University of California Press, Berkeley, 1983), p. 49.

4 For an analysis of Sung morality and its effect on elite Tokugawa education, see Dore, *Education in Tokugawa Japan*, especially pp. 34–7.

5 Dore, 'The legacy of Tokugawa education', pp. 122–3.

6 Fukuzawa Yukichi, *Ecouragement of Learning*, quoted in Herbert Passin, *Society and Education in Japan* (Columbia University Press, New York, 1965), p. 68.

7 Passin, *Society and Education*, p. 73.

8 ibid., pp. 103–4.
9 Mori, quoted in Passin, *Society and Education*, p. 68.
10 Passin, *Society and Education*, p. 104.
11 William K. Cummings, *Education and Equality in Japan* (Princeton University Press, Princeton, 1980), p. 21. The statistics cited are for the 1930s. For a summary of how the system of meritocratic competition developed to that point, see Kuroha Ryōichi, *Kyōiku kaikaku: tembō to kanōsei* (Kokudosha, Tokyo, 1984), pp. 11–13.
12 Ronald Dore, *The Diploma Disease: Education, Qualification and Development* (George Allen & Unwin, London, 1976), p. 42.
13 Passin, *Society and Education*, pp. 103–5.
14 For a discussion of the culture of pre-war higher schools in Japan, see Donald Roden, *Schooldays in Imperial Japan: A Study in the Culture of a Student Elite* (University of California Press, Berkeley, 1980).
15 In the 1870s, the American-influenced Education Minister Tanaka Fujimaro was arguing that teachers as well as localities should be allowed a fair measure of autonomy such that education would be made responsive to local needs. He argued that scholars and educators should never be forced to follow official orders but should be encouraged to express their own indpendent views: Passin, *Society and Education*, pp. 72, 82–3.
16 ibid., pp. 83–6.
17 For a profile of Mori, an important but complicated figure in the history of this period, see ibid., pp. 86–91. The system he established was a compromise between the liberal and nationalist currents in Meiji Japan and within Mori himself: it provided for a compulsory elementary sector with a heavy emphasis on nationalist and moral indoctrination and a university sector with a large measure of academic freedom and critical rationalism.
18 For the text of the Imperial Rescript, see ibid., pp. 226–8.
19 Benjamin C. Duke, *Japan's Militant Teachers* (University Press of Hawaii, Honolulu, 1973), p. 11. For further discussion of the idea of a 'Japanese ethic', see Robert Bellah, *Tokugawa Religion* (Free Press of Glencoe, New York, 1957). For a defence of the pre-militarist education ideology by a post-war Japanese conservative, see Kuroha, *Kyōiku kaikaku*, pp. 9–10.
20 Duke, *Japan's Militant Teachers*, p. 19.
21 Rohlen, *Japan's High Schools*, p. 56.
22 Yamazumi Masami, 'Educational democracy versus state control', in McCormack and Sugimoto (eds), *Democracy in Contemporary Japan* (M.E. Sharpe, Armonk, New York, 1986), pp. 90–3.
23 For detailed accounts of the activities and suppression of the pre-war teachers' unions, see Duke, *Japan's Militant Teachers*, pp. 14–26; and Donald R. Thurston, *Teachers and Politics in Japan* (Princeton University Press, Princeton, 1973), pp. 23–39.
24 Duke discusses the effect of the pre-war experience on the character of the post-war teachers' union. See *Japan's Militant Teachers*, pp. 28–41.
25 Nishi Toshio, *Unconditional Democracy: Eduation and Politics in*

Occupied Japan 1945–52 (Hoover Institution Press, Stanford, 1982), pp. 146–86.

26 The *kyōyō gakubu* is in most universities a separate department which offers a broad set of courses for students in their first and second years.

27 The Occupation's reform programme was outlined by the United States Education Mission sent to Japan in March 1946. For accounts of its visit and its proposals, see Nishi, *Unconditional Democracy*, pp. 187–96; and Duke, *Japan's Militant Teachers*, pp. 46–9.

28 For the text of the FLE, see Passin, *Society and Education*, pp. 301–4.

29 This list is based on the actions and statements of MOE bureaucrats and other conservatives in the period since the end of the Occupation – many of which are detailed in following chapters. It draws heavily on the recollections of MOE bureaucrats actually involved in implementing the Occupation reforms – collected in Kida Hiroshi (ed.), *Sengo no bunkyō seisaku* (Daiichi hōki, Tokyo, 1987), pp. 13–117.

30 Kennoki, as paraphrased by Tanaka Masataka, *Ushi no ayumi hachijūgonen: Kennoki Toshihiro kikigaki* (Nishi nihon shimbunsha, Tokyo, 1987), p. 42.

31 ibid., pp. 44–5; see also his recollections in Kida, *Sengo*, pp. 19–32. The degree to which such views of Occupation history are shared by other conservatives is clear from the comments of Prime Minister Nakasone in his preface to Kennoki's memoirs. The Prime Minister singles out Kennoki's account of his experiences under the Occupation for particular praise, describing his recollections as 'precious material in the process of setting right (*tōi naosu*) Japanese education'.

32 See the recollections of various MOE participants in the process of drawing up the FLE in Kida, *Sengo*, pp. 34–54. Again, the fact that the history of this document is important to conservatives is indicated by the fact that Nakasone appointed a young conservative historian known for his work on this particular issue (Takahashi Shirō) to sit as a specialist member on his Ad Hoc Council. For Takahashi's views, see 'Rinkyōshin to kyōiku kihon-hō', *Bunka kaigi*, no. 205 (1986): 34–54.

33 Interview with Kennoki Toshihiro, 13 August 1987.

34 Morito describes the mistakes made by the Occupation and takes responsibility for his role in the post-war reforms in his book, *Daisan no kyōiku kaikaku: chūkyōshin tōshin to kyōkasho saiban* (Daiichi hōki, Tokyo, 1973), especially pp. 4–6.

35 For a left-leaning historian's defence of the Japaneseness of the post-war settlement, see Suzuki Eiichi, *Nihon no senryō to kyōiku kaikaku* (Keiso shobō, Tokyo, 1983); and the same author's 'Sengo kyōiku kaikaku ni okeru kyōiku kihon-hō to 6–3–3–sei', *Kokumin kyōiku*, no. 64 (Spring 1985), pp. 104–14. For a more neutral account also emphasizing the role of Japanese, see the report on a government research project in *AS*, 14 September 1986.

36 Thurston, *Teachers and Politics*, p. 43.

37 Duke, *Japan's Militant Teachers*, pp. 79–81.
38 Nishi, *Unconditional Democracy*, p. 250.
39 T.J. Pempel, *Patterns of Japanese Policymaking: Experiences from Higher Education* (Westview Press, Boulder, Colorado, 1978), pp. 48–57.
40 Duke, *Japan's Militant Teachers*, pp. 123–7.
41 ibid., pp. 129–33.
42 ibid., p. 144.
43 Yamazumi, 'Educational democracy', p. 97.
44 Most prefectures decided not to link the rating results to salaries while many headmasters agreed either to give all teachers identical ratings or even let teachers fill in their own forms: Duke, *Japan's Militant Teachers*, pp. 138–54; Thurston, *Teachers and Politics*, pp. 205–9.
45 Thurston, *Teachers and Politics*, pp. 209–13.
46 Duke, *Japan's Militant Teachers*, pp. 144–5.
47 The two initiatives took place in 1952–4 and 1960–3: Pempel, *Patterns*, pp. 97–114.
48 For the MOE's refusal to negotiate with the union, see Duke, *Japan's Militant Teachers*, pp. 156 and 167–73. See also Ehud Harari, *The Politics of Labor Legislation in Japan* (University of California Press, Berkeley, 1973), especially ch. 8.
49 Kuroha, *Kyōiku kaikaku*, pp. 37–8.
50 Kuroha Ryōichi, *Sugao no sengo kyōiku* (Gakuji shuppan, Tokyo, 1974), pp. 163–4.
51 Kuroha, *Kyōiku kaikaku*, pp. 39–42; Yamazaki Masato, *Jimintō to kyōiku seisaku* (Iwanami shinsho, Tokyo, 1986), pp. 52–5.
52 Yamazaki, *Jimintō*, pp. 55–6.
53 Kuroha, *Sugao*, p. 160.
54 Mombushō daijin kambō chōsa tōkeika, *Shōwa 61-nendo gakkō kihon chōsa chokuhō (shotō-chūtō kyōiku)*, August 1986, p. 10.
55 MOE Higher Education Bureau, *Higher Education in Japan*, October 1984, p. 18.
56 Ronald Dore and Sako Mari provide an excellent description of the examination/selection process in their recent study entitled *How the Japanese Learn to Work* (Nissan Institute/Routledge Japanese Studies Series, London, 1989), ch. 2.
57 See Chapter 7 of this book.
58 Interview with Kennoki Toshihiro, 13 August 1987; Amagi Isao, quoted in Kida, *Sengo*, pp. 425–6.
59 The late 1960s *funsō* is considered to have started in 1965 with disturbances at Keiō and Hōsei Universities in Tokyo – reaching its peak in 1968 with the outbreak of disturbances at over seventy campuses (including Tokyo University). See Pempel, *Patterns*, pp. 114–25; Yagi Atsushi, *Mombu daijin no sengoshi* (Bijinesusha, Tokyo, 1984), pp. 187–8.
60 For analyses of the expansion in private university education and its effect on the quality of education in those institutions, see Yamazaki, *Jimintō*, pp. 75–7; Pempel, *Patterns*, pp. 147–52.
61 Yamazaki, *Jimintō*, pp. 79–80; see also Naitō Yosaburō, 'Naitō shian', *Gendai kyōiku kagaku* 11/11 (November 1968): 104–7.

62 Pempel, *Patterns*, pp. 121–2, 130–3.

63 *AN*, 1982, p. 474.

64 Attacks on teachers rose from 191 incidents in 1978 to 929 in 1983. Overall incidents of school violence rose from 1,292 to 2,125 during the same period. Keisatsuchō, *Shōnen no hodō oyobi hogo no gaikyō*, September 1986, p. 63. Benjamin Duke, puts these statistics in perspective by reporting comparative data from the United States: 282,000 students were physically attacked in a peak year while 1,000 teachers were assaulted seriously enough to require medical attention *each month – The Japanese School: Lessons for Industrial America* (Praeger, New York, 1986), p. 188. The Japanese media, politicians and even academics, however, tended not to refer to such international comparative data. They judged the rise in violence between 1978 and 1983 by Japanese standards, by which it was perceived to be precipitous.

65 *AS*, 13 February 1983.

66 *AS*, 16 February 1983.

67 Yagi, *Mombu daijin*, p. 211.

68 School violence, which peaked in 1983, fell in the following years to 1,492 total cases in 1985, just 200 more than in the low year of 1978: see Keisatsuchō, *Shōnen no hodō*, p. 63. At about the same time, the media began to focus on a new trend: the rapid growth in cases of students bullying fellow students. A few cases received media attention in 1985, but the problem began to be perceived as a 'crisis' in 1986 after a number of highly publicized suicides were linked to *ijime*; see *AN*, 1986, p. 209. In just seven months in 1985, the MOE announced, 155,891 cases of bullying had been reported, with reports coming from 69 per cent of state *chūgakkō*: *AS*, 22 February 1986. See also Keisatsuchō, *Keisatsuchō hakusho*, 1986, pp. 145–9, and Merry White, *The Japanese Educational Challenge* (Collier Macmillan, London, 1987), pp. 137–40.

69 In 1981, 95 per cent of student attack on teachers took place in the *chūgakkō*: *AN*, 1982, p. 474. Soeda Yoshiya, in a 1983 study of juvenile violence, attributed this imbalance to the fact that 'middle school represents a terrifying selection process for young people': 'Changing patterns of juvenile aggression', *Japan Echo* 10/3 (1983): 15. Several recent studies of Japanese education examine the effects – good and bad – of the system's concentration on selection. See Duke, *The Japanese School*; White, *The Japanese Educational Challenge*; and Rohlen, *Japan's High Schools*.

70 A quarter of elementary school students and almost half of *chūgakkō* students attend *juku*. See Mombushō, 'Jidō seito no gakkōgai gakushū katsudō ni kansuru jittai chōsa', reprinted in *Gendai kyōiku kagaku* 355 (June 1986): 104–7.

71 For an example of a popular critique of examination influence on the Japanese system, see Asahi shimbun shakaibu, *Kyōiku no hiroba* (Sōjisha, Tokyo, 1984). See also Duke, *The Japanese School*, pp. 200–6; and Rohlen, *Japan's High Schools*, pp. 77–110.

72 See Kitamura Kazuyuki, 'The decline and reform of education in Japan: a comparative perspective', in William Cummings *et al.* (eds), *Educational Policies in Crisis* (Praeger, New York, 1986). See

also Duke, *The Japanese School*, pp. 216–18; and John F. Zeugner, 'The puzzle of higher education in Japan', *Change*, January/February 1984, pp. 24–31.

73 Ronald Dore links many of the problems of Japanese education to its qualificationism, a trait of the system which, he argues, began to distort the quality of education even before the war; see his *Diploma Disease*, pp. 42–50. In 1971 he and other international education experts who reviewed the Japanese education system for the Organization for Economic Co-operation and Development urged Japan to address many of the problems linked to the distorting influence of examinations and qualificationism. See OECD, *Reviews of National Policies for Education: Japan* (OECD, Paris, 1971).

74 Amaya, paraphrased by Nishio Kanji in 'Naze rinkyōshin wa munaiyō ni owattaka', *Chūō kōron* 100/8 (August 1985): 144.

CHAPTER 3
INTERNAL ACTORS: THE LIBERAL DEMOCRATIC PARTY

1 Yamazumi Masami, 'Educational democracy versus state control', in Gavan McCormack and Sugimoto Yoshio (eds), *Democracy in Contemporary Japan* (M.E. Sharpe, Armonk, NY, 1986), p. 103.

2 Habara Kiyomasa, 'Jimintō bunkyōzoku no jitsuryoku', *Sekai* 444 (November 1982): 66.

3 *MS*, 29 August 1978.

4 Naitō Yosaburō, 'Naitō shian', *Gendai kyōiku kagaku* 11/11 (November 1968): 104–7.

5 *NKS*, 2 April 1984.

6 Yung H. Park, 'Kyōiku gyōsei ni okeru jimintō to mombushō', in Shimbori Michiya and Aoi Kazuo (eds), *Nihon kyōiku no rikigaku* (Yūshindō, Tokyo, 1983), p. 57.

7 The *Seirankai* was a maverick group of right-wing LDP members who objected in particular to Tanaka's decision to abandon Taiwan. They stood firmly in favour of constitutional revision and urged that the LDP return to its conservative roots; see Tokyo shimbun seijibu, *Seisaku shūdan: shin hoshutō e no taidō* (Tokyo shimbun shuppankyoku, Tokyo, 1983), pp. 148–52; 166–71.

8 For similar lists of *zoku* membership, see Satō Seizaburō and Matsuzaki Tetsuhisa, *Jimintō seiken* (Chūō kōronsha, Tokyo, 1986), p. 269; and 'Yūbenka-zoroi "bukyōzoku"', *Shūkan daiyamondo*, March 1986, p. 75. Membership in *Seirankai* is based on Nakagawa Ichirō, *Seirankai: keppan to yūkoku no ronri* (Rōman, Tokyo, 1973), pp. 209–19; and Tokyo shimbun seijibu, *Seisaku shūdan*, pp. 148–9. Membership in the Dietmen's League is based on lists in *Kempō*, its own newsletter, 15 April 1983.

9 *NKS*, 23 April 1984.

10 See for example Nakasone's answers to parliamentary questions about the need for an Ad Hoc Council, contained in Rinji kyōiku shingikai jimukyoku, *Rinkyōshin setchihō-hōan shingi tōben no gaiyō*, 14 September 1984, Section 1.

11 Jiyū minshutō, *Wagatō no kōyaku* (Jiyū minshutō shuppankyoku, Tokyo, 1986), p. 80.

12 LDP Dietmen intervened in the last stages of AHCE deliberations to have the council make a stronger recommendation on these matters. See *NKS*, 10 August 1987; see also Chapter 8 below.

13 See Donald Thurston, *Teachers and Politics in Japan* (Princeton University Press, Princeton, 1973). p. 15, for a discussion of the origins of this attitude.

14 See Yamazaki Masato, *Jimintō to kyōiku seisaku* (Iwanami shinsho, Tokyo, 1986), pp. 97–8, for a discussion of how pragmatism came to prevail.

15 ibid., p. 120.

16 Jiyū minshutō, *Wagatō*, p. 81.

17 Interview with Funada Hajime, 23 July 1987.

18 More has been written in recent years about the textbook issue than about any other education issue in Japan. See, for example, Kenneth B. Pyle and Yayama Tarō, 'Japan besieged: the textbook controversy', *Journal of Japanese Studies* 9/2 (Summer 1983): 297–316; Yamazaki, *Jimintō*, pp. 159–71; and Habara, 'Jimintō bunkyōzoku', pp. 65–71. According to Banno Junji, one of the authors of a textbook which is used in 65 per cent of upper secondary school history classes, the MOE review 'has actually become softer since the 1982 crisis. They tried to be tougher, but in the end had to back down to foreign pressure'. He himself is 'not worried about the review becoming too strict'. Banno explained that even in 1982, when he challenged the MOE's request that he change the term 'invasion', the ministry backed down. It could not dispute his exposition of the facts: interview, 2 March 1987.

19 Yamazaki, *Jimintō*, pp. 94–9; Makieda Motofumi, *Mombu daijin wa nani o shitaka* (Mainichi shimbunsha, Tokyo, 1984), pp. 180–4; Naka Mamoru, 'Zoku no kenkyū, 9: posuto rinkyōshin o ukagau ideorogî shūdan', *Gekkan seikai*, July–August 1986: 47.

20 Kobayashi Tetsuya, *Society, Schools and Progress in Japan* (Pergamon Press, Oxford, 1978), p. 163.

21 Jiyū minshutō seimu chōsakai bunkyō seido chōsakai, 'Kyōiku kaikaku shian', *Gendai kyōiku kagaku* 12/5 (May 1969): 105–9.

22 Interview with Nishioka Takeo, 23 July 1987.

23 *KS*, 17 December 1981.

24 Kondō published the plan on his own after it was rejected. See 'Kyōiku seido daikaikaku-ron', *Voice*, May 1982: 249–57; see also *KS*, 17 December 1981 and 5 July 1982; and Kuroha Ryōichi, *Rinkyōshin – dōnaru kyōiku kaikaku* (Nihon keizai shimbunsha, Tokyo, 1985), pp. 13–14.

25 *MS*, 22 July 1983.

26 *SS*, 11 September 1983; NKS, 18 June 1984.

27 Interview with Okuda Shinjō, 1 September 1987.

28 Interview with Usui Hideo, 23 July 1987.

29 'Jimintō "bukai" no kenkyū: bunkyōbukai', *Gekkan jiyū minshu*, July 1986: 174.

30 ibid., pp. 176–7.

31 See Nakasone's article in *MS*, 16 January 1969.

32 Nakasone was a leader of the effort to establish a cabinet-level Ad Hoc Council on the Education System (*Rinji kyōiku seido shingikai*) in the mid-1950s. The council, which was to review the post-war education laws and recommend revisions, became the subject of heated debate and did not obtain Diet approval: see *NKS*, 9 April 1984 and 4 June 1984.

33 *NKS*, 9 July 1984.

34 The Kyoto Group, 'Seven recommendations to revitalize school education, March 13, 1984', in *Discussions on Educational Reform in Japan* (Foreign Press Center, Tokyo, 1985), p. 31.

35 ibid., pp. 31–4. See further discussion in Chapter 5 below.

36 *NKS*, 11 June 1984. See also *NKS*, 21 May 1984.

37 *NKS*, 3 September 1984.

38 Quoted in *NKS*, 3 September 1984.

39 *NKS*, 21 May 1984.

40 Chairmanships of the Diet committees are awarded largely based on factional considerations. Thus chairmen are sometimes not members of the relevant *zoku*, as in the case of Aichi.

41 Interview with Aichi Kazuo, 30 July 1987.

42 Interview with Saitō Taijun, 13 August 1987.

43 Interview with Aichi, 30 July 1987.

44 Interview with Kaifu Toshiki, 3 September 1986.

45 ibid.

46 Yamazaki, *Jimintō*, p. 129.

47 Yagi Atsushi, *Mombu daijin no sengoshi* (Bijinesusha, Tokyo, 1984), pp. 194–5.

48 ibid., pp. 214–15.

49 As Table 3.1 reveals, while the education *zoku* includes relatively large numbers of Nakasone, Abe and Kōmoto faction members, it contains few Tanaka (now Takeshita and Nikaidō) and no Miyazawa faction members. Among the various theories offered in interviews and publications are the following: (1) the factions which have been in the mainstream for most of the past two decades (Tanaka and Miyazawa) have tended to neglect education in favour of the spheres more likely to produce votes and political funds, and (2) *zoku* elders have tended to recruit younger members from their own factions, thereby perpetuating the dominance of the Nakasone and Abe factions.

50 The recommendations were contained in various *Rinchō* reports. The basic philosophy on education cuts was outlined in *Daisanji tōshin (kihon tōshin)*, 30 July 1982, section on education.

51 The various *zoku* members cited in the LDP survey of *Bunkyōbukai* opinion repeatedly stressed the need for increased education spending – 'Jimintō "bukai" no kenkyū', pp. 170–7.

52 Satō and Matsuzaki trace the origins and development of PARC: *Jimintō seiken*, pp. 246–66.

53 Inoguchi Takashi and Iwai Tomoaki, *'Zoku giin' no kenkyū: jimintō seiken o gyūjiru shuyakutachi* (Nihon keizai shimbunsha, Tokyo, 1987), pp. 101–2.

54 Satō and Matsuzaki explain that there are no firm definitions of what these bodies do: *Jimintō seiken*, p. 250.

55 *Gendai seiji jōhō*, 1987, pp. 456–7.
56 Park, 'Kyōiku gyōsei', pp. 53–4; Kumatani Kazunori, 'Kyōiku seisaku ni kansuru kenkyū: yotō no jirei o chūshin ni', *Shakaigaku hyōron* 24 (December 1973): 44–6.
57 Inoguchi and Iwai, *'Zoku giin'*, p. 100.
58 Yung H. Park, 'Party–bureaucratic relations in Japan: the case of the Ministry of Education', *Waseda Journal of Asian Studies* 1 (1979): 55–8, and Naka, 'Zoku no kenkyū', pp. 40–2.
59 Interview with Kennoki Toshihiro, 13 August 1987.
60 Yamazaki, *Jimintō*, p. 115.
61 Interview with Kennoki, 13 August 1987.
62 Yamazaki, *Jimintō*, p. 80; Naka, 'Zoku no kenkyū', p. 43.
63 For a discussion of the 'Special Measures' law, see T.J. Pempel, *Patterns of Japanese Policymaking: Experiences from Higher Education* (Westview Press, Boulder, Colorado, 1978), pp. 132–3.
64 Interview with Nishioka, 23 July 1987.
65 Inoguchi and Iwai report that Nishioka in particular was 'recruited': *'Zoku giin'*, p. 113. They suggest that it was a Waseda University elder (probably Hasegawa) who recruited him. Whether or not it was true that he was recruited, Nishioka seems to have in turn taken on the role of convincing others to join: interview with Nishioka, 23 July 1987. He called on Fujinami and Kōno, both Waseda connections (elected in 1967), and later played a part in bringing in Mori and Matsunaga, also Waseda (elected in 1969). The *zoku*'s Waseda connection is one of its interesting characteristics. In addition to those listed above, Kaifu, Nakamura and Yanaga were also Waseda graduates – a total of nine out of twenty-one *zoku* 'members'. Kaifu, Nishioka, Mori, Fujinami and Mitsuzuka were all members of the famous Waseda *Yūbenkai* (a debating society known for producing talented politicians). When one notes that the PARC Education Division chairmanship was passed from Nishioka to Fujinami to Mori, with Kaifu taking possession of the ESRC, one realizes the degree to which the *zoku* has been controlled by this tightly-knit group. On the *Yūbenkai*, see Toyota Kōji, *Seishun kokkai gekijō: waseda yūbenkai ga unda asu o ninau senryō nain* (Bunka sōgō shuppan, Tokyo, 1976).
66 Yamazaki, *Jimintō*, p. 105; and interview with Nishioka, 23 July 1987.
67 Interview with Suzuki Shigenobu, 3 September 1987.
68 Interview with Okuda, 1 September 1987.
69 To say that most education *zoku* members worked their way up through party education posts is to employ the definition of a *zoku*; see, for example, Inoguchi and Iwai, *'Zoku giin'*, p. 99. Table 3.2 provides examples of both of the main *zoku* career paths: the early-start-and-work-your-way-up route is clearly more popular – exemplified by Nishioka, Ishibashi and Nakamura. In addition to Kaifu, there are, however, several others who joined the *zoku* only after serving as education minister (Okuno, Sunada).
70 Saitō Taijun, a top MOE official, emphasized the unusual character of education *zoku* Dietmen: *Bunkyō gyōsei ni miru – seisaku keisei katei no kenkyū* (Gyōsei, Tokyo, 1984), p. 84. See also Inoguchi and

Iwai, *'Zoku giin'*, pp. 126–7. The education *zoku* has a particularly large number of second-generation Dietmen: they include Nishioka, Tanikawa, Sunada, Matsunaga, Aoki, Nakamura and Funada (seven of twenty-one). Second-generation politicians tend to have a more stable political base (inherited from their fathers or fathers-in-law) and are therefore freer to become involved in policy issues. They also tend to get elected at a younger age, thereby allowing them time to develop policy expertise. See Suzuki Kenji, *Makete tamaruka!! daigishi nisei no gunzō* (Seikai shuppansha, Tokyo, 1984).

71 The particularly assertive character of education *zoku* members is evident, for example, in the comments of Nishioka about the proper role for the LDP in the policy-making process: 'The LDP's role should not merely be the passive one of approving or disapproving of legislation developed by the MOE. That just will not suffice. The majority party and the government must take joint responsibility in making policy' – Kumatani, 'Kyōiku seisaku', p. 48. More controversial than the *zoku*'s assertiveness *vis-à-vis* the MOE, however, has been its jealous defence of its control over education policy within the party. Aichi Kazuo described the *zoku* as extremely 'cliquish' (*haitateki*) – a kind of 'special village' which does not admit outsiders: interview, 30 July 1987.

72 Yamazaki, *Jimintō*, pp. 115–16.

73 See John C. Campbell, *Contemporary Japanese Budget Politics* (University of California Press, Berkeley, 1977).

74 Saitō describes the new budget process as it applies to the MOE: *Bunkyō gyōsei*, pp. 7–20.

75 ibid., pp. 84–5; also, interview with Watase Noriyuki, 29 August 1987.

76 Nakajima Akio described the personnel process as it relates to the MOE. He noted that due to seniority traditions the choice of the AVM, for example, was usually quite limited. Within these confines, however, he noted that the opinions of *zoku* leaders were one factor taken into account: interview, 1 September 1987.

77 See in particular his articles, 'Kyōiku gyōsei' and 'Party–bureaucratic relations in Japan'.

78 Interview with Nishioka, 26 August 1987.

79 Nakasone Yasuhiro, 'Reflections of a presidential prime minister', *Japan Echo* 15/1 (Spring 1988): 12–13.

CHAPTER 4 INTERNAL ACTORS: THE BUREAUCRACY

1 Interview with Kida Hiroshi, 22 July 1987.

2 Interview with Kuroha Ryōichi, 14 August 1987.

3 For a summary of the literature on *nemawashi* and the *ringi sei*, see Fukui Haruhiro, 'Japan's higher civil servants: issues and interpretations', unpublished manuscript, pp. 9–10. Much of the older literature describes the concepts as central to the Japanese bureaucracy; see Tsuji Kiyoaki, *Shinpan nihon kanryōsei no kenkyū*

(Tokyo daigaku shuppankai, Tokyo, 1970), pp. 158–60. Some recent studies, however, have questioned whether the system really works on a bottom-up basis in practice; see Albert M. Craig, 'Functional and dysfunctional aspects of government bureaucracy', in Ezra F. Vogel (ed.), *Modern Japanese Organization and Decision-making* (University of California Press, Berkeley, 1975), pp. 17–18; and Yung H. Park, *Bureaucrats and Ministers in Contemporary Japanese Government* (University of California Press, Berkeley, 1986), p. 11, 21–7. The importance of the two concepts within the context of educational administration, however, is that they remain as 'ideals' of the way policy should be made within the ministry. That they remain important in the MOE is clear, for example, in the work by Saitō Taijun, a ministry bureaucrat still active in 1987: *Bunkyō gyōsei ni miru: seisaku keisei katei no kenkyū* (Gyōsei, Tokyo, 1984), pp. 37–40.

4 Interview with Nakajima Akio, 1 September 1987.

5 ibid. The argument that the *ringi sei* inhibits reform is not original. Most of those who see the system as central to Japanese administration blame it at least partly for the conservatism of the nation's bureaucracy. See Tsuji, *Shinpan*, pp. 158–60; and Saitō, *Bunkyō gyōsei*, pp. 37–8.

6 While the discussion here has centred on the role of *newawashi* and the *ringi sei* in Japan, that should not be interpreted to mean that similar structures and patterns of bottom-up consensus-building cannot be found in other nations.

7 Yung H. Park, 'Party–bureaucratic relations in Japan: the case of the Ministry of Education', *Waseda Journal of Asian Studies* 1 (1979): 70.

8 Yung H. Park, 'Kyōiku gyōsei ni okeru jimintō to mombushō', in Shimbori Michiya and Aoi Kazuo (eds), *Nihon kyōiku no rikigaku* (Yūshindo, Tokyo, 1983), p. 63. Interviews conducted for this study confirmed Park's observations.

9 Park, 'Party–bureaucratic relations', pp. 70–1.

10 The MOE's CCE, for example, recommended in its 1983 report on educational content that students should be taught 'to understand the culture and traditions of our country': *Kyōiku naiyōra shoiinkai shingi keika hōkoku*, 15 November 1983, p. 12. See also Suzuki Isao's comments on moral education in 'Kyōiku kaikaku no kadai', *Kōdō* 927 (March–April 1987): 11–20.

11 Ishiyama Morio, *Mombu kanryō no gyakushū* (Kōdansha, Tokyo, 1986), p. 68.

12 According to several MOE officials interviewed, the idea originated with Nishida Kikuo – interviews with Nakajima, 20 July 1987; and Suzuki Isao, 30 July 1987.

13 Mombushō chūkyōshin, *Kyōin no shishitsu nōryoku no kōjō ni tsuite*, 16 June 1978.

14 Interview with Hirayama, 12 August 1987.

15 Interviews with MOE officials. Again, refer to Suzuki, 'Kyōiku kaikaku no kadai', pp. 11–20.

16 Ishiyama, *Mombu kanryō*, pp. 70–1.

17 See, for example, the CCE 1966 and 1971 reports. Relevant sections are reproduced in Saitō, *Bunkyō gyōsei*, pp. 111–12.

18 Saitō, in his article tracing the development of the MOE attitude towards diversification, calls such policies 'compartmentalization' (*kubunka*): *Bunkyō gyōsei*, p. 113.

19 MOE CCE, *Basic Guidelines for the Reform of Education*, 11 June 1971, pp. 11–12. The report tried to sound less elitist by calling for education to be provided according to students' 'abilities, aptitudes and *aspirations* (*kibō*)'.

20 Interview with Nakajima, 20 July 1987.

21 Interview with Suzuki Isao, 30 July 1987. Many officials interviewed expressed the idea that 'the public was not ready' for gifted education; the average member of the public was too committed to the egalitarianism of the established system.

22 Saitō, *Bunkyō gyōsei*, pp. 113–16. The ministry's 1983 CCE report endorsed the principle of increased selection at the secondary school level: *Kyōiku naiyōra*, pp. 11–12.

23 Tokutake Yasushi noted this trend in an interview, 27 July 1987.

24 Interview with Kuroha, 14 August 1987.

25 Mombushō shotō chūtō kyōiku kyoku, 'Wagakuni no shotō chūtō kyōiku', testmony before the AHCE on 23 January 1985, reproduced in *Gendai kyōiku kagaku* 341 (April 1985): 105.

26 Interviews with Nakajima, 20 July 1987; Kida, 22 July 1987, and Suzuki Isao, 30 July 1987.

27 Interview with Kida, 22 July 1987.

28 Yamazaki Masato, *Jimintō to kyōiku seisaku* (Iwanami shinsho, Tokyo, 1986), pp. 104–5.

29 Saitō Sei, Kida and Amagi all worked together in the MOE Research Bureau in the early 1950s, acquiring a taste for education reform through their work with the newly established CCE: interview with Kida, 22 July 1987.

30 Nakajima actually referred to the mainstream as a '*genjō iji* faction': interview, 20 July 1987. Other officials simply used the term *genjō iji* to describe the attitude of the majority of MOE bureaucrats in the immediate post-1971 period – interviews with Kida, 22 July 1987; and Suzuki Shigenobu, 3 September 1987. Suzuki Isao described his own views as opposed to the CCE, employing the 'guinea pig' argument – interview, 30 July 1987.

31 Ishiyama, *Mombu kanryō*, p. 173.

32 This description of the attitude of recent MOE bureaucrats is based on the observations of the various MOE officials interviewed for this study. These officials point out, however, that while virtually all recent bureaucrats have been more timid than the Amagi–Nishida group, some continue to be (at least quietly) more reform-minded than others: Sano Bunichirō (AVM, 1983–6), who had worked under Nishida in the Minister's Secretariat in the period of the CCE deliberations leading up to the 1971 report, was generally recognized to have inherited some of his mentor's style and opinions: Ishiyama, *Mombu kanryō*, pp. 192–3. Okuda Shinjō, Nishida's successor as Councillor in the Minister's Secretariat, was also considered to be

reform-minded – Takayama Yōji, 'Mombu kanryō – sono taishitsu to jinmyaku', *Sekai* 444 (November 1982): 81. Among those still active in the ministry in 1987, Nakajima Akio and Saitō Taijun were considered to be particularly 'internationalist': interview with Suzuki Isao, 30 July 1987.

33 Yung H. Park has been one of the stongest proponents of the idea that the MOE is largely a tool of the LDP *zoku*. See his works cited above in notes 7 and 8 as well as his book, *Jimintō to kyōiku kanryō* (Meiji daigaku gakujutsu kōryū iinkai, Tokyo, 1980).

34 Saitō, *Bunkyō gyōsei*, p. 94.

35 ibid., pp. 81, 87–95.

36 ibid., pp. 92–93.

37 Ishiyama, *Mombu kanryō*, p. 78.

38 Rinkyōshin, *Kyōiku kaikaku ni kansuru dainiji tōshin*, 26 June 1985, in *RD*, special edition 2–3 (June 1985): 71.

39 Several officials interviewed for this study used these arguments to defend the MOE's failure to implement the pilot project reform.

40 Interview with Nakajima, 20 July 1987. Other officials working with the advisory council, considering what to do about the six-year secondary-school proposal also pointed to numerous practical problems with implementing such a change: interviews, 26 August 1986.

41 The ability of councils to focus attention on the MOE's 'neutrality' and 'objectivity' fits perfectly with what Saitō described as the ministry's mission; see notes 34–6 above.

42 Gyōsei kanrichō, *Shingikai sōran*, 1983. The complete list includes the Distinguished Cultural Service Selection Council; Educational Curriculum Council; Private University Council; Special Council on University Problems; Copyright Council; Religious Corporations Council; Teacher Training Council; Science Council; University Establishment Council; Textbook Review Council; Japanese Language Council; Council for the Protection of Cultural Assets; Central Council on Education; Health and Fitness Council; Science and Industrial Education Council; Social Education Council; and the Geodesy Council.

43 Ehud Harari, drawing on case studies of Public Advisory Bodies (PABs) in England, Japan and the United States arrives at a three-fold categorization of council roles: securing policy guidance through policy analysis; co-opting certain interest groups and making them part of the formal public policy-making process; and legitimizing an administration's action or inaction. See 'Japanese politics of advice in comparative perspective: a framework for analysis and a case study', *Public Policy* 12/4 (Fall 1974): 542–6. The argument of this book is that, in the case of the MOE's councils at least, the third role (legitimization) seems to predominate.

44 T.J. Pempel, drawing primarily on examples in the education sphere, argues that councils are essentially manipulated by the bureaucracy – 'The bureaucratization of policymaking in postwar Japan', *American Journal of Political Science* 18/4 (November 1974): 656–63. Yung H. Park, also drawing on examples from

education, similarly points to the numerous ways in which Japanese bureaucrats manipulate councils – 'The governmental advisory system in Japan', *Journal of Comparative Administration* 3 (February 1972): 437–61. Harari has in some more recent work demonstrated that Japanese councils are more autonomous than generally believed – 'Turnover and autonomy in Japanese permanent public advisory bodies', *Journal of Asian and African Studies* 17/3–4 (1982): 235–46; and 'The institutionalisation of policy consultation in Japan: public advisory bodies', in Gail Lee Bernstein and Fukui Haruhiro (eds), *Japan and the World: Essays in Japanese History and Politics in Honour of Takeshi Ishida* (Macmillan, London, 1988), pp. 144–57. Given the conclusions of those studies concentrating on education councils and the analysis of education reform councils in this study, however, this author stands by the argument that education councils (at least) have indeed been manipulated by their parent ministry.

45 Kuroha Ryōichi, a man who has served on many MOE councils himself, openly acknowledges that most MOE councils are '*goyō shingikai*' (honorary councils). He explained: 'The office usually has a goal in mind from the very beginning. After all, it wouldn't do to have the council come up with a proposal which could not be implemented – so the office needs to conceive of an implementable one first. Then the office chooses members with this goal in mind. This is the pattern with most MOE councils, the CCE and others' – interview, 26 August 1986.

46 Ishiyama, *Mombu kanryō*, pp. 80–160.

47 ibid., p. 84.

48 ibid., pp. 96–103.

49 Again, see the two Park articles cited in notes 7–8 above.

50 Interview with Yamagishi Shunsuke, 15 August 1987.

CHAPTER 5
EXTERNAL ACTORS: INCORPORATED INTERESTS

1 The categorization of Japanese interest groups according to whether they are 'for' or 'against' the ruling camp reflects the framework used by Professor J.A.A. Stockwin in his lectures on Japanese politics at Oxford University, Michaelmas term 1985. He actually included a category of 'semi-incorporated interests' which has been left out in order to simplify the analysis in this study.

2 Yanaga Chitoshi, *Big Business in Japanese Politics* (Yale University Press, New Haven, 1968), p. 28.

3 Andō Yoshio, 'Zaikai no chii to yakuwari', *Ekonomisuto*, 21 December 1957, p. 16.

4 Gerald L. Curtis, 'Big business and political influence', in Ezra Vogel (ed.), *Modern Japanese Organization and Decision-making* (University of California Press, Berkeley, 1975), pp. 33–70.

5 Ogata Sadako, 'The business community and Japanese foreign policy: normalization of relations with the People's Republic of

China', in Robert Scalapino (ed.), *Japanese Foreign Policy*, (University of California Press, Berkeley, 1977), pp. 175–203.

6 John C. Campbell, *Contemporary Japanese Budget Politics* (University of California Press, Berkeley, 1977).

7 Curtis, 'Big business', p. 38.

8 Nikkeiren, *Kyōiku no kihon mondai ni taisuru sangyōkai no kenkai*, 18 September 1969.

9 Keizai dōyūkai, *Tayōka e no chōsen*, 24 October 1979; and *Sōzōsei, tayōsei, kokusaisei o motomeru*, July 1984.

10 Keizai dōyūkai, *Sōzōsei*, pp. 2–7.

11 List of education report supplied by Nikkeiren.

12 Nikkeiren, *Chokumen suru daigaku mondai ni kansuru kihonteki kenkai*, 24 February 1969.

13 Nikkeiren, *Kinnen no kōnai bōryoku mondai ni tsuite*, 7 May 1983, pp. 6–7.

14 See Ivan P. Hall, 'Organizational paralysis: the case of Tōdai', in Vogel (ed.), *Modern Japanese Organization and Decision-making*, pp. 304–30, for a more thorough discussion of the administrative problems facing national universities in Japan.

15 Keizai dōyūkai, *Kōji-fukushi shakai no tame no kōtō kyōiku seido*, 18 July 1969, p. 3. Almost identical criticisms can be found in Nikkeiren reports issued that same year. See Nikkeiren, *Chokumen suru daigaku mondai*.

16 Nikkeiren, *Chokumen suru daigaku mondai*.

17 Keizai dōyūkai, *Kōji-fukushi shakai*, pp. 20–3.

18 Nikkeiren, *Report of the Committee for the Study of Labor Questions*, 1984, p. 17.

19 Nikkeiren, *Report of the Committee for the Study of Labor Questions*, 1985, p. 17.

20 Keizai dōyūkai, *Gyōsei kaikaku: kongo no bunkyō seisaku ni nozomu*, January 1982.

21 Keizai dōyūkai, *Kōji-fukushi shakai*, pp. 19–25; and *Sōzōsei*, pp. 3–5.

22 Keizai dōyūkai, *Kōji-fukushi shakai*, pp. 26–28; and *Sōzōsei*, pp. 6–7.

23 Nikkeiren, *Kinnen no kōnai bōryoku*, pp. 19–33.

24 Nikkeiren, *Report of the Committee for the Study of Labor Questions*, 1986, p. 19.

25 See Yanaga, *Big Business in Japanese Politics*, pp. 49–51, for a general discussion of the Nikkeiren organization.

26 Keizai dōyūkai, *Keizai dōyūkai: What It Is; What It Does* (undated pamphlet). See Yanaga, *Big Business in Japanese Politics*, pp. 46–9, for a general discussion of the *Keizai dōyūkai* organization.

27 Keizai dōyūkai, *Keizai dōyūkai*.

28 Interview with Shimizu Kōichi, 28 August 1986.

29 Interview with Maeda Yōji, 2 September 1986.

30 ibid.

31 Lists of education reports provided by the two organizations.

32 Yung H. Park, 'The Central Council for Education, organized business, and the politics of education policy-making in Japan', *Comparative Education Review* 19/2 (June 1975): 304.

33 Aoki Satoshi, *Rinkyōshin kaitai* (Akebi shotoku, Tokyo, 1986), pp. 152–5. The membership of the Iwasa Committee included several academics who were to go on to serve on the AHCE (Ishikawa Tadao, Okamoto Michio, Ishii Takemochi and Kobayashi Noboru) as well as Kida Hiroshi, a former MOE bureaucrat who also went on to serve as a 'specialist' member of the Ad Hoc Council.

34 The Kyoto Group was set up and managed by the PHP Kenkyūjo, the publishing house (controlled by Matsushita) responsible for the publication of the journal *Voice* and numerous books – most of them representing the viewpoint of the reformist wing of the business community – the viewpoint advocated by Ushio Jirō and more broadly by *Keizai dōyūkai* calling for across-the-board deregulation, privatization, and reduced government spending. See Kuroha Ryōichi, *Rinkyōshin – dōnaru kyōiku kaikaku* (Nihon keizai shimbunsha, Tokyo, 1985), pp. 33–5; and Aoki, *Rinkyōshin kaitai*, pp. 156–7.

35 *NKS*, 25 June 1984.

36 Interview with Shimizu, 28 August 1986.

37 The chairman of the council's subcommittee dealing with higher-education issues pointed out that businessmen on his committee tended to base their arguments on anecdotal evidence like: 'College students these days don't seem to study. They're out playing all the time': interview with Iijima Sōichi, 4 August 1986.

38 Interview with Kuroha Ryōichi, 26 August 1986.

39 'Prefectural' is used here and elsewhere in this section to refer to the units of government immediately below the national government, variously called '*-to*', '*-dō*', '*-fu*' and '*-ken*'.

40 Teachers' salaries, for example, though technically under the jurisdiction of local bodies which actually employ teachers, are effectively tied to a national salary scale set by the government based on the recommendations of the National Personnel Authority: Benjamin Duke, *Japan's Militant Teachers* (University Press of Hawaii, Honolulu, 1973), p. 166.

41 See Nishi Toshio, *Unconditional Democracy: Education and Politics in Occupied Japan 1945–52* (Hoover Institution Press, Stanford, 1982), pp. 210–19, for details of the school board policy of the Occupation. Duke, *Japan's Militant Teachers*, pp. 129–33, discusses the 1956 reforms which rolled back that reform. One of the AHCE proposals in the latest round of reform called for a further reduction in local autonomy through the consolidation of small town and village authorities into larger units and through the appointment of professional superintendents right down to the local level (see Chapter 8 below).

42 Todōfuken kyōikuchō kyōgikai, *Kyōiku iinkai no unei no kasseika ni tsuite*, 26 June 1985, p. 1.

43 In 1984, 51 per cent of education superintendents were from a background in general administration, 19 per cent came from a background purely in education administration, and the remaining 30 per cent started as teachers: ibid., p. 10.

44 As recently as 1979, Minister of Education Naitō Yosaburō started a

policy whereby he required that all prefectural superintendents submit to an interview before obtaining his approval. He was seeking, he said, 'officials who will listen to what the ministry has to say'. Yamazaki Masato, *Jimintō to kyōiku seisaku* (Iwanami shinsho, Tokyo, 1986), p. 156.

45 For a discussion of the Tokyo reform effort and its lessons for other local high school reform efforts, see Thomas P. Rohlen, 'Is Japanese education becoming less egalitarian? Notes on high school stratification and reform', *Journal of Japanese Studies* 3/1 (Winter 1977): 62–8.

46 ibid., p. 67.

47 PESA official Takeyama Tetsu pointed out this pattern in an interview, 26 August 1986.

48 Todōfuken kyōikuchō kyōgikai kōtōkyōiku kaihatsu kenkyū puro-jekuto chîmu, *Kenkyū kekka hōkokusho*, 13 June 1979, pp. 12–13.

49 *RD*, special edition 2–3 (June 1985): 93.

50 Todōfuken kyōikuchō kyōgikai, *Rokunensei chūtōgakkō oyobi tanisei kōtōgakkō ni tsuite*, May 1986.

51 *RD*, special edition 2–3 (June 1985): 93.

52 Todōfuken kyōikuchō kyōgikai, *Kyōiku kaikaku ni kansuru chōsa*, December 1985.

53 ibid., p. 9.

54 *AN*, 1978, p. 511.

55 Interview with Suzuki Shigenobu, 3 September 1987.

56 Todōfuken kyōikuchō kyōgikai, *Kōtōgakkō nyūgaku senbatsu ni tsuite*, May 1984, pp. 1, 5.

57 Mombushō shotō chūtō kyōiku kyoku, *Kōritsu kōtōgakkō no nyūgakusha senbatsu ni tsuite (tsūchi)*, 20 July 1984.

58 Mombushō shotō chūtō kyōiku kyoku kōtōgakkōka, *Shōwa 61-nendo kōtōgakkō nyūgaku senbatsu no kaizen jōkyō ni tsuite*, undated internal document. See also *AS*, 10 December 1986.

59 Having worked for a year as an English teaching consultant in the Kumamoto Prefectural Office of Education, I returned to the pre-fecture as part of my research work to see how it had responded to education problems on a local level.

60 Interviews with officials in the Kumamoto Prefectural Office of Education, 9–14 July 1986.

61 The Kumamoto teacher-training programme was based on an MOE programme of grants to localities, the *Shinki saiyō kyōinra kenshū jigyō hojokin* programme initiated in 1976; the student camps were started after the MOE initiated another subsidy programme, the *Shizen kyōiku suishin jigyō hojokin* grant, in 1983; the *ijime denwa* was started after the MOE issued a *tsūchi* on 25 October 1985 suggesting the establishment of such a hot-line – *Ijime mondai ni kansuru shidō no tettei ni tsuite*; the guidance programme reflected the advice of the same *tsūchi* as well as a grant, *Kyōiku sōdan katsudō suishin jigyō hojokin* (1985).

62 Interview with the public relations officer, Kumamoto Office of Education, 9 July 1986.

63 Saitama-ken kyōiku kyoku shidōka, 'Tokushu aru kōkōzukuri

no suishin ni tsuite', undated internal document (probably 1985).

64 Kanagawa-ken kyōiku iinkai, *Kyōiku katei kaihatsu kenkyū-kō; koseika suishin-kō: kenkyū shūroku VI*, August 1985.

CHAPTER 6   EXTERNAL ACTORS: OPPOSITION GROUPS

1 These figures represent MOE estimates reported in Mombushō jōsei kyoku chihōka, *Kyōshokuin dantai no soshiki no jittai ni tsuite*, 1 October 1985, p. 16. *Nikkyōso* officials, however, point to several statistical devices used by the ministry to understate the union's strength. According to former union leader Makieda Motofumi, the total number of members is actually closer to 700,000 – including a full 80 per cent of public elementary and lower secondary school teachers. The MOE brings the figure down to 50 per cent by including groups of teachers (headmaster and upper secondary teachers) who subscribe in smaller numbers. Headmasters are legally barred from membership while many upper secondary teachers belong to the separate (but like-minded) *Nikkōkyō – Mombu daijin wa nani o shitaka* (Mainichi shimbunsha, Tokyo, 1984), p. 263.

2 The figure on membership is again from the MOE survey. The same report lists the membership of other teachers' unions as follows: the Japan Upper Secondary School Teachers Union (*Nikkōkyō*) – left faction, 2.5 per cent; its right faction, 1.4 per cent; and the National Association of Teacher-Manager Groups (*Zenkankyō*), 0.4 per cent.

3 See for example *Zennikkyōren*'s testimony before the AHCE – *RD*, special editions 2–3 (June 1985): 82.

4 After decades of government efforts to suppress it, *Nikkyōso* is finally beginning to suffer. Its membership, as high as 86.3 per cent in 1958, is now listed as just under 50 per cent (see note 2 on MOE stats, above).

5 Makieda Motofumi, leader of the union at the time of the CCE report, recalled this issue as being one of those which most concerned *Nikkyōso*: interview, 21 August 1986.

6 See the union's testimony before the AHCE – *RD*, special edition 5 (April 1986): 161, as well as its reaction to the second AHCE report: 'Rinji kyōiku shingikai no kyōiku kaikaku dainiji tōshin ni taisuru bunseki hihan oyobi watakushitachi no motomeru kyōiku kaikaku e no teigen (dainiji hōkoku)', (hereafter 'AHCE no. 2 analysis and proposals'), *Minna de kyōiku kaikaku o* 9 (1 June 1986): 14–15.

7 The *Nikkyōso* position on teacher training is detailed in its *Report of the Second JTU Council on Educational Reform* (summarized edition), October 1983, pp. 26–30. With regard to the AHCE proposals in particular, see its 'AHCE no. 2 analysis and proposals', pp. 18–20.

8 *Nikkyōso*, 'Rinji kyōiku shingikai "kyōiku kaikaku ni kansuru, dainiji tōshin" ni taisuru nikkyōso kenkai', (hereafter 'AHCE no. 2 critique') *Minna de kyōiku kaikaku o* 9 (1 June 1986): 4.

9 ibid.

10 See, for example, the union's testimony before the AHCE – *RD*, special edition 5 (April 1986): 161–2.

11 *Nikkyōso*, 'AHCE no. 2 critique', p. 2.

12 *Nikkyōso* regularly publishes its own programme for education reform. Recent reports include the first and second reports of the JTU Council for Studying the Education System (1974 and 1983) and the first and second reports of the JTU Council for Research into Education Reform (1984 and 1986). The union's proposals have not in fact changed much over this time. The proposals cited here may be found in any of the reports, most recently the 1986 report as published in 'AHCE no. 2 analysis and proposals', pp. 29–48.

13 *Nikkyōso*, 'AHCE no. 2 analysis and proposals', p. 30.

14 *Nikkyōso*, 'Nihon no kyōiku o dō aratameru ka (daiichiji hōkoku)', *Minna de kyōiku kaikaku o* 5 (1 December 1985): 11.

15 ibid., pp. 11–13.

16 ibid., p. 9.

17 ibid., pp. 9–10.

18 *Nikkyōso*, of course, has policy aims other than those described above. One additional aim requires at least footnote treatment: teachers' salaries. While *Nikkyōso* remains concerned about salary levels, it has not made them a major issue since teachers received their last major salary hike in the mid-1970s. Recently, the union's concerns in this area have centred on its effort to achieve a five-day work week for teachers.

19 *Nikkyōso*, *RD*, special edition 5 (April 1986): 161.

20 *Nikkyōso*, 'AHCE no. 2 critique', p. 5.

21 Ōmori Kazuo, 'Sutāto shita rinkyōshin', *AN*, 1985, p. 208.

22 Interview with Tamaru Akiyo, 29 August 1986.

23 Initially quite flexible regarding the question of JTU participation in the Ad Hoc Council, Tanaka was first forced to retreat slightly in April 1984 when, at an extraordinary conference of union leaders, he was forced to agree (unofficially) to rather rigid terms for participation. Facing an ever more serious revolt from the left at the union's regular conference in June, Tanaka was forced to make the above terms official – effectively closing off the possibility that the union would let an official representative sit on the council – see *NKS*, 2 July 1984.

24 Yamazaki Masato, *Jimintō to kyōiku seisaku* (Iwanami shinsho, Tokyo, 1986), pp. 153–4.

25 See *AS*, 9 August 1986.

26 For an analysis of the leadership struggle, see *AS*, 25 December 1986.

27 See Duke's account of *Nikkyōso* strikes during this period, *Japan's Militant Teachers* (University Press of Hawaii, Honolulu, 1973), pp. 149–56.

28 *AN*, 1972, p. 513.

29 *Nikkyōso*, 'Daisanjūgoji nikkyōso kyōken zenkoku shūkai hōkoku', *Minna de kyōiku kaikaku o* 7 (1 April 1986): 2–3.

30 Interview with Soejima Takeyoshi, 19 August 1986.

31 Interview with Morita Tomio, 19 August 1986.

32 Calling education a 'broad public-type issue' (*habahiroi kokuminteki kadai*), Nakasone emphasized in a February 1984 public statement that his council would depend on the advice of experts and 'will not violate the political neutrality of education': Adachi Takuji, 'Ugokidashita shushō shudō no kyōiku kaikaku', *Gendai kyōiku kagaku* 329 (April 1984): 51.

33 Thurston, *Teachers and Politics in Japan* (Princeton University Press, Princeton, 1973), pp. 207–9.

34 Thurston notes the gap between attitudes of officials at local and national levels: ibid., p. 218.

35 Superintendents were most divided in their reaction to proposals for: (1) special boards to weed out 'bad' teachers, (2) the most severe teacher-training proposals, and (3) six-year secondary schools, all proposals which would spark severe disruptions by union teachers. See Todōfuken kyōikuchō kyōgikai, *Kyōiku kaikaku ni kansuru chōsa*, December 1985.

36 The chairman, Okamoto Michio, was a former president of Kyoto University who was very involved in the ANUP effort to reform the university entrance system in the 1970s. The subcommittee chairman was Iijima Sōichi.

37 T.J. Pempel, *Patterns of Japanese Policy-making: Experiences from Higher Education* (Westview Press, Boulder, Colorado, 1978), pp. 108–10.

38 Interview with Iijima Sōichi, 4 August 1986.

39 Iijima himself admitted that he was picked largely due to MOE pressure: interview, 4 August 1986. See Chapter 8 for background on the appointment process.

40 Kaifu expressed 'full support' for freeing up higher education: interview, 3 September 1986. Kida said the idea of more independent universities was 'all right since the government cannot actually control universities': interview, 13 August 1986.

41 Interview with Iijima, 4 August 1986.

42 While officials like Kida speak about the desirability of eventually allowing public universities greater autonomy in budget and planning decisions, they always qualify these statements by noting that universities now are not yet 'ready': interview, 13 August 1986.

43 Interview with Iijima, 4 August 1986.

44 See, for example, Duke's account of the debate over the 1956 school board revision plan, *Japan's Militant Teachers*, p. 133.

45 The two amendments were incorporated into the law as Article III, Section 2 and Article V, Section II. See the text of the law in *RD*, special edition 2–3 (June 1985): 153–4. See also *AS*, 29 June 1984, for background on the negotiating positions of the various sides. On the 'spirit of the FLE' clause, see Yagi Atsushi, *Mombu daijin no sengoshi* (Bijinesusha, Tokyo, 1984), pp. 216–17. A 'memo' prepared by one of Nakasone's education advisors makes it clear that the Prime Minister's side decided to make that compromise fairly early in the process: *NKS*, 21 May 1984.

CHAPTER 7   EDUCATION REFORM IN THE 1970s

1 Interview with Kennoki Toshihiro, 13 August 1987.
2 Mombushō, *Chūō kyōiku shingikai yōran*, 8th edn, 1979.
3 Interview with Kida Hiroshi, 22 July 1987.
4 Kida gives Amagi a great deal of credit as well: interview, 22 July 1987. His name was also the one most often mentioned by journalists who observed the initiation.
5 Interview with Kida, 22 July 1987.
6 The accompanying text is quoted in Kuroha Ryōichi, *Kyōiku kaikaku: tembō to kanōsei* (Kokudosha, Tokyo, 1984), p. 53.
7 See the CCE's midterm report: Mombushō chūkyōshin, *Chūkan hōkoku: meiji hyakunen no kyōiku bunseki*, 30 June 1969.
8 See Kuroha Ryōichi, *Sugao no sengo kyōiku* (Gakuji shuppan, Tokyo, 1974), pp. 222–3, for a discussion of how the 'facts' presented in the 1967 report were arranged to support the 'internationalist' preference for structural reform.
9 Interview with Suzuki Shigenobu, 3 September 1987.
10 Ishiyama Morio, *Mombu kanryō no gyakushū* (Kōdansha, Tokyo, 1986), pp. 171–2, also emphasizes Nishida's role in guiding the council with documentary evidence.
11 Interview with Suzuki Shigenobu, 3 September 1987.
12 Kuroha, *Sugao*, p. 223.
13 *AS*, 29 May 1970.
14 Suzuki reports that the idea was only fully developed after he discovered – during the course of a fact-finding tour of Europe – that such a programme of experimental schools was being operated in Germany: interview, 3 September 1987.
15 Interview with Kida, 22 July 1987, and with Nishioka Takeo, 23 July 1987.
16 Interview with Suzuki Shigenobu, 3 September 1987.
17 See *AS*, 11 August 1970.
18 Ishiyama, *Mombu kanryō*, pp. 172–3.
19 MOE Central Council for Education, *Basic Guidelines for the Reform of Education: On the Basic Guidelines for the Development of an Integrated Education System Suited for Contemporary Society*, 11 June 1971, pp. 9–11; the *AS* evaluated this change in wording as a 'retreat': 8 October and 6 November 1970.
20 *AS*, 29 May 1970.
21 *MS*, 6 and 7 November 1970.
22 See *MS*, 29 May, 11 August and 6 November 1970.
23 *MS*, 12 June 1971.
24 MOE CCE, *Basic Guidelines*, pp. 16–17, 53 and 62. See also Nishijima Takeo, 'Chūkyōshin tōshin sono ato', *Kikan kyōikuhō* 3 (March 1972): 173.
25 Kuroha, *Sugao*, pp. 226–7.
26 Interview with Tokutake Yasushi, 27 July 1987. See Kuroha, *Sugao*, pp. 227–8, for a description of how the initially ambitious plans were watered down.
27 MOE CCE, *Basic Guidlines*, pp. 28–9.

28 ibid., p. 36.
29 ibid., pp. 38–40.
30 Yamazaki Masato, *Jimintō to kyōiku seisaku* (Iwanami shinsho, Tokyo, 1986), p. 105.
31 Interview with Suzuki Shigenobu, 3 September 1987, and with Nakajima Akio, 20 July 1987.
32 The proposal was not even listed, for example, in the *AS* summary of the report's contents: 12 June 1971.
33 MOE CCE, *Basic Guidelines*, pp. 19, 22, 48.
34 For the May draft see *AS*, 29 May 1970; for the final recommendation see MOE CCE, *Basic Guidelines*, pp. 20–2, 47–8, 62.
35 *MS*, 6 November 1970.
36 MOE CCE, *Basic Guidelines*, pp. 20–1, 47–8, 62.
37 Kida Hiroshi (ed.), *Sengo no bunkyō seisaku* (Daiichi hōki, Tokyo, 1987), p. 312.
38 Interview with Oguchi Kōichi, 13 August 1986.
39 MOE CCE, *Basic Guidelines*, pp. 20–2, 47–8, 62. The *AS* called the final recommendation a 'retreat' from earlier proposals, 12 June 1971.
40 MOE CCE, *Basic Guidelines*, pp. 11–15.
41 ibid., pp. 40–2, 48–50, 63.
42 Makieda Motofumi, *Mombu daijin wa nani o shitaka* (Mainichi shimbunsha, Tokyo, 1984), p. 185.
43 *MS*, 12 June 1971.
44 ibid. See also the editorial in *AS* (12 June 1971) as well as an interesting article by Nagai Michio in the same issue. Nagai, the *Asahi* and even the *Nihon keizai shimbun* (12 June 1971) criticized the council for failing to address the basic problem of Japanese education – its over-emphasis on the selective function of the system.
45 *MS*, 12 June 1971.
46 *YS*, 12 October 1971.
47 ibid. For a comprehensive summary of the views expressed by various organizations, see Suwa Takashi, 'Kewashiku tōi kyōiku kaikaku no michi', *Gendai kyōiku kagaku* 15/3 (March 1972): 88–92.
48 Yagi Atsushi, *Mombu daijin no sengoshi* (Bijinesusha, Tokyo, 1984), p. 194.
49 *AS*, 12 June 1971.
50 Yagi, *Mombu daijin*, p. 195.
51 Satō Eisaku, the Prime Minister during the entire course of CCE deliberations, also retired one year after the CCE report. His replacement, Tanaka Kakuei, was also less committed.
52 Interview with Suzuki Shigenobu, 3 September 1987.
53 Interview with Amagi Isao, 3 September 1986.
54 Ishiyama, *Mombu kanryō*, pp. 162–5.
55 *AS*, 19 September and 4 December 1971; *Nihon keizai shimbun*, 21 October 1971; and interviews with various MOE officials.
56 See *Nihon keizai shimbun*, 27 August and 8 September 1971, and *AS*, 19 September 1971, for details of the ministry's original request; see also Suwa, 'Kewashiku tōi', pp. 88–92, and Nishijima, 'Chūkyōshin', pp. 169–70.

57 See *Nihon keizai shimbun*, 6, 10 and 13 January for details of the MOF cuts and the renegotiation process; *Nihon keizai shimbun*, 27 November 1972; see Mombushō, *Kuni to chihō no bunkyō yosan*, 1972, for details of the final government budget.

58 *YS*, 30 July 1972.

59 For the findings of the Co-operative Council, see Mombushō shotō-chūtō kyōiku kyoku, *Yōji, jidō, seito no shinshin hattatsu ni tsuite*, June 1977.

60 *Nihon keizai shimbun*, 27 August 1971.

61 Mombushō, *Kuni to chihō no bunkyō yosan*, 1971 and 1972; *Nihon keizai shimbun*, 6, 10 and 13 January 1972.

62 Mombushō, *Kuni to chihō no bunkyō yosan*, issues 1971–86. Assistance for the establishment of kindergartens had increased to ¥11 billion by 1980 while the low-income assistance programme had grown to ¥13.7 billion. Both budgets were frozen and began to be reduced shortly afterward.

63 Nishijima, 'Chūkyōshin', pp. 172–3.

64 Mombushō, *Kuni to chihō no bunkyō yosan*, issues 1970–80. See Nihon shiritsu daigaku kyōkai, *Shōwa 61-nendo jigyō keikakusho*, 28 March 1986, pp. 40–50, for a concise history of the government's increasing support for private universities. The same organization's *Kōtōkyōiku no genjōra ni kansuru shiryō*, 31 May 1986, p. 14, provides a graphic illustration of the growth in government grants as a share of private university operating expenses.

65 In the immediate post-war period, the government (including the MOE) refused to finance private universities with the argument that Article 89 of the Constitution forbade aid to private organizations. By the 1960s, however, the government was providing aid on a limited scale to cover two-thirds of their costs of research and equipment: Nihon shiritsu daigaku kyōkai, *Shōwa 61-nendo*, pp. 40–50.

66 Yamazaki, *Jimintō*, pp. 75–7.

67 See Kuroha, *Sugao*, pp. 192–3.

68 Nihon shiritsu daigaku kyōkai, *Shōwa 61-nendo*, pp. 46–7; Yung H. Park, 'Kyōiku gyōsei ni okeru jimintō to mombushō', in Shimbori Michiya and Aoi Kazuo (eds), *Nihon kyōiku no rikigaku* (Yūshindo, Tokyo, 1983), p. 67.

69 See Yamazaki, *Jimintō*, pp. 136–8, for an account of the passage of this legislation – the Promotional Aid to Private Education Law (*Shigaku shinkō jōsei hō*).

70 Grants to cover a share of the operating expenses of private schools, initiated in 1975 at a level of ¥8 billion, grew to a level of ¥80 billion by 1982 before fiscal constraints began to force budget cuts: Mombushō, *Kuni to chihō no bunkyō yosan*, issues 1975–86. Spending for handicapped education also increased at a rapid rate, and in 1979 school attendance by compulsory school-aged handicapped pupils was made mandatory. See Mombushō shotō chūtō kyōiku kyoku tokushu kyōikuka, 'Yōgo gakkō no jisshi', *Mombu jihō* 1226 (July 1979): 48–59.

71 See *AS*, 25 June 1971 and 14 December 1973.

72 Yamazaki, *Jimintō*, p. 138.
73 MOE Higher Education Bureau, *Higher Education in Japan*, October 1984, pp. 2, 8 and 12. See also Ronald Dore and Sako Mari, *How the Japanese Learn to Work* (Nissan Institute/Routledge Japanese Studies Series, London, 1989), Chapter 5.
74 *AS*, 27 June 1972. This Discussion Group produced a report in March 1976 which laid the groundwork for the MOE's first detailed five-year plan (1976–80). This planning process was subsequently formalized as part of the regular work of the MOE (through its University Chartering Council) which went on to issue further plans covering 1981–6 and 1986–92. This formalization of the planning process for higher education – first proposed by the CCE – was one of the concrete changes which was successfully implemented. See MOE Higher Education Bureau, *Higher Education*, pp. 8–10.
75 Details of the Tsukuba legislation (the *Kokuritsu gakkō setchihōra no ichibu o kaisei suru hōritsu*) are given in Hamabayashi Masao and Hatakeyama Hidetaka, *Tsukuba daigaku: sono seiritsu o meguru tatakai to genjō* (Aoki shoten, Tokyo, 1979), pp. 129–30.
76 See William K. Cummings, 'The conservatives reform higher education', in Edward Beauchamp (ed.), *Learning to Be Japanese* (Linnet Books, Hamden, Conn., 1978), pp. 316–28, for a concise account of the Tsukuba debate in English. In Japanese, Fukuda Nobuyuki, *Tsukuba daigaku no bijiyon* (Zenhonsha, Tokyo, 1983), tells the story from the perspective of one involved in promoting the reform while Hamabayashi and Hatakeyama, *Tsukuba daigaku*, give a more progressive account of the debate.
77 The group was brought together by MOE University Bureau Planning Director Kida Hiroshi. Members included Miyajima, Fukuda, and Ōjima from TEU as well as leading reformist faculty from the University of Tokyo, Waseda, and other universities: Kida Hiroshi, quoted in Fukuda, *Tsukuba daigaku*, p. 121.
78 Fukuda, *Tsukuba daigaku*, pp. 161–2; also Yamazaki, *Jimintō*, p. 90.
79 Fukuda, *Tsukuba daigaku*, p. 128.
80 ibid., pp. 162, 131.
81 Hamabayashi and Hatakeyama, *Tsukuba daigaku*, p. 118.
82 Interview with Kida Hiroshi, 13 August 1986. He did add, however, that Tsukuba was nevertheless 'hearing things from outside'. The administrator cited below also discussed the reality of the advisory board. He explained that it did get heard at the top level of administration but that its reach did not extend down to the working level of the university. Asked if Tsukuba could still be considered an 'ivory tower', he admitted that it could.
83 The administrator asked that his name not be used. In all of the interviews conducted for this study his was the only such request.
84 *Nihon keizai shimbun*, 1 July 1974. Ivan P. Hall, 'Organizational paralysis: the case of Tōdai', in Ezra F. Vogel (ed.), *Modern Japanese Organization and Decision-making* (University of California Press, Berkeley, 1975), pp. 304–30, discusses the attempt at reform at the University of Tokyo.

85 Interview with Kida, 22 July 1987.
86 The *shiho* system died quickly: *Nihon keizai shimbun*, 27 November 1972. The goal of strengthening teacher-training courses at regular universities was a major focus of MOE activity during the 1970s and early 1980s, but the effort stalled in 1984 when licensing reform legislation died before it could be considered by the Diet. Murayama Matsuo discusses the difficulties the MOE encountered in seeking to reform the teacher-training and licensing system in Kida (ed.), *Sengo*, pp. 311–17.
87 Interviews with MOE officials.
88 Kida (ed.), *Sengo*, pp. 346–7.
89 Yamazaki, *Jimintō*, pp. 107–9.
90 Iwama gives a colourful account in Kida (ed.), *Sengo*, pp. 348–51; Yamazaki, *Jimintō*, pp. 116–18.
91 Yamazaki, *Jimintō*, p. 119; Iwama in Kida (ed.), *Sengo*, pp. 351–6.
92 The union defended its decision to ask for the salary rise while opposing the legislation by arguing that 'even a poison cake (*doku manjū*) was edible if you removed the poison': Yamazaki, *Jimintō*, p. 121.
93 Kida (ed.), *Sengo*, pp. 356–7; Yamazaki, *Jimintō*, pp. 122–3.
94 Iwama in Kida (ed.), *Sengo*, p. 350.
95 'Shunin modai to seitō no gyōsei kainyū', *Gendai kyōiku kagaku* 19/2 (February 1976): 105. The *Jinkakuhō*, while directing the government to provide funds for a substantial rise over three years, had left it to the MOE and the Personnel Commission to decide exactly how the rise should be distributed. While the increase allocated for the first two years had been awarded without controversy (largely on an across-the-board basis) the third-year allocation became the focus of the *shunin* dispute when the MOE requested that it be allowed to use part of the allocation to create the *shunin* bonus.
96 'Shunin mondai', p. 106; Yamazaki, *Jimintō*, p. 139; Park, 'Kyōiku gyōsei', p. 69.
97 See Yamazaki, *Jimintō*, pp. 131–3, for background on Nagai and his assumption of this cabinet post.
98 'Shunin mondai', pp. 106–7; Kida (ed.), *Sengo*, p. 359.
99 Makieda, *Mombu daijin*, pp. 230–1, describes the union's campaign.
100 Interview with Suzuki Isao, 30 July 1987.
101 *Nihon keizai shimbun*, 8 December 1971.
102 A whole range of opinions are summarized in Suwa, 'Kewashiku tōi', pp. 90–1.
103 *AS*, 9 June 1977.
104 See note 44 above.
105 The other three 'horses' were to be examination reform, a reduction in the differences between universities, and a change in the societal emphasis on educational background: Yagi, *Mombu daijin*, p. 202.
106 *AS*, 22 June 1978: Mombushō shotō-chūtō kyōiku kyoku kōtō-gakkōka, 'Kōtōgakkō no shin-kyōiku katei hensei jōkyō ni tsuite', *Mombu jihō* 1261 (June 1982): 79.

107 Mombushō shotō-chūtō kyōiku kyoku kōtōgakkōka, 'Kōtōgakkō', pp. 79–80.

108 The rationale for the *Kyōtsu-ichiji* exam was contained in a report issued by the ANUP committee charged with drawing up a proposal for examination reform: see *AS*, 18 November 1976. While it was the ANUP committee which issued the detailed proposal for reform, the MOE had actively encouraged the ANUP to propose a unified examination.

109 Okuda Shinjō, one of the MOE architects of the 1970s curriculum reforms, admitted that the changes had failed to spark much of an increase in specialization at the upper-secondary-school level – 'largely because of examinations'. He pointed out that Kanagawa and Saitama Prefectures had established several diverse schols (*tokushu aru kōkō*), but added that this was only happening on a small scale: interview, 1 September 1987.

CHAPTER 8   EDUCATION UNDER NAKASONE

1 *MS*, 5 December 1980; *AS*, 24 January 1981.

2 Jiyū minshutō seimu chōsakai bunkyōbukai kyōin mondai ni kansuru shoiinkai, *Kyōin no shishitsu kōjō ni kansuru teigen*, 16 May 1981. The report referred to the *shiho* system as a long-term goal but noted that it was too expensive for the short term.

3 As noted in Chapter 3, the 'Kondo Plan' failed to win the support of the whole Education System Research Council, indicating that many *zoku* members considered Kondō's ideas too radical.

4 The three Dietmen were quoted calling for system reform in *AS*, 5 April 1982.

5 Mombushō kyōiku shokuin yōsei shingikai, *Kyōin no yōsei oyobi menkyo seido no kaizen ni tsuite*, 22 November 1983.

6 Mombushō chūō kyōiku shingikai, *Kyōiku naiyōra shoiinkai shingi keika hōkuku*, 15 November 1983.

7 The subject of a continuing conflict between the *zoku* and the ministry, system reform became a particularly contentious isse in the period after the *zoku* began its reform offensive in 1980. While leading *zoku* members demanded action, top MOE officials insisted that system reform should be considered as a last resort. See *MS*, 29 March 1982; Ishiyama Morio, *Mombu kanryō no gyakushū* (Kōdansha, Tokyo, 1986), p. 20. In March 1982 the *zoku* finally succeeded in extracting a promise from MOE AVM Morosawa Masamichi that the ministry would initiate a study of the question of system reform: *MS*, 29 March 1982. Under Morosawa's direction, a group of senior ministry officials studied the issue for several months. The CCE subcommittee was then given its assignment to examine the issue: Ishiyama, pp. 20–1. In July 1983 the ministry formally set up a 'project team' of bureau chiefs to further develop the ministry's position: *MS*, 22 July 1983.

8 Tsūsanshō sangyō kōzō shingikai, *1980-nendai no tsūshō sangyō seisaku (bijiyon)*, 17 March 1980.

9 Keizai dōyūkai, *Sōzōsei, tayōsei, kokusaisei o motomeru*, July 1984.

10 Kyoto Group for the Study of Global Issues, 'Seven recommendations to revitalize school education, March 13, 1984', in Foreign Press Center, Japan (ed.), *Documents on Educational Reform in Japan* (Foreign Press Center, Tokyo, 1985), pp. 31–4.

11 See Chapter 2 above.

12 Nakasone Yasuhiro, 'Seven-point proposal for education reform, December 10, 1983', in Foreign Press Center, Japan (ed.), *Documents*, pp. 13–14.

13 He first expressed support for a supra-cabinet education council in 1981; see *NKS*, 16 April 1984.

14 He expressed a lack of faith in the CCE and the need for a more independent council in the book he prepared for the 1983 general election: *Atarashii hoshu no ronri* (Kōdansha, Tokyo, 1983) – cited in *NKS*, 14 May 1984.

15 On several occasions in late December 1983 and early January 1984, Nakasone expressed his desire to refer the issue to a new session of the CCE: Adachi Takuji, 'Ugokidashita shushō shudō kyōiku kaikaku', *Gendai kyōiku kagaku* 329 (April 1984): 49–54.

16 It is difficult to determine exactly when Nakasone decided to insist on his original plan. He openly expressed renewed interest in a supra-cabinet council on 17 January during meetings with DSP leader Sasaki who had encouraged him to establish a broad-based council: *AS*, 18 January 1984. According to various journalists' reports, however, Nakasone had by that time already expressed his intention to establish a council to Mori Yoshirō (the Education Minister) and to several education *zoku* members of his own faction (including Fujinami Takao): Ishiyama, *Mombu kanryō*, p. 27, and Yagi Atsushi, *Mombu daijin no sengoshi* (Bijinesusha, Tokyo, 1984), p. 214. On the other hand, both Mori and Fujinami made public statements on 17 January insisting that the CCE was still going to be used: Adachi, 'Ugokidashita', p. 50, and Yagi, *Mombu daijin*, p. 213.

17 Yagi, *Mombu daijin*, p. 214.

18 ibid.

19 ibid., pp. 214–15.

20 *NKS*, 21 May 1984.

21 Adachi, 'Ugokidashita', p. 51.

22 According to an account given by Ishiyama Morio, *Mombu kanryō*, pp. 26–8, senior MOE officials were not aware of the Prime Minister's decision until 24 January. The most senior official, Sano Bunichirō (AVM, 1983–6) was informed by Mori at an earlier date. He did not, however, inform others in the ministry until they heard rumours about Nakasone's plan.

23 These provisions were included in the original bill, *Rinji kyōiku shingikai setchi-hōan*. The provisions were not altered during Diet deliberations and remained in the final law.

24 *NKS*, 9 April 1984.

25 The JSP drew up its own plan for a 'People's Education Council'

organized under the MOE. The text of the proposal is contained in *RD*, special edition 2–3 (June 1985): 174–6.

26 Yagi, *Mombu daijin*, pp. 222–4; Ishiyama, *Mombu kanryō*, pp. 218–21.

27 Okamoto, whose credentials as a leader of the 'education world' might have made him a member of the 'MOE Camp', was also close to Nakasone, thus making him more of a neutral member.

28 According to Ishiyama, *Mombu kanryō*, p. 223, Nakasone chose five members not on the original MOE-supplied list: Sono, Kōyama, Nakauchi, Miyata and Dōgakinai.

29 Article II of the AHCE Establishment Law.

30 Kōyama Kenichi, *Kyōiku kaikaku no kihon hōkō ni tsuite no teian*, cited in Yamazaki Masato, *Jimintō to kyōiku seisaku* (Iwanami, shinso, Tokyo, 1986), p. 176. His ideas are elaborated in greater detail in his book *Jiyū no tame no kyōiku kaikaku* (PHP kenkyūjo, Tokyo, 1987).

31 *NKS*, 22 October 1984.

32 The NHK poll, conducted 3 September before the council had even met, found that five members agreed with the statement that the FLE was 'definitely a subject for re-examination' while at the other extreme, seven felt 'it must be respected': cited in *NKS*, 15 October 1984.

33 *NKS*, 22 October 1984. Fujio Masayuki, the head of PARC, was even more direct. 'It is imperative,' he said, 'that the FLE – drafted while Japan was under the Occupation – be radically revised': *NKS*, 12 November 1984.

34 Kōyama presented his case at the 14 November 1984 general meeting of the council: *NKS*, 4 February 1985. Shortly before that date, the Minister of Education, Mori, had pointed in the same direction, arguing that 'the FLE is actually quite well made': *NKS*, 12 November 1984.

35 Interview with Ōmori Kazuo, 21 August 1986.

36 *AS*, 26 January 1985. Arita's subcommittee on that day adopted a position paper which attacked Kōyama's liberalization proposals in detail. See *NKS*, 11 February 1985, for a summary of the document.

37 The text of Kōyama's position paper is included in *NKS*, 11 February 1985. Over the following few months this battle between the first and third subcommittees – in effect a surrogate battle between the MOE and *zoku* on the one hand and Nakasone on the other – filled the pages of Japan's monthlies and weeklies. Just a few of the articles, all abridged translations of articles in Japanese periodicals, include Kōyama Kenichi, 'An end to uniformity in education', *Japan Echo* 12/2 (1985): 43–9; Kida Hiroshi, 'Can education survive liberalization?', *Japan Echo* 12/2 (1985): 57–61; and Amaya Naohiro and Nishio Kanji, 'Education reform: how far, how fast?', *Japan Echo* 12/2 (1985): 50–6.

38 *AS*, 24 January 1985.

39 *AS*, 31 January 1985 (evening edition).

40 *RD*, special edition 2–3 (June 1985), pp. 74–116.

41 Rinji kyōiku shingikai, *Shingi keika no gaiyō (sono ni)*, 24 April 1985, in *RD*, special edition 2–3 (June 1985): 35–6.
42 Benjamin Duke, 'The liberalization of Japanese education', *Comparative Education* 22/1 (1986): 37–44, discusses the terminology of this debate.
43 *AS*, 25 April 1985 (evening edition); and *NKS*, 15 July 1985.
44 Yamazaki, *Jimintō*, p. 179, gives an account of this discussion. The meeting included Arita, Iijima, Ishikawa and Uchida from the AHCE and Kaifu, Aoki, Sunada and Ishibashi from the *zoku*: *NKS*, 12 August 1985.
45 *NKS*, 12 August 1985.
46 Yamazaki, *Jimintō*, p. 179.
47 Yamazaki, *Jimintō*, p. 178, details the earlier Nakasone statements on liberalization.
48 See *NKS*, 12 August 1985, for an account of this debate.
49 This case was made by a *zoku* study group in 1983: *NKS*, 25 February 1985.
50 *NKS*, 4 March 1985.
51 The Third Subcommittee expressed this opinion in the same brief in which it attacked the liberalization line. See *NKS*, 11 February 1985.
52 Tsukuba University was the main institution taking advantage of this provision: *NKS*, 25 February 1985. The case against a forced, total changeover was made by an official of the Japan Private Junior College Association: *NKS*, 4 March 1985.
53 Nakasone made the reform of the examination system one of his seven education reform promises during the December 1983 elections and spoke of 'abolishing' the *Kyōtsū-ichiji* exam on repeated occasions after that date.
54 Rinkyōshin, *Shingi keika no gaiyō (sono ni)*, pp. 38–9.
55 Nakasone, quoted in 'Sengo seiji no sōkessan o kataru', *Gekkan jiyūminshu*, August 1985.
56 Nakasone never actually spelt out what he hoped would follow the abolition of the *Kyōtsū-ichiji* exam. The rationale outlined in the text was that offered by Kanasugi at about the same time Nakasone was engaging in his final offensive aimed at convincing the council to abolish the exam: *NKS*, 2 September 1985.
57 It was this last point which he emphasized in council debates: *NKS*, 2 September 1985. See also Okamoto's comments cited in *NKS*, 26 August 1985.
58 *NKS*, 9 September 1985.
59 *NKS*, 2 and 9 September 1985, gives accounts of the Akasaka meeting followed by these changes.
60 This last paragraph apparently reflected last-minute pressure from the *zoku*. It was inserted after the AHCE executive committee had agreed on a draft: *NKS*, 15 July 1985, and Yamazaki, *Jimintō*, p. 180. The council's philosophy was spelt out in Part I of its First Report: Rinkyōshin, *Kyōiku kaikaku ni kansuru daiichiji tōshin*, 26 June 1985, in *RD*, special edition 2–3 (June 1985): 7–12. The report is also available in English as Provisional Council on Educational Reform, *First Report on Educational Reform*, 26 June 1985.

61 Rinkyōshin, *Daiichiji tōshin*, pp. 16–21.
62 *NKS*, 21 October 1985.
63 *YS*, 31 August 1986.
64 Rinkyōshin, *Kyōiku kaikaku ni kansuru dainiji tōshin*, 23 April 1986, in *RD*, special edition 5 (April 1986): 71–2.
65 Rinkyōshin, *Kyōiku kaikaku ni kansuru daisanji tōshin*, 1 April 1987, in *RD*, special edition 7 (April 1987): 32–3.
66 Rinkyōshin, *Shingi keika no gaiyō (sono san)*, 22 January 1986, in *RD*, special edition 4 (January 1986): 100–4.
67 Rinkyōshin, *Dainiji tōshin*, p. 71.
68 ibid., pp. 34–7, 71.
69 Mombushō chūkyōshin, *Kyōiku naiyōra*, pp. 11–12, 21–2.
70 Rinkyōshin, *Dainiji tōshin*, pp. 72–5.
71 Rinkyōshin, *Shingi keika no gaiyō (sono yon)*, 23 January 1987, in *RD*, special edition 6 (January 1987), pp. 29–36, 92–7. See *NKS*, 3 November 1986, for background.
72 Rinkyōshin, *Daisanji tōshin*, pp. 19–21. See *NKS*, 14 and 20 April 1987, for analysis.
73 Rinkyōshin, *Dainiji tōshin*, pp. 45–6; for other recommendations, see *Daisanji tōshin*, 38–9, 41.
74 Rinkyōshin, *Daisanji tōshin*, p. 40.
75 Rinkyōshin, *Dainiji tōshin*, p. 54.
76 See *NKS*, 6 October and 1 December 1986 and 1 June 1987, for stories of early conflicts.
77 Rinkyōshin, *Daisanji tōshin*, pp. 36–7.
78 ibid., pp. 24–6.
79 Rinkyōshin, *Kyoiku kaikaku ni kansuru daiyoji tōshin (saigo tōshin)*, 7 August 1987, pp. 51–3. See *AS*, 8 August 1987.
80 All of these proposals were included in the Second and Third Reports.
81 Rinkyōshin, *Saigo tōshin*, pp. 41–2. See *NKS*, 6 April and 18 May 1987, for background on the debate over this phrase.
82 Rinkyōshin, *Dainiji tōshin*, pp. 18–21.
83 Rinkyōshin, *Saigo tōshin*, p. 11.
84 Rinkyōshin, *Dainiji tōshin*, pp. 32–3.
85 ibid., pp. 40–1.
86 Kanasugi had originally sought to convince the council to draft a new 'education charter' (*kyōiku kenshō*) to supplement and explain the FLE to the people of Japan. For his version of such a document, see *21-seiki o tenbō shita kyōiku no arikata ni tsuite*, published by the First Subcommittee, 23 January 1985. When this idea failed to gain support, he and other nationalists on the council sought to include a reinterpretation of the FLE in the philosophical section of the Second Report. The final text, however, did not contain much which could be called 'reinterpretation'. After protests from *Nikkyōso* and others, statements about the role of the Occupation in the promulgation of the FLE and the controversial views of then Minister of Education, Tanaka Michitarō – both mentioned in the AHCE's interim report (Rinkyōshin, *Shingi keika no gaiyō (sono san)*), pp. 12–13 and pp. 34–45) were dropped from the final report.

An even more controversial approach focusing on the abolition of the Imperial Rescript – advocated by Takahashi Shirō – was not even included in the interim report. See *NKS*, 25 November and 2 December 1985.

87 For a comparison of the AHCE and CCE proposals, see Kito Yoshizumi, 'Shoninsha kenshū seido no jittai o saguru', *Gendai kyōiku kagaku* 367 (June 1987): 20–1.

88 Kuroha Ryōichi ('Gutaiteki teigen wa sukunakutomo', *RD* 30 (June 1987): 15) and others have argued that the council's main contribution to education reform was to point out the long-term directions for education reform in Japan. The council focused, for example, on the need for Japan to move from a where-did-you-go-to-school-society to a what-do-you-know-society: what it termed a 'lifelong learning society' (*shōgai gakushū shakai*). It thus recommended, for example, that employers consider more than a candidate's university and that universities consider more than a student's exam scores. It suggested that graduate schools be opened to mid-career adults, and that schools be opened to people in the community. In general, it said, Japan needed to move from a single-dimensional school-background centred society to a more multi-dimensional one. The difficulty of measuring the effectiveness of the council's recommendations in this area was my justification for largely ignoring this aspect of the AHCE's work.

89 *NKS*, 31 August 1987.

90 The question of whether to establish a new supra-cabinet organ was the subject of intense debate inside the AHCE in its final months and within the government after the AHCE issued its last report. See *NKS*, 27 July and 31 August 1987 and *AS*, 8 and 13 August 1987. In October Nakasone finally convinced the cabinet to endorse a vague statement committing the government to the setting up of a new council: *NKS*, 10 and 24 October 1987. With his departure, however, action was delayed, and the formulation of the plan for the council was essentially left to the MOE. As outlined in January 1988, the new council (although technically an organ of the Prime Minister's Office) was to have its office in the MOE and was to refrain from further reform planning. It was unclear whether the Diet would pass the legislation needed to establish it: *NKS*, 16 and 23 January 1988. As all of this was happening, it was the MOE which was in charge of acting on the AHCE recommendations.

91 In October 1987 the MOE decided not to include provisions to allow six-year secondary schools in legislation it was submitting in 1988: *NKS*, 17 October 1987. The generally negative attitude of MOE officials towards this idea and the September start proposal was revealed in interviews with MOE officials.

92 *NKS*, 25 May 1987.

93 Mombushō kyōiku katei shingikai, *Kyōiku katei no kijun no kaizen ni tsuite: shingi no matome*, 27 December 1987, in *NKS*, 28 November 1987 (pullout section). See *NKS*, 3 and 24 October and 28 November 1987.

94 *NKS*, 10 and 31 August 1987.

95 *YS*, 31 August 1986, describes the failed effort of *zoku* leaders to win the exemption in 1986. See also *NKS*, 8 December 1986.

96 The government's 1988 budget provided for only a 0.66 per cent increase in the education budget: *NKS*, 16 January 1988.

97 Adachi Takuji, 'Tetori ashitori no shoninsha kenshū ga sutāto', *Gendai kyōiku kagaku* 365 (April 1987): 95–100, and Kito, 'Shoninsha kenshū', pp. 20–6.

98 Mombushō kyōiku shokuin yōsei shingikai, *Kyōin shishitsu nōryoku no kōjō hōsakura ni tsuite*, 18 December 1987, in *NKS*, 26 December 1987 (pullout section), p. 5. The final implementation of the programme depended on the government's willingness to provide an eventual budget of ¥80 billion (US$640 million) a year for the salaries of supervisory staff and other expenses: *NKS*, 26 September 1987.

99 *NKS*, 26 September and 7 November 1987.

100 *NKS*, 21 November 1987.

101 Mombushō kyōiku katei shingikai, *Kyōiku katei*; *NKS*, 28 November and 26 December 1987.

102 Lower-ability interests were emphasized in the Curriculum Council reports: Mombushō kyōiku katei shingikai, *Kyōiku katei*, p. 19. The concrete plans to set up such schools (in Ishikawa and Iwate) were aimed at part-time students: *NKS*, 26 September and 24 October 1987.

103 *NKS*, 12 and 16 December 1987.

104 *NKS*, 23 January 1988.

CHAPTER 9   FINAL CONCLUSIONS

1 See the discussions of the way Nakasone sought to use 'outside' forces to promote change in these areas in Muramatsu Michio, 'In search of national identity: the politics and policies of the Nakasone administration', *Journal of Japanese Studies* 13/2 (Summer 1987): 307–42.

2 Interview with Amaya Naohiro, 1 September 1986.

3 Harada Saburō, 'Mombu kanryō no tanagokoro no ue de: maboroshi ni owatta kyōiku kaikaku', *Sekai* 500 (April 1987): 95.

4 Interview with Amagi Isao, 3 September 1986.

5 Interview with Amaya, 1 September 1986.

6 Interview with Kida Hiroshi, 22 July 1987. Kida was particularly critical of the lack of interest in education policy on the part of the Parent Teacher Associations (PTAs). He described them as having changed little since the pre-war days when they were called *Fukeikai* (Parents' Associations) and served as 'little more than cheering organizations' for individual schools. For similar evaluations of the PTA's role, see Albert Novick, 'Japan's marginal PTA', *DY*, 2 September 1987 and Fujita Kyōhei, 'Konna PTA ni dare ga shitanoka', *Chūō kōron* 89/11 (November 1974): 120–7.

7 To reiterate the point made in Chapter 1, this book has not taken a position on the question of whether or not Nakasone was correct in seeking reform. It merely sought to explore why he was not able to achieve change.

References

NEWSPAPERS AND SERIALS (with their abbreviations)

AN: *Asahi nenkan*, annual
AS: *Asahi shimbun*, daily
DY: *Daily Yomiuri*, daily
        Gendai seiji jōhō, annual
        Jinji kōshinroku, annual
        Kokkai benran, reissued with each session of the Diet
KS: *Kyōiku shimbun*, weekly
MS: *Mainichi shimbun*, daily
        Nihon keizai shimbun, daily
NKS: *Nihon kyōiku shimbun*, weekly
RD: *Rinkyōshin dayori*, monthly during the course of the Ad Hoc
        Council's deliberations
SS: *Sankei shimbun*, daily
YS: *Yomiuri shimbun*, daily

BOOKS, PERIODICALS AND GOVERNMENT DOCUMENTS

Aberbach, J.D., R.D. Putnam and B.A. Rockman (1981) *Bureaucrats and Politicians in Western Democracies*, Harvard University Press, Cambridge, Mass.

Adachi Takuji (1974) 'Bunkyō seisaku no seiji rikigaku: mombushō wa jimintō mombukyoku ka', *Gendai kyōiku kagaku* 17(1): 84–8.

—— (1984) 'Ugokidashita shushō shudō no kyōiku kaikaku', *Gendai kyōiku kagaku* 329: 49–54.

—— (1987) 'Tetori ashitori no shoninsha kenshū ga sutāto', *Gendai kyōiku kagaku* 365: 95–100.

Amaya Naohiro and Nishio Kanji (1985) 'Education reform: how far, how fast?', *Japan Echo* 12(2): 50–6.

Andō Yoshio (1957) 'Zaikai no chii to yakuwari', *Ekonomisuto*, 21 December.

Aoki Satoshi (1986) *Rinkyōshin kaitai*, Akebi shotoku, Tokyo.

Asahi shimbunsha shakaibu (1984) *Kyōiku no hiroba*, Sōjisha, Tokyo.

Beauchamp, Edward (ed.) (1978) *Learning to Be Japanese*, Linnet Books, Hamden, Connecticut.

Bellah, Robert (1957) *Tokugawa Religion*, Free Press of Glencoe, New York.

Campbell, John C. (1975) 'Japanese budget *baransu*', in Vogel (ed.), pp. 71–100.

—— (1977) 'Compensation for repatriates: a case study of interest group politics and party–government negotiations in Japan', in Pempel (ed.), pp. 103–42.

—— (1977) *Contemporary Japanese Budget Politics*, University of California Press, Berkeley.

—— (1984) 'Policy conflict and its resolution within the governmental system', in Krauss *et al.* (eds), pp. 294–334.

Craig, Albert M. (1975) 'Functional and dysfunctional aspects of government bureaucracy', in Vogel (ed.), pp. 3–32.

Cummings, William K. (1978) 'The conservatives reform higher education', in Beauchamp (ed.), pp. 316–28.

—— (1980) *Education and Equality in Japan*, Princeton University Press, Princeton.

Cummings, William K., *et al.* (eds) (1986) *Educational Policies in Crisis*, Praeger, New York.

Curtis, Gerald L. (1975) 'Big business and political influence', in Vogel (ed.), pp. 33–70.

Donnelly, Michael W. (1977) 'Setting the price of rice: a study in political decisionmaking', in Pempel (ed.), pp. 143–200.

—— (1984) 'Conflict over government authority and markets: Japan's rice economy', in Krauss *et al.* (eds), pp. 335–74.

Dore, Ronald (1965) *Education in Tokugawa Japan*, University of California Press, Berkeley.

—— (1969) 'The legacy of Tokugawa education', in Jansen, Marius, (ed.) *Changing Japanese Attitudes Toward Modernization*, Princeton University Press, Princeton, pp. 99–131.

—— (1976) *The Diploma Disease: Education, Qualification and Development*, George Allen & Unwin, London.

Dore, Ronald and Sako Mari (1989) *How the Japanese Learn to Work*, Nissan Institute/Routledge Japanese Studies Series, London.

Duke, Benjamin (1973) *Japan's Militant Teachers*, University Press of Hawaii, Honolulu.

—— (1986) *The Japanese School: Lessons for Industrial America*, Praeger, New York.

—— (1986) 'The liberalization of Japanese education', *Comparative Education* 22(1): 37–44.

Foreign Press Center, Japan (ed.) (1985) *Documents on Educational Reform in Japan*, Foreign Press Center, Tokyo.

Fujita Kyōhei (1974) 'Konna PTA ni dare ga shita ka', *Chūō kōron* 89(11): 120–7.

Fukuda Nobuyuki (1983) *Tsukuba daigaku no bijiyon*, Zenhonsha, Tokyo.

Fukui Haruhiro (1972) 'Economic planning in postwar Japan: a case study in policy making', *Asian Survey* 12(4): 238–47.

—— (1977) 'Studies in policymaking: a review of the literature', in Pempel (ed.), pp. 22–59.

—— (1977) 'Tanaka goes to Peking: a case study in foreign policy-making', in Pempel (ed.), pp. 60–102.

—— (undated) 'Japan's higher civil servants: issues and interpretations', unpublished manuscript.

George, Aurelia (1988) 'Japanese interest group behaviour: an institutional approach', in Stockwin *et al.* (eds), pp. 106–40.

—— (1988) 'Japan and the United States: dependent ally or equal partner?', in Stockwin *et al.* (eds), pp. 237–96.

Gyōsei kanrichō (1983) *Shingikai sōran.*

Habara Kiyomasa (1982) 'Jimintō bunkyōzoku no jitsuryoku', *Sekai* 444: 65–71.

Haley, John O. (1987) 'Governance by negotiation: a reappraisal of bureaucratic power in Japan', *Journal of Japanese Studies* 13(2): 343–57.

Hall, Ivan P. (1975) 'Organizational paralysis: the case of Tōdai', in Vogel (ed.), pp. 304–30.

Hamabayashi Masao and Hatakeyama Hidetaka (1979) *Tsukuba daigaku: sono seiritsu o meguru tatakai to genjō*, Aoki shoten, Tokyo.

Harada Saburō (1982) 'Sengo mombu gyōsei no kiseki', *Sekai* 444: 55–64.

—— (1987) 'Mombu kanryō no tanagokoro no ue de: maboroshi ni owatta kyōiku kaikaku', *Sekai* 500: 89–100.

Harari, Ehud (1973) *The Politics of Labor Legislation in Japan*, University of California Press, Berkeley.

—— (1974) 'Japanese politics of advice in comparative perspective: a framework for analysis and case study', *Public Policy* 12(4): 537–77.

—— (1982) 'Turnover and autonomy in Japanese permanent public advisory bodies', *Journal of Asian and African Studies* 17(3–4): 235–49.

—— (1988) 'The institutionalisation of policy consultation in Japan: public advisory bodies', in Gail Lee Bernstein and Fukui Haruhiro (eds), *Japan and the World: Essays in Japanese History and Politics in Honour of Takeshi Ishida*, Macmillan, London, pp. 144–57.

Inoguchi Takashi (1983) *Gendai nihon seiji keizai no kōzō*, Tōyō keizai shimpōsha, Tokyo.

Inoguchi Takashi and Iwai Tomoaki (1987) *'Zoku giin' no kenkyū: jimintō seiken o gyūjiru shuyakutachi*, Nihon keizai shimbunsha, Tokyo.

Ishida Takeshi (1984) 'Conflict and its accommodation: *omote-ura* and *uchi-soto* relations', in Krauss *et al.* (eds), pp. 16–38.

Ishiyama Morio (1986) *Mombu kanryō no gyakushū*, Kōdansha, Tokyo.

Itō Daiichi (1988) 'Policy implications of administrative reform', in Stockwin *et al.* (eds), pp. 77–105.

Japan Teachers Union (1983) *Report of the Second JTU Council on Educational Reform*, summarized edition, October.

'Jimintō "bukai" no kenkyū: bunkyōbukai' (1986) *Gekkan jiyū minshu*, July: 170–7.

Jishu kempō kisei giin dōmei (1983) *Kempō*, 15 April.

Jiyū minshutō (1986) *Jiyū minshutō-shi shiryōhen*, Jiyū minshutō shuppankyoku, Tokyo.

—— (1986) *Wagatō no kōyaku*, Jiyū minshutō shuppankyoku, Tokyo.

Jiyū minshutō seimu chōsakai bunkyōbukai kyōin mondai ni kansuru shoiinkai (1981) *Kyōin no shishitsu kōjō ni kansuru teigen*, 16 May.

—— (1983) *Kyōin no yōsei, menkyora ni kansuru teigen*, 19 May.

Jiyū minshutō seimu chōsakai bunkyō seido chōsakai (1969) 'Kyōiku kaikaku shian', in *Gendai kyōiku kagaku* 12(5): 105–9.

Johnson, Chalmers (1975) 'Japan: who governs? An essay on official bureaucracy', *Journal of Japanese Studies* 2(1): 1–28.

—— (1982) *MITI and the Japanese Miracle: The Growth of Industrial Policy, 1925–1975*, Stanford University Press, Stanford.

Kanagawa-ken kyōiku iinkai (1985) *Kyōiku katei kaihatsu kenkyūkō; koseika shuishin-kō: kenkyū shūroku VI*, August.

Kanasugi Hidenobu (1985) *21-seiki o tenbō shita kyōiku no arikata ni tsuite*, published by the AHCE First Subcommittee as a separate opinion, 23 January.

Keisatsuchō (1986) *Shōnen no hobō oyobi hogo no gaikyō*, September.

—— (1986) *Keisatsuchō hakusho*, Tokyo.

Keizai dōyūkai (undated) *Keizai Dōyūkai: What It Is; What It Does*.

—— (1969) *Kōji-fukushi shakai no tame no kōtō kyōiku seido*, 18 July.

—— (1979) *Tayōka e no chōsen*, 24 October.

—— (1982) *Gyōsei kaikaku: kongo no bunkyō seisaku ni nozomu*, January.

—— (1984) *Sōzōsei, tayōsei, kokusaisei o motomeru*, July.

Kida Hiroshi (1985) 'Can education survive liberalization?' *Japan Echo* 12(2): 57–61.

Kida Hiroshi (ed.) (1987) *Sengo no bunkyō seisaku*, Daiichi hōki, Tokyo.

Kitamura Kazuyuki (1986) 'The decline and reform of education in Japan: a comparative perspective', in Cummings *et al.* (eds), pp. 153–70.

Kito Yoshizumi (1987) 'Shoninsha kenshū seido no jittai o saguru', *Gendai kyōiku kagaku* 367: 20–6.

Kobayashi Tetsuya (1978) *Society, Schools and Progress in Japan*, Pergamon Press, Oxford.

Kondō Tetsuo (1982) 'Kyōiku seido daikaikaku-ron', *Voice*, May, pp. 249–57.

Kōyama Kenichi (1985) 'An end of uniformity in education', *Japan Echo* 12(2): 43–9.

—— (1987) *Jiyū no tame no kyōiku kaikaku*, PHP kenkyūjo, Tokyo.

Krauss, Ellis S. (1984) 'Conflict in the Diet: toward conflict management in parliamentary politics', in Krauss *et al.* (eds), pp. 243–93.

Krauss, Ellis S., Thomas Rohlen and Patricia Steinhoff (eds) (1984) *Conflict in Japan*, University of Hawaii Press, Honolulu.

Kubota Akira and Tomita Nobuo (1977) 'Nihon seifu kōkan no ishiki kōzō', *Chūō kōron* 92(2): 190–6.

Kumatani Kazunori (1973) 'Kyōiku seisaku keisei katei ni kansuru kenkyū: yotō no jirei o chūshin ni', *Shakaigaku hyōron* 24 (December): 38–58.

Kuroha Ryōichi (1974) *Sugao no sengo kyōiku*, Gakuji shuppan, Tokyo.

—— (1984) *Kyōiku kaikaku: tembō to kanōsei*, Kokudosha, Tokyo.

—— (1985) *Rinkyōshin – dōnaru kyōiku kaikaku*, Nihon keizai shimbunsha, Tokyo.

—— (1987) 'Gutaiteki teigen wa sukunakutomo', *RD* 30: 15.

Kyoto Group for the Study of Global Issues (1985) 'Seven recommendations to revitalize school education, March 13, 1984', in Foreign Press Center, Japan (ed.), pp. 31–4.

Makieda Motofumi (1984) *Mombu daijin wa nani o shitaka*, Mainichi shimbunsha, Tokyo.

McCormack, Gavan, and Sugimoto Yoshio (eds) (1986) *Democracy in Contemporary Japan*, M.E. Sharpe, Armonk, New York.

McKean, Margaret A. (1977) 'Pollution and policymaking', in Pempel (ed.), pp. 201–38.

—— (1981) *Environmental Protest and Citizens Movements in Japan*, University of California Press, Berkeley.

Ministry of Education, Science and Culture (1986) *Education in Japan: A Brief Outline*, Tokyo.

MOE Central Council for Education (1971) *Basic Guidelines for the Reform of Education: On the Basic Guidelines for the Development of an Integrated Educational System Suited for Contemporary Society*, 11 June, Tokyo.

MOE Higher Education Bureau (1984) *Higher Education in Japan*, October, Tokyo.

Misawa Shigeo (1973) 'An outline of the policy-making process in Japan', in Itoh Hiroshi (ed.) *Japanese Politics: An Inside View*, Cornell University Press, Ithaca, pp. 12–48.

Mochizuki, Mike (1982) 'Managing and influencing the Japanese legislative process: the role of parties and the National Diet', unpublished PhD dissertation, Harvard University.

Mombushō (annual) *Kuni to chihō no bunkyō yosan*, Tokyo.

—— (1979) *Chūō kyōiku shingikai yōran*, 8th edn, Tokyo.

—— (1985) *Mombushō*, Mombushō, Tokyo.

—— (1986) 'Jidō seito no gakkōgai gakushū katsudō ni kansuru jittai chōsa', in *Gendai kyōiku kagaku* 355: 104–7.

Mombushō chūō kyōiku shingikai (1969) *Chūkan hōkoku: meiji hyakunen no kyōiku bunseki*, 30 June, Tokyo.

—— (1978) *Kyōin no shishitsu nōryoku no kōjō ni tsuite*, 16 June, Tokyo.

—— (1983) *Kyōiku naiyōra shoiinkai shingi keika hōkoku*, 15 November, Tokyo.

Mombushō daijin kanbō chōsa tōkeika (1986) *Shōwa 61-nendo gakkō kihon chōsa chokuhō*, August, Tokyo.

Mombushō jōsei kyoku chihōka (1985) *Kyōshokuin dantai no soshiki no jittai ni tsuite*, 1 October, Tokyo.

Mombushō kyōiku katei shingikai (1987) *Kyōiku katei no kijun no kaizen ni tsuite: shingi no matome*, 27 November, in *NKS*, 28 November 1987 (pullout section).

Mombushō kyōiku shokuin yōsei shingikai (1983) *Kyōin no yōsei oyobi menkyo seido no kaizen ni tsuite*, 22 November, Tokyo.

—— (1987) *Kyōin shishitsu nōryoku no kōjō hōsakura ni tsuite*, 18 December, in *NKS*, 26 December 1987 (pullout section).

Mombushō shotō-chūtō kyōiku kyoku (1977) *Yōji, jidō, seito no shinshin hattatsu ni tsuite*, June, Tokyo.

—— (1984) *Kōritsu kōtōgakkō no nyūgakusha senbatsu ni tsuite (tsūchi)*, 20 July, Tokyo.

—— (1985) 'Wagakuni no shotō chūtō kyōiku', *Gendai kyōiku kagaku* 341: 102–6.

Mombushō shotō-chūtō kyōiku kyoku kōtōgakkōka (undated) 'Shōwa 61-nendo kōtōgakkō nyūgaku senbatsu no kaizen jōkyō ni tsuite', internal document.

—— (1982) 'Kōtōgakkō no shin-kyōiku katei hensei jōkyō ni tsuite', *Mombu jihō* 1261: 77–82.

Mombushō shotō-chūtō kyōiku kyoku tokushu kyōikuka (1979) 'Yōgo gakkō gimusei no jisshi', *Mombu jihō* 1226: 48–59.

Morito Tatsuo (1973) *Daisan no kyōiku kaikaku: chūkyōshin tōshin to kyōkasho saiban*, Daiichi hōki, Tokyo.

Muramatsu Michio (1981) *Sengo nihon no kanryōsei*, Tōyō keizai shimpōsha, Tokyo.

—— (1987) 'In search of national identity: the politics and policies of the Nakasone administration', *Journal of Japanese Studies* 13(2): 307–42.

Muramatsu Michio and Ellis Krauss (1984) Bureaucrats and politicians in policymaking: the case of Japan', *American Political Science Review* 78(1): 126–46.

—— (1987) 'The conservative policy line and the development of patterned pluralism', in Yamamura and Yasuba (eds), pp. 516–54.

Naitō Yosaburō (1968) 'Naitō shian', *Gendai kyōiku kagaku* 11(11): 104–7.

Naka Mamoru (1986) 'Zoku no kenkyū, 9: posuto rinkyōshin o ukagau ideorogî shūdan', *Gekkan seikai*, July–August: 38–51.

Nakagawa Ichirō (1973) *Seirankai: keppan to yūkoku no ronri*, Rōman, Tokyo.

Nakane Chie (1970) *Japanese Society*, Wiedenfeld & Nicolson, London.

Nakasone Yasuhiro (1983) *Atarashii hoshu no ronri*, Kōdansha, Tokyo.

—— (1985) 'Seven point proposal for education reform, December 10, 1983', in Foreign Press Center, Japan (ed.), pp. 13–14.

—— (1985) 'Speech made at the first meeting of the provisional council on education reform', in Provisional Council on Education Reform (ed.), pp. 68–9.

—— (1988) 'Reflections of a presidential prime minister', *Japan Echo* 15(1): 8–16.

Nihon keieisha renmei (1969) *Chokumen suru daigaku mondai ni kansuru kihonteki kenkai*, 24 February.

—— (1969) *Kyōiku no kihon mondai ni taisuru sangyōkai no kenkai*, 18 September.

—— (1983) *Kinnen no kōnai bōryoku mondai ni tsuite*, 7 May.

—— (1984–6 editions) *Report of the Committee for the Study of Labor Questions*.

Nihon kyōshokuin kumiai (1985) 'Nihon no kyōiku o dō aratameru ka (daiichiji hōkoku)', *Minna de kyōiku kaikaku o* 5: 3–18.

—— (1986) 'Daisanjūgoji nikkyōso kyōken zenkoku shūkai hōkoku', *Minna de kyōiku kaikaku o* 7: 2–23.

—— (1986) 'Rinji kyōiku shingikai "kyōiku kaikaku ni kansuru dainiji tōshin'' ni taisuru nikkyōso kenkai', *Minna de kyōiku kaikaku o* 9: 2–5.

—— (1986) 'Rinji kyōiku shingikai no kyōiku kaikaku dainiji tōshin ni taisuru bunseki hihan oyobi watakushitachi no motomeru kyōiku kaikaku e no teigen (dainiji hōkoku)', *Minna de kyōiku kaikaku o* 9: 10–48.

Nihon shiritsu daigaku kyōkai (1986) *Shōwa 61-nendo jigyō keikakusho*, 28 March.

—— (1986) *Kōtōkyōiku no genjōra ni kansuru shiryō*, 31 May.

Nishi Toshio (1982) *Unconditional Democracy: Education and Politics in Occupied Japan 1945–52*, Hoover Institution Press, Stanford.

Nishijima Takeo (1972) 'Chūkyōshin tōshin sono ato', *Kikan kyōikuhō* 3 (March): 168–74.

Nishio Kanji (1985) 'Naze rinkyōshin tōshin wa munaiyō ni owattaka', *Chūō kōron* 100(8): 144–150.

Novick, Albert (1987) 'Japan's marginal PTA', *DY*, 2 September.

Ogata Sadako (1977) 'The business community and Japanese foreign policy: normalization of relations with the People's Republic of China', in Robert Scalapino (ed.) *Japanese Foreign Policy*, University of California Press, Berkeley, pp. 175–203.

Ōmori Kazuo (1985) 'Sutāto shita rinkyōshin', *AN*, p. 208.

Organization for Economic Co-operation and Development (1971) *Reviews of National Policies for Education: Japan*, OECD, Paris.

Park, Yung H. (1972) 'The governmental advisory system in Japan', *Journal of Comparative Administration* 3: 435–67.

—— (1975) 'The Central Council for Education, organized business, and politics of education policymaking in Japan', *Comparative Education Review* 19(2): 296–311.

—— (1979) 'Party–bureaucratic relations in Japan: the case of the Ministry of Education', *Waseda Journal of Asian Studies* 1: 48–75.

—— (1980) *Jimintō to kyōiku kanryō*, Meiji daigaku gakujutsu kōryū iinkai, Tokyo.

—— (1983) 'Kyōiku gyōsei ni okeru jimintō to mombushō', in Shimbori and Aoi (eds), pp. 49–78.

—— (1986) *Bureaucrats and Ministers in Contemporary Japanese Government*, University of California Press, Berkeley.

Passin, Herbert (1965) *Society and Education in Japan*, Columbia University Press, New Nork.

Pempel, T.J. (1974) 'The bureaucratization of policymaking in postwar Japan', *American Journal of Political Science* 18(4): 647–64.

—— (1978) *Patterns of Japanese Policymaking: Experiences from Higher Education*, Westview Press, Boulder, Colorado.

—— (1982) *Policy and Politics in Japan: Creative Conservatism*, Temple University Press, Philadelphia.

—— (1987) 'The unbundling of "Japan, Inc.": the changing dynamics of Japanese policy formation', *Journal of Japanese Studies* 13(2): 271–306.

Pempel, T.J. (ed.) (1977) *Policymaking in Contemporary Japan*, Cornell University Press, Ithaca.

Pempel, T.J., and Tsunekawa Keiichi (1979) 'Corporatism without labor? The Japanese anomaly', in P.C. Schmitter and G. Lehmbruch (eds) *Trends Toward Corporatist Intermediation*, Sage, London.

Provisional Council on Educational Reform (1985) *First Report on Educational Reform*, 26 June.

Pyle, Kenneth B., and Yayama Tarō (1983) 'Japan beseiged: the textbook controversy', *Journal of Japanese Studies* 9(2): 297–316.

Richardson, Bradley M. (1977) 'Policymaking in Japan: an organizing perspective', in Pempel (ed.), pp. 239–68.

Rinji gyōsei chōsakai (1982) *Daisanji tōshin (kihon tōshin)*, 30 July.

Rinji kyōiku shingikai (1985) *Shingi keika no gaiyō (sono ni)*, 24 April, in *RD*, special edition 2–3 (June 1985): 31–40.

—— (1985) *Kyōiku kaikaku ni kansuru daiichiji tōshin*, 26 June, in *RD*, special edition 2–3 (June 1985): 6–20.

—— (1986) *Shingi keika no gaiyō (sono san)*, 22 January, in *RD*, special edition 4 (January 1986): 2–109.

—— (1986) *Kyōiku kaikaku ni kansuru dainiji tōshin*, 23 April, in *RD*, special edition 5 (April 1986): 5–77.

—— (1987) *Shingi keika no gaiyō (sono yon)*, 23 January, in *RD*, special edition 6 (January 1987): 2–130.

—— (1987) *Kyōiku kaikaku ni kansuru daisanji tōshin*, 1 April, in *RD*, special edition 7 (April 1987): 5–68.

—— (1987) *Kyōiku kaikaku ni kansuru daiyoji tōshin (saigo tōshin)*, 7 August.

Rinji kyōiku shingikai jimukyoku (1984) *Rinkyōshin setchihōhōan shingi tōben no gaiyō*, 14 September.

Ripley, Randall B., and Grace A. Franklin (1976) *Congress, the Bureaucracy, and Public Policy*, The Dorsey Press, Homewood, Illinois.

Rix, Alan (1988) 'Dynamism, foreign policy and trade policy', in Stockwin *et al.* (eds), pp. 297–324.

Roden, Donald (1980) *Schooldays in Imperial Japan: A Study in the Culture of a Student Elite*, University of California Press, Berkeley.

Rohlen, Thomas P. (1977) 'Is Japanese education becoming less egalitarian? Notes on high school stratification and reform', *Journal of Japanese Studies* 3(1): 37–70.

—— (1983) *Japan's High Schools*, University of California Press, Berkeley.

Saitama-ken kyōiku kyoku shidōka (undated) 'Tokushu aru kōkōzukuri no suishin ni tsuite', internal document.

Saitō Taijun (1984) *Bunkyō gyōsei ni miru: seisaku keisei katei no kenkyū*, Gyōsei, Tokyo.

Satō Seizaburō and Matsuzaki Tetsuhisa (1985) 'The Liberal Democrats' conciliatory reign', *Economic Eye* 6(4): 27–32.

—— (1986) *Jimintō seiken*, Chūō kōronsha, Tokyo.

Scalapino, Robert A., and Masumi Junnosuke (1962) *Parties and Politics in Contemporary Japan*, University of California Press, Berkeley.

'Sengo seiji no sōkessan o kataru' (1985) *Gekkan jiyū minshu*, August.

Shimbori Michiya and Aoi Kazuo (eds) (1983) *Nihon kyōiku no rikigaku*, Yūshindo, Tokyo.

'Shunin mondai to seitō no gyōsei kainyū' (1986) *Gendai kyōiku kagaku* 19(2): 105–10.

Soeda Yoshiya (1983) 'Changing patterns of juvenile aggression', *Japan Echo* 10(3): 9–16.

Stockwin, J.A.A. (1982) *Japan: Divided Politics in a Growth Economy*, 2nd edn, Weidenfeld & Nicolson, London.

—— (1988) 'Dynamic and immobilist aspects of Japanese politics', in Stockwin *et al.* (eds), pp. 1–21.

Stockwin, J.A.A., *et al.* (eds) (1988) *Dynamic and Immobilist Politics in Japan*, Macmillan, London.

Steslicke, William E. (1973) *Doctors in Politics: The Political Life of the Japan Medical Association*, Praeger, New York.

Suwa Takashi (1972) 'Kewashiku tōi kyōiku kaikaku no michi', *Gendai kyōiku kagaku* 15(3): 88–92.

Suzuki Eiichi (1983) *Nihon no senryō to kyōiku kaikaku*, Keiso shobō, Tokyo.

—— (1985) 'Sengo kyōiku kaikaku ni okeru kyōiku kihon-hō to 6–3–3–sei', *Kokumin kyōiku* 64: 104–14.

Suzuki Isao (1987) 'Kyōiku kaikaku no kadai', *Kōdō* 927: 1–24.

Suzuki Kenji (1984) *Makete tamaruka!! daigishi nisei no gunsō*, Seikai shuppansha, Tokyo.

Takahashi Shirō (1986) 'Rinkyōshin to kyōiku kihon-hō', *Bunka kaigi* 205: 34–54.

Takayama Yōji (1982) 'Mombu kanryō – sono taishitsu to jinmyaku', *Sekai* 444: 72–86.

Tanaka Masataka (1987) *Ushi no ayumi hachijūgonen: Kennoki Toshihiro kikigaki*, Nishi nihon shimbunsha, Tokyo.

Thurston, Donald R. (1973) *Teachers and Politics in Japan*, Princeton University Press, Princeton.

Todōfuken, kyōikuchō kyōgikai (1984) *Kōtōgakkō nyūgaku sembatsu ni tsuite*, May.

—— (1985) *Kyōiku iinka no unei no kasseika ni tsuite*, 26 June.

—— (1985) *Kyōiku kaikaku ni kansuru chōsa*, December.

—— (1986) *Rokunensei chūtōgakkō oyobi tanisei kōtōgakkō ni tsuite*, May.

Todōfuken kyōikuchō kyōgikai kōtōgakkō kyōiku kaihatsu kenkyū purojekuto chīmu (1979) *Kenkyū kekka hōkokusho*, 13 June.

Tokyo shimbun seijibu (1977) *Seisaku shūdan: shin hoshutō e no taidō*, Tokyo shimbun shuppankyoku, Tokyo.

Toyota Kōji (1976) *Seishun kokkai gekijō: waseda yūbenkai ga unda asu o ninau senryō nain*, Bunka sōgō shuppan, Tokyo.

Tsuji Kiyoaki (1984) 'Public administration in Japan: an overview', in Tsuji (ed.) *Public administration in Japan*, Tokyo University Press, Tokyo.

Tsuji Kiyoaki (ed.) (1970) *Shinpan nihon kanryōsei no kenkyū*, Tokyo daigaku shuppankai, Tokyo.

Tsūsanshō sangyō kōzō shingikai (1980) *1980-nendai no tsūshō sangyō seisaku (bijiyon)*, 17 March.

van Wolferen, Karel G. (1986/87) 'The Japan problem', *Foreign Affairs* 65(2): 288–303.

Vogel, Ezra F. (ed.) (1975) *Modern Japanese Organization and Decision-making*, University of California Press, Berkeley.

White, Merry (1987) *The Japanese Educational Challenge*, Collier Macmillan, London.

Yagi Atsushi (1984) *Mombu daijin no sengoshi*, Bijinesusha, Tokyo.

Yamamura Kōzō and Yasuba Yasukichi (eds) (1987) *The Political Economy of Japan, Vol. 1: The Domestic Transformation*, Stanford University Press, Stanford.

Yamazaki Masato (1986) *Jimintō to kyōiku seisaku*, Iwanami shinsho, Tokyo.

Yamazumi Masami (1986) 'Educational democracy versus state control', in McCormack and Sugimoto (eds), pp. 90–113.

Yanaga Chitoshi (1968) *Big Business in Japanese Politics*, Yale University Press, New Haven.

Yuasa Hiroshi (1986) *Kokkai 'zoku giin'*, Kyōikusha, Tokyo.

'Yūbenka-zoroi "bunkyōzoku" ', (1986) *Shūkan daiyamondo*, March: 74–8.

Zeugner, John F. (1984) 'The puzzle of higher education in Japan', *Change*, January/February: 24–31.

INTERVIEWS

Aichi Kazuo (LDP Dietman; chairman of the Diet Education Committee), interview, 30 July 1987.

Amagi Isao (Special Advisor to the Minister of Education; MOE AVM, 1969–71), interview, 3 September 1986.

Amaya Naohiro (Special Advisor to the Minister of International Trade and Industry and former senior MITI official; member of the Ad Hoc Council on Education – chairman of the First Subcommittee), interview, 1 September 1986.

Araki Shirō (Democratic Socialist Party Policy Deliberations Council Chief Officer; formerly Education Officer), interview, 2 September 1986.

Banno Junji (Tokyo University professor; textbook author), interview, 2 March 1987.

Fukuda Nobuyuki (former Tsukuba University president), interview, 19 August 1986.

Funada Hajime (LDP Dietman), interview, 23 July 1987.

Ienaga Saburō (former Tokyo Education University professor; textbook author), interview, 4 September 1986.

Iijima Sōichi (former president of Nagoya University; member of the Ad Hoc Council on Education – chairman of the Fourth Subcommittee), interview, 4 August 1986.

Inai Keijirō (MOE AVM, 1978–80), interview, 10 August 1987.

Kaifu Toshiki (LDP Dietman; Minister of Education, 1976–7 and again 1985–6), interview, 3 September 1986.

Kennoki Toshihiro (former Dietman; Minister of Education, 1966–7), interview, 13 August 1987.

Kida Hiroshi (Director of the Japan Society for the Promotion of

Science; MOE AVM, 1976–8), interviews, 13 August 1986 and 22 July 1987.

Kitai Yoshihiko (editor of *Seiron*; former *Sankei shimbun* education reporter), interview, 24 July 1987.

Kitamura Minoru (secretary-general of the Japan Scientists' Association), interview, 27 August 1986.

Kobayashi Tetsuya (Kyoto University professor; member of MOE Teacher Training Council), interview, 31 July 1986.

Kudō Iwao (LDP Dietman; MOE political vice-minister, 1985–6), interview, 29 July 1987.

Kuroha Ryōichi (Tsukuba University professor; until 1986, education and editorial writer for *Nihon keizai shimbun*; specialist member of the Ad Hoc Council on Education), interviews, 26 August 1986 and 14 August 1987.

Kusuyama Mikao (former *Sankei shimbun* education reporter), interview, 29 July 1987.

Maeda Yōji (*Nikkeiren* education officer), interview, 2 September 1986.

Makieda Motofumi (chairman of *Nikkyōso*, 1971–83), interview, 21 August 1986.

Morimoto Shinshi (head of the People's Committee for the Normalization of Textbooks), interview, 25 August 1986.

Morita Tomio (LDP Policy Affairs Research Council Education Officer), interview, 19 August 1986.

Nakajima Akio (MOE Elementary and Secondary Education Bureau Councillor), interviews, 26 August 1986, 20 July 1987 and 1 September 1987.

Nishioka Takeo (LDP Dietman; chairman of the LDP Policy Affairs Research Council Education Division, 1971–4), interviews, 23 July and 26 August 1987.

Oguchi Kōichi (planning director of MOE Educational Assistance and Administration Bureau Teacher Training Division), interview, 13 August 1986.

Okuda Shinjō (Yokohama National University professor; former MOE Minister's Secretariat councillor), interview, 1 September 1987.

Ōmori Kazuo (*Asahi shimbun* MOE reporter), interviews, 21 August and 3 September 1986.

Ōsaki Hitoshi (MOE Commissioner for Cultural Affairs; formerly Higher Education Bureau Chief), interview, 21 August 1986.

Saitō Taijun (chief of the Ad Hoc Council Secretariat), interviews, 27 August 1986 and 13 August 1987.

Shimizu Kōichi (*Keizai dōyūkai* education section chief), interview, 28 August 1986.

Shimizu Yoshirō (PTA National Association office chief), interview, 5 September 1986.

Soejima Takeyoshi (*Nikkyōso* University division vice-chief), interviews, 19 and 28 August 1986.

Suzuki Isao (director-general of the National Institute for Educational Research; former MOE Elementary and Secondary Education Bureau chief), interview, 30 July 1987.

Suzuki Shigenobu (former superintendent of the Kanagawa Prefecture

Education Office; specialist member of the Central Council on Education, 1967–71), interview, 3 September 1987.

Takahashi Shirō (Meisei University associate professor; specialist member of the Ad Hoc Council on Education), interview, 18 August 1986.

Tamaru Akiyo (elementary-school teacher; member of the Ad Hoc Council on Education), interview, 29 August 1986.

Tokutake Yasushi (former Jiji Press education reporter), interview, 27 July 1987.

Usami Nobuyuki (Private Universities Association office chief), interview, 4 September 1986.

Usui Hideo (LDP Dietman), interview, 23 July 1987.

Watase Noriyuki (chief secretary to Dietman Sakata Michita), interviews, 11 August 1986 and 29 August 1987.

Yamagishi Shunsuke (*Asahi shimbun* social section reporter), interview, 15 August 1987.

Yano Shigenori (MOE Elementary and Secondary Education Bureau High School Division vice-chief), interview, 26 August 1986.

Zeniya Masami (MOE Elementary and Secondary Education Bureau High School Division vice-chief), interview, 26 August 1986.

Index